THE POLITICS AND STRATEGY OF NUCLEAR WEAPONS IN THE MIDDLE EAST

SUNY Series in Israeli Studies
Russell Stone, editor

THE POLITICS
AND STRATEGY OF
NUCLEAR WEAPONS
IN THE MIDDLE EAST

Opacity, Theory, and Reality, 1960-1991
An Israeli Perspective

SHLOMO ARONSON
with the assistance of Oded Brosh

STATE UNIVERSITY OF NEW YORK PRESS

Published by
State University of New York Press, Albany

© 1992 State University of New York

For information, address State University of New York Press,
State University Plaza, Albany, N.Y., 12246

Production by Marilyn P. Semerad
Marketing by Theresa A. Swierzowski

Library of Congress Cataloging-in-Publication Data

Aronson, Shlomo, 1936-
    The Politics and strategy of nuclear weapons in the Middle East :
opacity, theory, and reality, 1960-1991 : an Israeli perspective /
Shlomo Aronson with the assistance of Oded Brosh.
        p.   cm. — (SUNY series in Israeli studies)
    Includes bibliographical references and index.
    ISBN 0-7914-1207-5 (cloth). — ISBN 0-7914-1208-3 (paper)
    1. Middle East—Military policy. 2. Israel—Military policy.
3. Nuclear weapons—Middle East. 4. Nuclear weapons—Israel.
5. Nuclear nonproliferation. I. Brosh, Oded. II. Title.
III. Series.
UA832.A77 1992
355'.033056—dc20   91-46244
                                                                         CIP

10 9 8 7 6 5 4 3 2 1

Contents

Preface

This book was originally part of a larger manuscript entitled "Jewish Wars." In "Jewish Wars" I attempted to describe and analyze Zionist and Israeli behavior pertaining to war and peace since Hitler's rise to power. The sociocultural history of the Yishuv and the formative years of contemporary Israel were studied in some detail, in order to understand the Yishuv's political behavior and several crucial decisions made by Israeli leadership.

The Holocaust loomed heavily over that earlier manuscript, the sociocultural and domestic political issues, when combined with Israel's War of Independence, with regional and international developments, and with decisions of great complexity and autonomous ramifications such as Israel's nuclear program, were too much for one book.

I have, therefore, separated the nuclear issue from the much broader context, even if not entirely, and offer it here as a separate book. Nuclear weapons are important enough to be dealt with as a central topic, especially when major actors in the Middle East drama consider them as such.

This book began as a historical-theoretical discourse, then contemporary history intervened. I completed the first version of the book in 1989, but developments in 1990 and 1991 added to the manuscript two full chapters and a revised conclusion, which the reader—using a book that was completed in July 1991—may further revise, using some of the data, arguments, terminology, and the perspective offered here.

Dr. Oded Brosh, who was my research assistant at the time this book was being written, was very helpful in gathering the primary and secondary sources used here and in offering his own ideas.

I am also indebted to Avner Cohen and Ben Frankel, who cooperated with me for some time in dealing with what I originally called "semicovert" nuclear proliferation. It was Frankel who renamed the phenomenon "opaque." Since our original work together, we have disagreed on several basic issues related to the subject of this book and the methods of studying it. We have continued our work separately. Very few common ideas remain in the first chapter, and I alone carry the responsibility for the book as a whole.

I am especially indebted to Dr. Warren H. Donnelly, Senior Specialist in the Congressional Research Service of the U.S. Library of Congress; and to Professor Russell Stone, general editor of the SUNY Series in Israeli Studies, to Clay Morgan, my editor at SUNY Press, and to Janice Byer, who edited the entire manuscript, my wise and patient collaborators from the inception of our common enterprise: the transformation of my Hebrew-German English into a readable book.

My wife, Dalia, was the only real victim of the nuclear war waged for five years between me, the sources, and the computer; I am not sure the outcome will reassure her.

Introduction

In May 1991, United States President George Bush announced an arms control initiative for the Middle East. His main targets were nuclear weapons, missiles capable of carrying them, and other weapons of mass destruction, such as chemical and biological warheads. Mr. Bush's public initiative was rather short; but in it, he declared the Middle East to be especially dangerous in regard to nuclear weapons, and he promised action.

The presidential initiative seemed to be the tip of the iceberg—or of several icebergs, whose emergence and development are the subject matter of this book. Bush's initiative—when specifically aimed at the Middle East—remained general and universal, at least on the face of it. It addressed itself to phenomena that proliferation scholars sometimes call "undeclared bombs."[1] We shall call them "opaque" nuclear cases.

The adjective "opaque" is derived from physics. In this context, it can be used to describe what happens when one looks at an object through a certain type of crystal. Depending on how you hold the crystal, you might not see the object clearly—it will be distorted. But if you hold the crystal "properly," you will see the object very clearly indeed.

This is the challenge: to inquire into very important phenomena—the most important in the nuclear age—when the available, official information is incomplete, sometimes missing, and many times purposely misleading.

I have used three sources of information, so that when all sources were compatible, an agreed-upon version could be offered. First, I have used official information—from various sources, public and archival, at home and abroad. In spite of the veil of security and censorship that usually covers sensitive subjects like ours, a wealth of firsthand information can now be found in the American presidential archives, in the Library of Congress, in private freedom of information institutions, and even in memorabilia that must be carefully compared to the primary sources themselves. True, this is not the whole story. Therefore, as a second source, I have studied the actions as well as the words of various actors in the arena; and thus their behavior—as far as it could be reconstructed—was added to their public stances and to the archival sources. And third, I have used a very large body of secondary sources related to the issue.

My methodology was empirical-historical and inductive. I began with only one preconceived assumption; that nuclear weapons meant a new phase in human history, not only because of their power of destruction but also because of the symbolism and the emotions attached to them. I started with the facts and developed from them a larger picture in which some basic features could be seen repeatedly. Patterns emerged. These patterns could then be used—with much care—to study further developments and deviations from the patterns. None of the patterns, however, became a universalistic law—except in very broad and probabilistic terms—because of the uniqueness of the profound change imposed on human history by nuclear weapons, and because of their historical, cultural, and political uses.

Mr. Bush's initiative has seemingly closed a circle that began in Eisenhower's and Kennedy's days. At that time, proliferation became a source of concern to the superpowers—and Israel did not escape their attention. Since then, however, "undeclared bombs" have been added to the declared ones in the Middle East and in the Subcontinent. Something like a worldwide nuclear underground is in the making, and it is possible that previous efforts to limit or ignore it have failed. In this connection, we must ask whether opacity, or the undeclared status of existing bombs, had seemed to be better than a declared status until it seemed clear that proliferation, declared or not, had reached such dimensions that it might prove dangerous to the international order. According to Mr. Bush, by the end of the century many countries may possess nuclear bombs, in the fashion that is the subject of this book— probably undeclared.

Our problem is to inquire into the relationship between proliferation and the nonproliferation campaign. But first we must study the initial motives for the acquisition of "national nuclear options" by countries such as Israel in comparison to the motives of the official members of the "nuclear club."

There have been a number of contextual solutions to proliferation, such as the Non-Proliferation Treaty (NPT) of 1968, the London Supplier Group (LSG) controls over nuclear materials of 1976, and the 1987 Missile Technology Control Regime (MTCR). And now we have Mr. Bush's initiative. We will discuss these efforts in the political-cultural context of the Middle East. We will study their technical-abstract nature in the context of historical conflicts and the various cases of the behavior of "elites," who may have perceived in these solutions an unacceptable infringement of freedom of action, national interest, and basic values. We shall study the very issues that usually belong to the political history of the Middle East rather than to the study of nuclear proliferation per se. We are interested not just in the bomb but in the people who are interested in having it. We are not only interested in the strategic aspects of nuclear thinking, because we have come to believe, as a result of this study, that in the nuclear age strategy and politics are linked much more than was so in the past. In Chapter 1, we will inquire into the nature of politics and strategy. This will explain the Middle Eastern reality better than any discussion of Israeli and Arab politics and history in isolation from nuclear proliferation.

We must examine the existing literature very critically and be aware of the motives of writers who excelled in either technical or pure strategic analysis but were innocent of the political and cultural aspects of Middle Eastern reality. Some of these writers may even have been interested in exposing technical data while ignoring its strategic and political value. For example, the British nuclear physicist and antinuclear activist Frank Barnaby attempted to analyze the Israeli case by using photographed and oral data given to him by Mordechai Vanunu (the nuclear technician who had photographed the underground Israeli facility at Dimona). Barnaby painstakingly disclosed every detail of plutonium production at Dimona, the location of each installation and its mode of technical operation, and information on assembling bombs and assessing their power—presenting Israel as a thermonuclear nation with capabilities comparable to those of Great Britain and China.[2] He gives us detailed technical information without giving any political-historical framework.

We will look into the historical development of "undeclared bombs" from various viewpoints. This will bring us to the question of whether opacity is a clear-cut breach of internationally accepted norms or whether it is (or was at least for some time) a deviation from the norm which is not obvious—and therefore does not fully break international norms. Then we will look into the question of whether opaque nuclear weapons could fulfill a strategic-political function, or whether they could be at least halfway ignored.

We are dealing with phenomena that are sometimes concealed by governments—partially or fully—and sometimes denied by scholars. We must create the time frames in which to study these problems in relation to global developments. For example, if the Israeli option preceded NPT, whereas Arabs had to operate within the norms created by the treaty, the problem might have been aggravated by a sense of discrimination, or it may be that NPT itself made it easier for Arabs to acquire military nuclear potential.

We shall also look into the problem of whether the nonproliferation regime itself, as agreed upon by the superpowers in the late 1960s, generated—maybe even deliberately—the opaque solution that recently proved to be unacceptable to the Bush Administration.[3] In other words, if Israel's opaque case was somehow tolerable for a time, the fear that others would follow suit (and might not even remain opaque) revived the efforts initiated by Eisenhower and Kennedy—now that enough experience has been gained with NPT and other measures to cast doubt on their effectiveness.

The changes in the international environment—that is, the end of the cold war—must be studied as well, as a reason to tackle proliferation in the Middle East and as an explanation of why proliferation, especially in the Israeli case, was not prevented earlier. We must further look into the discrepancy between a change of heart and the resolution of the conflict between the great powers who realized that in the nuclear age it had become impossible to carry on as they were—especially in a region in which even an open discussion of nuclear weapons is difficult due to opacity.

We shall dwell on the origins of the issue. When it comes to Israel, our problem will be to trace the origins of what is perceived to be Israel's official opaque stance. The questions will be whether the Israelis were pushed to adopt an opaque stance against their better judgment or adopted such a stance by themselves for a number of reasons, requiring a detailed study of the political system and of internal debates. We shall bring this analysis together with the relations between the superpowers leading to and following NPT. And we shall examine the merits of the opaque posture as a factor influencing Arab behavior.

The case of Israel's opacity could, of course, be perceived as an incentive for many other nations in the region (and beyond) to follow in Israel's undeclared footsteps. But we must ask ourselves why proud and ancient nations, such as Egypt, and new-old ones, such as Iraq, Syria, and Libya, would refrain from seeking the most striking symbol of power in the nuclear age. We shall ask ourselves whether some Arab states adopted changed or interchangeable attitudes in this regard, especially when confronted with the Israeli nuclear option, and consciously decided not to pursue a nuclear option.

Finally, we shall look in some detail at the Gulf War of 1991 in the context of Iraq's nuclear ambition and in the context of the efforts to eliminate it, which may have spilled over into Bush's initiative. And we shall try to analyze the chances of this initiative's success, both in the context of the Middle East peace process and outside of it.

CHAPTER ONE

Strategy, History, and Politics

Nuclear strategy—both in regard to proliferation and nonproliferation—must be studied within a political-historical context. Yet one of the original assumptions behind the nonproliferation campaign can be sought through deductive and apolitical thinking, as Robert Jervis argued about Western deterrence theories ten years ago.[1] An apolitical approach harbors many of its supporters' values and status quo biases, some of which characterize not only nonproliferation thinking in the West but also General Pierre Gallois' and Kenneth Waltz's "pro-proliferation" thinking.[2] These arguments neutralize each other, leaving only one direction for fruitful discussion, that of historical analysis.

Like many deductive theories of human behavior, non- and pro-proliferation thinking harbor contradictory assumptions about human nature. Thomas C. Schelling, otherwise a liberal thinker, is pessimistic about humankind's common sense and responsibility with regard to nuclear weapons, and he bases his opinion on the assumption (discussed in Chapter 2) that madmen and children cannot be deterred. In Schelling's view, the more people with access to nuclear weapons, the greater the likelihood that one of "them" will be prepared to use these weapons, even in the face of counternuclear threats. The rather conservative French General Gallois, on the other hand, as well as his American colleague Waltz, take the optimistic view that nuclear elites are forced to socialize with each other, because they realize that each has the power to destroy the other. Such generalizations, I believe, require examination in contemporary historical terms. But we must always be conscious of the way these theories have *already* influenced reality.

Let us start our argument with the contention that nonproliferation thinking is based, among other things, on deterrence-theoretical thinking, and on what we will call the "strategic" approach. This approach is highly technical and relies on a specific terminology. Furthermore, nonproliferation is anchored in a moral-political commitment against the bomb, whose historical roots should be studied from the vantage point of the 1990s. Finally, nonproliferation is, of course, an obvious tool used by the possessors of nuclear weapons for their own purposes; however, as a result of the open nuclear race and nuclear threats of the past, possessors have developed various kinds of responsibilities toward each other, as well as toward third parties.

As we have already stated, nuclear proliferation, including its opaque pattern, is politically motivated, and must be studied as a political-historical, culture-bound phenomenon.[3] The actual scholarly work in this regard requires a good knowledge of the cultures and histories of the nations involved. Such a very broad study could not be offered here; the political aspects are the main focus of this book. The reader can consult history books and other sources of such information to put my political science into the utterly necessary framework of historical analysis.

In the context of cultural-historical values and beliefs, "political" is understood here as the use of power to acquire and maintain control over people, over territory and natural resources, or to influence human behavior. "Political" can be divided into two categories: "high politics," referring to basic values, as one understands them and scholars may judge them to be; and "low politics," referring to personal, partisan, and prestige calculations (when we grossly simplify these matters for our purposes). Still, the question remains as to whether the nuclear age has not transformed this complex from that of a mere power game to a struggle whose results are more predictable. In other words, whereas a conventional power game could be efforts to attain and use power at all costs, because at least one party believed that the results were undeterminable in advance, the nuclear age may have transformed politics into an effort to acquire those things of value in an individual cultural-historical context with power, which must be used with care, as a major item among them. In this connection, we must ask ourselves which power has an opaque posture due to its peculiar character. But, before discussing this, let us return to our definition of politics, which, in our view, may include the well-known goal of "grand strategy": to influence the enemy's will to fight.[4] The values and the history, the psychology and the cultural aspects of the enemy's existence, are no less important to our understanding than the "means," the actual subject matter for many strategic-military thinkers.

"High politics" could mean, for great powers, a high degree of influence over the international order, by spreading one's values in order to secure and develop an international economic order or to secure natural resources (both inside and outside of one's territory). All of these aspects may also become intertwined with domestic political variables that could be perceived by us as "low." The wasteful use of untaxed, imported oil in the United States could belong to such a category, as could the reelection of a congressman or even the election of a president who promises no tax increases. Yet these examples are related to "high political" ones too, such as preventing Saddam Hussein's Iraq from seizing control over Kuwait's oil to fuel its military-political ambitions. "High political" goals are therefore complex, when great powers and even regional powers are involved. And since they are always mixed with "low political" goals, the politicians involved in them sometimes have great difficulties in explaining them to their own people, especially in democracies.

In the case of Israel, as in the case of other small powers, the main "high political" issue can be that of the survival of old and new societies. Sheer survival seems relatively easy to define, yet even this simple concept is subject to various interpretations, including one relating specifically to the nuclear age. We, the scholars, must study the "low political" aspects hidden behind arguments coined in terms of survival, and discern the cultural-historical, possibly the psychological, reasons that lend them "high political" significance in the eyes of their consumers (and maybe in the eyes of the politicians who use them).

At this early stage, we must address one of the most difficult problems tackled in this book: the issue of Israeli and Palestinian statehood. Viewed in terms of survival, the problem can only be fully understood if we add to it historical-cultural and a variety of psychological aspects. Jews perceive themselves to be not just a nation but a civilization connected to a certain territory that gave it its significance and was later taken over by other civilizations. This civilization adopted a variety of interpretations, including a modern secular one that stresses the role of emancipation and independence in terms of survival, as well as offering a refuge for Jews and a political base for the future development of that civilization. Palestinians, on the other hand, belong to a larger civilization and a larger nation, divided into separate political entities. Their quest for independence may be perceived by them as an issue of survival, i.e., of emancipation and independence among other Arab nations. Another basic difference is that although many Jews in the Diaspora support Israel, they will not move to Israel and live there—in fact, they would even defend their right to be citizens of the world or of their respective countries. Palestinians, on the other hand, usually have the support of other Arabs. And yet under some circumstances Arab Palestine might be claimed by other Arab entities (such as Syria and its Arab inhabitants, declared to be "Southern Syrians"). History plays an important role here when the past—sometimes the very remote past—is invoked to define boundaries and to serve claims for territory, such as in the case of Iraq's claim to Kuwait or militant Israelis' claims to the West Bank. This process can assume a variety of "low political" motives when someone such as Saddam Hussein needs Kuwait's money or when the Likud Party in Israel must defend its ideological essence in the polls.

Historically, Israel is a given fact in the nuclear age, and its destruction would require the use of force. Therefore, the nuclear factor must be studied as a variable that is independent of and yet related to all of the other factors (historical, cultural aspirations, and so on) mentioned above.

The strategic aspect of nuclear proliferation, that is, its deterrent value, and the counterstruggle to defeat the bomb's role as a deterrent in the hands of proliferators, were both shaped to a considerable extent by nuclear strategic theory, which was born in the original, open nuclear nations. Nonproliferation policies were accompanied by a variety of "political" features, such as the use of carrot-and-stick measures to prevent proliferation, an array of secret diplomatic moves and leaks, and possibly—especially in the case of the United States—the "opaque" pattern itself. This "opaque" pattern was thus a mixture of political measures combined with strategic-theoretical elements. "Political" should be understood here in terms of secret diplomacy, of avoiding open confrontations, of offering conventional weapons and economic aid and the like; and "strategic" understood in terms of avoiding military dangers related to the bomb in principle and in particular when the superpowers could have drawn to a regional conflict. "Strategic" can also mean here the denial of political-strategic advantages from the bomb for the proliferator.

But proliferation always carries with it the connotation of being expansionary, even if it is used as a deterrent only and its role can actually be aimed at preserving the status quo, which could hardly be maintained by invoking conventional deterrence alone. Further proliferation, by anti-status quo powers, might serve as a tool to regain the freedom of, at least, conventional action. And yet, the nonproliferation "regime" may transform all these activities to less visible, half-hidden— i.e., "opaque"—ones, at least as far as the general public is concerned. The questions remain, then: Did this opacity influence military decisions and political processes in the Middle East? Did it obscure facts that otherwise would have contributed to stability and peace? Or did it conceal developments that may soon lead to instability and war? Has opacity given the politicians involved better tools to handle Middle East crises? Apparently, President Bush's initiative in May 1991 expresses dissatisfaction with the present state of affairs (even if the initiative itself was expressed in rather opaque terms).

Israel can be perceived as having invoked opaque nuclear deterrence either to maintain the status quo or to try to resolve its conflict with the Arabs and make peace. Israel can also be viewed as having used conventional means to change the status quo because it did not believe in nuclear deterrence. Therefore, Israeli policymakers felt that they needed strategic depth and territorial trump cards for peace. This, however, was not the whole picture. Other considerations—both domestic and foreign, related to Israeli-American relations and to ideological and conventional-military priorities—intervened with the "pure" strategic-political calculations in regard to the nuclear option. Arabs, on the other hand, have tried (some may still be trying) to change the status quo by neutralizing Israel's nuclear option—if not physically, then through deterrence-theoretical terminology and other political and military tools. Several Arab states might have used Israel's nuclear threat, opaque though it might be, to justify their own nuclear ambitions beyond the Arab-Israeli dispute. In the nuclear age, nuclear weapons can be perceived by some Arab leaders as the key to their own, to their state's, and to the Arab nation's power and glory.

The "opacity" of some of the Arab parties involved in nuclear proliferation has been motivated by many considerations. Some of them seem to have been drawn into playing Israel's own game of opacity. A few members of the Arab camp have been quite open on the subject, however; others have adopted interchangeable positions, acting directly or discreetly as they see fit. Nuclear strategy, as it was born in the West, is also a historical-cultural way of thinking, but it has a life of its own as a sort of autonomous paradigm.[5] Yet autonomy doesn't produce concurrence. An important question to resolve is whether the Soviets, and later the Chinese, refused to adopt the Western view of nuclear weapons and nuclear strategy, at first at least, and whether they influenced other nations in their own initial efforts to maintain high-level conflicts in the nuclear age. Yet another question is how nuclear weapons were regarded by others in the world who wanted to use power to achieve value-bound goals, enhance their interests, and give vent to their drives—the contents of politics, in the nuclear age and before. These value-bound goals, these interests and drives, must be studied historically in order to compare what nuclear weapons and their actual workings mean to "undeclared nations" and to those already declared. These factors must be studied across the spectrum of the foreign and domestic politics of the countries involved in undeclared proliferation in a specific region, with some comparisons to other regions, such as the Subcontinent.

Nuclear proliferation could be taken as being the first development of bombs beyond the original party in possession of one, as no real consensus had been reached worldwide on a distinction between those nations "entitled" to bombs and those not entitled. And yet, the rise of Soviet Russia during World War II to its seemingly ever-growing status as a world power, had de facto given it the "right" to pursue the bomb, once the Baruch Plan and other ideas regarding the possible sharing of the new energy among nations proved to be futile.

The original nuclear nations, while providing an example of how and why nuclearization could be achieved, objected to further nuclearization by other nations in their nonproliferation policies, which reflected both domestic and foreign considerations. With the export of these opposing ideas—active nonproliferation and nuclearization by example—the ideas and policies of the original nuclear nations (and their behavior vis-à-vis each other) all became part of the study of proliferation itself. As we have already argued, proliferation and its effects must not be separated either from the nations, cultures, and people involved in it—whether successfully or not—or from the strategic and political thinking of the nuclear powers themselves.

Our question, however, concerns "undeclared bombs," which seem to be a new form of proliferation. Has their development been inspired by the same considerations that have led to the acquisition of nuclear weapons in the past, or are they a response to something else? Could they be a response to the changed international environment created by the nuclear stalemate between the superpowers themselves, and to the resulting insecurity? Or are they the result of smaller nations' growing power of bargaining? In other words, did undeclared bombs emerge as a result of the agreement between the great powers among themselves to curb proliferation? Did this agreement, a byproduct of the superpowers' own nuclear stalemate, leave various clients of one of them frustrated in their own regional conflicts, or even in their drive to use superpower rivalry for their own goals? Did that stalemate, and the ensuing decline of Soviet power, give some Arabs the feeling that they must develop their own, independent nuclear power? Did some radical Arab leaders feel "naked" because Soviet power had declined, or did they feel encouraged to pursue their own way? Did they start their nuclear effort under conditions, now changed, of superpower rivalry, which some of them had hoped would give them enough leeway to "go nuclear," at least in opaque terms, in spite of the declared nonproliferation policy of the superpowers?

Did standing and prestige, the quest for regional hegemony, the maintenance of a regional conflict on its own merits, or in order to serve purposes of nation-building and modernization, play a decisive role here? How could this be achieved in an "undeclared" fashion? This is even more of a problem when, in the Arab-Israeli context, Arab states pursued changes in the status quo by invoking military means—e.g., in 1973—in a region that already contained "undeclared" bombs. Have the specific uses of military means in such cases, such as the Yom Kippur War of 1973 and even the Gulf War of 1991, emerged as a result of the inputs of the superpowers? Or was Arab behavior in these cases constrained or enhanced by any strategic thinking and behavior originated in the superpowers' approach to limited wars in the nuclear age, or in other nations such as China and Vietnam? What role was played here by Israel's "undeclared" nuclear option?

This brings us back to the problem of defining "undeclared bombs" and opaque nuclear proliferation within the context of Western strategic thinking and actual behavior. First, opaque proliferation is technically a process of nuclear research and development that is believed by foreign governments and by most of the scholarly community to be comparable to full-fledged nuclear status, including delivery means. Yet, such governments and proliferation scholars may refuse to acknowledge the process as such, and declare the deterrent and/or the political value of nuclear weapons in this case to be almost nil.[6]

Second, because opacity is an undeclared nuclear status, it cannot have visible means of demonstrating technical perfection, such as open testing or missile launching. This undeclared state does not allow clear-cut nuclear threats by the possessor government. As such, opaque proliferation can leave totally contradictory impressions: either that it is a status that is more manageable than an open one because the lack of clarity allows maneuverability, or that it is even less manageable because it is a lie, a breach of an international norm, or a desperate effort of a pariah state to maintain its untenable existence. Thus, it is an advance warning of the likelihood of unconstrained behavior by such a nation. It could also be perceived, especially in the Israeli case, as being highly impractical, because no final borders are defined and the territory to be protected by nuclear threats is disputed by many members of the international community. And yet Israel may think that this is the only way to make that border secure. Still, it would only be able to do this in opaque terms.

Third, opaque proliferation is an opportunity for the enemies of a possessor nation to forgo a policy of complete hostility toward the traditional, but now nuclear, enemy; it is even possible to accept it, while retaining the freedom to find the political rationale for this shift in policy. These enemies are able to justify making peace without mentioning the bomb—even though it is the main reason for pursuing peace. But even partially admitting that the bomb was the reason can be suffered without too much humiliation, if other reasons, such as winning back occupied territory, are used as the main reasons for peacemaking. A conflict can be maintained on a level beneath one of possible nuclear devastation by capitalizing on several aspects of the opaque posture: its deviation from the nonproliferation norm, which could imply superpower support of the proliferator's enemy; greater maneuverability due to its less clear meaning in terms of "red lines"; and the consequent ability to assume protection only of specific territory by the possessor nation. And because of this opaqueness, there is often the real possibility of working in accord with the domestic disagreement among the decision makers of the possessor nation. In such cases nuclear weapons might not even be regarded as a real political-strategic tool in the eyes of their possessors; but if they are construed as such a tool, their range could be from full to minimal to "last resort" only.

Fourth, opaque proliferation may indeed entail considerable confusion within the states who have adopted such a posture. It certainly allows for division about nuclear weapons as political tools and as strategic deterrents, although a unified backing to an opaque front is equally possible. In Israel's case, Shimon Peres, the Labor leader, argued that in the nuclear age, the reasons for the previous Middle East wars and the quest for territory have become obsolete. He dismissed the old doctrine that assumed that Israel should prepare for a conventional war, preempt and occupy territory to use as a trump card for peace. He said that "no economy can sustain the cost of modern weaponry. Thus the modernization of the army endangers the economy. And of course, the price of war should not be forgotten, beyond the maintenance of the army: *no territory justifies the losses that the preempting party will have to sustain in order to occupy it, in a world of nuclear weapons. The conclusion is that we should depart from military confrontations . . . in the Middle East* [italics added] . . ."[7]

Peres further stated that the nuclear stalemate between the superpowers had rendered Soviet aid to Arabs in their bid to destroy Israel impossible. But he did not go beyond a certain formulation, which made his language appear general and "opaque." Since most Israelis had only a vague idea of what Peres was talking about, his approach could be ignored by Yitzhak Shamir, the leader of the nationalist Likud bloc, whose ideological quest for territory remains supreme. This did not mean that Shamir had no opaque nuclear concept of his own; he most likely had one supporting his political-ideological refusal to give up territory in the West Bank, Gaza, or the Golan Heights. However, his approach remained half-hidden as well, relying on popular sentiment in favor of Israel's presence in that territory to give it weight. However, both Labor and Likud might have invoked opaque nuclear threats vis-à-vis Syria's, Libya's, or Iraq's chemical weapon threats, even before the Gulf War in which such threats became almost fully open. They could even have agreed, in the past, on common efforts vis-à-vis implied Soviet nuclear threats, when Soviet-Arab relations gave such threats a certain role to play. This, however, requires a detailed investigation. Other elements, especially several groups of Israeli radicals, may abhor the very idea of relying on nuclear weapons at all, whether Israel has them or not.

The approach of such groups is a different kind of opacity: the deliberate denial of nuclear options as if they never existed, until peace—or even nuclear disarmament agreements without peace—either solves the conflict or allows the region to become nuclear-free. A milder version of such opacity acknowledges the existence of nuclear options in Israeli hands, but denies them any or much deterrent value by invoking academic deterrence theories and other practical-historical arguments.

Thus, we return to the presumed effect of "opaque" nuclear postures on an enemy or several enemies. In cases where nuclear weapons are regarded as "last resorts" or as hardly applicable political-strategic tools, the assumed low credibility of nuclear threats could allow major wars to occur. Undertaken by conventional nations against nuclear ones, such wars could trigger the actual use of the bomb. Another possibility is the assumption by the enemies of an "opaque" nuclear nation of an "opaque" counterthreat, which would allow the same results: a high-level conflict and major wars that could deteriorate into an exchange of nuclear blows. Yet another possibility, though not likely to lead to the use of the bomb, is a conventional guerrilla war, or low-density war, as the answer to nuclear threats in the post-Hiroshima age. These might be waged even more successfully against an opaque nuclear nation than against an open one. When several of these possibilities combine, the final outcome could be the maintenance of a high-level conflict, which indeed may deteriorate to the actual use of nuclear weapons by one party when challenged by several hostile and uncoordinated conventional—and one day nuclear—enemies.

Thus, undeclared bombs—whose credibility seems to be in doubt because of domestic disagreement, the lack of clearly stated threats, and other reasons — may be perceived as a new danger to the world. Making them "declared," however, can be seen as an unmitigated disaster. "Declaring" would lead to the unavoidable collapse of the nonproliferation regime, resulting in the complete loss of control over nuclear weapons.

This might have been the idea behind President Bush's May 1991 initiative. The possible open introduction of the bomb may complicate the Middle East peace process, because it can add to it various and complementary issues. Israel itself, or important outside powers, may wish to prevent open nuclear threats in that complex and sensitive region. On the other hand, it may be seen that just such threats are necessary to make peace acceptable, including territorial and political concessions that must accompany a peace process—or that may in fact be the very substance of such a process. As a result of the desire to avoid open threats, however, the domestic and foreign political processes related to peace negotiations may assume a different, largely distorted character, due to the "hidden" or "opaque" nature of the nuclear options involved. In Israel, a political faction that hates to make concessions—such as giving up the occupied territories—or to lose American conventional and financial aid, and so forth, may believe, or at least argue, that such goals are related to nuclear strategy, to its limitations, and to the "opaque" nature of its own nuclear options. In any case, the outcome of this situation could still be an "undeclared bomb," only fully dealt with by those among the scholarly community who study proliferation—and whose attitude toward such a phenomenon is mostly negative. We shall deal separately with governments and intelligence agencies that are very much interested in these phenomena. They are certainly politically motivated.

Proliferation experts have not been totally apolitical. There has been a predominant notion that proliferation in the form of an undeclared nuclear posture took root, or threatened to take root, specifically among "pariah states," such as Israel, South Africa, Taiwan, and South Korea.[8] At the time this terminology was first promulgated, Egypt, which could not quite be called a pariah, had already been toying with unconventional capabilities, not necessarily because of the Israeli challenge, but in the interests of its long-held aspirations to lead a new, Arab world power. Iraq was actually in the process of acquiring nuclear weapons production capabilities for quite some time without some proliferation experts taking much notice. It escaped notice among other reasons because the focus was concentrated on pariah states, and its motives were clearly not pariah, but rather, deeply embedded in Arab politics.

India, meanwhile, had even exploded a nuclear device in 1974. But the explosion was claimed to be for peaceful use, so the users of the pariah terminology—and some members of the nonproliferation lobby as well—could ignore this case. Pakistan's nuclearization has also been well under way. And Israel's options could have been seen as the precedent that halfway legitimized Pakistan's "Islamic bomb," although the real reason was more likely to have been the Indian challenge.

Thus the very use of the term "pariah state" by scholars in regard to Israel could have been enough to justify both Pakistan's and Iraq's efforts in the eyes of some scholars and officials whose attention was focused rather myopically on Israel. Whereas others tended to keep Israel—without having any serious remaining doubts about the nature of its nuclear efforts—outside as a sui generis case. Still, most scholars of both schools tended, until recently, to treat Israel's nuclear arsenal and its nuclear strategic and political options in several ways: i.e., by questioning facts or at least leaving them open to various interpretations; by arguing against the strategic-political value of nuclear weapons in Israel's case; or by limiting it to the "last resort" formula, which by itself is rather unclear. This was the picture during the 1960s, 1970s, and early 1980s, when Iraq embarked upon the first serious effort in the Arab world to acquire the bomb within the rules of NPT. Israel, alone, had to tackle the potential Iraqi threat by introducing a novel method of dealing with proliferation: i.e., knocking out the enemy's reactors, even though they were under International Atomic Energy Agency (IAEA) control and built within the framework of NPT. Iraq then continued its effort by invoking other means. That effort became a major factor, in conjunction with oil, considered by the United States in responding to Saddam Hussein's invasion of Kuwait. While the results of the American-led effort remain uncertain, the Bush Administration tried to make the whole region free of nuclear weapons, and thus focused attention on Israel again. This brings us back to the earlier discussion of the Israeli case.

The pariah thesis used a deductive method for political analysis, assuming that Israel was a pariah state at that stage in its history, and arguing that countries like South Africa and Taiwan should be categorized as similar phenomena. The argument went on to question the value of nuclear solutions for pariah states by using strategic-technical arguments. This was part of the work of Robert Harkavy (cited above), and he used his strategic-technical assumptions in a typically deductive fashion. He calculated the possibility that the Soviets would administer a nuclear blow to Israel, and even considered whether Israel, having absorbed a Soviet "first strike," should consider hardening nuclear silos in order to deliver a "triangular second strike capability" against Arab cities. At the same time, Harkavy could seriously ask whether

> Israel would ever have embarked on such a [presumably] expensive and [with regard to the United States] politically dangerous nuclear weapons program if it had not felt reasonably optimistic about the *technical possibilities for effective deterrence, despite the Soviet counterthreat* [italics added].[9]

Is this emphasis on "technical possibilities for effective deterrence" enough to explain Israeli or Soviet behavior? We have argued that the issue is primarily political, not technical. Therefore, while nuclear weapons and delivery means are, of course, "technical" by their very nature, the main key to understanding their possible role in Israel's case is the origin, the nature, and the development of Arab politics and behavior vis-à-vis Israel, and vice versa, in the context of Soviet-Arab, Soviet-Israeli, Soviet-American, and Arab-Arab relations. Other nations, such as China, North Korea, and especially Vietnam, must not be forgotten in the Arab context. The political dimensions of this complex go far beyond the technical ones when the subject matter is nuclear weapons and their means of delivery. This would make Israel's case perforce different from any other cases of proliferation. Of course, other proliferating nations' behavior is also the result of their specific political circumstances, and each one of them must be evaluated as a case in itself. But Israel's situation with regard to the Soviet Union must be further studied in terms of Soviet ideology, history, and domestic policy, and in terms of the relations between the Soviet Union and nations such as China and the West—as well as in terms of Israel's own behavior.

Thus let us examine a more recent strategic-technical scenario, published in the United States in 1988 by Kurt Gottfried and Bruce Blair. This scenario argues that a rather large Israeli nuclear arsenal exists (based on Mordechai Vanunu's revelations to the London *Times* two years before). It also calculates Syrian chemical weapons, and a possible conventional Syrian advantage that might, under certain circumstances, allow President Assad a surprise conventional attack, covered by chemical missiles. The scenario then describes the ensuing threats to vital Israeli centers such as Haifa, a possible Israeli nuclear counterthreat, a Soviet nuclear "surgical" strike against Israeli nuclear facilities, American intervention to save the Israelis and restore the status quo, the Soviet refusal to do so, and so forth.[10] This scenario is based solely on capabilities, or "means," and is totally innocent of any political-historical argument, except for the often-used Cuban Missile Crisis. In his 1989 book, British physicist and antinuclear activist Frank Barnaby also argues against the Israeli nuclear program by invoking all conceivable anti-bomb arguments, including Soviet guarantees to the Arabs, and technical arguments against the neutron bombs that Israel had supposedly developed for battlefield use.[11] In contrast to these arguments, my contention is that the political-historical framework must be added to the above-mentioned technical- and capabilities-based argument in order to create the proper context.

Here, it should not be forgotten that Israel was born as a result of World War II, when the Jewish claim for at least a part of Palestine was finally legitimized by many members of the international community. Even Soviet Russia supported this claim for the creation of a Jewish state in a part of Palestine, and contributed to its survival. But this in itself is not the only reason to make a "Soviet nuclear counterthreat" in the service of an Arab war of destruction against Israel— at the time of the "pariah" argument's proposition—a rather questionable endeavor. When combined with American commitments to Israel (which may have been in turn related to the undeclared Israeli bomb that had been described abroad), with the "rules of the game" that emerged between the superpowers themselves regarding nuclear threats and nuclear sharing with third parties, and finally with Soviet foreign policy preferences and war fighting doctrines in the nuclear age, a "Soviet nuclear counterthreat" became rather difficult to prove. Indeed, highly qualified American analysts evaluated the possibility and rejected it as early as 1963. As far as further developments in this area are concerned, we must study them historically the best we can, because even such "counterthreats," if they were made at all, could have been "opaque" as well.

The more recent scenario (as described by Barnaby) disregards the major changes in Moscow's international behavior that have occurred since Gorbachev's takeover, including rather visible changes in the Kremlin's attitude toward Israel. This may be partially explained by the foreign news about the launching of Israeli missiles allegedly capable of striking at Moscow, and by a variety of domestic-foreign political developments in the Soviet Union itself. These political developments are nuclear-weapons-related in that they resulted, among other reasons, from the Soviet refusal to maintain a high-level worldwide conflict with the West in the nuclear age, because no victory proved possible in this race. Here, the "means," i.e., the related technologies, might have played a very important role. One may even speculate that the Soviets acknowledged that an enormously expensive nuclear race with a power whose GNP was double that of its own was leading nowhere, and that nuclear weapons at the hands of smaller powers could endanger it seriously, if it maintained a high-level international and even regional tension. Other reasons, of course, were general economic, domestic-political, and psychological, such as the emergence of a more liberal elite or elites in the Soviet Union.

In other words, deductive, technically inspired, deterrence-strategic-dominated thinking (such as the scenarios described above) seems to miss the political background involved in the emergence of Israel's nuclear development. Ironically enough, however, it was just this sort of technical, deductive thinking that was adopted by a number of Israeli politicians and even scholars later on. A group of them used it to produce the "ambiguous" Israeli posture of the 1960s and 1970s, a posture that was kept alive in the 1980s and early 1990s.[12] And this kind of thinking was even used to formulate the antithesis to the "ambiguous" posture—to wit, as suggested by me and later by Shai Feldman,[13] an Israeli student of Kenneth Waltz's—that an open Israeli nuclear posture would decisively guarantee its security, if Israel only withdrew to the pre-1967 lines and—as Feldman recommended—adopted a "launch upon warning" posture. Both approaches, when they remain deductive, abstract, and primarily based on logic and technical means, obviously only contradict each other and lead to no fruitful conclusion.

It is the purpose of this book to first explore the politics of Israel's nuclear behavior as perceived by others and as it became known within the rules of official opacity; second, to explore Arab behavior in this regard; and third, to study extra-regional inputs.

At the same time, the argument is put forward that "opaque" proliferation is not just an "ambiguous" nuclear posture, even if both terms are semiotically identical. "Ambiguity" is understood here as a historical phase in developing a nuclear-based, or -supported, foreign policy and strategy. In the ambiguous stage, capabilities are not yet ready—or are only partially ready—but efforts to achieve them are underway and there is a political need to hide them, but not always completely. That is, one uses them even at this stage for strategic and political purposes, and to meet domestic needs, even if in an ambiguous form. The ambiguous language could serve its users by avoiding foreign complications and staying within the rules of NPT, if necessary. Such was the case with Iraq; whereas, in Israel's case, the ambiguous stage preceded NPT itself. However, ambiguity may also represent a genuine desire—in practical terms, not just as the result of foreign pressure—to minimize the role of nuclear weapons in a nation's foreign policy and strategy for fear of the consequences in its foreign policy. Or else, an ambiguous nation could even be rejecting any serious role for its own nuclear potential on technical-practical and deterrence-theoretical grounds.[14]

"Opacity," on the other hand, is a deliberate decision not to assume an open nuclear posture when the capability to do so is fully developed, or regarded as such by foreign powers. This posture may be adopted for any of several reasons, among them foreign pressure to stay "undeclared," the enemy's perception of open threats as blackmail and humiliation, and possibly moral-cultural motives. Domestic political motives may also play an important role in presenting one's nuclear options to the general public in an opaque fashion, and thus they have little to do with foreign policy and with security considerations. Yet an opaque nation could, in fact, be seen as a full-fledged nuclear nation—with a peculiar status. And while a country's elites disagree on the exact role nuclear weapons play in that country's foreign and security policy, the general public has difficulty in following its own government's behavior. The enemy or enemies of such a nation may use the opaque posture for their own purposes.

The packaging of opacity for foreign consumption may be done by using opaque language, such as making nuclearlike threats disguised on the surface, or by demonstrating capabilities but calling them by other names—for example, by launching research satellites by means of nuclear-capable missiles. Opacity assumes a higher degree of credibility for nuclear options, in spite of theoretical and practical arguments to the contrary. But people who give opacity higher credibility have various political goals in mind and are motivated by various drives and interests while assuming such a posture. These motives, however (though not fully spelled out), might or might not have been chosen by them but were imposed on them by outside powers. Still, the ways and means toward opaque nuclear postures require a historical study, a comparison with the behavior of open nuclear nations, and a consideration of the countermeasures that have been used to prevent opaque nations from "going nuclear" at all, or at least openly.

Nations can be both ambiguous and opaque in today's world; whereas in the past they were simply covert until they became open. It may well be that only France and Israel, who happened to cooperate,[15] had a purely ambiguous phase in their nuclear history, whereas India intended from the beginning to be opaque.

We will, however, concentrate on only one region at the outset of this book, and will deal with India, Pakistan, Iran, North Korea, and some other would-be proliferators only at the end, in order to see to what extent their behavior can be compared with—or had any influence on—Middle Eastern actors.

An understanding of open behavior, as it influenced other nations, will illuminate our discussion. Therefore, we will begin with a short look at the open nuclear model, which was, historically, the first to emerge.

CHAPTER TWO

The American Paradigm and Early Efforts to Limit Proliferation

The Americans developed nuclear weapons because they believed that the Nazis were making an effort to gain control of such weapons in conditions of total war.[1] The road to World War II and the onset of war itself combined to produce theory and praxis in the West concerning the bomb. Nazism had deliberately broken the rules of international behavior before the war and had brutalized them in various spheres to such a degree that winning a possible nuclear race against Hitler in the middle of a world war seemed a matter of life and death. The Nazis had invoked "conventional" means and new technologies, such as cruise and ballistic missiles, and through their use of "revenge weapons," had shown that they were ready to use anything—even nuclear weapons (had they been available). Despite Hitler's beliefs in the racial superiority of the German people, one wonders whether even he would have regarded that superiority as an asset at the outset of a conflict involving nuclear weapons; in such a conflict racial qualities have no meaning. In the unique circumstance of a conventional war during which Hitler might have gained unilateral access to nuclear weapons the issue seemed, rightly, to be that of survival not only for the United States but for all human civilization.

Another point in our paradigm is that the American covert effort was made public by the dropping of two atomic bombs on Japan, an ally of the already-defeated Hitler, with the ostensible purpose of concluding World War II as early as possible and, thereby, saving many Allied and enemy lives. Even without reviewing the serious arguments presented against these bombings, we are well aware that they were

17

seen as setting a precedent instead as a warning or demonstration of a power that must never be actually used. The ensuing call was to share the new power with the Soviets, or even to use it to create some kind of world government to control global order, in the fear that otherwise the world might not survive this deadly invention.[2]

Among American policymakers, however, as we are told by McGeorge Bundy and John Newhouse in their works about the nuclear age, the use of the bomb was entirely justified in terms of shortening the war; it was anticipated that the atomic bomb would succeed where firebombing had failed.

Winston Churchill later formulated the Hiroshima decision as follows:

> The President invited me to confer with him forthwith . . . Up to this moment we had shaped our ideas towards an assault upon the homeland of Japan by terrific air bombing and by the invasion of very large armies. We had contemplated the desperate resistance of the Japanese fighting to the death with Samurai devotion, not only in pitched battles, but in every cave and dug-out . . . To quell the Japanese resistance man by man and conquer the country yard by yard might well require the loss of a million American lives and half that number of British . . . For we were resolved to share the agony. Now all this nightmare picture had vanished. In its place was the vision—fair and bright indeed it seemed—of the end of the whole war in one or two violent shocks. I thought immediately myself of how the Japanese people, whose courage I had always admired, might find in the apparition of this almost supernatural weapon an excuse which would save their honour and release them from their obligation of being killed to the last fighting man . . .
>
> At any rate, there never was a moment's discussion as to whether the atomic bomb should be used or not. To avert a vast, indefinite butchery, to bring the war to an end, to give peace to the world, to lay healing hands upon its tortured peoples by a manifestation of overwhelming power at the cost of a few explosions, seemed, after all our toils and perils, a miracle of deliverance.[3]

The Japanese did not respond immediately to the Allied nuclear challenge. The Japanese cabinet was hopelessly split on accepting defeat, even though, conventionally, Japan was in extremely bad shape. It took the emperor to make the actual decision for them. Hirohito's decision allowed the institution and the person of the mikado to remain in power in the shadow of occupation, and thereby, legitimize it for the Japanese people. In another situation, where there is no emperor to settle the matter for quarreling cabinet members, it is unlikely that a nation would be so quick to accept unconditional surrender.

Yet Churchill introduced here a psychological-cultural factor in dealing with the Oriental culture that other statesmen, such as Israel's David Ben-Gurion, might have examined on their own and found useful in dealing with a non-Western culture.

During World War II, the Jews did not escape Hitler's wrath; they could not fight back as the Allies did. This fact, combined with other political lessons, drove them back to a country they had left thousands of years before, back to a traditional environment in which their presence was deemed culturally and politically unacceptable. If we look at the Arab states as competing brotherly entities, sovereign and half-sovereign, whose potential for conventional warfare was potentially great and who had no strong cohesive leadership, we can see that Ben-Gurion's fear was the emergence of an Arab Hitler who (in Ben-Gurion's words) could unite the Arab states before Israel had entrenched itself.

So, Ben-Gurion would not allow Israel to go about its business without pursuing a nuclear option. Ben-Gurion was conscious of the fact that Zionism was something that could fit into the category of "subjective rationality"—a specific set of values, history, and psychology. It was the cultural-historical logic of Jews that Ben-Gurion accepted as the right one. But he was able to understand that others would not accept it and would fight it instead. Still, in his view, he was "right" and they were "wrong"—by itself an important substantive matter.

In the West this logic, when combined with positive efforts—some unique, such as the Kibbutz—was somewhat accepted before the Holocaust but was widely endorsed after the Holocaust. Not so among Arabs, whose own subjective rationality, plus political-military events that had occurred before and during the Israeli War of Independence, would reject the notion of Israel outright. To this we must add what we characterize as "low politics" of Arab leaders, states, and groups; "low politics" is inseparable from history and psychology—and in some cases it could become the most important problem. Israel's problem, therefore, was to develop objective tools that would be forced on Arab subjective rationality. This subjective rationality was mixed with several other dimensions—both "high political" and "low political." The very existence of Israel, for example, could be seen as "high political" to Jews but not to Arabs; Arab unification or hegemonic aspirations of Arab nations such as Egypt or Iraq could seem to be "high political" to some, if not to us; and the personal ambitions of leaders such as Gamal Abdel Nasser or Saddam Hussein could be regarded as "low political." Therefore, taking into account these various high and low political goals, we can see that, even at this stage, the term "rationality" was not enough to understand Arab behavior so that Israeli strategy could be shaped accordingly.

In Ben-Gurion's eyes, the toils and perils of the Jewish people during World War II might have seemed to have exceeded the suffering of the Allies in the war—suffering that had justified, in Churchill's words, a "nuclear respite" to subdue Japan. And parts of the historical-cultural argument could have seemed applicable to a degree to the Arab situation, though Ben-Gurion would have developed it independently before Churchill's remarks quoted above were published in the early 1950s. He might well have drawn conclusions from Hiroshima itself, and from the lessons he learned from Israel's 1948 War of Independence. The use of nuclear weapons against the Japanese played a political role. That is, the bomb provided an "excuse" for surrender: the proud and fighting tradition of the Samurai culture was being defeated not by men in the field but by "almost supernatural powers." For Israel, defending itself against the somewhat similar Islamic tradition, the bomb, if and when acquired, could serve the same purpose of making peace, or at least of allowing Arabs to accept Israel de facto, although with important adjustments.

In this context, the "political" use of nuclear weapons becomes clear: it is a technical-psychological, strategic measure aimed at making an enemy forgo war. Yet the usual meaning of "politics" is almost the opposite. As opposed to "strategic" calculations—which are aimed at fighting wars, winning them, or imposing one's will on the enemy by deterring him from pursuing his goals by force—"politics" has to do with one's prestige, standing, domestic political calculations, and the various tools related to pursuing these purposes.

My argument, however, as proposed in Chapter 1, is that when it comes to nuclear weapons, this distinction, when seen historically, is not always valid. In the case of Israel and Egypt, for example, nuclear capabilities—the implied threat of nuclear weapons—contributed heavily to something close to conflict resolution; the same can be said of the end of the cold war between Gorbachev's Soviet Union and the United States, at least in the heyday of Gorbachev's *perestroika*. In the case of Qaddafi's Libya and Saddam's Iraq nuclear weapons seem to be the precondition to continuing conflicts. Since these countries are in the process of trying to acquire the bomb, we do not know whether its acquisition can be prevented, or turned at least into opaque postures. And we must ask what will happen when and if they do acquire the bomb. Will the conflicts around these nations become worse, or will they accept the logic of mutual destruction and agree at least to some

kind of a stable, low-level conflict, on the way to eventual conflict resolution, a situation similar to that which developed between the two
original nuclear nations? In order to study these options, we must first
return to the nuclear history of the world since Hiroshima.

Churchill's view of Hiroshima was related solely to the situation in
1945, but it colored his opinion on the use of nuclear weapons in the
post-Hiroshima world. He argued against Clement Attlee's proposition that the United States should make an "act of faith" by offering its
atomic knowledge for the benefit of the whole world.[4] Churchill
believed that the American nuclear monopoly could be further used,
possibly in cooperation with the British, to restrain the Russians in
Europe, and possibly come to some political agreement with them. His
formulation at that early stage of the cold war was that since the Americans had a "two or three year lead" in the nuclear field, "in this short
interval they and we must reach some form of security based upon a
solemn covenant backed by force viz. the force of the atomic bomb,"
and only then a United Nations conference should be convened to deal
with the bomb itself. Churchill argued further that

> Nothing will give a foundation except the supreme resolve of all
> nations who possess or may possess the weapon to use it at once unit-
> edly against any nation that might use it in war. For this purpose the
> greater the power of the US and GB in the next few years the better are
> the hopes. The US therefore should not share their knowledge and
> advantage except in return for a system of inspection of this and all
> other weapon-preparations in every country, which they are satisfied
> after trial is genuine.[5]

This quotation introduces us to two elements in Western nuclear behavior relevant to our understanding of Israel's pursuance of a nuclear
option: first, the issue of the "nuclear lead" aimed at reaching a political
settlement based on "some form of security," arrived at through
"nuclear sharing"—in this case, of course, between the United States
and Great Britain, and second, the issue of international norms prohibiting the use of the bomb by any state. Israel's very acceptance by the
Arabs as a "state" would be the main issue at first. Thus for Ben-Gurion
"deterrence" and "conflict resolution" were close to one and the same
thing. Once the Arabs accepted Israel as a given, with or without formal
peace—which might indeed follow—a basic "high political" aim would
be secured. Allowing the Arabs to acquire the bomb first would be suicidal, so Israel had no other choice but to win the race and use its lead
the best it could. Paradoxically enough, Ben-Gurion's basic, pessimistic
assumptions about Arab belligerence and its reasons were intertwined

with optimistic assumptions about the impact of the bomb on them, if accompanied with a variety of other, "high political," measures including the maintenance of the partition of Palestine. His adversaries, such as General Yigal Allon, postulated conventional deterrence and compellence. Allon tended to believe that the introduction of the bomb and the following "balance of terror" would play into Arab hands. Others came to believe that Israel must add a new element to the nuclear history of the world: that of preventing adversaries from developing their own nuclear infrastructure at all.

Churchill was at first in the opposition, and actual British nuclear policy was decided upon by others. The 1989 study by Ian Clark and Nicholas Wheeler provides information that revises the "dismissive attitude toward the role of strategy in the formation of British atomic policy."[6] Here "strategy" is understood in the terms that we have attributed to "high politics"—aimed at preserving or enhancing elementary value-bound goals as opposed to sheer self-interest, prestige calculations, and seeking power for its own sake, even though such "strategy" may have had limited goals. The role of strategy was conceived, indeed, in terms of defending the British Isles by deterring the Soviets from attacking them; it did not pursue any further goals, such as changing Soviet behavior in other spheres.

In this connection, Clark and Wheeler tell us that if it is now anachronistic to read the decline of Britain as a superpower, as an extant and recognized condition, back into the period 1945-1947, it would seem to follow that the primarily political explanations of the British deterrent that emphasize the nostalgic quest for great power eminence are equally anachronistic. Thus, whatever it was to become in the longer term, "British nuclear strategy in its origins was *not* simply a reflection of political and economic decline." Rather, "it was based on a hardheaded analysis of Britain's strategic predicament as it confronted policy-makers in 1945"—even though Britain had no nuclear weapons at the time. And yet, Britain became "the first nation to base its national security planning almost entirely upon a declaratory policy of nuclear deterrence."[7]

The case of Israel seems to have been somewhat similar, except that what Clark and Wheeler call the "myopic vision" of the British chiefs of staff—which was finally accepted by Prime Minister Attlee, "whose initial reaction to the atomic bomb was little short of apocalyptic"—was, in the Israeli case, "the steady purpose of Prime Minister David Ben-Gurion," according to McGeorge Bundy.[8] Yet what Clark and Wheeler call "strategic thinking" was not necessarily the common view among Israeli generals and influential strategic thinkers. Bundy oversimplified a more complex picture.[9] We do not know whether Ben-Gurion would have adopted a "declaratory policy of nuclear deterrence." But military men, some already influenced by British- and American-inspired nuclear strategic ideas, combined these ideas with their perceptions of Arab behavior and developed serious doubts about their validity in the Israeli case. The most prominent among such military men was Yigal Allon, probably the best general in Israel's War of Independence (1947-1949), whose book *A Curtain of Sand*, first published in 1959, was the first open, clear-cut antinuclear strategic treatise in Israeli history.

We cannot prove in detail whether Allon was exposed to modern deterrence-theoretical thinking before he published the first version of *A Curtain of Sand* in 1959, but at least he was in principle interested in such literature. Since becoming a war leader, he had admired the writings of Captain B. H. Liddell-Hart. As early as 1946, Liddell-Hart had published a rather skeptical work on the limited utility of nuclear threats.[10] Hart stressed that Britain's vulnerability had to be reduced first in order to make the British nuclear deterrent credible.

As Allon saw it, Israel, in its 1949 boundaries, was much more vulnerable than were the British Isles. Hart underlined "the diminution of a country's vulnerability [as] the best deterrent to aggression—far better than a relatively feeble power of counterattack."[11]

Allon might also have read the collection edited by American strategic thinker Bernard Brodie and published in 1946 under the title *The Absolute Weapon*.[12] In this collection, Brodie argued that ultimately other countries besides the United States would have atomic weapons; he predicted that there would be no reliable means of defense against such weapons. In such a context, the role of military power would fundamentally change—a phrase that Allon used almost verbatim in his own book, echoing, and dismissing as bad for Israel, Brodie's conclusion that "Thus far, the chief purpose of the military establishment has been to win wars. From now on its chief purpose must be to avert them." Allon, in other words, wanted to maintain for Israel the option to fight conventional wars, when necessary, win them, and achieve strategic and territorial goals that went beyond those that were fixed as a result of Israel's War of Independence. Allon's main aim was one of "deterrence-compellence." That is, should deterrence fail, conventional compellence—rather than massive nuclear retaliation or sophisticated nuclear strategy (as developed later in the West)—plus territorial changes principally in Israel's favor should be pursued as trump cards.

Clark and Wheeler,[13] however, discuss interesting differences between early American and British nuclear strategic thinking; Allon might have been exposed to the British side of this thinking rather than the American. G. Herken tells us that "in retrospect it is somewhat surprising not how quickly but how slowly deterrence theory, and even clarity about the concept, developed after WWII."[14] We shall return to Churchill himself, in this regard, but first we will look more closely at what influenced Allon.

Allon went to England in the early 1950s to study at Oxford. There he had access to the military and to leftist Labour leaders. He might have endorsed the British concept of deterrence, but in contrast to that concept—which emphasized declaratory nuclear deterrence—Allon was working for deterrence by invoking conventional means, to be followed by using the same means to make peace. From leftist Labourites, he might have learned later, as we shall see, that "national bombs" were to be regarded as a prospect for disaster, since any "national bomb" in Europe might become available to the West Germans in due course, which would challenge the Soviet Union to take extreme countermeasures.

Yet, this was still to come. American thinking about the bomb developed rather slowly following Brodie's initial contribution. The Americans, "for about five years after the end of the war . . . lacked any systematic strategy or theory linking military planning to foreign policy objectives."[15] Or rather, "the United States was slow to embrace deterrence at the official level because it was torn between the conception that atomic bombs made little strategic difference and the conception that they made all the difference in the world"[16] (in the sense that they could decisively win wars and change Soviet behavior with or without wars).

"In Britain, precisely the reverse was the case . . . the concept of deterrence was one that had long since been embraced . . . Such a British doctrine of deterrence . . . was limited in scope and specific in intention . . . It was not a doctrine of compellence, seen as having great potential for shaping the general diplomatic behavior of the Soviet Union."[17] One could speculate that Allon followed British logic in this regard, in the sense that he had adopted the very concept of deterrence, however conventional, and added to it conventional compellence, rather than the limited British goal of maintaining the status quo. Nor would he endorse early American nuclear war-fighting doctrines or Ronald Reagan's or rather Edward Teller's later "defensive" version of nuclear "compellence." For Allon, compellence could be achieved by invoking conventional means in a conventional environment. Nuclear weapons meant, in the case of the Middle East, a dangerous status quo, which the Arabs could use for their own purposes.

At the same time and again later, Israeli politicians and generals-turned-politicians, such as Allon, were influenced not only by British strategic concepts but also by political considerations short of the "high political" ones—such as American pressure in regard to nuclear proliferation. Added to this was the fact that they were also influenced by domestic political and partisan interests and by personal reasons and drives. Foreign inputs to Israeli thinking were also grounded in Western strategic nuclear concepts as they developed later on. And these concepts, as Clark and Wheeler tell us, were based on the more "political" and integrated British approach to nuclear weapons, which entailed a serious discussion of the proliferation problem in relation to the issue of nuclear "sharing" with countries like West Germany. On the other hand, the early American approach, which had been adopted by some members of the military such as General Curtis LeMay,[18] was less integrated and more military-oriented.

Both the United States and Great Britain took it for granted that the Soviets would have their own bomb sooner or later. So the real issue was what could be done in the meantime while the Americans still held the nuclear monopoly. We have no evidence that the United States seriously planned the elimination of the Soviet nuclear weapon production industry in order to maintain its monopoly; however, the Americans were not ready to agree to a far-reaching political-strategic sharing in the nuclear weapons field with the British government, despite the initial scientific cooperation among the United States, Great Britain, and Canada in developing the American bomb. Thus, from the beginning, the British under Attlee pursued the bomb on their own—a secret that was kept not only from Parliament but certainly from the public as well. Due to the American McMahon Act, which prohibited nuclear sharing almost entirely, and also due to their own desire to acquire the bomb, the British, upon Churchill's return to power in 1951, completed their atomic "national bomb." Later, following a still-secret agreement with President Eisenhower,[19] and an amended version of the McMahon Act, the British developed a hydrogen bomb. This, of course, was the first breach of the exclusive dual membership rule of the Soviet-American nuclear club. Moreover, the renewed American-British cooperation was bound to enrage the French, if not the Soviets.

Yet, in my view, Churchill's public and private ideas about the bomb were still an important British contribution, which had a profound influence on the Americans, at least in shaping Western deterrence postures.[20] As the cold war reached its peak in Europe in the late 1940s, Churchill referred to the bomb as our "only hope as usual,"[21] and stressed the "deterrent" role of the atomic bomb. He popularized the term and drew a parallel with the lessons of the inter-war period: if the democracies had acted on time, Hitler could have been deterred, Nazi Germany could have been stopped, and "the unnecessary war" avoided.

As long as the atomic bomb was the sole nuclear weapon and the United States had a clear lead in the nuclear race, the American government under President Truman was bound to an extent by the document known as "NSC 68," of which Paul Nitze is said to have been the main author.[22] This document called for the containment of Soviet expansionism and rejected isolationism. Assuming that the United States must lead the free world by strengthening both its economy and its military forces, NSC 68 read "as though war, and nuclear war at that, was just around the corner, [and] ended by calling for a large scale build-up of American nuclear and conventional forces. A national shelter policy was also recommended."[23] President Truman, however, was careful not to use the bomb—both at the outset of the Korean War and when General MacArthur pushed for a major war with China. (The latter—a direct American involvement in continental Asia including the use of nuclear weapons against the largest and most important nation in that part of the world—by itself would have stood in direct contradiction to American traditions.)

Soon enough the Soviets had not only atomic weapons but also followed the United States in developing hydrogen bombs. And before long, it seemed, wrongly, that they had won the missile race. This is the third step in our paradigm: that the virtual American nuclear monopoly of 1945—supported by a growing arsenal, a variety of bombers, and foreign bases—was replaced by a growing nuclear and missile race with the Soviet Union, which exposed the United States itself to the hazards of virtual extinction. Deterrence, rather than warfighting doctrines, seemed to have carried the day, although as both McGeorge Bundy and John Newhouse stress, President Eisenhower's policy in regard to nuclear war-fighting was "enigmatic" from the beginning. Bundy aptly describes this policy as "the instructive difference between doctrine and behavior, theory and practice, in the time of Dwight Eisenhower."[24]

The vehement rivalry of the cold war saw Soviet defense doctrines that dismissed Western deterrence thinking as irrelevant to the Marxist-Leninist view on just wars, and explained away Western moves and countermoves in terms of class warfare initiated by imperialistic powers. In turn, Marxist-Leninist doctrine seemed to the West to be only a justification for Soviet expansionism. What was worse, however, was that Soviet doctrinaire thinking seemed to consider nuclear war as a practical, as well as a theoretically sustainable, possibility. The enormity of Soviet-controlled space, the habits and education of the vast Soviet population, and the political framework within which they were ruled, all seemed to justify Stalin in conducting a deliberate campaign to minimize the challenge of the atomic bomb.[25]

The public approach of the Soviets to the Western nuclear threat was also officially assumed by the Chinese even before they had any nuclear weapons of their own. This was demonstrated by Mao's dismissal of the United States as a "paper tiger," and by his actual military confrontations with the Americans in Korea and over the islands of the Formosa Straits.

Here we are introduced to two phenomena relevant to the Israeli-Arab case. The first is that of the official posture adopted by conventional adversaries of nuclear powers denying that the bomb would have a decisive impact on a conflict between them. A similar posture could be adopted by manpower-rich, territorially vast nations whose nuclear options are weak, such as the U.S.S.R. in the 1950s. Yet even Mao's risk-taking policies were not clear-cut; the Korean War was concluded when Eisenhower started to show nuclear impatience at the same time that the Soviets failed to support the Chinese with a credible nuclear guarantee. And this is the second problem relevant to the Middle East: that of the credibility of a nuclear guarantee given by a third party to a non-nuclear nation involved in a conflict with another party.

Mao maintained his "paper tiger" doctrine, however, for several more years while trying, unsuccessfully, to get Soviet nuclear aid and while developing his own bomb. Similar military-doctrinaire thinking in both respects may have taken root in time in the Third World, including among Arab military thinkers.[26] We do not know whether the introduction of the hydrogen bomb and the Soviet familiarity with it brought about a profound change in official Soviet treatment of the bomb as a threat to humanity, and led to their worldwide campaign to eliminate it (leaving them with overwhelming conventional superiority). But we shall find somewhat similar approaches among Arabs.

In reality, the Soviet Union vacillated between war by proxy and open, even if limited, challenges to the West, without finding a satisfactory compromise among its prenuclear Communist mission, its strategic-national motives, its domestic problems, and the reality of the post-Hiroshima world, which made the United States such a powerful opponent. The Soviets carefully considered the developing American policy as it culminated in what McGeorge Bundy describes as "what became known inaccurately but indelibly" as John Foster Dulles' doctrine of "massive retaliation."[27] This doctrine, by itself, was a deviation from the diversified deterrents and war-winning assets recommended in NSC 68, and was accompanied by a major cutback in all military expenditure. It also was supposed to enhance some agreement with the Soviets, now that the hydrogen bomb overshadowed the globe. Yet at the same time, John Foster Dulles, President Eisenhower's secretary of state, maintained a "roll-back" challenge toward the Soviets, which they rejected, declaring themselves undeterred in every other respect.

The doctrine of "massive retaliation" as it was formulated by Dulles—and as it was understood by others, if not by Eisenhower himself—was a classic case of open, binding, wholesale nuclear threats. (Later, we will discuss a case in which an Israeli scholar advocated that a similar policy be adopted by his government, and we will see why this option has not been adopted.) Dulles felt it necessary to convince the Soviets that despite the notorious weakness of democracies (as it had expressed itself in the 1930s) and the role of the public (which had no meaning in totalitarian regimes), the United States had learned its lesson. It was ready to retaliate "massively" by using its overwhelming nuclear might against Soviet acts of aggression, especially in Western Europe, while refusing to be drawn to limited wars favoring the Soviets or to the enormous expenditures involved in a variety of other deterrents.

The deterrent capacity of these American threats was soon subjected to much scholarly analysis. The question became: Were these threats "credible" considering (1) the growing Soviet nuclear might, and (2) the fact that by the late 1950s, the power of preemption emanated first from a supposed "bomber gap" and later from a "missile gap" in the Soviets' favor? This issue was brought to light by Albert Wohlstetter, a RAND mathematician whose work had reportedly impressed nuclear strategist Paul Nitze and many others. The idea Wohlstetter articulated was simply that a "first strike" could be deterred by maintaining a "credible second strike." This idea came to dominate American nuclear strategy, despite the fact that President Eisenhower himself, as we are repeatedly told by Newhouse and Bundy, was far from sharing Wohlstetter's view of the Russians or his quantitative system of analytical tools. The general-turned-politician thought more in terms of perceptions—i.e., of credible threats related to his view of Soviet behavior—than in terms of capabilities—i.e., of actual means and their practical use. Several rather influential civilians (Nitze among them), on the other hand, emphasized the means, the numbers of nuclear bombs, and other quantifiable elements of "nuclear strategy."[28]

Nuclear analysts were at first drawn more and more into discussing Nitze's beloved numbers (as Lord Zuckerman put it), and then later to other technical issues, such as silos, nuclear submarines (in which Eisenhower himself was very much interested), hardening silos, MIRVs, and the like. The emphasis was placed on the "strategic" value of these means, i.e., mainly as deterrents, and not on the economic and the political meaning of the arms race for both sides. No one, I suspect, had predicted the collapse of the Soviet economy, owing in part to the enormous costs of the nuclear build-up. And the stability of the Soviet regime seemed to be a constant that no one expected to change along with changes in Soviet society.

In the late 1950s Herman Kahn, also originally a mathematician, entered the scene with his peculiar terminology and methods of discussing escalation and "thinking about the unthinkable." His contemporary, Thomas Schelling, on the other hand, was a proponent of achieving a "non-use" situation of nuclear weapons among the great powers. Here we enter the stage in which American academic "conflict theory" impacted on the nuclear age. Wohlstetter, Kahn, and Schelling were key players in this development, despite the well-known differences in their theories. Schelling, as we will soon discuss, seems the most important of these academics in various respects.

The final step in our paradigm is the development of deterrence theory since the late 1950s, and especially toward the end of the 1960s—the period during which Israel, in its peculiar way, joined the club, as described by Bundy and by our French sources.

The hydrogen bomb and the cold war produced both the "massive retaliation" doctrine and deterrence-theoretical discussions of conflict in the nuclear age—leading to the doctrine of "flexible response"—and with them the first U.S. efforts to curb nuclear proliferation. Deterrence theory's direct influence over nonproliferation began not with President Eisenhower, but rather with President Kennedy. The publication of Thomas C. Schelling's *Strategy of Conflict*, a major work on conflict management in the nuclear age, almost coincided with Kennedy's election campaign.

In 1961, Schelling ran simulation games related to his theories, in which Henry A. Kissinger, a nuclear strategist at the time, and Robert W. Komer, among others, are reported to have participated. McGeorge Bundy, a future national security adviser, was close to Schelling's circle. Bundy and Komer would soon play a major role in Kennedy's National Security Council (NSC) with regard to the Middle East—especially in trying to curb Israel's nuclear program.[29]

Schelling's works are of great interest here because of his explicit desire to construct an apolitical theory of conflict based on the notion of the "rational behavior" of the partners in a conflict. This notion is not simplistic,[30] nor does it create a scale of rationality in which highly rational actors are positioned on one end and totally irrational ones on the other. It requires the participants primarily to be able to calculate profits and losses rationally in a situation in which they are dependent on each other's behavior. "Irrationality," as defined by Schelling, embodies the following characteristics: an unorganized and nonconsequent value system, wrong calculations, the inability to get information and pass it on, marginal and accidental influences over decision making and over further transmission of decisions to others. It could be the reflection of a decision taken by individuals who did not share a common value system, and whose organizational and communicative arrangements would prevent them from working as a unit. In addition, decision makers must be aware of their own "subjective rationality"—a notion that Schelling left rather open but that can be understood as considerations important to the calculations of one partner in a conflict, but considered not acceptable as such by the other. For example, ideological and domestic political considerations could be "subjective rationalities"— that is, they could influence a conflict that could destroy both partners. Schelling's theory postulates, moreover, that "small children and madmen," who are lacking the ability to behave in a reasonably rational fashion, could not be deterred. Neither would they have the sense to avoid the "zero sum games" that strive for an absolute benefit to either party in a conflict.

This game-theoretical theory, seemingly value-free and behavioristic, stresses the importance of communication between partners to a conflict, and further suggests normative methods of controlling credible threats in order to maintain a balance between them. Besides the idea of making threats openly, Schelling stressed the importance of having a commitment, such as national prestige, to support the threats and "red lines" to define them. At the same time, he warned that it was essential to bear in mind the other party's red lines in order to: (1) make credible threats in a way in which the enemy would be unlikely to preempt them, and (2) to ensure that the enemy not be pushed behind its own red lines. "Signalling" and other modes of sophisticated communication were added as alternatives to open threats in order to minimize the dangers inherent in one of the greatest paradoxes exposed by the theory's system: that the overwhelming benefit of *not* executing one's threats can thoroughly undermine the credibility of the threats. Thus, the "players" must use an exact dose, form, and method to achieve the desired credibility and play without ruining the game.

As the theory applies to nuclear strategy, "non-use" of nuclear weapons as an agreed norm might reduce the risks involved to a bearable minimum.[31] This theory was basically limited to two actors. And when applied to Washington and Moscow, it was drawn, among other things, from their experiences with each other and with China up until that time. Though the theory denies any dependence on American values, it clearly reflects the behavior of Americans, as observed by Schelling—but stripped of their national identity and culture as such. It also, implicitly, includes previous American experiences, such as the perception of Hitler as a madman.

The problem is, of course, whether Schelling's definitions of "rationality" and "irrationality" are valid for human beings whose "value systems" are different from his own. Can Schelling's definitions be broad enough to encompass complex situations between alien cultures, that is, cultures different from those known to him when he constructed his theory in the late 1950s? Schelling emphasized forms of decision making, rather than substance, except for the American tendency to seek trade-offs and maintain rules of profit and loss in political life. Therefore, his theory created a built-in doubt about forms of decision making that deviated from what seemed to be the American bipartisan, unified, consensual approach to foreign affairs at the time. It further reflected a view of the world as a highly dangerous place, mired in constant high-level conflict, and thus it was more concerned with conflict management than with conflict resolution.

Yet in retrospect, one may argue that historical-cultural substance, rather than "rational" decision making, played an enormous role in shaping the behavior of the superpowers themselves in regard to nuclear affairs. And therefore, Schelling's theory's emphasis on forms of decision making contributed positively to "rationalizing" the dialogue between the superpowers on nuclear matters, and to restraining proliferation; it also had to address itself to the mechanisms of "rationalizing" conflicts, including nuclear risk taken by people in cultures about which he knew little.

The obvious result—once Schelling's ideas were adopted by the politicians—was a renewed American effort to limit proliferation. This made him, or people like him, the referees of "rationality" in a universalistic and abstract fashion that was typical of American social sciences of the time. This view of "rationality" could hardly cope with diversified realities, but was supported by American power or American involvement in a complex and not always viable mode. Moreover, the theory, when combined with its initial goal of seeking for "credibility" in a game of chicken—and with a built-in refusal to allow the bomb to destroy civilization—helped to escalate conventional conflicts such as the Vietnam War, and possibly also contributed to the outbreak of the

Israeli Six-Day War. The theory also ignored the economics of the nuclear race: one party could incur insufferable costs in order to maintain the game of chicken. It also ignored the possibility of domestic political changes. For example, the changes that occurred in the Soviet Union under Gorbachev—which reflect a complex process of economic, ideological, and organizational inputs—may have made previous conflict with the West suddenly seem less important. A somewhat similar process had taken place in Egypt, as we shall see. A "high political" study of the elementary value-bound goals of both Egypt and the Soviet Union, together with a study of their economic difficulties, might have been useful in anticipating the behavior of these countries. In the absence of such a study, conflict theoreticians and military-inspired analysts put the emphasis on the countries' "strategic" potential, based on what seemed to be the experience of the past. Yet, the military-strategic pressure on their societies and economies might have proved very important—not as a tool to keep a conflict manageable, but maybe to transform the nature of the conflict altogether.

"Political" analyses are less rigid than "strategic" ones, which accept high-level conflicts as givens. "High political" analyses would seek sometimes to resolve conflicts altogether, or at least would be flexible and broad enough to examine more of the variables necessary for conflict resolution—if the analysts had the vision and the reason to do so. The cases of Iraq and Libya may seem to be different when compared to Egypt's, but here too cultural-historical, personal, and political factors, which Schelling deliberately sought to avoid, must be studied to understand these countries' behavior in regard to the bomb and its uses.

Schelling's theory, a splendid construction, can also be used as a negative model: as a tool to measure conditions that must prevail if disaster is to be avoided in the nuclear age. As such, it was used—almost immediately after its publication in the early 1960s—by Middle Eastern actors to argue that their enemies were madmen and, therefore, were capable of the most extreme behavior. And since in Schelling's theory, madmen cannot be deterred, their anticipated acts had to be preempted. Also, some of these actors could *purposely* adopt signs of "irrational behavior" in order to achieve the image of a "crazy state"—a notion developed, not surprisingly, by an Israeli decision-making theoretician. Here, the theory could indeed perceive "us" as "rational," and "them" as "irrational," and thus influence reality in a fashion that requires more than Schelling's value-free definition of "rationality." In the Arab-Israeli case, as used in the 1960s, the theory required knowledge of the contents, or the substance, of the cultures and subcultures involved. It required knowledge of the way these cultures and subcultures combined in the political setup and in the political tradition of given Arab countries, within the changing framework of the Arab world, and of a changing Israel. It was (and is) important to realize (even if the notion is unfashionable) that Arabs are a historical-cultural entity, very much self-focused, sometimes used to invoking barbaric methods, mired in their own past and struggling with a difficult present, while following foreign inputs at the same time.

Israeli analysts such as General Allon—who were of course conscious of these factors—could take the theory out of its nuclear, Soviet-American context and use it to develop a conventional strategy that included conventional preemption, due to Arab "irrationality," while perceiving their own nation as perfectly "rational." The outcome was, in connection with many contributing factors, the Israeli occupation of East Jerusalem and the West Bank in 1967, which helped transform the Israelis into highly emotional people, whose own ancient past interfered with their present more than ever before.

For General Allon, Arab "irrationality" dictated forgoing nuclear weapons or making them a "last resort" option only. The theoretical and practical difficulties involving a "last resort" option could be derived from Schelling's theory itself. "Last resorts" are sometimes difficult to define, especially in the Middle East where international boundaries are not always historically legitimized. One cannot always tell the enemy's definition of a "last resort." And in some cases one's definition of "last resort" may invite probes of an escalating nature by the enemy. Even the drawing of "red lines," in conventional terms, as Allon did in public, would hardly expose the nuclear last resort. In conflict theoretical terms, used by Schelling and other American theoreticians, the status-quo could be seen as the last resort.

But even then the problem of creating credible threats to maintain the status quo tortured the theoreticians no end. This problem led among other things to the development of "theater nuclear weapons" and the like, which enabled the United States to make a credible threat to fight in Europe against overwhelming Soviet conventional superiority and nuclear power; thereby avoiding a military confrontation that might endanger the American homeland—a proposition which seemed to lack credibility.

In retrospect, then, Schelling neglected many historical and political determinants that could influence the behavior of nuclear powers toward each other. From our perspective in the early 1990s, one can argue that these other, ignored, determinants have influenced the behavior of the superpowers and contributed to the stability of their conflict more than Schelling's recommended open or highly sophisticated threats. For example, the status of the superpowers as marginal, continental conglomerates, well separated from each other and hegemonic in their immediate environments—a distinct difference from the European situation that gave birth to two world wars—could have contributed to stability. Despite later controversies about Yalta and Potsdam, Europe itself was divided as a result of World War II to the basic satisfaction of the Soviets, who had no historical, national, or cultural interests in the military occupation of Western Europe. The Berlin problem and the issue of Germany's future did remain dangerously open. And in regard to these two issues Moscow took several risks to try to protect its cordon sanitaire. Still, it agreed to the neutralization and virtual Westernization of Austria. And earlier, the Soviets did not support Communist insurgents in Greece, and left others behind in Iranian Azerbaijan. Within their own sphere, the Soviets also had to put up with Tito in Yugoslavia; but when it came to Prague, they put their foot down.

In other parts of the world the Soviets seldom confronted America directly. Perhaps they deliberately chose, or were driven, to confront America indirectly in "gray areas" such as Korea. Or, in some cases, they were drawn into confrontation, as occurred in Vietnam and was the result of a much more complicated process involving local clients and China. This lack of direct confrontation is due simply to the fact that the superpowers share no common boundaries and have no direct territorial claims on each other; neither do they have an old national hatred or any other reason to fight each other to defend their right to exist. At first, the Soviets were seen as the "Evil Empire," the Americans were understood to be classic imperialists, and several moves on the parts of both countries did create an atmosphere of constant crisis. However, it was only upon the introduction of the bomb—and perhaps just the introduction of the hydrogen bomb—that the superpowers became vulnerable to mutual destruction in their own eyes.[32] Only since the introduction of nuclear weapons has there been any need for abstract conflict theories dealing with the prospect of premeditated, complete, mutual destruction, or conflicts resembling the game of chicken.

Communism is grounded in an extremely materialistic-technological world-view; from its inception it emphasized the role of capitalism as maximizing technological development. Therefore, the Soviets recognized the bomb as a major change in world affairs long before first admitting it. Perhaps this pragmatic bent as regards the bomb was a Soviet historical-ideological subjective rationality, which might have helped maintain the basic historical status quo in Europe. Soviet ventures in Europe could mainly have been efforts to preserve the post-

World War II status quo, as they perceived it, against America's presence and nuclear might, rather than attempts to change it in Russia's favor by invoking military means in the nuclear age. On the contrary, their Marxist-Leninist ideology expected the socioeconomic process to win anyway, as far as the future of capitalism was concerned, but stressed adequate defense from imperialistic threats and convulsions.

This historical-ideological subjective rationality, which did not necessarily strive for Soviet occupation of Western national states, could be seen as colliding with commitments to communism in general, and to "freedom movements" in the Third World. It was at odds, also, with other domestic and national priorities and values. To the extent that the United States was not committed to nations in the Third World, the Soviets were free to act; even so, however, as a consequence of exactly these sorts of calculations the Soviets had their major rift with China, a struggle that was related in part to Moscow's refusal to lend Mao nuclear aid.

These various, highly complex inputs were not necessarily governed by American game-theoretical use of threats, by the simple drawing of red lines by the United States, or by signalling. The Soviets had their own conflicting priorities. The bomb, of course, has a language of its own; the Russians used their judgment and historical-cultural tools, among other things, to respect its voice. In regard to Western Europe, which had never been an integral part of the Soviet empire, once they built the Berlin Wall, the Soviets were ready to maintain the status quo. Their restraint has been due, in part, to American strength, but they have been less deterred from their goal of becoming a major world power. They were ready to take advantage of Fidel Castro's regime and its fear of an American invasion. They were willing to build missile bases in Cuba aimed at the U.S. mainland, even with the conditions of nuclear disparity in America's favor, hoping to thereby change it and create a perfect game of chicken in which they might gain more freedom of action.

This brings us back to the Kennedy era, which we touched on briefly above. Here, for the first time, deterrence theory appears to have influenced the president's behavior, by pushing him to close some alleged "missile gaps" and to return to a massive program of nuclear rearmament. On the other hand, he exercised extra care not to push the Soviets behind their own red lines. He offered to remove obsolete missiles from Turkey as a gesture of compensation for his demand that they withdraw missiles from Cuba. We could inquire here whether Kennedy's men did not try to restore a balanced game of chicken in the nuclear field, while getting involved conventionally in Vietnam, by using signals that failed to make an impression on Hanoi, due to the theoretical biases of American theoreticians. This is the point in time at which Israel's nuclear options were drawing attention abroad.

Kennedy's efforts to curb nuclear proliferation had started before the Cuban missile crisis. And that incident gave his administration yet another reason to oppose proliferation: to prevent the Russians from deploying nuclear missiles in client states from which their removal would have been much more difficult than had been the case in Cuba. At least, the Kennedy Administration had the opportunity to use that argument to prevent proliferation per se. But it seems that in any case, deterrence-theoretical thinking—which assumes a world in a constant high-level conflict—might have pushed Kennedy to his own extension of Eisenhower's campaign to prevent nuclear proliferation. The basic ideas behind Kennedy's campaign seemed to be as follows:

1. The apparent deterrence of the Soviets in Europe—including the building of a wall around East Berlin (which could have been perceived as a defensive posture)—and later in Cuba seemed to indicate that their leaders had the ability to behave rationally. Due, among other things, to historic and strategic reasons, such as the lack of proximity between the superpowers themselves and their growing nuclear arsenals, the Russians had the freedom to be rational and the means to be "credible." Other nations, however, could have "madmen or children" for leaders. And these leaders, in close proximity to each other and in control of some crude nuclear devices, could use crude threats against each other and invite nuclear disasters. They might even establish such behavior as a norm in international relations. Or they could even try to influence the behavior of the superpowers themselves. In invoking their parochial interests, these third parties could further cause the superpowers to get involved in situations more complex than in the relatively manageable European situation or in the isolated Cuban missile crisis. In this event, the superpowers could lose control of the stability they had at least to some degree established between them. (As we shall see, such thinking partially governed American fears with regard to a nuclear Israel.)

2. A bipolar nuclear world was difficult enough to manage, but there was no theory available to handle the affairs of a multipolar nuclear world, except (according to existing theory) to live in a growing state of conflict. "Madmen and children" were expected to emerge "out there" as a matter of course, or rather, of time.

The concept of "rationality" itself could lose its meaning in situations involving many partners having complex relationships with each other and with the competing superpowers. For example, in a typical complication characterizing the Middle East situation, it would be perfectly "rational" for a nuclear Egypt under President Nasser, or for a nuclear Iraq, to support a guerrilla war against Israel. In this "rational" scenario, Egypt or Iraq would give Palestinian commandos some kind of a nuclear guarantee—either through an implied or an open threat—to cover the Palestinians' bases of operation in a third Arab country, such as Lebanon or Jordan. This scenario assumes that Egypt or Iraq were safe from Israel's retaliation. It is impossible to predict how likely this "rational" calculation would be, but it does make sense in that it transports the Vietnam example to the Middle East—if one believes that the U.S. was deterred from using nuclear weapons in that conflict due to Soviet and Chinese support of Hanoi. This scenario makes nuclear retaliation seem "irrational." Yet, however "irrational" retaliation would seem at the beginning of such a process, as it would entail increasing, insupportable pain to Israel, Israel might "rationalize" very risky efforts, including facing a nuclear threat, to stop the guerrilla warfare. Other nuclear Arab actors, such as Libya, would then join to defend Egypt or Iraq, and each country would have ties with rival superpowers who would simultaneously supply them with conventional weapons (or such weapons would be supplied by other nations in any case). We can further complicate this scenario by suggesting a nuclear umbrella offered by Libya to a conventional Egypt in competition with a nuclear Iraq, when all these parties are committed to the cause of the Palestinians. This cause is, of course, carried out by rival Palestinian groups, whose base may be a Soviet-oriented Syria, and so forth.

Another scenario could calculate Arab nuclear threats aimed at the United States itself, in terms of threats against its local client—Israel—and a resulting Israeli response, as well as a Soviet threat (even if the main issue would seem to be Arab-American relations). Another scenario would calculate the transfer of nuclear weapons by an Arab state directly to Arab guerrillas, and the ensuing, uncontrollable blackmail aimed at whoever one may imagine. The number of variables here does not lend itself to the construction of a theory of conflict management, nor could such a theory account for the ironical transformation of a perfectly rational calculation into a multiparty version of the "prisoners' dilemma."

Clearly, the theory of deterrence—as Robert Jervis puts it—was basically deductive, abstract and status quo-bound.[33] Yet, it reflected America's fundamental satisfaction with its national status and the realization of its values and interests. These American values became, in deterrence theory, an implied subjective rationality favoring rational (i.e., based on calculations of profit and loss), businesslike, one-on-one relations with a partner in an ongoing conflict. The theory was, however, anchored in a historical situation in which both sides were supposed to adopt such calculations; both sides had assets to trade off, even if they first had to learn how to do so without risking their very survival. Both sides also had allies and various interests in every corner of the globe.

In this sense, the situation of the superpowers was even more complicated than the situation of Israel, a nation whose very survival has been at stake from the day of its birth, a nation that has not been accepted as legitimate by its neighbors in their environment. These neighbors, therefore, were politically committed to each other to destroy Israel. But, for the Americans the issue seemed to be limited to "rational" calculations of profit and loss—although in reality it was a much more complicated process. Partially, it was governed by historical realities, such as facts created by World War II, especially in Europe. Partially, this process was governed by "domino theories," of which liberals as well as conservatives were not free due to the Hitler experience. And, assuming a pessimistic view of human nature, one might even have developed a number of scenarios in which the contradictory logic of partners involved in a conflict would lead to "theoretical" disasters detached from real-life situations. In fact, the calculations were primarily political-historical, even if the logic of the theory and of nuclear strategy was added to the politics of the nuclear age. As such, these calculations require a treatment in which deterrence-theoretical terminology, rather than its logic, played its role. So, if we acknowledge the limitations of the theory, it can be extremely useful for our own purposes.

Yet American deterrence thinking, grounded as it was in the cold war, would perforce desire that the rest of the world remain nonnuclear. The only way to continue the game of chicken, with its technique of open, credible threats and flexible give-and-take rules—a difficult yet manageable situation—was to do everything possible to cut down on the number of players. Two were plenty, but more, such as China and France, not to mention Great Britain, was a grave annoyance. This argument, coupled with American power, prevented proliferation, or at least made it illegal—the value of illegality being to make the open, binding, and less flexible characteristics of nuclear threats seem to disappear, even if that does not seem to have been the original aim of those who tried to stop proliferation. Illegality of nuclear arms, and consequently of nuclear threats, also allowed for intervention behind the scenes before such threats could publicly come into play. Illegality also prevented the complication of the praxis of the use of nuclear weapons as it had established itself in an open fashion between the relatively "rational" superpowers, at least for the time being.

Nonproliferation may also have been influenced by the residue of the moral, largely liberal, rejection of nuclear weapons after Hiroshima and the cry to outlaw the use of the bomb. There is evidence that it may have been closely connected with public sentiment against Dulles's doctrine of massive retaliation, and with the emotional counterargument of the time: "Better Red Than Dead." In publicly adopting nonproliferation, Kennedy was demonstrating a liberal desire to "Ban the Bomb."

Regardless of Kennedy's motives, his approach seems to have had results. Nonproliferation was the order of the day, and proliferation may have been prevented in some cases. In other cases, his policy created the need for "ambiguous" nuclear postures; some nations could not afford France's and China's stubborn open testing and building of arsenals, which indeed prompted American intervention.

Even without the open postures of France and China, Israel's case was also a subject of Washington's attention. Later, nonproliferation policy and the related scholarly discussion of the issue could take credit, along with other reasons, for the phenomenon of "opaque" threats. Furthermore, the fear of the bomb itself, combined with deterrence techniques previously developed in the nuclear context, contributed to the conventional disaster in Vietnam, which had begun during the Kennedy Administration and was escalated by the same group of officials, Bundy among them. Under Kennedy, something like nuclear "self-deterrence" came into being—that is, the use of the bomb for any purpose whatsoever except to deter direct Soviet nuclear attacks in given areas was rejected by Bundy and his associates, and this policy continued under Johnson. As we shall see, the same people contributed to Israel's conventional, unnecessary war in 1967.

CHAPTER THREE

The Israeli Paradigm:
American Controlled Opacity?

The second Eisenhower Administration was confronted with two cases of covert proliferation: the French case and the Israeli case. Although one generally associates Kennedy with the nonproliferation program, actually the first serious crisis between Washington and Jerusalem in this regard took place under Eisenhower. Kennedy inherited the problems of both France and Israel. He also took over the problem of West German Gaullism, which, however, could have given him a major trump card vis-à-vis the Soviets. The sharing of nuclear weapons with West Germany was, for Moscow, an unmitigated disaster, and using it as a bargaining chip could have prevented the Soviets from dangerous acts of a similar nature with their own clients. In the early 1960s, the two other major problems looming in the horizon were first China, and in relation to it, India.

We do not know when the United States learned of the Chinese nuclear effort, but once evidence was received, it caused grave deliberations in Washington, and some kind of common action with Moscow was considered. Washington also had to deal with India's response to the Chinese challenge, and to take seriously Nehru's open warnings that India would not tolerate a world dominated by the nuclear superpowers. Delhi's demands for superpower self-restraint in this and other fields played a role in delaying an already agreed upon United Nations-sponsored formula on banning proliferation in the early 1960s; the Non-Proliferation Treaty (NPT) itself and the superpower monopoly inherent in it were later described by Indira Gandhi as "nuclear apartheid."[1]

Information about American deliberations regarding China and

India, the early history of the NPT, and the establishment of the International Atomic Energy Agency (IAEA) in 1957 can be deduced from the sanitized and censored documentation available in the Library of Congress and in Kennedy's and Johnson's presidential libraries. There must have been connections between the West German nuclear sharing problem, the nonaligned position (in regard to the proliferation problem at that time), and the Israeli nuclear program. Obviously, we will concentrate on the Israeli aspect. At least the Limited Test Ban Treaty (LTBT) of 1963 signified a growing degree of understanding between the superpowers, and one may speculate that the LTBT played a role in making Israel's nuclear option less visible a little later, when Ben-Gurion's successor, Levi Eshkol, officially endorsed it.[2]

As one can readily see, the French and the Chinese were left to pursue their own ways. The latter exploded their first bomb in 1964. India, meanwhile, was building reactors supplied by Canada for "peaceful use" in the spirit of Eisenhower's Atoms for Peace program. This program was the positive side of the nonproliferation concept of the time, and its general premises were also used later to resolve, for appearances' sake, the crisis with Israel.

In this respect, Indian and Israeli behavior seems to have been rather similar; they both claimed their reactors were for peaceful use. Actually, though, their means of acquiring nuclear potential, their motives, and the final results of their efforts, including their relations with Washington, were different. India's case will be discussed briefly in Chapter 13. However, at the outset of our historical review of Israel's opacity, we should mention that India's introduction into nuclear weapons development involved deceiving its suppliers—an act that might have been inspired by India's self-image as a great power and by China's nuclear challenge. India acquired its reactors directly from antiproliferation powers within the framework of their norms prohibiting the use of those reactors for arms development. First Canada, then the United States, supplied reactors to India after 1969, and Indian-built units were later added. In contrast Israel's nuclear acquisition, according to our French sources, began with a modest cooperation agreement with France in the early 1950s, at a time when nonproliferation was not yet even an accepted international norm, much less cemented in the NPT.[3] In fact, this relationship almost preceded the birth of the IAEA itself.

The French, themselves, who had pioneered nuclear research for peaceful use, began their scientific-industrial effort immediately following the Manhattan Project, in which several French scientists were involved in Canada. In the mid-1950s, the French were able to construct natural-uranium-plus-heavy-water reactors to produce plutonium and separation or reprocessing plants for making the plutonium weapons-grade, although, at that time, they had not yet devised triggering mechanisms.[4]

France's decision to "go nuclear" was deferred due to domestic differences typical of the Fourth Republic, and to its complex foreign political inclinations, among which was the Israeli connection, rather neglected by historians. The connection was implemented, finally, in 1957 by a Socialist government that was an ideological and political ally of Israel's. Both governments were dominated by Social-Democrats, whose attitude toward the Anglo-Americans was rather ambiguous: The French remembered the 1930s well, including British appeasement policy and American isolationism vis-à-vis Hitler, and the Israelis believed that the Anglo-Americans could have done more to stop Hitler and help save the lives of countless Jews. Furthermore, following the Holocaust, British promises to the Zionists were broken several times—an experience that added to Ben-Gurion's lessons from the Holocaust itself—while American support was always tentative and sometimes nonexistent.

Both recognized Fascist traits in Arab nationalism. And their basic opposition to it aligned them, even though the French were taking advantage of Arab nationalist ideology to fight Nasser's Egypt and its support of the Algerian claim for independence. They could use negative opinion about the ultranationalistic traits of Nasserism, its pan-Arab and populist-socialist ideology, and its subversive activities against opposing Arab regimes to defend their own colony, Algeria. Nasser's anti-Israeli rhetoric was phrased many times in anti-Semitic terms, a reminder of the Fascist syndrome of the 1930s. When such a person was supporting the Algerians, he could be targeted by the French as a Fascist, as in fact Ben-Gurion perceived him, rather than as Third World freedom fighter. The same French Socialist government, and later a radical Socialist cabinet, is reported to have promised Israel a complete nuclear weapons production system in late 1957, including a plutonium separation plant. Reliable sources reveal that this process was begun before, and was solidified as a result of, France and Israel's combined, abortive campaign against Nasser's Egypt in 1956.[5] Several versions of this explanation are still circulating in Israel itself. According to former minister of transport Yitzhak Ben-Aharon, the 1957 agreement was just a "framework agreement" that did not provide for bomb production.[6] Other sources, such as Matti Golan and Michael Bar-Zohar, even maintain that Ben-Gurion promised General de Gaulle later that "no bomb will be produced" at Dimona. Yet Jean-Francis Perrin, the then director-general of the French Atomic Energy Commission, claimed later that the French did promise Israel a reactor and a "chemical" plant, in an agreement flexible enough to allow both sides enough room for interpretation, while binding them as firmly as possible to each other.

Israel was not obligated to the United States or to Canada (as India was) concerning the development of nuclear options, but the French were under an obligation to the United States regarding the transfer of "nuclear secrets" and materials such as heavy water to third parties.[7] But American behavior vis-à-vis the French when they were exposed to Soviet nuclear threats during the 1956 campaign against Egypt, and in relation to Israel, whose very survival was threatened in the most explicit terms by Moscow during that campaign, might have helped the French feel released from their obligations to Washington.[8]

Ben-Gurion's Israel—whose forces were withdrawn from the Sinai Peninsula following the 1956 Suez War due to combined American-Soviet pressure—had incentives to "go nuclear" before the French connection was established, according to our French source.[9] The Arab situation certainly warranted a close evaluation of the nuclear options. As mentioned above, Israel was not obligated to America in any way at that time. Ben-Gurion had tried hard but failed to gain access to one of the regional treaty systems sponsored by Washington, just as he failed to gain a binding American security guarantee. The recent publication of the 1955-1956 volumes of *Foreign Relations of the United States*, dedicated to the Arab-Israeli dispute,[10] reveals that the United States was involved in complex efforts to solve the Arab-Israeli conflict. (Because these events preceded Israel's nuclear efforts, we will not go into them here, but will return to them briefly in Chapter 4.) So, although Israel had reason to be grateful to the United States—and reason to be cautious in acting at cross-purposes with a great power—a dispassionate analysis of America's position vis-à-vis Israel reveals that the United States was no more than a very reluctant patron of Israel's during the mid-1950s.

David Ben-Gurion was very conscious of America's positive role in supporting the Zionists' claim for a Jewish state in a partitioned Palestine, and its crucial economic aid to the newborn nation. But he had reason to believe that the support given by Washington to Israel's birth emanated from a unique combination of circumstances, including American-Jewish pressure on President Truman during an election year. Truman was an inexperienced and dependent president whose basic morality may have moved him to support Israel against the British and Arab refusal to accept any political compromise. Notwithstand-

ing, that same American government withdrew its support from the
U.N. partition plan for Palestine and refused to supply an almost
unarmed, infant nation with the arms necessary to win its independence against the invading armies of the Arab world, who were themselves armed by the West.[11] Moreover, it seemed clear that American
interests were aimed in the long run on winning the Arabs over, and not
only because of Arab oil or the importance of the Middle East in the
context of Soviet-American rivalry. Important government circles in
Washington were also impressed by the Arabs themselves—their numbers, vast spaces, national culture, and potentially violent habits.[12] These
aspects, as well as the Arab bid for unity and refusal to accept defeat
from a handful of Jews, made it obvious to Ben-Gurion that Israel's
War of Independence was only the first round, and that in this first
round the most friendly nation—the United States—had stood aside.

Israel had had to create itself, and having done so, became a fact of
life that both Washington and Moscow were ready to recognize immediately. Yet as a nation that created itself, it stood alone. No one would
join in Israel's fight, or even guarantee to supply the necessary arsenal
for the country to defend itself against an angry, possibly united, Arab
world. For Ben-Gurion, Arab unification was a legitimate, difficult, and
logical course for Arabs to pursue. The necessary modern ideology—
such as the Ba'ath Party's pan-Arabism—was already at hand when
Israel was born. Nasserism—combining the strongest Arab state with
mass support and enthusiasm across the Arab world—could present an
immediate danger. Western "appeasement" policy toward quasi-Fascist
forces was nothing new, and even the war against Hitler had not been
readily embarked upon, especially when perceived to be a "Jewish
War." Having matured as a statesman during the 1930s, Ben-Gurion
perceived Western interests and values as having combined with
Japanese and German actions to push the democracies to fight. And he
further perceived that the emergence of the United States as a great
power following the war imposed on Washington responsibilities and
burdens—including in the Middle East—that could run heavily against
Israeli interests.

Israel, however, was not a "pariah state"—that is, it was not totally
unaccepted and isolated. The country had qualified support abroad,
which was enormously important, but no more. Following the Holocaust, Israel's cause seemed justified if problematic, and its Socialist,
pioneering spirit seemed fresh and interesting. Thus, Ben-Gurion, in
contrast to his rival Menachem Begin, the future leader of the right-
wing Likud Party, accepted the changing international arena as a basic
framework for his own operations. He saw it as a given that he had to

use anything he could to enhance Israel's own interests, while avoiding unnecessary political confrontations and maintaining a middle-of-the-road course in regard to territorial issues and military actions. He refused to go too far and occupy the Arab territory in the West Bank, whereas Begin pursued an ideological commitment to Jewish control over all of Western Palestine. (This Begin held in common with an important leftist group, to be discussed later.)

Following Israel's War of Independence, Ben-Gurion refused to invest too much in a huge, conventional army. And he was satisfied with the 1949 armistice demarcation lines imposed by the great powers through the U.N., without formal peace. The armistice gave him time—precious time—to absorb mass immigration and develop the country and to evolve a plan for reforming traditional Jewish politics and introduce a British-like cabinet system and ballot law. Yet these efforts always collided with immediate and long-range security priorities. Arab hostility did not die with the 1949 armistice agreements. The Israeli dilemma was anchored in the discrepancy between "high political" support for its cause, backed by Jewish power in the United States, and strategic and political calculations in the West, and later in the Eastern bloc, favoring the Arabs. These calculations were partially related to oil, to East-West rivalry, and to a potential Arab role in international affairs. Here, too, the distinction between high politics and other considerations supporting the Arabs was blurred. Of course, neither the whole international community nor the superpowers perceived Israel's existence as illegitimate; but the Arabs did, with some support from major Third World nations such as India, Pakistan, and later Moslem nations such as Indonesia. This imposed severe restrictions on Israel's very ability to sustain itself.

Therefore, it was imperative that Israel use the precious time available to establish itself before the Arabs got ready. According to Steve Weissman and Herbert Krosney, Ben-Gurion said rather early on: "It is not impossible for scientists in Israel to do for their own people what Einstein, Oppenheimer, and Teller have done for the United States." The three scientists were, of course, all Jews, as McGeorge Bundy, who used this quote in his book, wryly asserts.[13]

A "war of destruction" against the Jews in Palestine was a traditional goal of local Arab leaders. In their opposition to Jewish immigration, they had forced the British to close the gates of Palestine to Jewish refugees in 1939 almost completely. Later, the most influential Palestinian leader, Amin al-Husseini, went so far as to collaborate with Hitler and enthusiastically support his "Final Solution of the Jewish Question."[14] This "Final Solution"—a carnage of unprecedented scope, devised to eradicate Jews entirely and exclusively—was not at first recognized properly in the West and was carried out by simple, conventional means. The Jews were Hitler's principal civilian victims, as an entire ethnic group picked out for systematic slaughter. Moreover, the Jews were totally unable to defend themselves. Despite the West's humanistic and universal war aims, the Jews received almost no benefit from the Allies' war effort. It developed too slowly to save most of them. It is possible to argue that the Allies' effort might have suffered if one of its main objectives had been the rescue of Jews. The West was fighting for its values and interests alike. It refused to fight a "Jewish war" at the same time, and the sad reality is that very little was done to save Jews.

Ben-Gurion was cautious not to blame the West for Hitler's atrocities, as Menachem Begin and Yitzhak Shamir did. Shamir was one of the leaders of the Stern Gang, an extreme, terroristic group, in the 1940s, which saw in the British the main enemy during World War II. But later he joined Begin's party. That party maintained a strong nationalistic, emotional as well as legalistic, defiant attitude toward "the World," anchored in the immediate pre-Holocaust European reality and in various rightist and national-liberal ideological inputs. Yet Begin perceived himself to be first a statesman, believing in Jewish rights and power. He was aiming at securing Western—especially American—support against the British, and later against what he perceived to be primitive, barbaric, and anti-Western Arab nationalism.

Ben-Gurion was a pre-World War I social-democrat, a product of the nineteenth century's world. He educated himself to change reality within its constraints. As a social reformer, he was rather critical of Jewish habits and behavior, as well as of non-Jewish treatment of Jews. In addition to his social mission and his interest in a cultural renaissance, he aimed at transforming the Israeli Jews into "political people," i.e., bringing them out of their actual and mental Diaspora and back into history and real life. This required, among other things, the study of non-Jewish reality (whether one liked it or not) and the pursuit of realistic, sometimes risky, goals to create Israel and sustain it. He recognized the logic of the "triple trap" into which the Jews had been maneuvered since 1933: between Hitler, who wanted, at first, to deport them; the Allies, who could not accept millions of aliens without endangering their domestic order and later the national consensus necessary to fight Hitler; and the Arabs, who finally blocked their access to Palestine. Ben-Gurion understood that Hitler had courted the Allied masses with anti-Semitic arguments, making Western and Soviet Jews seem responsible for the Allied war effort. This despite the fact that, as a group, Jews living in Allied nations had no influence over Allied high politics, and as individuals unconditionally supported the mobilization to fight Hitler, and thus facilitated reprisals against their compatriots under his control. Nevertheless, Nazi arguments that the war was "Jewish" could not be ignored by the Allies if Hitler was to be fought with the necessary broad support at home. Later, when Hitler began the "Final Solution," Ben-Gurion was also able to perceive the other tragic trap into which the Jews had fallen: Had Hitler been pressed to stop the slaughter, he might have considered it, depending on his strategic situation, but only in exchange for concessions that the Allies would not make — and the Jews could not have asked them to make. Or else Hitler would have used the issue to try and drive a wedge between Allied leaders and their own people, or between the Allied powers.[15] One way or another, the Jews, most of whom refused to emigrate in time or were refused when they did, were alone and could not count on anyone to come to their aid until it was too late.

This description is rather simplistic in that it does not take into account the role played by anti-Semitism in the West. In actuality, opinions were expressed in the West that Germany had proved to be less capable than Britain or the United States in "handling the Jews." The Jews (so this argument went) had brought trouble on themselves by provoking the German people to such a degree that a nationwide, anti-Jewish hatred existed; Hitler capitalized on this hatred and used it to assume power. A more vicious version was that Hitler was indeed a threat to the West, but that the Jews, who contributed to his rise to power, were partially responsible for making the West the victim of his threat; therefore, the West had to take care of its own civilization and interests first.[16] However, there is no reason to assume that the principal Allied leaders were making decisions based on personal anti-Semitic motives, though they did have to calculate the anti-Semitic sentiments all around them. And although these sentiments were widespread, it did not change the fact that even the best of intentions on the part of the Allies could not have saved the Jews from Hitler's traps.

The situation in the Arab world was complicated. Some traditional and Westernized Arab leaders were tied to the West. But even some of them—let alone the emerging group of nationalistic leaders—not only did not oppose the Fascist powers but attempted to woo them with more enthusiasm than they at first received from Nazi Germany in return. Part of the Arabs' sympathy for the Axis powers was due to their anti-Semitism and to the German unification model, which was neither democratic nor liberal, and thus seemed to suit their needs better than the hated Western model. The West became, for many Arabs, the incarnation of their own decline. And the Jews, as the "masters" of the West, had been represented to them as also being responsible for their decline by Fascist and anti-Semitic propaganda since the 1930s. The Palestinian and even traditional Arab leaders outside of Palestine did their part by trying to prevent Jewish survivors from finding a haven in Palestine during and following the Holocaust. Despite the Holocaust, Arabs maintained anti-Jewish emotions of contempt and fear and sustained feelings of actual victimization requiring revenge.

Ben-Gurion, therefore, concluded that none of the values and goals that the Allies had fought for during the war seemed to be operative among Arabs—except the right to self-determination, and that only for themselves. Once the Arabs recovered from their defeat in the Israeli War of Independence—"won by us not because the Israeli Defense Forces (IDF) were so brilliant, but because the Arab armies were so rotten," as Ben-Gurion told his proud commanders in private, having praised the IDF endlessly in public—Ben-Gurion was sure that Israel would face revenge.[17]

His solution at the time was to pursue a scheme of political-military maneuvers aimed, in the long run, at an "Arab-Israeli alliance." This would be accomplished once the Arabs had accepted Israel's independence as a fait accompli, absorbed the Arab refugees who had left or were forced to leave the Jewish part of the partitioned country, and realized that cooperation with Israel would be beneficial to all parties concerned.[18] Yet Ben-Gurion also considered the worst: the Israeli population was concentrated in a narrow strip along the Mediterranean around Tel-Aviv and could be destroyed by means of "a single bomb." Therefore, he took a keen interest in the post-Hiroshima world, which was, for him, a world that had allowed the Holocaust to happen but was also capable of all kinds of change.

The problem in such a world was to find the right mixture of morality and power, of daring action within limits, and of gestures and offers toward the enemy—a kind of mixture that would work in the eyes of Western democracies. Perhaps the enemy, or rather enemies—given time, the right leadership, the necessary domestic structure, and the right international circumstances—could be persuaded to make peace by at least accepting Israel's existence. However, at the time, most of these conditions were missing in the Arab world. Ben-Gurion therefore considered several limited territorial changes in Israel's favor in the West Bank, but was defeated by his own cabinet. As far as the nuclear option was concerned, his initial thinking might have been defensive. It seemed likely that the oil-rich Arabs would lay their hands on an atomic bomb first; but Ben-Gurion expected Jews to use their own scientific skills sooner than Arabs would be able to buy the most revolutionary technologies abroad. (In line with this aim he created a "Science Corps" in the Israeli Army as early as 1948.) But even when the Arabs failed to purchase such technologies for the time being, Ben-Gurion still found Arab conventional potential enough to worry about.

Although very much interested in self-produced nuclear facilities Ben-Gurion saw that attempts in this area were rather premature. Instead, he concentrated his attention on mass immigration from North Africa (against the inclinations of many of his colleagues), and tried hard to make the large, empty, and relative secure Negev Desert Israel's main target of settlement and development. He meanwhile decided to refrain from making the Arab-populated, Jordanian-controlled West Bank of the Jordan River a target of Israeli expansion and future settlement, although it was very close to Israel's vital centers and carried a great historical significance for Jews.

For the time being, Israel's vulnerable heart was not exposed to immediate danger, because the West Bank and the East Bank approaches to it were in the control of the relatively friendly Hashemite regime in Jordan. Yet the Hashemites were weak; they soon came under pressure from their own Palestinian population and from stronger Arab nations. The likelihood of a conventional war was multiplied by the Arab bid for unity—which was rife with inter-Arab competition for control. Israel's destruction would have given all a legitimate political goal with which to achieve unity, demonstrate leadership, mobilize their masses, and modernize. The necessary ideology—the "social Fascism" of the Ba'ath Party—was already at hand.[19] As mentioned earlier, Nasserism later carried the day and served the same purpose, with some deviations—namely, Egypt's claim to leadership, Egyptian interests, and Nasser's constraints and style. The conclusion seemed obvious and inevitable: the manpower ratio was about thirty to one, which, although far from military realization, could only improve in favor of the Arabs.

In conventional terms, the "catch" situation inherent in this enormous discrepancy was later formulated by Ben-Gurion thus: The Arabs could afford to lose all rounds against Israel, while Israel could not afford to lose any. Arab marginal losses would always be tolerable, whereas even an uninterrupted series of Israeli victories would add up to a virtual defeat, or rather to the disintegration of Israeli society.

Israel could find no dependable conventional resistance to this demographic might, nor could the country offer any peaceful incentive to the Arabs, save one. Israel could offer its brain power as a potential resource to the whole region: "Scientific achievement in the nuclear age, which has changed history beyond recognition."[20] Ben-Gurion mentioned this in his 1948 war diaries, seemingly as an opportunity to use nuclear energy for peaceful purposes in cooperation with Arabs.

Immediately after the 1948 war, Israel sought uranium in the Negev Desert and found it in poor but extractable quantities. Then the first Israeli scientists were sent abroad to study the new phenomenon.[21]

Ben-Gurion's strategic thinking seems to have been high political rather than purely military—even if, in the Israeli case, the two were quite close—and was, in this sense, "Churchillian." (Ben-Gurion had a genuine admiration for Churchill's personality and views.) Possibly, he hoped not just to deter the Arabs—as did the British military with regard to the Soviets. Maybe the proud, oriental nations surrounding the "illegitimate" Jewish entity needed a reason to reconcile themselves completely to its presence among them. Once Israel was seen by the Arabs as indestructible, positive incentives could be added to the nuclear one. Israeli conventional military might would not be enough. In the early 1950s, when Ben-Gurion was contemplating the strategic dilemma, the IDF itself—the conventional army—had its own problems. Waves of Jewish immigrants from all over the world, in particular from the Arab countries, made Israel's army become more of a huge absorption agency than a professional military machine. However, for the time being, the Arabs were absorbed in their own affairs. As Ben-Gurion put it in his 1948 war diaries, Israel had to secure its existence before the Arabs recovered, modernized to a sufficient degree, and possibly even united, and the opportunity was lost.[22]

As far as practical help with a nuclear option was concerned, nothing could be expected from the United States. And the French had not yet even developed their own nuclear infrastructure. Still, seemingly as early as 1948, Israel was headed in the direction of a nuclear option through the combined "Churchillian" vision of David Ben-Gurion, the practical direction of Ernst Bergmann (a major biochemist and a rather controversial scientific eminence), and the assistance of Shimon Peres, who later joined them as an executive officer and eventually developed the French connection. This early sequence of events was perceived by the Arabs as the beginning of Israel's interest in the bomb.[23]

So, for Ben-Gurion, the Arab-Israeli conflict was a high political issue, seen in terms of right and wrong, of interests and power. It was unique, as Jewish history was unique, and yet it was rather a simple case of sheer survival for one side, involved in an unequal race to win the nuclear option first. The terminology—but not the logic—of Thomas Schelling's conflict theory would have been useful for Ben-Gurion, although it was developed from a historical situation in which both sides had the means, but not the reasons, to destroy each other.

Of course Ben-Gurion was not exposed to Schelling's conflict theory when he made his initial decisions in regard to the nuclear option (it was not yet even published), but it is useful to suggest his possible criticism of it here, because he would eventually be confronted with it at home and from abroad. Moreover, Arab nuclear thinkers would be influenced directly by it and would use premises of the theory directly for their own purposes.

By all accounts, Ben-Gurion's problem with Schelling's theory would have been how to combine Schelling's concept of rationality, which was abstract and value free, with what Schelling called "subjective rationality" but never truly defined. Schelling probably meant history, values, cultures, and substances of conflicts, which might have meant nothing to him in comparison to nuclear risks and threats in a game of chicken. Controlling the game was Schelling's problem. Ben-Gurion, on the other hand, would not have had any use for abstract social science or deterrence-theoretical games, detached from the history and politics of the nations involved. And he could well have perceived parts of Schelling's methodology as dangerous. An amateur philosopher and a profound admirer of Plato, Ben-Gurion would have developed a "Bloomist" (to place Allen Bloom's arguments many years before Bloom published them) criticism of any value-free theory, especially when implemented in terms Schelling himself warned his readers of misusing.

Schelling's theory postulated conflict in the nuclear age in terms that were either those of mutual high risk or of "rational profit and loss calculations." Both were as yet irrelevant to the Middle East, because Israel was at high risk and the Arabs were not. Schelling's conflict theory could have applied to the Middle East if Arabs accepted the profit and loss logic, once Israel made the price of its destruction equal to the destruction of the Arabs. However, Israel did not want to destroy the Arabs, but to prevent them from destroying Israel. In this sense, the Arab-Israeli conflict could hardly be described as a game of chicken. Schelling tried to transform the game of chicken, a zero-sum game, into a rational calculation of profit and loss. The terminology of conflict theory was not an official lingo in this part of the world (or in fact elsewhere at this point). But if it had been, Arabs would not have accepted the profit-loss terminology (they despised such Western terminology), but might have learned that if they played a game of chicken well, the other side—the Jewish chicken—would lose its nerve because its logic was "commercial." Worse still, the theory could have taught one to pretend to be a "madman" or to endorse the traits of a "madman state."

It postulated that madmen could not be deterred—that one must yield to them because they were ready to take much higher tolls. Of course, it isn't necessary to have a theory to behave like that, but the theory postulated "undeterrable" enemies, even in the nuclear age, and did not offer any intellectual way out of their challenge except nonproliferation—for other nations. True, the theory was conscious of this and tried indeed to make deterrence credible as far as possible within the deterrence dilemma for the two superpowers. But it took for granted that even in the nuclear age, in spite of the nuclear revolution, some would never be deterred, and phrased this in typical abstract, generalized terms. Thus the scare of "madmen" might encourage Middle East politicians to act as "madmen," even if we do not know whether they would involve themselves in a no-way-out situation, once the bomb entered the scene. The only remedy to this would be to obtain it ahead of them, not to forgo it, and not to minimize its meaning or make it a "last resort" option in public or even in private.

With regard to third parties and even to domestic public opinion, the total depoliticization of the Arab-Israeli conflict to a game of chicken would focus the attention of the "players" and of the involved bystanders on some behavioral aspects of such a basic, in fact simplistic, human situation. This would transform the conflict into a discussion of the engines, then maybe the number of the cars involved in the game, and teach the drivers some behavioral skills, which they might or might not accept. One could therefore try to force the parties to forgo nuclear weapons altogether, and thus give the Arabs the full advantage of their potential, conventional superiority.

High politics, on the other hand, was something elementary in a different sense—and much more complicated, one may say richer and indeed more important. The game would not be value-free, when the issues were *who* the drivers were and *why* they took to the road, and whether alternative roads must be found, and the theory expressed American values, and in fact, American interests.

Instead of dealing with deterrence-theoretical threats, Ben-Gurion was inclined to approach Arabs on several levels—some emanating from their own history and culture (Schelling's "subjective rationality"), which would make it possible for them to accept Israel without admitting defeat at the hand of the Jews in the battlefield. On the other hand, he took it for granted, as one may argue, that as long as the Arab-Israeli conflict remained conventional, the Arabs would be politically obliged to destroy Israel. The main issue for him was the lead—the possibility of Israel's victory in a nuclear race, due to its more advanced scientific skills and connections abroad (as we were told by Bundy).

After gaining a lead, the issue became what should be done with that lead in order to entrench Israel in the area, as a positive, relatively small, less-threatening entity in various ways—especially in terms of territory and by refusing to rule over Arabs.

We do not know what Ben-Gurion thought about an Arab bomb, and the ensuing, possible game of chicken between Israel and one or several nuclear Arab states. It is possible that he counted on something like NPT to stop them—or at least to complicate their efforts and make their threats illegal—after he had already secured the option for Israel. The Arab existence was not at stake, but the Arabs would have to use offensive, anti-status-quo arguments. And the status-quo was in fact the very, indisputable historical foundation of Schelling's conflict theory, based on the praxis that gave birth to the theory without admitting it.

Yet following Ben-Gurion's way of thinking about similar, American behavioristic deductive thinking, the ahistorical premises of the theory and its logic were not necessarily true. He must have had his doubts about whether games of chicken could start in the Middle East, just as American teen-agers started them in their adolescent environment. This was not, after all, the way international relations worked. "Madmen" may reach for power and obtain it, but this is different from, and more complicated than, getting into two cars on a deserted road. There were other issues—economic considerations, the aid of others, the stages of the conflict in which one starts to behave as a god—and looking at these and other factors in relation to Hitler or Stalin could show similarities and differences to the Arab-Israeli conflict. "Children" never took power in any modern state, and in medieval or ancient ones they were the nominal rulers only. But the jargon of the theory could have been used by Arabs to argue that their enemies were "madmen"; that Israel was a criminal and suicidal phenomenon. And this, combined with the "children and madmen" argument, would give future Israeli nuclear threats the image of "madmen's threats"—which may have a very high degree of credibility but also invites preemption rather than stabilization.[24] On the other hand, Arabs may perceive Jews in traditional terms—as a commercial, not very brave, historically extinct civilization that would shrink back to its "normal" status as a tolerated minority if the Arabs used their enormous power properly. Modern anti-Semitic terms could be added to these, calling the Jewish presence in the Middle East expansionary, "cancerous" by definition, seeking to dominate the whole Arab world. Thus this threat must be answered by Arab force. Yet this Arab power was still exclusively conventional—manpower, oil, and territory—while Arab motives were historical-cultural. Some of these motives were relatively new, such as the European-imported, fierce nationalism. And some were very old, such as the pride and exclusivity, the inward focus of Islam, which seeks victory on earth and does not, by all means, perceive life as a corridor to the real, spiritual life after death. Thus, Arabs were brave and proud, due to their numbers and self-perception as a world power in the past, and they were divided and in some cases corrupt. The same historical-cultural reasons may further explain their current frustration and sense of victimization. These historical-cultural and psychological factors, even the political ones, could be neutralized by virtue of the same factors, if the nuclear incentive were added to them, if Israel reduced its challenge to Arabs to the minimum, dictated by its own interests and priorities. But Israel could not rely on these factors alone. Competition among Arabs, the nondemocratic nature of their regimes, and the temper and drives of their particular leaders were problematic. Still, once the Arabs understood the meaning of the nuclear revolution, they might leave Israel alone.

The terminology that Ben-Gurion might have used is important. The term "rational," in the Western sense, does not necessarily apply in a sensitive area such as the Middle East, and could obscure the historical scene. Western measures of "rationality" might prove "irrationality" on the Arab side, even though they behaved—in historical terms, say— within the bounds of their culture, politics, and interests, which are indeed a "subjective," but the decisive, "rationale" of their behavior.

Coming back to Ben-Gurion, however, Arabs' acceptance of the alien Jews in their midst as an independent polity seemed possible to him for the same reason that made Israel's acceptance in their eyes impossible—first, as a matter of principle, and also in light of Israeli territorial expansion since 1948 and the plight of the Palestinian refugees. In Ben-Gurion's view, Arabs could perceive themselves as a proud, courageous nation and perceive Jews as weak and wicked. In the Arab view, the Zionist adventure, moreover, is a crime against the Jews' own history. It forced them to live in exile as a sort of religious community, but not in Palestine as a nation. Therefore, following a massacre, the Jews might be forced back to their "natural" state of existence in the Diaspora. But if Arabs were given an unconventional reason *not* to demonstrate their self-perceptions in the traditional, conventional, cultural-historical fashion—that of a holy war, or any other kind of conventional warfare—they might accept Israel. This might be possible if Israel did not add insult to injury, for example, by taking control over the whole of Western Palestine or of sovereign Arab territory elsewhere.

However, deterrence theory recommends fighting fire with fire—or invoking credible threats against threats that seem rather credible a priori, or against threats that might escalate to action due to less effective responses. So, rather than Arabs learning from an Israeli nuclear option to leave Israel in peace, deterrence theory could teach them to get their own bomb. Deterrence theory itself emerged from a historically given situation, in which the bomb was already present on both sides, and its initial goal was to preserve a status-quo. This was not the case in the Middle East. But this imported theory—emanating from a different situation, politically and culturally—could be used for various purposes, including low political ones, such as enhancing the personal interests of an Arab dictator, who would skillfully play the nuclear "madman." Moreover, thus armed, the Arabs could either try to erode the credibility of the Israeli threats, or even of Western adversaries such as the United States, or start a game of chicken with regional and maybe extraregional adversaries under conditions more favorable to them than the roughly equal game played between the Americans and the Soviets. Why? Because they were braver, or held bravery above other values, or would not admit—as a matter of tradition—any defeat as final. Theoretically, leaders among them would create a no-win situation from the beginning; whereas the other side—the fat Western democracies, the Jews, etc.—would give in because (invoking their own profit and loss terminology) they would believe that they had more to lose.

The very intense discussion among Westerners of their own nuclear threats as doubtful and their self-imposed taboos in this regard (such as Schelling's "non-use" formula) could be useful to a more determined party. The Vietnam experience and earlier Chinese and Soviet challenges to the West could be interpreted thus (even if Schelling's theory was invented to meet challenges mainly from the Soviet Union). Furthermore, in the case of Israel—with a limited number of atomic bombs combined with the calculations of profits and loss that would be introduced in such a game—Arab numbers and space would undermine the "Churchillian" excuse for the Arab culture to defer from eradicating the alien entity in its midst.

Thus deterrence theory, which totally ignored politics and history while creating relatively simple mutual threat situations, would seriously impair the "Churchillian" strategy. Arabs may use the theory for their own purposes, which would be entirely different from those of Schelling.

There is little doubt that Ben-Gurion had cultivated a profound rejection of American behaviorism and deductive methods; whereas some Israeli scholars and politicians perceived in them a form of modern, unalterable, scientific wisdom that could serve their various low political goals.[25]

The French military strategist General Pierre Gallois believed that nuclear weapons could act as the "big equalizer" for smaller nations against much bigger and stronger opponents, according to what he called "the balance of terror."[26] But Gallois' writings were not necessarily known to Ben-Gurion when he made his major decisions about Israel's nuclear options. And they clearly had no effect on Ben-Gurion's early interest in the bomb, since they were published years later. In any event, the Israeli prime minister did not think that "the balancing of terror" should be the issue for Israel, nor was it exactly the case elsewhere. Nuclear weapons did not "equalize" entities whose relations were different. France, even when occupied, remained a grand civilization; it had friends, a solid national base, and a long history as well as a future that might well survive communism itself. France had faced serious problems, but Israel faced extinction. Without a nuclear option, the last chance of the Jewish people to regain a homeland and sovereignty, with all the obligations and hopes attached to it, would be over; its population could face mass killings, something the French did not suffer even under the Nazis.

Israel's situation was more difficult, and yet clearer and more elementary, than the case of France. The Arabs transformed it to a sheer life-and-death question, thereby creating a unique high political drama. No one threatened France in such terms, nor had regional conflicts anywhere in the Western world assumed such a definite character. Unless, of course, one accepted the Arab argument that Israel was a colonial phenomenon, an argument that even the Soviet Union did not endorse. On one hand, Israel's problem was that of imposing its will—to a "reasonable" degree—on the Arabs, especially when they started to receive a lot of conventional Soviet military aid. And on the other hand, this very expectation was elementary and lacking hegemonic, regional-political interests and even economic expectations. These same factors— along with France's complex relationships with Great Britain and the United States—played various roles in France's own decision to "go nuclear" vis-à-vis West Germany, for example, and to develop nuclear reactors for peaceful use on a very large scale. Thus, all the complicated deterrence-strategic considerations emerging from the politics of the Western Alliance at the time—the issues of discrimination, great powers' "collusion," the reliability of superpowers' nuclear guarantees, and even the issue of theater nuclear weapons—were different from Israel's own basic dilemma, except perhaps for the French notion of having nuclear weapons as "triggers" to ensure American nuclear

involvement. These considerations would not have had the same meaning for David Ben-Gurion as for the leaders of the European powers
and for nuclear strategists in the West.

Ben-Gurion's main idea—as I interpret it—was to give the Arabs a
way to climb down from their ladder of hostility and be able to justify
peace or at least coexistence in their own eyes. He did not pursue Gallois' "balance of terror," nor did he try to equalize Israel's power with
Arab power, due to the enormous differences between Arab and Jew in
historical-political and economic terms. He accepted that Israel should
remain a small Jewish entity in a partitioned Palestine. But even for
that purpose, Israel needed something to make the Arabs accept it.
Without the fabrication of a nuclear-scaled excuse, Ben-Gurion might
well have seen no other reason for the Arabs to accept Israel. On the
contrary, Arab politicians willing to accept a conventional Israel would
be committing a major political mistake, and in this sense would indeed
be behaving "irrationally." But the "supernatural" and "objective"
power of the nuclear option would be an asset in rationalizing recon-
ciliation. By yielding to the bomb's elemental forces of nature rather
than to Jewish swords, Arabs' "surrender" would be to forces beyond
their control. Again, abstract nuclear strategy may blur this picture,
and rationalize a deliberate "irrational" behavior by Arabs, even if its
very purpose was to achieve the opposite result.

Of course Israel could not ignore the problems inherent in the very
technical nature of nuclear research and development, such as missile
development, or the problem of credibility, especially when the bomb
would eventually appear on the Arab side.[27] For Ben-Gurion, however,
"credibility" emanated from the high political nature of the Zionist venture, as can be seen in his public speeches in the 1950s. In those
speeches, he praised the pioneering, selfless sacrifice of individuals and
devoted communities in transforming an old civilization into a new
nation, in reversing current trends such as urbanization by settling in
barren land and "making the desert bloom." All these efforts, which
he praised and tried to accomplish as best he could, would prove the
serious, positive nature of Israel to Arabs in the long run, when combined with the nuclear option. Credibility was, of course, also a military
matter. It required strategic territory, to a degree; conventional deterrence, achieved by means of "controlled conventional retaliation" (limited, and usually short, night raids); and due to endless difficulties in
conventional weapon procurement abroad, it required efforts at self-
produced arms. Meanwhile, the nuclear option loomed heavily above
every other thing Ben-Gurion did. But the actual issue of credibility in a
nuclear chicken game seemed not to have bothered him too much. The

Arabs were able, like anyone else, to understand that nuclear weapons revolutionized the military history of the world, even if they might not admit it at first—and perhaps even more so, given that they were the only powers in the world resolved to destroy an adversary.

Ben-Gurion also provided for the limitation that Israel neither rule over too many Arabs in territories inhabited solely by them, such as the West Bank, nor occupy sovereign Arab land. This last principle was not honored for a short time in 1956, due to the specific problem of Egyptian control over the Gaza Strip. The strip was part of British Palestine, and many Palestinian Arabs found a miserable refuge in that territory, occupied in 1948 by Egypt. They were not allowed to settle in Egypt proper, but were kept in refugee camps. The Palestinians in Gaza were permitted by the Egyptians to launch guerrilla attacks against Israel. Yet even then, the main goal of the 1956 war, in cooperation with France and Great Britain, was to gain access to French-made nuclear reactors, according to an Israeli source,[28] following a short period of Israeli occupation of the Sinai.

Summing up, one may argue that Ben-Gurion assumed that even Israeli nuclear options would not be enough to cause the Arabs to give up their self-imposed rules, due among other things to the rivalry among them. Nor would nuclear options prevent the enormous complications inherent in such situations as under-the-threshold wars and the mobilization of third parties (such as the Soviets) to end this anomaly. But it seems that he hoped that despite this, nuclear options in Israel's hands would be the tool that Arabs needed to reconcile themselves to the Israeli phenomenon—if limited to a partitioned Palestine—without losing face. It would not be the Jews who made them "surrender," but nature itself. And thus neither "terror" nor a "balance" would have been a part of Ben-Gurion's vocabulary. One may speculate that he did not forget the Soviets, but that according to the Israeli analyst Avigdor Haselkorn, he could see no solution to the problem of their growing—conventional—support of Arabs, other than nuclear threats aimed at Moscow itself. And yet, Ben-Gurion would have rejected as totally deductive and ahistorical Kenneth Waltz's arguments that nuclear weapons socialize elites and in general contribute to stability and peace; because Ben-Gurion's aim was to win the race—not to achieve a "balance of socializing terror." And he attributed the utmost importance to the time factor, i.e., to what Israel could do when it won the race, and to what the superpowers and the Arabs would do then. He refused to generalize, or to forget other political aspects accompanying nuclear politics. The nuclear option itself was not enough to resolve the conflict, but several related issues, such as the partition of Palestine and the

refusal to rule over Arabs, were necessary to achieve peace in this particular case. When combined with feelings like humiliation and revenge,
pride and a sense of victimization, the nuclear option could allow Arabs
to excuse themselves. This option was a precondition, and the decisive
one, if it was first gained by Israel and denied from Arabs. Of course
one could argue that it would just drive them to the other extreme and
cause at least some Arab leaders to become obsessed with the bomb. But
in Ben-Gurion's view, as I interpret it, Arabs would pursue the bomb on
their own. It would be hard to prevent a culture that perceives itself as
the just and prevailing religion, or as an old world power seeking
revival, from pursuing the most important tool in the nuclear age. At
any rate, Israel could not prevent the Arabs from so doing by adopting
nuclear self-denial. Thus Israel had no other choice but to pursue the
nuclear option first, and then seek a political settlement.

The outcome would not be simple, and not necessarily the same
across the Arab world, but it would serve as a base for further political
processes, combined with economic developments, whose final outcome would be more promising than anything else.

As for whether this option of nuclear "excuse" should be delivered
openly—that is, whether Arab culture would allow open threats to be
officially accepted or whether they should be implied—and how exactly
threats should be combined with other positive and negative efforts
were issues that Ben-Gurion did not resolve in his time, as we shall see.

Ben-Gurion began (as we are told by Bundy and our French
sources) to take action based on this understanding of the bomb's
potential role. And his approach could have been seen by some quarters
in Israel—and in Washington and London—not only as sheer nonsense
but as a threat to Israel's own security and to the regional and global
interests of the United States.

CHAPTER FOUR

American Intervention

The Israeli-French nuclear connection of the late 1950s could be interpreted in terms of nuclear "sharing."[1] This followed the American-British sharing earlier in the 1950s, which may have made sharing with Israel seem justified to the French. They may have seen Washington's "collusion" with Moscow in regard to the abortive Suez War as further justification. Also, a French-West German-Italian nuclear program was discussed in 1957 (following the very same war).[2] And it is possible that this connection was fully known to the Americans.[3] In any event, it focused Israel's attention on Bonn as a rather important partner in France's own nuclear plans. The German link could complicate Ben-Gurion's domestic politics. Also there could be a possible Soviet campaign against such a development; and it could affect American deliberations in regard to West Germany—that is, how to give Adenauer some, but no real, nuclear "sharing," without pushing the Soviets too much. This very complex process was in the making when General de Gaulle took over.

By all appearances, the Israeli-French connection was working well following de Gaulle's ascendancy in 1958, despite his insistence on a French "national bomb" (which by definition should be exclusive and for French interests only). According to available French sources, de Gaulle's own plutonium separation plant did not produce weapons-grade plutonium before 1959, and the "national bomb" was not ready before 1960.[4] Israel reportedly helped design it with the use of American-made computer equipment that Washington had refused to supply to the French.[5] This alone may have justified de Gaulle's reciprocity, but it was not enough to win his fundamental support. At about this

61

time, the French concluded that the secret French-Israeli cooperation agreement had become known, and de Gaulle's foreign minister presented Israel with an ultimatum: Jerusalem must make its nuclear plans public and agree to inspection by the IAEA (which came into being in 1957, the year that the original French-Israeli nuclear agreement had been signed) to safeguard the Dimona reactor against weapons production. If the Israelis disagreed with this ultimatum, the French would break the cooperation agreement. And, according to our French sources, without the cooperation agreement Israel would forfeit the missing reactor parts, the whole plutonium separation plant, and the deliveries of uranium for their half-finished reactor.[6]

This behind-the-scenes crisis with the French took place a couple of years after internal dissension had shaken the Israeli Atomic Energy Commission (IAEC) to its foundations. Though attached at that time to the Ministry of Defense, the IAEC had been created in the early 1950s, before the French connection with its intrinsic military potential was made. Several members of the IAEC were major scientists who were sworn enemies of the nuclear option, if misused. Other members were interested in basic research rather than in costly applied science. And still others wanted the Israeli nuclear effort to develop under their own control, or at least in their full knowledge and thus in cooperation with their opinions. In March 1958, the commission resigned, leaving behind Ernst Bergmann in his role as chairman.[7]

Professor Julio Rackach, doyen of Israeli theoretical physics and the mentor of many Israeli nuclear physicists, was among the prominent natural scientists who resigned. We know the official nature of Rackach's objections: He refused to serve as a rubber stamp. For other Israeli scientists, of mainly German origin, nothing could justify the introduction of a nuclear option to the Middle East, a step that could portend a holocaust for everyone. Several of them, such as professors Markus Reiner and Shmuel Sambursky, were politically active among radical minority groups before Israel was born and either rejected the very concept of a Jewish state in Palestine or resented what they perceived as Ben-Gurion's "Jewish nationalism." Such people, after the Holocaust, could be mobilized to help create the Jewish state in a partitioned Palestine, but they still harbored doubts about the price of statehood and were, therefore, prone to set limits to that state. At the same time, Rackach and other intellectuals may have discerned threatening dictatorial traits in Ben-Gurion's behavior. They feared that, encouraged by Ernst Bergmann (a sort of "Dr. Strangelove" in their eyes) and his apparatchik, Shimon Peres, and in collaboration with the nationalist French, Ben-Gurion would be a danger to Israeli democracy—or might even use the bomb rather than save it for deterrence only. Bergmann was the problem for some scientists; whereas Peres created doubts among domestic and foreign leaders, such as British Labour leaders Richard Crossman and Dennis Healey, to whom he openly talked about Israel's nuclear ambitions. The year of the French-Israeli nuclear agreement—1957—happened to be crucial for Great Britain. It had embarked at the time upon a conservative doctrine of "massive retaliation" of its own. This doctrine was ridiculed by moderate Labour left-wing leaders such as Crossman, who advocated the renunciation of nuclear weapons by the British and their neighbors within the framework of a nonproliferation agreement. Crossman preferred "a state of bipolar nuclear deterrence as more stable than a multipolar system.[8] He had ties with the left wing of the Israeli labor movement, which perceived in Peres a sort of amoral whiz kid, playing with dangerous toys without deep understanding of their strategic nature. Crossman's colleague Dennis Healey emphatically referred to Peres as "Fascist" at the time.[9]

The issue was further complicated by its West German implications. John Newhouse refers to a secret agreement early in 1958 between Jacques Chaban-Delmas, a Fourth Republic minister of defense, and his West German counterpart Franz Josef Strauss regarding Bonn helping France develop nuclear warheads and the means for their delivery.[10] At this time, Shimon Peres developed his own military ties with Strauss, and had already developed intimate ties with the French, including the French nuclear-weapons-related establishment. Hans-Peter Schwarz tells us that Konrad Adenauer himself was interested in tactical nuclear weapons for the *Bundeswehr* from the beginning—1957 being the "crucial year" for the rearmament of the Federal Republic. Adenauer described the absence of German nuclear might as "discriminatory."[11] And his first minister for atomic energy, later his minister of defense, Strauss, never disguised his own plans for German nuclear might. The various German, French, and American deliberations in this regard are more complicated than the scope of this discussion. But British left-wing politicians such as Crossman wanted to give up their own independent nuclear power in order to prevent the French and the Germans from transforming Europe into a multipolar, and hence less manageable, theater. It seems clear that to these British politicians (and to the German Social-Democrats as well) the idea of German nuclear weapons, or French-German cooperation in this field, was seen as an unmitigated disaster—especially if right-wing politicians such as Strauss controlled them. The Peres-Strauss connection thus smelled bad, even if Adenauer did not go beyond the idea of tactical nuclear weapons, which he perceived as modern artillery for his army. It smelled bad in spite of the fact that Adenauer was very conscious of his dependence on the Americans and NATO at large, and of major difficulties at home, which imposed far-reaching constraints on German nuclear ambitions.

The German-French-Italian nuclear cooperation experiment of 1957-58 could, however, be perceived by the British and by leftists in Germany as a way out for Bonn, and if Peres was involved in this with Strauss and Chaban-Delmas, Israeli left-wing politicians would have been informed about it. For many Israelis such a connection was anathema (even though de Gaulle had eliminated it immediately after his ascendence). Moreover, a multipolar, nuclear Middle East would have been seen by Israelis as more dangerous even than a multipolar Europe—although they seemed to disregard the fact that Egypt appeared to be willing and capable of trying to unite the Arabs and pursue the bomb.

Peres was the most visible Israeli contact with Strauss, although Ben-Gurion had expressed interest in West German aid for "establishing heavy industries in Israel and in the field of guided missiles" in 1957.[12] It should be mentioned here that Israel appeared to be interested in ballistic missiles earlier. Israeli chief of staff General Moshe Dayan had returned from a visit to the United States in August 1954, and had discussed weapon-procurement abroad with Ben-Gurion. Ben-Gurion summed up their conversation in his diary by stating that the Arabs could buy everything. "We must procure as well, especially guided missiles [V-2s—spelled out in the original] and rockets."[13] But Peres cultivated special relationships with both the French and West German defense ministries, and thus became the easier target of domestic criticism in this regard. For too many Israelis, Strauss represented the revival of the old German army with the addition of nuclear aspirations. This was bound to push Moscow to a severe, possibly anti-Israeli, reaction. The fear of Soviet Russia, combined with ongoing sympathy for its achievements, was common among the Israeli Left and among some intellectuals.[14] At the least, this apprehension of Moscow's reaction was a good political argument to use against Ben-Gurion and his aides.

About a year after the resignation of the IAEC in 1958, General Yigal Allon—the leading Israeli military thinker and political figure of the nationalist Left and leader of a small but influential political party—published his book *A Curtain of Sand*. In it, Allon called for a purely Israeli conventional strategy of preemption and territorial expansion—mainly in the West Bank, which he claimed for historical-cultural and political reasons coupled with strategic ones.[15] (The rejection of Palestine's partition had been the old plank of his group since the 1930s.)

Allon envisaged a coup aimed in several directions. But his main targets were personal and political enemies, such as Ben-Gurion. As prime minister and minister of defense, Ben-Gurion had brought about Allon's resignation from the IDF, and had brought about the downfall of a whole group around Allon, because of their ideology and their political ties to the then-pro-Moscow elitist Left. Allon's group was opposed to the 1949 armistice boundaries, and to the armistice regime itself. As we know, Ben-Gurion was ready to accept an armistice as an interim stage toward peace; whereas Allon wanted peace, right away, contractual peace, and perceived occupied Arab territory as the major trump card toward imposing it. Ideologically, Allon's group was committed to Israeli rule in the country as a whole and rejected partition even after the 1948-1949 War of Independence, during which the group tried to challenge Ben-Gurion's direction of the war and his control over the IDF. Early in 1948, this group joined another leftist group, and both adopted a pro-Soviet orientation—inherent beforehand in both of them—which later isolated them politically.

In 1954 the groups separated again, and then both joined Ben-Gurion's parliamentary coalition, which involved them in collective responsibility for his cabinet's decisions. Traditionally, both groups, now organized as separate political parties, had difficulties in accepting majority decisions, whether in the Histadrut (the General Federation of Labor) or in other institutions in which they were represented on the basis of the common proportional ballot. But did Ben-Gurion bring the nuclear arrangements with France to the cabinet's attention early on? According to one leftist minister at the time, he did not: Ben-Gurion "had started the reactor construction . . . without the knowledge of the Knesset's Foreign Affairs and Security Committee and without approval of its Finance Committee."[16]

If Ben-Gurion did withhold knowledge from these committees, he had his reasons. The leftist ministers in the cabinet were expected to vehemently oppose the project. And, due to the peculiar power of minorities in Israel's multiparty coalitions, they were able to torpedo issues. Also, they were well known for forming personal or group vendettas when their sense of self-righteousness was inflamed. Eventually, the issue, however, did become known to most ministers. A staunch minority remained totally opposed to the venture.[17] The majority of representatives of the Left played a double game by adopting a sympathetic view toward antinuclear groups—including, in due course, the Americans and the Soviets—while accepting Dimona itself either as a "last resort" option or, as formulated later in public by Allon, as a safety measure in case Arabs acquired the bomb.[18]

Allon himself was not a member of the cabinet at the time. But as the most visible antinuclear strategist, he could blur his pro-Soviet past and return to mainline Israeli politics aimed at American support and friendship. At the same time, he was trying to cultivate a special relationship with the Russians, gain sympathy among liberals and the scientific community, and denounce Shimon Peres and his political ally, General Moshe Dayan. Allon saw Peres and Dayan as irresponsible French-influenced "technocrats" or, worse, as Gaullists and German-oriented at the same time. He seemed to be genuinely afraid of a sharp Soviet reaction to the Israeli-German military cooperation.

Allon tried to find sympathy among leading members of Ben-Gurion's own party, the middle-of-the-road Social-Democratic Mapai, especially Foreign Minister Golda Meir. Meir was known to resent Dayan and Peres, the latter personally, as contenders for Ben-Gurion's succession; and she feared Washington's wrath over the nuclear issue. She was doubtful about the Bonn connection, because the West Germans refused to take visible action to stop the activities of German experts in Egypt who were hired by President Nasser to build missiles carrying so-called unconventional warheads.[19] Other Mapai leaders were opposed to the cost of the enterprise, in addition to having doubts about its real value and fearing trouble with Washington. And they heard criticism from their British Labour colleagues.

The British government was informed by its Tel Aviv embassy in April 1959 about internal Israeli deliberations in regard to the nuclear option. This was when Peres cemented his secret arms deals with Bonn.[20] A secret report from the British Embassy in Tel Aviv, dated April 10, 1959, states:

> We noted, but did not report at the time, a speech made by Shimon Peres . . . at a symposium in the Weizmann Institute on February 1 in which he criticized the theoretical nature of the research being done at the Institute and referred briefly to a "secret weapon" which Israel was trying to obtain . . .
>
> The veil of security which was immediately pulled over this speech—one of Peres' typically indiscreet efforts—prevented us from finding out to which weapon Peres referred . . .
>
> At dinner with the Ambassador a few days ago Meyer Weisgal, the Director of the Weizmann Institute where Israel's atomic research is carried out, shed a little more light on the subject. He told the Ambassador that there had for some time been a heated argument within the Ministry of Defense as to whether Israel should or should not try to acquire the atomic bomb. Brigadier [Dan] Tolkowsky, who was moved on last year from heading the Air Force to be a "planner"

in the Ministry, had apparently been set to carry out a review of Israel's atomic policy. He had concluded that it would be foolish for Israel to try and get an atomic bomb, both because of the expense and because even if Israel were successful, the Soviet Union would undoubtedly arm the Arab countries in similar fashion. Tolkowski's view was supported by the majority of senior professional soldiers in Israel who thought it wise that the Middle East should be kept bomb-free. Peres on the other hand was extremely keen to have the bomb and had been saying he was sure that he could get it from the French. Ben-Gurion's view was that Israel should first concentrate on a nuclear reactor for atomic power but might thereafter achieve her own bomb as a by-product from it.[21]

Such opinions, about an issue which had seemingly been resolved since 1957 by the agreement with France to build the Dimona reactor, circulated in Israel and fueled the hidden debate when, in May 1960, de Gaulle had his own bomb ready and the French were suddenly withdrawing from the deal.

The crisis with de Gaulle took place, partly, following leaks from Israel, particularly by Bergmann and Peres[22] and by some ex-members of the IAEC who were involved because of their moral or political concerns. These individuals joined others in establishing a public body "for a nuclear-free Middle East" to continue their fight against the Israeli nuclear option. Allon was reported to have covertly cooperated with this group, several members of which were also involved in a parallel domestic crisis situation known as the "Lavon Affair."[23]

In short order, most of Ben-Gurion's cabinet were reported to have opposed the nuclear project for one reason or another. Ben-Gurion, in return, finally financed Dimona outside of the parliamentary-approved budget, through private fundraising.[24] Yet despite this activity, the project remained virtually unknown to most Israelis; the only information consisted of various rumors and the activities of the antinuclear committee.

Ben-Gurion was determined to have his own way with the project, but by 1960 he was confronted with a quadruple domestic-foreign crisis, and it seemed that he would not be able to go through with it. First, he was embroiled in the Lavon Affair.

Pinchas Lavon was a Socialist thinker and Mapai politician who became Israel's second minister of defense during Moshe Sharett's premiership in the early 1950s. He was an opponent of the nuclear program.[25] His political campaign in the early 1960s was targeted against Shimon Peres and Moshe Dayan—and later also against Ben-Gurion. The inner-party scandal was related to the style and substance of Ben-

Gurion's leadership, to the problem of his succession, and—because of
timing and Mr. Peres' person and methods—to the nuclear issue. The
whole affair became a public scandal of the first order.

Publicly, the Lavon Affair revolved around the question of who,
during Lavon's tenure as minister of defense in 1954, had authorized a
subversive Israeli operation in Egypt that ended in disaster. Lavon
claimed innocence at the time. He demanded the removal of the director of Army Intelligence, Colonel Benjamin Givli, and also of Peres,
who was director general of the Defense Ministry, based in part on
what Lavon perceived as Peres' disloyalty. Lavon's demands brought
about his own downfall, as his own loyalty to Prime Minister Sharett
and to the cabinet as a whole proved rather questionable. His behavior
in the Egypt operation seemed dubious; in similar cases he was proved
beyond doubt to have acted radically and without authorization.[26]

Peres had been appointed by Ben-Gurion, who returned to the
Defense Ministry when Lavon was forced to leave and then resumed
the premiership as well. When Lavon reopened the case of the Egyptian
operation in 1960, he demanded to be exonerated from any responsibility. He implicated Givli, Peres, and (less so) Dayan as those who
were directly and indirectly responsible—and Ben-Gurion, himself, as
their mentor. Soon enough Lavon blamed the defense establishment as
a whole for what he regarded as closed, immoral, dictatorial behavior.
At the same time, Lavon broadened the issue into a general quest for
neosocialist reform, a return to the voluntary roots of Labor Zionism,
and a general attack on Ben-Gurion's "statism," e.g., against his emphasis on the state's role, its civil service, and the role of the IDF in the
nation-building process.[27]

The second element of Ben-Gurion's four-part crisis was that he
seemed to be involved in an unmitigated disaster with the tricky
French, who were apparently deserting Israel in regard to Dimona.[28]

And third, Ben-Gurion had a full-blown falling out with President
Eisenhower, and shortly afterward with John Kennedy, regarding
Dimona. And he soon had to deal with a fourth challenge—Egypt's
"answer" to the Dimona reactor, described as Egyptian missiles armed
with "unconventional" warheads made by German experts.[29]

Ben-Gurion did finally extricate himself from this net of crises. We
will not go into the details of how he extricated himself; however, it
began with a state visit to France in 1960 and an open discussion of the
nuclear issue with de Gaulle. It appears that the general was indeed
moved by Ben-Gurion's arguments, and was satisfied with assurances
that Israel would not use its nuclear option to assert supremacy in the
fragile Middle East or to expand beyond its existing boundaries.

According to Matti Golan, the French had initially insisted upon a series of agreements, partially tying Israel's hands regarding Dimona, before the original agreement was signed in October 1957.[30] Accordingly, the French Foreign Ministry demanded that the atomic energy commissions of both nations sign a technical agreement to the effect that France was committed to give Israel the blueprints, the technical assistance, and the materials necessary to build the reactor, and that Israel was committed to consult with France on every matter related to it. Political assurances were necessary before this "technical" agreement was signed by both parties on October 3, 1957.[31] In the meantime, the crisis with de Gaulle on Dimona took place, which prompted Ben-Gurion's 1960 visit.

About this visit, Matti Golan tells us that Ben-Gurion promised the French president that "there would be no bomb produced" in Dimona.[32] Golan adds, however, that the agreement finally reached by Peres with de Gaulle's government stated that "Israel would continue to build the reactor by herself and France would refrain from demanding international inspection."[33] Israel, however, had neither industrial capabilities in this respect nor the technical know-how to proceed with the construction "by herself." Pierre Pean and Jean Francis Perrin tell us that, in fact, the French continued to construct the reactor itself, but they "froze" the plutonium reprocessing plant—or the most "sensitive" part of it—for about two years. Later, the French claimed that that part of the project was delivered from France behind de Gaulle's back.[34] According to the same source, however, the plant had been delivered with the knowledge of one of the general's close aides, and that under de Gaulle's rule France was actually building ballistic missiles for Israel.[35]

Pean and two American writers, Herbert Krosney and Steve Weissman[36] (the latter two quoting Israeli sources), suggest that the 1957 agreements were broadened in 1960, and that the French were given their alibi by the Israelis regarding the reactor itself. They claim that the separation plant was frozen because de Gaulle refused to give Israel an independent reprocessing capability. But Israel found a way to do some reprocessing in France. Though it is not clear whether this was done with de Gaulle's knowledge and cooperation. In any event, according to Pean, the Israeli-French connection finally provided Dimona with the plutonium separation plant and allowed it to start production of weapons-grade plutonium in 1965. According to Mordechai Vanunu, as quoted by Frank Barnaby, actual production began in 1966.[37]

The meeting between de Gaulle and Ben-Gurion included discussion of the political and not just the military aspects of the Arab-Israeli conflict. The general slyly asked about Israel's expansionist ambitions and was reassured that Israel would not repeat France's own tragedy (ruling over many hostile Arabs in Algeria). Ben-Gurion did not need any warnings to that effect; he feared Israel's "Algerization"—the occupation of the Arab-populated West Bank—as early as 1948. And for this reason he was firmly opposed to the return of Arab refugees to Israeli territory. As we may infer from our French source, however, the real reasons the French decided to drop their demand for international safeguards and agree to publicly separate themselves from Dimona (while in fact continuing construction of the reactor itself) are numerous.[38]

First, de Gaulle might have used the nuclear connection with Israel to neutralize the close ties between the defense establishments of France and Israel, so that they could not endanger his withdrawal from Algeria in 1962. He kept the Israelis tied to him by refraining from dropping the previous cooperation altogether and by continuing the missile program.[39] At the same time, he managed to isolate the "French-Algerian" element in his own army and finally dropped Algeria itself.

Second, he might also have believed that Israel and West Germany were able to cooperate in several sensitive spheres; as we have discussed, Ben-Gurion wanted Bonn's help in regard to "guided missiles."[40]

A third reason the French changed their initial uncompromising demands put forward in May and then agreed with Peres upon the much more moderate deal of November 1960 can be deduced from Wilfrid Kohl's *French Nuclear Diplomacy*, and the more recent works of McGeorge Bundy and John Newhouse. Also, as early as 1968, American writer William Bader offered his ideas on the subject (though not fully developed).[41] De Gaulle's early efforts to secure nuclear cooperation with America were finally rebuffed, as he understood it, even though he had demonstrated to the world his own capability by testing France's first atomic bomb early in 1960.[42]

In May 1960, when de Gaulle prepared for the ill-fated Paris summit conference between East and West, which collapsed as a result of the U-2 incident, he was loyal to Eisenhower as the leader of the Free World. But afterward he demanded from the president no less than "an equal voice in joint [presumably tripartite] decisions on the use of nuclear weapons." The Americans were ready to give him less than that. And "in the autumn of 1960 the negative American response was clear."[43] The United States was unwilling to risk offending its other European allies by accepting de Gaulle's demands for a formal triumvirate over NATO and was "unprepared to share America's world power to the extent sought by de Gaulle."[44] But the United States did share nuclear secrets with the British, much to France's displeasure, and might have been drawn to do more with the West Germans—something that de Gaulle wouldn't tolerate. Thus we can speculate that some nuclear sharing with Israel seemed inadvisable to de Gaulle as long as he hoped for a tripartite nuclear agreement with the Americans. However, once these hopes vanished, he might have played the Israeli card to demonstrate to the Americans that they had no monopoly on sharing. The next move would have to be Washington's. But now the end of 1960 was in sight and with it the end of Eisenhower's second term.

Considering the thorny problem of the negative publicity in the United States and Great Britain that would result from news of the Israeli nuclear option—particularly after information about it was leaked, possibly from Israeli and French sources—the French and the Israelis seem to have officially agreed to end their cooperation and declare that the Dimona reactor was completed by Israel alone "for peaceful use."[45] Thus, the French renounced responsibility; but they were still sufficiently involved. According to Pean, soon after making the project publicly known in the Knesset in December 1960, and describing it as a reactor for peaceful development of the Negev Desert,[46] Ben-Gurion was able to proceed with the reactor construction as before. The French halted the supply of the separation plant; they could calculate that now the Americans would intervene and Washington would assume international responsibility for France's basic "crime." In other words, since Israeli-French cooperation was officially, but not fully, over, Israel remained publicly responsible vis-à-vis Washington for its own nuclear affairs. Therefore, Washington, not France, would be blamed for any further developments regarding Israel's nuclear option, even if enough sharing continued to give France whatever advantage it sought from the Israeli connection. Sure enough, the Americans bit, and Ben-Gurion had to deal with them—once he overcame his initial troubles at home with Lavon and Dimona and abroad with de Gaulle.

In the meantime, Ben-Gurion had a full-blown crisis with the Americans over Dimona, as we are told by Mordechai Gazit.[47] President Eisenhower was on his way out in December 1960, and Washington, while awaiting the new administration, apparently saw no danger in the Israeli reactor. But Kennedy, once in office, wasted no time in getting involved.[48] Eisenhower's administration wanted to inspect the reactor and verify its peaceful nature. It also sternly warned Israel not to develop it for military purposes. Kennedy's problem was to find a common ground with the Soviet Union when possible, oppose it at the same

time, and devise a viable method for dealing with nuclear proliferation. He ended up trying to combine the Israeli nuclear effort with
Egypt's "answer" to it in order to kill them both by means of-trilateral
negotiations.[49] In this connection, Kennedy gave Foreign Minister Meir
the first American executive promise to guarantee Israel's boundaries,
and agreed to supply the country with conventional, at first defensive,
weapons to strengthen its non-nuclear option.[50] This aid, in the form of
Hawk SAMs, was badly needed to protect Dimona itself; therefore, the
promise of aid was made conditional on Israeli concessions regarding
the nuclear issue. According to McGeorge Bundy, Kennedy's national
security adviser, in 1962:

> Kennedy's assistant Myer Feldman negotiated a simultaneous agree-
> ment that the United States would sell Hawk . . . missiles, and that in
> return Israel would permit regular visits by Americans to Dimona,
> where they could judge for themselves whether or not the installa-
> tion was part of a weapons program. These bilateral visits continued
> until 1968, but they were not as seriously and rigorously conducted as
> they would have had to be to get the real story. My recollection is that
> close concern with this issue ended with the death of Kennedy.[51]

Later, we will discuss Johnson's presidency, during which Bundy's
own interest in Dimona would lead to interesting developments, which
he did not mention above. In the meantime, Kennedy's team, including
Bundy, was rather active. The promise of more aid strengthened the
anti-Ben-Gurion-Peres-Dayan forces in Israel, who emphasized conventional warfare. And several of them, such as Allon who aspired to
border changes in the West Bank, were encouraged. Thus the Israeli
nuclear option, while not yet born, had already started to draw the
United States more and more into the Middle East and made it intervene in Israel's murky domestic affairs. The same interest in Israel's
nuclear program later compelled the Americans to supply Israel with
modern weaponry, which, indeed, supported its 1967 preemptive conventional strike and the West Bank occupation. The effort to prevent
nuclear war, which was grounded among other things in deterrence
theory, actually encouraged conventional wars, which found support in
nuclear deterrence theory taken out of its nuclear context. And by not
accepting on time the American proposal to "trade off" its unconventional missiles with the Israeli nuclear effort in the framework of something like trilateral arms control, Nasser's Egypt actually encouraged
this American aid to Israel.[52]

Under heavy pressure from Kennedy to allow American inspection of Dimona, Ben-Gurion deferred as long as he could—for about a

year. This was long enough to complete some construction and dis-
guise the control panels, according to our French source.[53] In the meantime, he awaited the construction of the plutonium separation plant.
This vital component reportedly arrived sometime in 1962 and was
built underneath the reactor itself, hidden from foreign inspectors.[54]

While this was being accomplished, Foreign Minister Meir was
shifting alliances. She was very sensitive to Israel's new and promising
American ties, and was personally both a foe of Shimon Peres and tired
of Ben-Gurion's long rule and methods. Following the crisis with the
Americans and public controversy over Israel's relations with Bonn,
she was drawn toward Allon's path. Though, if we accept the testimony of one of her closest allies at the time, she never rejected Dimona
in principal.[55] Allon's political party was much smaller than Mapai, but
it was an influential factor in the Histadrut, the General Federation of
Labor. With its sister party Mapam (which produced some visible antinuclear activists), Allon's group could deprive Mapai of control over the
Histadrut, demand wage raises among workers, and thereby destabilize
the economy. This was the main concern of Mapai's "bosses" Levi
Eshkol and Pinchas Sapir. Also, Mapai's "doves" in the Israeli cabinet,
such as Sapir, felt able to associate with these conventional "hawks"
because of their traditional enmity toward Dayan and Peres, Ben-
Gurion's "technocrats." They were worried about a scandal with the
United States over Dimona, yet hardly dared to challenge Ben-Gurion
himself. The most influential among the "doves" was Pinchas Sapir, at
that time minister of commerce and industry. Sapir was one of Mapai's
most powerful party bosses, a friend and ally of Pinchas Lavon, and
personal enemy of Peres and Dayan—and a relative of Herman Kahn,
the American nuclear theorist.

Kahn visited Israel several times in the 1960s, but we have no evi-
dence that he influenced Sapir. We do know that Sapir's allies, Allon and
Galili, argued that Kahn's deterrence-technical thinking was limited to the
conflict between the superpowers only and did not apply to Israel's case.
Israel Galili was a close political associate of Allon's and a former pro-
Soviet leftist. In 1948 he had been fired from his post as deputy minister of
defense by Ben-Gurion. However, it is clear that both Schelling's and
Kahn's treatment of escalation, and the signalling necessary to control
it, helped guide Allon's and Galili's conventional strategic thinking. These
same methods were later employed by Allon's disciple, Chief of Staff
Yitzhak Rabin, on the eve of the Six-Day War.[56] According to secondary
Israeli sources, a coalition of several groups within Mapai was emerging
behind Ben-Gurion's back. This coalition leaned toward Allon's nationalist Left, and was reported to be ready to give up the nuclear option.[57]

Sometime in 1962, as we are told by Yair Evron, a "small group of decision makers" met to openly discuss Israel's nuclear option.[58] Allon stressed Israel's conventional advantage, which he believed would prevail "and would not disappear at all," unless nuclear weapons were introduced to the region, causing the possible decline of the IDF (due to the allocation of resources and because of the army's self-perception). Both Allon and his political ally Galili used American deterrence theory—thanks to the work of Galili's aide Arnan Azariahu, "who had personally inquired into the nuclear issue"—to argue that the Arabs would obtain their own bomb once Israel did, and that Nasser would then strike first. Due to its small size, Israel did not have a second strike capability, and therefore no "balance of terror" was possible in the Middle East. They repeated Allon's public arguments that in order for the bomb to act as a deterrent one's enemies must be "rational," and the Arabs fit Schelling's definition of "madmen and children" in the nuclear age. They further argued in favor of an enhanced conventional effort, whereas Dayan and Peres argued in favor of an "enhanced nuclear development." In his published version of these events, Yair Evron alleged that Ben-Gurion "tended to accept Allon's and Galili's approach." This decision had two consequences: First, it was decided that Israel should not adopt a nuclear strategy; second, that in the struggle over financial resources, more would be allocated to the procurement of conventional weapon systems. The outcome of that meeting was, in fact, without the participants consciously aiming at it, the adoption of Israel's ambiguous option.[59] Evron's version could be acceptable, if we use our definition of "ambiguity," rather than his.

Ambiguity was inherent in this interim phase, when the nuclear research and development process and the whole system were in the making, and Ben-Gurion did not need to make choices. Evron's interpretation of the meeting is totally incompatible with our findings in the official American archives, and hence it represents his own interest in "continued ambiguity," or in "academic opacity."

The same meeting is described somewhat differently by then= minister of transportation Yitzhak Ben-Aharon of Allon's party.[60] According to Ben-Aharon, Moshe Dayan was the one who asked for the reduction of conventional capabilities in favor of nuclear options, and raised the issue of an open Israeli nuclear policy in the future. His view was rejected, but Galili did not demand anything further and did not necessarily adopt Allon's totally negative view of the matter. He did not dare to forgo that option, says Ben-Aharon. But the actual result, according to Evron, was a compromise—an undeclared option—"rather the adoption of a nuclear doctrine as the foundation of Israel's national security," combined with an enhanced conventional effort.[61] In Evron's view this was the de facto source of the "ambiguous" nuclear stance Israel still follows today.

Still, Evron happens to be very skeptical about the possible advantage of nuclear options in Israel's case, based on deterrence-theoretical arguments. It was for the Left a political-moral burden—if not an impractical tool, and very possibly a dangerous one—once Kennedy and the Soviets put pressure to bear on Israeli representatives abroad, and on Ben-Gurion directly. Ben-Aharon was told by the Russian representatives at U.N. conferences, including the Geneva Arms Control Talks, that "once Israel will have the bomb, the Arabs will have it, too." He interpreted this to mean direct or indirect Soviet nuclear aid to the Arabs, a proposition that was totally dismissed by the CIA's Board of National Estimates. We shall return to the board's Middle East related arguments, but the reasons for this estimate could have been twofold: the perception of Moscow's fear that any move on its side might cause American nuclear sharing with West Germany, and a principled refusal to embark upon Soviet nuclear sharing with Moscow's own allies. According to Michael Beschloss's book on the Kennedy-Khrushchev relations, in October 1963 Soviet Foreign Minister Andrei Gromyko repeated to Secretary of State Dean Rusk the Soviet suggestion to create "nuclear-free-zones around the world. Rusk said the United States would not object, as long as the idea won the consent of the countries involved. In Latin America, for example, Cuba would be the main problem. In Africa, the stickler would be Egypt. As for the Middle East, Rusk went on to suggest that 'perhaps something could be worked out' to deal with Israel."[62]

I believe that Ben-Gurion expected American politicians and experts to do one or even both of the following: to think in their national-behavioral fashion, emphasizing their responsibilities and interests first; or to adopt a simplistic view of Israel's problems, of Arab motives and intentions in a conventional conflict, and of Soviet behavior in such a conflict. He was not one to be impressed by the foreign theoreticians quoted by Allon and Galili in their debate. In this connection, a confidential memo by Walt W. Rostow, then counselor and chairman of the Department of State's Policy Planning Staff, dated November 19, 1964, is illuminating:

A Way of Thinking About Nuclear Proliferation:
. . . the Israelis, with their extraordinarily heightened sense of vulnerability, are worried about an Arab attack conducted so swiftly as to make U.S. or Western support too late to be effective. This narrow but

intense anxiety brings the Israelis close to the point of ignoring the
negative arguments of a general pacific kind; and the possible play-
back effects of what it does on the decisions of Cairo. It does not con-
template a confrontation with one of the superpowers; and, therefore,
the relationship with the U.S. and possible damage to that relationship
are the only major restraints on proceeding to achieve a national
nuclear capability.[63]

This assessment was simplistic, at least as far as Ben-Gurion was
concerned: Israel did not expect "U.S. and Western help" to arrive on
time. And the reasons for this belief were rooted in history: the memory
of the Holocaust, U.S. behavior during Israel's War of Independence,
and U.S. behavior later, during the 1950s, when London and Washington seriously contemplated a "general settlement" between Israel and
several Arab states—the Alpha and Omega initiatives.[64]

These initiatives did not include formal peace, but were based
entirely on Israeli territorial concessions, on the principle of the right
of Palestinian refugees to return or accept compensation for loss of
land, and on Western guarantees promised to Israel once the border
lines were finally settled. The main territorial concessions were supposed to be made in the Negev Desert—the only open space left to
Israel in the 1949 demarcation lines. Israel needed this open space to
pursue settlement, keep the southern gate at Eilat open to the Indian
Ocean, and to work on the nuclear project. Moreover, Nasser's growing prestige, and Soviet support supplied to him since the mid-1950s,
generated Western initiatives toward compensating him at Israel's
expense. Any or all of the issues contained in the Arab-Israeli conflict—the Palestinian refugee problem, border questions, the issue of
freedom of navigation, and retaliatory policy (open and subject to
serious disputes between Washington and Jerusalem)—could spark a
general war.

Also, Israel was exposed to Soviet nuclear threats, as were its allies.
Based on historical experience and Ben-Gurion's vision of the future
as a constantly changing reality, he would not trust anything but Israel's
own deterrence power should another "confrontation with a superpower," provoked by the Arab clients of that superpower, loom on the
horizon.

The Arab response to the nuclear development of Israel was very
much in the mind of the Allon school, perhaps because of Rostow's
recommendation:

> . . . With respect to Israel, the familiar question is whether there is a
> combination of stick and carrot, of pressure and reassurance, we can

mount without wrecking either our relation to Israel or our tenuous links to the Arabs. *A heightening of Israeli anxiety about an Arab nuclear capability is an asset we can and should use* [italics added].

It is possible, however, that Ben-Gurion agreed to an enhanced conventional effort not because he suddenly recognized the problems involved in the nuclear one but as an interim strategy until the nuclear option was ready. (And, as we are told by Pean, the plutonium separation plant was delayed at the time.) Furthermore, once the nuclear option was ready, he might have opted for a more subtle, rather than an open, nuclear policy vis-à-vis the proud and sensitive Arabs. And he, of course, realized that the issue was entangled with superpower deliberations at that juncture.

An article published in the *Jewish Observer and Middle East Review* on December 28, 1962, a periodical regularly used by Mr. Peres to express his own views abroad (often mixed with others', notably Ben-Gurion's) supports the assumption that Peres himself wanted at the time to make the nuclear option known, rather than make it undeclared, "ambiguous," or even "opaque." Entitled "An Independent Deterrent for Israel," the article argued that the recent tough exchange between President Kennedy and Nikita Khrushchev meant that "since last October [the Cuban missile crisis] we have not only been *talking* about living in the nuclear age but also experiencing it . . . and against this background, it may seem rather unrealistic, if not plain silly, even to discuss the production and maintenance—let alone the operation—of an Israeli independent deterrent." The lead article continued to argue that Britain could not maintain such a deterrent due to its costs, and France did it "due to a tremendous effort of will by her President." But to put the question in this way to Israelis "who support the development of an independent deterrent—*and they include the Prime Minister, Mr. Ben-Gurion* [italics added]—is to invite the answer that Israel, unlike Britain and France and unlike every other country, cannot pose her problems in this manner. For Israel the question is whether she needs an independent deterrent in order to ensure her national survival . . . The Israeli decision to proceed was based on two conclusions . . . The first was . . . political. It was based on similar reasoning to that of the French General Gallois, who . . . had demonstrated effectively that by the very nature of nuclear warfare, the Americans will not be able to engage their own massive deterrent unless they are themselves directly threatened . . . The second—and far stronger—specifically Israeli justification [is:] Israel . . . is not arguing a purely hypothetical case. It is not yet twenty years since millions of Jews died because they could not fend for them-

selves . . . many hundreds of thousands who might have been saved
died because of the higher interests of winning the war, or 'not antagonizing Britain's Arab friends'—because, understandably, the Russians,
the British and the Americans had to put their own national interest
and national existence before that of the threatened Jews."

This description of the Holocaust and the trap situation into which
the Jews were pushed at the time is simplistic and has been discussed
briefly above. But the argument that the Jews must be able to defend
themselves, and that Ben-Gurion and his aides did not blame the West
for the Holocaust (a tendency that was widespread among Menachem
Begin's and Yitzhak Shamir's followers), is echoed here when the writer
concluded: "The Israelis are not complaining about this . . . here is the
dangerous precedent, and one that was—unintentionally—given its
sharpest formulation by President Kennedy . . . if a nuclear conflict will
produce . . . a hundred million dead during the first exchanges of missiles, the President would . . . justifiably pause before engaging in a
conflict in the Middle East which might seem marginal to the larger
stakes and which might escalate into a total war . . . Israel . . . is not
threatened by Soviet missiles, but by Arab threats of total destruction. In
these circumstances, a much smaller and much more sophisticated
deterrent with strictly limited consequences for the potential attacker is
something the Israelis now consider to be essential for their security
and survival . . ."

We can not judge what here was a presentation for American consumption—a "much smaller and sophisticated deterrent" could mean
tactical nuclear weapons only, no threat to Arab cities, no threat to the
patron power of Arabs, the Soviet Union itself, and so forth—and what
was the real strategy conceived at that time. We shall try to answer
such questions in due course. The point is that Peres' mouthpiece (the
newspaper article) was at the time far from being ambiguous or opaque
in regard to nuclear matters.

In the midst of these deliberations, on June 16, 1963, Ben-Gurion
resigned as prime minister and minister of defense. The resignation
was caused by several domestic reasons; mainly, Ben-Gurion's growing
isolation among his party colleagues with regard to his policy of cooperation with West Germany, and as a result of the coalition that Eshkol
and Meir pursued with the parties of the Left in order to maintain control over the Histadrut. His resignation was also related to the unresolved succession issue, and to his quest to reform the Israeli multiparty government system. (He wanted to introduce public "rules of the
game," something close to British cabinet rule based on majority-con-
stituency balloting.)

The resignation happened to be submitted following an internal decision by President Kennedy formulated in a "National Security Action Memorandum" (NSAM 231), in which Kennedy "instructed the Department (of State) to develop proposals for forestalling the development of advanced weapons in the Near East."[65] There had also been recent intensive diplomatic activity regarding the Arab-Israeli dispute as a whole and especially the nuclear issue. The Americans examined the best possible means to convince Ben-Gurion and Nasser to give up their unconventional efforts. These activities, which were partially mentioned by General Dayan in public in April 1963,[66] culminated in a crucial Middle East visit by John J. McCloy, Kennedy's arms control aide.[67] McCloy first went to Egypt to begin negotiations with President Nasser on the link between Dimona and the Egyptian missiles, hoping to develop it into some kind of mutual arms control negotiations. According to Gazit: "Central to the McCloy mission was the idea that *the United States would attempt to convince the Israelis to agree to international supervision of the Dimona reactor in return for Egyptian flexibility regarding their missile program* [italics added]."[68] But before McCloy could get to Israel, he was rebuffed by Nasser, Gazit tells us, seemingly because the Egyptian President would not enter into any American-sponsored talks with Israel. At the time, he was leaning toward Moscow and had reason to fear other Arab competitors—such as Ba'athist Syria and revolutionary Iraq, with whom he had concluded a pact of confederation shortly before. According to a more recent interpretation, McCloy was not fully rebuffed, but Nasser gave him vague, or at least insufficient, answers.[69] The Egyptian president seems to have hoped to bring enough American pressure to bear on Israel regarding its nuclear program without sacrificing his own missile program (having concluded a large arms deal with the Soviets in 1963). In Nasser's mind, the Israeli nuclear effort, not his own missiles, should have been Washington's main concern. After all, Egypt had no nuclear capabilities at all.

And then, shortly afterward, President Kennedy was assassinated. The Israeli nuclear option seemed to have survived, despite the Israeli elite, and against American "better judgment" and interests.

Kennedy's main concerns had been: Israeli high-handedness toward the Arabs and its position as a regional power once it had the nuclear option; Arab counterefforts; and particularly, the growing involvement of the Soviet Union as a protector of the Arabs against a nuclear Israel. The chairman of the CIA's Office of National Estimates, Sherman Kent—a highly qualified OSS veteran who offered his views to the president—did not believe that Arab nuclear counterefforts would materialize. He based his belief on the assumption that the Arabs were not advanced technologically and that Israel would undoubtedly take countermeasures. Likewise, he did not consider the possibility of Soviet nuclear protection of the Arabs as something to be taken seriously.[70] However, Kent did expect Israel to assume a much more aggressive policy toward the Arabs once in possession of public nuclear tools. He even imagined Israel trying to have a voice in the Soviet-American arms control talks. Kennedy may well have been greatly worried by the vision of Soviet-American rivalry being complicated by semi-independent nuclear clients, who were primarily preoccupied with their own parochial affairs. In this sense, he might have agreed with Nasser that Israel's nuclear option was a matter of American concern wider than the Middle East dispute itself. Nevertheless, the Israelis argued in Western capitals that Egypt had been first to add the missile factor to the unconventional race, which made it somewhat difficult for America to act on that concern to the benefit of the Egyptians. The Kennedy Administration could not ignore these arguments.[71]

In fact, Egypt's German-made missiles were not taken seriously, at least at first. They had no guidance system and carried no real unconventional warheads.[72] Egypt had hoped to buy some radioactive waste, such as cobalt and strontium 90, for that purpose,[73] but nothing ever came of it. Yet the very threat sent shock waves through the whole Israeli security establishment and caused problems for Mr. Peres, whose German connection seemed to have been used by Bonn to cover up its missile (and maybe even unconventional warhead) aid to Egypt. At least this is how Mossad director Isser Harel—the man who had just caught Adolf Eichmann—preferred to see it,[74] especially when this view could be used in the succession struggle against Peres.

Kennedy's main concern was to somehow use Israel's and Egypt's unconventional efforts to stop them both, while achieving his primary aim—to block Russian influence in a dangerous, vital region. He wanted to prevent the Soviets from capitalizing on the Israeli bomb, when and if it became a reality, by becoming the guarantee power of the Arabs. His goals were to prevent this from happening so that the United States could reach an agreement with Moscow to curb proliferation and to stabilize East-West relations in the nuclear and, possibly, other areas (thanks, among other things, to Kennedy's own Nitze-Wohlstetter-inspired, massive nuclear rearmament).

The German scientists scare—along with Ben-Gurion's bids for superpower guarantees for peace and for limiting arms exports to the Middle East and his alternative bid for an American-Israeli NATO-like defense treaty—were perceived in Washington as "a part of a campaign to justify Israeli development of nuclear weapons, or to threaten this as an alternative if we didn't come through with a security pact."[75]

This American pressure was keenly felt by Ben-Gurion, according to his biographer Bar-Zohar. He felt compelled to complete his nuclear option in spite of his domestic problems.[76] He realized, though, that he had become a problem to the Americans and Israelis alike, and so he resigned. With his resignation Ben-Gurion left the completed (according to Pean's and Barnaby's dates), partially hidden nuclear complex to Levi Eshkol and Mrs. Meir to negotiate with McCloy, while Shimon Peres maintained his job as deputy defense minister. Before he left office, Ben-Gurion had agreed to American inspection visits at Dimona,[77] but this agreement pertained to a just-finished, though disguised, production unit—and thus to a nonexistent (as yet) nuclear capability.

Here, the Krosney-Weissman version of the reprocessing in France, if true, becomes irrelevant, as Israel had (according to Pean, and as photographed in place later by Vanunu) its own means to reprocess, if given time and enough freedom of action. Ben-Gurion's own position and style may have been seen to have endangered the project. The Americans perceived in him a sort of "mini de Gaulle"; and they also had to deal with de Gaulle himself, who gave them enough trouble and who was much less dependent on them. It may have seemed that Ben-Gurion should have given up on the nuclear option—which he wouldn't do—or try tricks and bluffs—which, from a domestic political viewpoint, he might not have been able and willing to try. (At home, he was facing Lavon, Isser Harel, and Golda Meir.)[78]

Once in power, Levi Eshkol, Meir, and even Allon, by now an important ally in their cabinet, would have to use real options as best they could. Ben-Gurion must have had his doubts about this coalition, but it seems that he hoped the clever Eshkol might deal better with Kennedy. Eshkol was an accomplished wheeler-dealer, a quality that Ben-Gurion saw in Kennedy too. Eshkol might be able to argue better with the president and his determined antiproliferation "whiz kids," including Kennedy's National Security Council chief McGeorge Bundy, who was the driving force behind the unusual interest in Dimona shown by Robert Komer, an NSC Middle East executive.[79] But their interest and work was deflected—by Nasser and Lee Harvey Oswald, who made the issue of Dimona less immediate for them.

The recently opened American (and British) documents relating to Nasser's foreign policy clearly reflect his efforts to create a great Arab power. He tried to exploit East and West rivalry for that purpose, and yet, was highly responsive to challenge—real and less real—from the West and by Israel. Ben-Gurion, on the other hand, expected the superpowers to woo the Arabs at Israel's expense, especially in regard to the Negev, which he needed to establish Israel as an indestructible entity. The 1956 Suez War helped him in this direction and later pushed the debate to new horizons—due to the Dimona reactor, which he was able to secure because of the Suez campaign. Nasser himself might have been trying to reach these same horizons. And thus he was reluctant to agree on any final settlement with Israel beforehand. Egypt's "destiny" as a great power might have entailed unconventional ambition from the start, but it helped legitimize Israel's nuclear efforts, at least in the "opaque" fashion. But this was yet to come, when Ben-Gurion (temporarily) left the scene.

Upon assuming office as prime minister, Eshkol made a statement to the Knesset that was seen as a significant public signal. He was immediately quoted by the American Embassy in Tel Aviv, as follows: "'It would be ridiculous if debate should leave impression we now have new parties: a conventional arms party and an unconventional arms party . . . Key criterion is nature of weaponry likely to be used against Israel, and for the sake of somewhat remote danger . . . [Arab unconventional weapons] . . . some tens of years ahead . . . we cannot disregard the danger that exists here and now—the conventional arms.'"[80] This was Eshkol's public stance, but not necessarily his personal policy or reflective of his actual behavior.

CHAPTER FIVE

The 1967 War

Just before Lyndon Johnson inherited the problem of Israel's nuclear option, President Kennedy gave Prime Minister Eshkol written assurances of Israel's boundaries in order "to influence Israel's behavior in regard to the reactor in Dimona."[1] Executive agreements like this are usually secret and, therefore, not as binding as open agreements, let alone defense treaties requiring Congressional approval. In this case, however, the president also made a public announcement on the subject, although it seemed vague and not binding.[2] With this written agreement, Israel managed to emerge from its isolation and gain super-power support; yet the Israeli public knew nothing about the agreement or the reasons for it.

Israel was hardly ready to trust American promises of aid or support, although striving to gain them. From the country's birth it had been subject to a continuing series of American rebuffs and unacceptable demands. We have already discussed how President Truman withdrew American support from the U.N. partition plan for Palestine and placed an embargo on American weapons to the Middle East in 1948. For a while he also endorsed the idea of an international trusteeship for the country as a whole. Washington never recognized West Jerusalem de jure as the capital of Israel. Further, it refused to intervene with Jordan to allow Israelis to visit the holy places in East Jerusalem. The United States saw the division of Jerusalem as an inevitable situation, until the general border problem was resolved. We must remember that Israel had no borders in the legal sense, only armistice demarcation lines (drawn after the War of Independence). And even after boundaries were drawn, the issue was complicated by

Arab sensitivities prohibiting formal peace. Washington placed ongoing demands on Israel to cede territory, especially in the sensitive Negev, to the Arabs. And every now and again the Americans demanded that Israel admit Palestinian refugees into the pre-1967 territory. Such demands were not put forward to Soviet Russia and Poland even during the worst years of the cold war, although both had pushed millions of Germans into Western-occupied Germany in 1945, and Bonn, an American ally, had absorbed them later on. The Arab countries refused to absorb Palestinian refugees. And the West seemed to accept their refusal to do so, as though the rules and realities that came into being as a result of World War II were not applicable to Israel.

The Palestinian problem combined two issues in a difficult way. The first issue—which was the main point during Nasser's heyday—was that of pan-Arabism, according to which all Arabs belonged to the same *uma*, or "nation." And second, several Arab entities claimed their own national rights as well. No one emphasized Palestinian statehood at the time, or resolved the tension between nationalism, say Egyptian nationalism, and pan-Arabism. In practical terms, Egypt's union with Syria in the late 1950s proved to be unacceptable to the Syrians, but all Arabs claimed to support the "rights of the Palestinians" as exiled people. Thus, one could have concluded that the "rights of the Palestinians" at the time might mean annexation of Palestinian territory by a hostile pan-Arab regime supported by the Palestinians themselves, a development Ben-Gurion feared.

There were attempts at foreign intervention in these complex issues. For example, the Kennedy Administration suggested making Israel give Palestinians the option to assert their "right of return" to their homes in Israel. Of course this gesture was of a symbolic nature. But giving Palestinians the right to settle in Arab exile and be compensated for their property left behind in Israel would have exposed them as making an unacceptable concession in terms of Arab perceptions of their historical rights. Or it would have exposed Nasser as a partner to such an unacceptable deal. Fearing Egyptian predominance, his numerous rivals in the Arab world—especially the conservative, in fact pro-Western, regimes and the revolutionary Iraq—would have accused him of treachery. Moreover, his home base and standing in an excited Arab world—to a large extent excited by him—was based on a noncompromising attitude on such questions. This was supported by Arab legal claims and the Arab legal turn of mind, which emphasized Israel's "illegality," and also by several U.N. resolutions, which Arabs made use of when such resolutions enhanced their cause.

When Nasser secured Soviet military aid, Israel seemed once again to be the loser in an unequal race involving the strategic political interests of a united West. London and Washington demanded concessions from Israel, and these concessions did not wholly disappear following the rupture of the Western alliance in the Suez War. Western calculations related to the oil supply and the growing race with the Soviets in the area also led to Kennedy's own initiatives toward a solution of the Palestinian refugee problem, partially, at least, within Israeli territory. Washington, however, did not interfere with Nasser's policy of blockading the Suez Canal to Israeli shipping—and severely censured Israel's retaliatory policy. The Americans traditionally refrained from supplying weapons to Israel,[3] although, under Eisenhower, Nasser's flirtation with the Russians and his activities against Western interests in black Africa and in the Arab world allowed a more flexible approach toward Israel in Washington. These traditional constraints on U.S.-Israeli relations changed with direct arms supplies and secret military guarantees under Kennedy, due to a large extent to the nuclear factor—of which most Israelis were unaware.

When Lyndon Johnson entered the scene, he continued the basic policy of his predecessor and retained the group of officials—especially McGeorge Bundy, his "front man" Komer, and others—who worked hard to stop Israel's nuclear program; although Johnson himself—and later President Nixon—was much less sensitive to the issue of Israel's actual nuclear efforts than was the Bundy group.[4]

During the Johnson Administration, more American conventional aid was promised to Israel, and was added to ongoing French supplies. Soviet aid to Egypt, Syria, and Iraq continued to flow, supplying them all with large amounts of firepower and confidence. Meanwhile, these three countries were endlessly quarrelling among themselves and with the pro-Western Arab states about who was most opposed to Israel, while professing their support for each other and the Palestinian cause—a competition whose outcome was always feared by Israel.

Under Chief of Staff Yitzhak Rabin, appointed in 1963, Israel built a conventional striking force capable of preemption, as called for by Allon's doctrine of preemptive conventional war. Rabin was a professional soldier who stayed in the IDF when his mentor Allon left following the 1949 armistice. He represented the interests of a conventional army vis-à-vis Eshkol. But Rabin maintained his ties to Allon's group, the political influence of which grew in direct proportion to the decline of Ben-Gurion's power. Shimon Peres, meanwhile, seemed to have been willing to align himself with the new governing coalition, as did Moshe Dayan who remained a member of Eshkol's cabinet until his resignation two years later. It was only then that Dayan warned

Eshkol publicly against American inspections at Dimona,[5] although he had already (as quoted in the previous chapter) expressed himself publicly in favor of Israeli missiles carrying nuclear warheads. At this stage, and in their dealings with the Americans through Minister Gazit, Eshkol and Golda Meir seemed to have followed up on some of Ben-Gurion's main worries. They even endorsed Dayan's and Peres' quest for a "limited military action" in the West Bank, and "demanded the demilitarization of the West Bank" if King Hussein fell out of power[6]—an action Ben-Gurion had rejected beforehand, refusing to get involved in that area.[7]

Years later, it was reported that Eshkol's cabinet decided in 1963 not to build missiles at home, but to rely solely on the French for them. This decision was made public in an article in *Ha'aretz* on February 6, 1976. The article was written by Yuval Ne'eman, a physicist and a military-political figure of some importance to any inquiry into Israel's military history. Ne'eman argued that the 1963 decision to build missiles abroad was a precedent that should have taught Israel not to rely on foreign nations—as evidenced by de Gaulle's refusal to supply the missiles later, following the 1967 war.[8] According to Ne'eman: "It is enough to remember the security misdeed which happened in 1963, when the then Prime-Minister and Minister of Defense [Eshkol] had forgone the development of the 'Jericho' missile in Israel, and the order went to France *(which has learned the subject thereby on our account)* [italics added]." One could deduce from this that de Gaulle, in spite of his reluctance to cooperate with Israel on the nuclear issue itself, had something to gain in developing missiles for it. Ne'eman referred to the French-built missiles with the general name "Jericho"; Pean and foreign analysts and diplomats referred to them as MD 620 (for Marcel Dassault), or the Jericho 1, and MD 660, or the Jericho 2.[9] The Jericho 1 is described as a short-range ballistic missile (with a range of 300 to 450 kilometers); the Jericho 2 (probably meant to be the MD 660) could reach 850 to 1,000 kilometers, and thus the southern region of the Soviet Union.

In a 1977 conversation with General H. Toufanian (the Iranian viceminister of war), General Ezer Weizmann (then Israeli defense minister and former IAF commander) talked about one missile system that "we started working on . . . in 1962,"[10] following a public demonstration of Egyptian missiles made by German experts, which in his words created a "panic" in the Israeli defense establishment.[11] In the same meeting, Professor Pinchas Sussmann, Weizmann's director-general in the Defense Ministry, said that "the missile [which was demonstrated to the Iranian visitor the next day] was originally a French missile." Thus we can assume—if this demonstration was successful—that an Israeli demonstration of missiles was carried out from Israeli soil in 1977.

Foreign sources believe that the Jericho 2 was visibly test flown over the Mediterranean in 1987, and that a boosted version thereof, the Jericho 2b, or a Jericho 3 missile, was used by Israel to launch its first satellite in September 1988.[12] With the acquisition of these missiles, the Soviet nuclear threats of 1956 bore the appropriate fruits (even if these fruits ripened when *glasnost* was ripening as well—an issue we will discuss later). But in 1963 it was a long time before any of this would happen. According to Pean, the MD 660 was expected to be delivered not before 1967. De Gaulle was keeping the key to it, having regarded Ben-Gurion's departure with caution and having taken up business with the Arab world as well.[13]

Early in 1966 details about missiles made in France for Israel were published in the Western press. The publication of the details followed a long behind-the-scenes battle fought in Washington and Jerusalem to prevent Israel from "purchasing" the missiles from the French altogether—or at least to prevent Israel from openly demonstrating a missile capability. According to a *New York Times* report of January 7, 1966, "The United States believes Israel ordered 30 intermediate-range ballistic missiles from France, a move seen as indicating an intention to develop atomic weapons."

A memorandum to the president from McGeorge Bundy, President Johnson's National Security Adviser, and Myer Feldman, the White House "Jewish expert," March 13 and March 14, 1964, provides interesting insight into the behind-the-scenes battle.[14] Feldman declared himself to be sympathetic with those who would not agree to a U.S. tank sale to Israel unless the Israeli government gave up "its intention to purchase ground-to-ground missiles. However, it is difficult to tell a sovereign power what weapons it needs for her defense." Feldman reminded the president of Egypt's missile program and "the fact that the Israeli Government has already contracted 25 experimental missiles from France [which] make it impossible to condition the sale of tanks upon the renunciation of missiles." Feldman suggested two alternatives: to link the renunciation of Israeli missiles, including anti-aircraft Hawk SAM (surface-to-air) missiles promised by Kennedy, to Egyptian willingness to do the same; or to persuade Israel "to refrain from any further purchases of missiles without prior consultation with us." He volunteered to intervene with American Jewish leaders—who, he wrote, had already demonstrated their discretion—to ask them to persuade Eshkol to accept his proposal.

We do not know which alternative was finally endorsed by Johnson, but in February 1965 he authorized an official visit to Israel by W. Averell Harriman—the American "roving ambassador"—and Robert Komer—the NSC official who, since Kennedy's days, had played an operative role in American efforts to curb Dimona. Harriman and Komer were sent to discuss both the nuclear and the missile issues with Eshkol in connection with U.S. conventional weapons sales to Israel. This was the high point of several efforts undertaken at the time, efforts which will be discussed in more detail below.[15]

Without missiles or even without demonstrating missile capability or having suitable aircraft to deliver the bomb, Israel seemed to have deferred the decision to "go nuclear," as Israeli antinuclear activists put it.[16] Actually, Eshkol was simply trying not to have his cake and eat it too. He might have realized that an antiproliferation campaign of renewed intensity was taking place in America, partially in public and partially behind the scenes.[17] We do not know exact details about the behind-the-scenes campaign, but the public documents are worth quoting.

On January 7 and January 8, 1965, the President's Committee on Nuclear Proliferation met to discuss the options open to the United States. Johnson had already publicly committed the United States as a guarantee power to nonnuclear nations "blackmailed" by nuclear powers. And now China had gone its "nuclear way" (following de Gaulle's France), and India was accordingly alarmed.

This group, previously known as the "Task Force on Proliferation," was made up of various prominent Americans. From the following excerpts from the censored and sanitized version of their discussion we learn that they were presented with two models, "Model A" and "Model B," and several specific options (offered by Secretary of Defense Robert McNamara, by the chairman of the Atomic Energy Commission Glenn Seaborg, by Secretary of State Dean Rusk, by the Chairman of the Joint Chiefs General Earl Wheeler, and by ACDA director William Foster).[18] It is not easy to identify the "models" and "options" themselves from the censored document. However, they become more clear if we follow the debate itself. The committee's chairman, Roswell Gilpatric, a former deputy secretary of defense under Kennedy and Johnson, "stated his preference for a world with a limited number of nuclear powers, *finding it implausible that additional proliferation could be compartmentalized, quarantined, or regionalized and comparing the consequences for the world of the Sarajevo incident* [italics added]. "This was very much in the spirit of Kennedy's views, which were partially influenced by Barbara Tuchman's *Guns of August* and by Schelling's conflict theory. "He found it all the more unlikely," the document continues, "that a nuclear conflict involving 1.5 billion Chinese, Indian and Japanese could not affect our own security . . ."

William Webster, president of the New England Electric System, "felt a rearguard action to keep proliferation to the minimum is to some extent inevitable . . . He questioned whether we should be prepared to pay the ultimate price to stop proliferation [censored]. On the other hand, he favored the taking of all steps reasonably necessary to slow proliferation, to approach the problem on a case-by-case basis. He felt he was nearer to Secretary McNamara's 'Model A world . . .'" This could be interpreted to mean allowing a few more powers such as China to go their own way in regard to nuclear weapons, but to try and minimize their threat as nuclear powers (and the number of such nations).

John J. McCloy cautioned the committee in regard to the American guarantees to nonnuclear nations, arguing that American guarantees in regard to Berlin were "convincing, but the character of our determination will be diluted if we have 20 such commitments . . . McCloy went on to discuss the problems of NATO, including de Gaulle's semindependence in and outside the alliance: "We are going to have to confront de Gaulle's belief that a return to nationalism in the Twentieth Century is appropriate; nationalism isn't adequate for conventional weapons and is not adequate for nuclear weapons . . ."

McCloy's view of "nationalism" in the twentieth century was not just his understandable reaction to the Gaullist challenge to U.S. leadership and to European integration. It was also his basic view of the old European nation-state. This view would have been skeptical toward Zionism (i.e. Jewish nationalism) and yet would perceive Arab nationalism—due to the large number of parties involved, their enormous space, and common but different ground—as something understandable, less "narrow" and not necessarily bad for America and the world. McCloy and liberals of his school would not have tolerated the idea of an Israeli bomb in this picture. But their attention was focused elsewhere at the same time.

Arthur Watson, chairman of the board of IBM, was in favor of "Model A," but "was puzzled by how we were to get it going without participation by the French. Soviet cooperation . . . would be desirable, at the price of overcoming their historical fears of Germany. Mr. Gilpatric suggested that perhaps at some time we may give up the 'Holy Grail' and move to a 'Model B' world [censored]." One may guess that the "move over to a 'Model B world'" meant a move over to a multinuclear world—in which American allies would be given access to American nuclear weapons, in order to localize dangers and avoid the problems of direct guarantees, without the French and without negotiations with the Soviets. In this model, further proliferation could be seen as being almost inevitable and yet localized and contained.

These assumptions of what was meant by "Model B" seem indeed to be justified when we read McCloy's argument later that "we did the same before on both the Common Market and NATO and . . . the Russians will adjust once again . . ."

Dr. George Kistiakowsky, the designer of the first plutonium bomb and later a presidential adviser on nuclear matters, was strongly in favor of "Model A," which was termed "rearguard action" by others, but he believed that their approach was "a concession of defeat . . . *We must wage a campaign to keep proliferation at a minimum and be prepared to lose individual battles, but not the overall war* [italics added] . . . Our own example will be essential . . . We should press measures of arms limitations and increasing understanding with the Soviet-Union." This was a strong advocacy in the spirit of the Eisenhower-Kennedy nonproliferation campaign, in spite of the many obstacles that hindered Soviet-American cooperation, such as the discovery of the alleged "bomber and missile gaps" by Al Wohlstetter and others and capability problems that emerged as preconditions to serious arms limitation talks— although the "gaps" seemed now to have been taken care of, and MAD (mutual assured destruction) to a certain extent guaranteed.[19]

Two important remarks were made at the end of the official record of the committee's deliberations by Professor Fisher and Dr. Kistiakowsky. These remarks are the substance of what seems to have guided nonproliferation thinking since its inception. Fisher desired "a policy to make nuclear weapons appear bad and the undertaking of progressive policies to eliminate United States reliance on nuclear weapons." Kistiakowsky said that "our hopes to stop proliferation are based on two basic 'ifs': Soviet cooperation and future Chinese behavior."

Robert W. Komer and W. Averell Harriman were preparing to leave for Israel soon after the above discussions took place. And they both may have seen Israel's nuclear efforts as worth stopping according to both "Model A" and "Model B," which in fact were not tailored to meet Israel's problems at all; and yet Israeli behavior might have jeopardized both models.

So, whether known to Eshkol or not, these were the constraints within which he had to work. In 1963, Eshkol joined the Limited Test Ban Treaty, and in 1964, he was reported to have issued an ambiguous statement to the effect that Israel would not be "the first to introduce nuclear weapons" to the Middle East. Later, following a domestic battle with Ben-Gurion, which he won, Eshkol transferred the IAEC from the Defense Ministry to the Prime Minister's Office. He got rid of Ernst Bergmann, its staunch chairman, while pursuing negotiations with the United States on the purchase of safeguarded reactors for peaceful use.[20]

Yet, the Dimona reactor remained rather busy. The plutonium for the first bomb was made ready between 1965 and 1967, according to our French source—precisely in 1966 according to Barnaby and Vanunu—and the first successful test of a French-made missile for Israel took place on French soil in 1966, according to our American source. This, however, could have been seen by foreign analysts as just the initial stage of the bomb's production, requiring several more years of work before the actual production of "crude" and later of "refined" weapons and the actual possession of missile capabilities. One can speculate, however, that Israel might have acquired from the French enough know-how to significantly shorten the bomb production procedure and skip the testing. That is, Israel could have relied on France's own tests of plutonium bombs produced by the same method. (In this way, it could have later avoided difficulty under the terms of Senator Stuart Symington's amendment, adopted in the mid-1970s, which made American foreign aid conditional on the prohibition of nuclear testing.)

The missile issue was thus of great importance, and influential members of the Johnson Administration continued to address the nuclear issue itself with both Israel and Egypt. Early in 1964, about half-a-year after Eshkol's takeover and McCloy's initial failure in Cairo, the United States returned to the issue of Israel's nuclear capabilities and the Egyptian missile program, which required some kind of unconventional weapons to be effective.

As far as the Israeli nuclear program itself was concerned, the Americans did not seem to be overly optimistic about their ability to stop it, unless some kind of gesture came from Egypt, too. On May 31, 1964, on the eve of Eshkol's visit to the United States, Under-Secretary of State George Ball cabled the American Embassy in Cairo:

> We particularly want you to emphasize mischievous role of UAR [Egypt's] missile program in pushing arms rivalry to new and dangerous levels . . . We recognize of course thin line between insuring Nasser understands and appreciates nature of this escalation and on other hand giving him impression Israel is about to go nuclear with our understanding and tacit support. We therefore leave to you best means of convincing Nasser this is game he cannot win because of Israel's technological development and access to outside financial sources . . .[21]

Ball went on to criticize Nasser for not keeping the Israeli issue in the "ice box," as he apparently had promised to do at least for the time being, and for not seeking other areas of understanding with the United States. "His periodic opening of 'icebox' door . . . has let out blasts of cold air that put great psychological pressure on Israelis to obtain deterrent." Here Ball was referring to Nasser's repeated public threats to obliterate the "Zionist enemy" and "foreign base" on Arab soil. Ball then concluded:

> We are not trying to justify Israeli actions . . . [but] merely explaining them and his responsibility.
> Essential facts are:
>
>   1. UAR [Egypt] was first to opt for surface-to-surface missile force.
>
>   2. UAR is continuing to develop SSMs.
>
>   3. Reports are that Israel in response is also acquiring SSMs . . .
>
>   5. *We believe Israel can be persuaded not to proceed further with SSM development if UAR is willing to demonstrate restraint* [italics added].

The emphasis on the missiles can be explained by a second visit to Egypt by John McCloy in the summer of 1964. This visit was preceded by Nasser's letter of July 26, 1964: "In that letter Nasser assured you [President Johnson] the UAR would not introduce or develop weapons of total destruction. " In reference to McCloy ' s second "Mission on Near East Arms, " Secretary of State Dean Rusk wrote to President Johnson on August 12, 1964:

> The purpose of the present probe is to pursue the question of restraining the surface-to-surface missile rivalry between the UAR and Israel. Mr. McCloy's objective is to let Nasser know we believe we can convince Israel to exercise nuclear and missile *self-denial* [italics added] if Nasser will limit his acquisition of major offensive missiles to the number he now has or to a low ceiling.[22]

There is no evidence that Eshkol was convinced to exercise "self-denial." But we can assume that Eshkol refused to commit himself, and thus the Americans had to continue inspections at Dimona to create the impression of "self-denial." The inspection technique was used by the Americans to make Dimona "peaceful." This, however, required repeated inspection visits, which had not been made public yet. The method of making Dimona "nonexistent" in military terms was thus confined to Eshkol's public statements, to be followed by secret American inspection tours. The American emphasis on the missile issue, also conducted behind the scenes, was related to Nasser's efforts to arm his missiles with nuclear waste such as cobalt. Futile as these efforts were, they were made public and only gave Israel a good (though nonpublic) argument regarding its own missiles.

Nasser was not only unwilling to start arms control negotiations with Israel, but John S. Badeau, the American ambassador in Cairo, told Washington that despite Nasser's basic policy of not risking a real war with Israel,

> the only circumstances in which the Egyptians would even contemplate a surprise attack on Israel would be *if it became clearly apparent* [italics added] that the Israelis had or were shortly to obtain nuclear weapons. In such a case the Egyptian objective would be to destroy the Israeli facilities as quickly and as effectively as possible and then retire behind the frontier counting on international public opinion and pressure to prevent Israel from retaliating. But in such a contingency, the Egyptians would be acting for defensive rather than aggressive considerations.[23]

Washington had this and possibly other complications—such as some kind of Soviet involvement to balance out Israel's nuclear threat—on its mind during Eshkol's official visit to America from June 1 to 12, 1964, and, according to a State Department circular telegram dated June 26, 1964, told him the following:

> c) US reiterated its commitment to safeguard territorial integrity and political independence of Israel and other Near Eastern states against aggression, use or threat of force.
>
> d) US conveyed its belief Israel's concerns over its security should be largely allayed by US undertakings oppose aggression.
>
> e) US expressed hope that reassurances given to Israel will permit progress toward our mutual goal of damping down arms race . . .

In another part of the document, it was stated that:

> b) [the administration] estimates UAR missile capability will remain primarily psychological threat and that there will be no UAR nuclear capability.
>
> c) US concerned about escalation of Near East arms race and opposes proliferation missiles and nuclear weapons.

In quoting Eshkol's views, the document tells us:

a) Israel appreciates US support but convinced *it must maintain independent deterrent to Arab attack* [italics added]; US commitments believed sincere, but US might be involved elsewhere at critical moment of need.

b) UAR missile threat real to Israeli man-in-street; *nevertheless Israel will postpone demonstration missile capability 1-2 years* [italics added].[24]

This information was given to all American embassies in the Arab world and to the IAEA and American embassies in Paris and Rome.

The decision to postpone the demonstration of Israel's missile capability, and perhaps to limit it to the twenty-five missiles already purchased—or even simply to their delivery (as opposed to an actual demonstration)—did not, however, constrain the French-Israeli missile program itself. We can infer this from a cable sent on March 3, 1965, by the U.S. air attaché in Tel Aviv to U.S. Air Force headquarters in Washington. In this cable an Israeli source who had just returned from a visit abroad "confirmed that the testing of French-designed SSM for Israel has already begun on Ile de Levant," and that the missile appeared to be satisfactory after some initial trouble. The "source" also stated that Israel would probably concentrate on fixed launching positions, because of the country's small size and due to

the fact that enemy targets are known and fixed. To counter-argument that Israel's SSM would not be materially significant with conventional warhead, source blurts out: "don't worry, when we need the right kind of warhead we will have it . . . and after that, there will be no more trouble in this part of the world."[25]

One can infer from the above that this was a dangerous juncture: Israel had a working, vulnerable reactor, which it had publicly declared for peaceful use only, and then had said it would not be "the first to introduce nuclear weapons" into the area. And behind the scenes, Israel was subject to American inspections that officially, but not publicly, outlawed its real products. According to Pean, some weapons-grade plutonium was already available in 1966 (as far as everybody except the Israeli people were concerned). But the enemy may well have believed that no bombs were ready yet, and Israel had no apparent means of delivery except several subsonic French light bombers.

By March 1966, the Arabs had suspicions about plutonium production at Dimona and convened a high-level conference to discuss the issue. This followed the summit conference of 1964, during which a unified Arab military command was reestablished. The 1966 meeting was secret, yet many open warnings against Israel's nuclear threat followed and were published in the Arab press. A sanitized and heavily censored State Department copy of a document dated December 12, 1964, illuminates this point. The document originated either in the White House or the CIA and was circulated among the relevant officials; it carried the heading "Background Paper on Factors Which Could Influence National Decisions Concerning Acquisition of Nuclear Weapons."[26] Regarding Israel, the paper tells us the following:

> As of January, 1964, Israel's nuclear energy program seemed directed to research, but was adaptable to a weapons making program. Prime Minister Eshkol has told us orally that Israel's nuclear activity is peaceful. Nevertheless, neither he nor Ben-Gurion before him ever ruled out Israel's developing a nuclear weapon if the Near Eastern situation warrants.

After several omissions from the original text due to censorship, the next paragraph tells us only that "Israel now has the technical capability to develop a bomb" (p. 17). The next two pages were also heavily censored, but contain the following statements:

> We believe Israel, without outside assistance, could detonate its first nuclear device two or three years after a decision to develop a nuclear capability. If Israel wished to concentrate on producing at the earliest moment an unsophisticated weapon . . . it could probably produce it two to three years after a decision to do so. Production of a refined weapon . . . would require a year or two more.

The writer or writers continue:

> Meanwhile, we have convincing evidence that a French firm is developing for Israel a 250- to 300-mile solid propellant, two-stage missile. The 1,500- to 2,000-pound warhead is designed for either a high explosive or nuclear payload . . .
>
> *Israel regards maintenance of an independent military deterrent as vital to its survival. Given this attitude, the arms rivalry in the Near East has reached a dangerous stage* [italics added]. As Arab unity advances and as UAR missile technology improves, Israel seeks to develop an unmatched, economical counter-deterrent. This seems destined to lead to development of nuclear warheads for Israeli missiles purchased from France.
>
> *Lower level Israeli officials speak frankly about Israel's strategy toward the UAR: (a) surface-to-surface missiles targeted on the Nile Delta and (b) a*

capacity to bomb and release the waters behind the Aswan High Dam.
Destruction of the Aswan High Dam would require a nuclear warhead [italics added].

Turning to Egypt, the paper states:

Of all the countries in the Near East, the UAR is the most vulnerable to nuclear attack. A single well-placed nuclear device would bring a sheet of water 400 feet high cascading down the narrow Nile valley where the entire Egyptian population is concentrated. Israel is also vulnerable but the peculiarities of its boundaries would cause a nuclear attack to hurt neighboring Arab states almost as much as itself. Thus, *for its own survival, the UAR probably sees advantages in preventing the use of nuclear weapons, and therefore also their introduction into the area* [italics added].

Soon afterward President Nasser had to give up his own missile program. Hassnein Heikal tells us that the reason was "the deflationary measures of 1965-6." In fact, Egypt's economy was on the verge of collapsing at that time, due among other things to its population explosion, deteriorating relations with the West, and foreign ambitions—especially its involvement in Yemen.[27] Under these circumstances Nasser was forced to switch from his own "unconventional" schemes to some kind of preemptive war, or at least to making public threats in this direction, following the March 1966 Arab conference.

On March 19, 1966, the American Embassy in Cairo informed Washington about the conference: ". . . conference uncovered concern and deep Arab suspicion Israel developing nuclear armaments. (We have already reported in Embtel 2363 statement by Iraqi premier Bazzaz that report Israel on way to producing atomic weapons most serious item confronting conf.)" After a censored half-line, the cable continues:

. . . very confidentially told me . . . [censored] had reported to him conversation between [censored] Pres Nasser [during which latter] expressed his concern Israel threat and included remarks Israelis now have "eight kilos plutonium" . . . [censored] expressed the view, which he identified as general in Cairo, that situation would be very dangerous if Egypt failed to accept *US assurances re Israeli nuclear activity* [italics added].[28]

Seeking American "assurances" behind the scenes, the Egyptians continued to issue public warnings of a forthcoming, preventive war. Both before the conference (on February 2, 1966) and immediately afterward Nasser proclaimed something like an official doctrine of preempting Israel's nuclear program.[29] Since this information was censored in Israel—or at least played down by the Israeli press—the public had no idea of the new Arab casus belli. Israeli decision makers had several options. They could repeat Eshkol's public statement that Israel would not be the first to introduce nuclear weapons to the Middle East (and Eshkol indeed did so in May 1966). They could allow yet another American inspection of Dimona to publicly create the impression that the Americans were interested in maintaining—that Dimona was not producing nuclear weapons. (And an inspection was reported this time by the *New York Times* on June 28, 1966.) Or they could refrain from taking delivery of the French-made missiles when ready—as suggested by White House adviser Myer Feldman—and not engage in missile demonstration.

Ben-Gurion, on the other hand, had reason to be greatly worried. The Arabs seemed ready to go to war to destroy Dimona and, should it come to a general war, Israel itself. He could have argued that the Americans had intervened in such a way as to encourage the Arabs to attack and liquidate the nuclear reactor—the only means that could prevent the Arabs from making war and force them to accept Israel as a fait accompli. Even worse, if we follow the logic of the Israeli analyst Avigdor Haselkorn, Israel could also be exposed to Soviet threats in the form of guarantees to the Arabs before the installation of the MD 660, the meager answer to those threats.[30]

These being the lines of Ben-Gurion's approach, we can understand why he publicly accused Eshkol of a major "security blunder" which should disqualify Eshkol from further carrying the responsibility for Israel's security. However, it can also be argued that Ben-Gurion used the nuclear issue, among other things, to disqualify Eshkol because of Eshkol's failure to follow Ben-Gurion's domestic reform schemes, coupled with the Lavon Affair (which in Ben-Gurion's view had exposed the Eshkol regime as unjust and inefficient) and Eshkol's "unholy" alliance with the Allon group. That group, as we have seen, was neither united nor completely opposed to Dimona, especially as it was an established fact. It did, however, reject a "nuclear doctrine"—i.e., actual targeting or any serious use of nuclear threats as an integral part of Israel's foreign policy, let alone as a part of its war-fighting doctrine—as Yair Evron puts it.[31] This approach was ascribed to Shimon Peres and to his adoption of French nuclear deterrence concepts. The Allon group adopted a "last resort" nuclear option approach instead. Their main concern, however, was to win a war if necessary by invoking conventional means, and if possible to change the boundaries and impose peace.

Ben-Gurion must have perceived this as nonsense, because the Arabs were better suited, conventionally, to oppose Israel; and no further territorial expansion would force them to make peace. Furthermore, Allon's argument, following Schelling, was that the Arabs were "irrational" and "irresponsible" and thus couldn't be deterred by the bomb, but would desperately seek a bomb of their own and then probably use it. And this argument did not explain why the Arabs could be expected to be deterred by conventional means, or to make peace if their territory was occupied. If they were "madmen"—which, of course, they were not—how could a tiny conventional Israel deter them, and impose peace by first occupying their land, creating therein "new defensive lines," and then using the rest of the land for peace negotiations? The "madmen" argument obscured political-cultural and personal elements—attached to real-life situations and to real people—and elevated the discussion to an abstract, almost mystical, level. In order to assess the adversaries' motives and ways of thinking, the real issues had to be studied on their own merits and evaluated with historical-cultural and political tools and imagination.

As we can assume on the basis of above-cited foreign sources, Ben-Gurion did not want any more wars. He wanted some kind of peace, or at least coexistence, which could not be guaranteed by conventional means alone in the present boundaries. On the other hand, he was not bothered by "French-like" doctrines, such as war-fighting strategies Peres might have learned about from General Paul Ely or from General Gallois.[32] De Gaulle himself was far from both Ely and Gallois. He saw nuclear weapons as primarily political tools; and apparently, so did Ben-Gurion. As I interpret his behavior, Ben-Gurion saw nuclear weapons as an excuse for the Arabs to leave Israel alone, and as a measure to make Soviet aid to the Arabs less plausible and binding, thus making the Arabs pragmatically accept a Jewish state in a partitioned Palestine. At least this would be the case if proper political steps accompanied Israel's lead in the nuclear arena, a lead that could not be sacrificed in any way, even in response to Bundy's pressure. However, Dayan—and Peres—did not bother much about Arabs; the main problem in their eyes were the Soviets, then and later, until after 1973.

At this juncture Allon and Galili greatly feared a Soviet "nuclear guarantee" to the Arabs in response to an Israeli nuclear doctrine. And this fear was "encouraged" by the Bundy group. They were willing to offer Israel conventional tools; whereas Ben-Gurion refused to fight conventionally—unless a foreign power would help to limit the war and minimize losses that the tiny Israeli nation could not afford, for many reasons, including its domestic weaknesses. In the absence of this kind of help from a foreign power, Israel had to give the Arabs other excuses not to attack. If this was, in fact, his view, achieving it required a clear concept, time, and no Israeli-initiated conventional wars.

Early in 1966, an ambiguous Soviet "nuclear guarantee" was publicly made to the Egyptians. According to a report in the *New York Times* of February 4, 1966, "Soviet Deputy Defense Minister [Andrei] Gretchko, in his December visit to Cairo, reportedly refused to send nuclear weapons to Egypt, but pledged protection if Israel developed or obtained such arms." Nasser, however, was not completely assured. He convened the March 1966 Arab conference and continued to threaten Israel openly.

Here we can make an interesting comparison between an Egyptian-inspired version of the February 1966 meeting between President Johnson and Anwar el-Sadat (at the time president of the Egyptian National Assembly)[33] and American primary sources. Sadat was quoted in the Egyptian-inspired report as having told Johnson that Israel was still working toward the development of nuclear weapons according "to the reports Egypt receives," and that General de Gaulle himself

> admitted in a [recent talk] with [the Egyptian minister of war, Field Marshal Abd el-Hakim] Amer [during a visit to Paris] that Israel is capable of producing nuclear weapons . . . Following this, and Israel's refusal to allow American observers to control the Dimona situation, [a fact] which confirmed the information at Cairo's hands, President Johnson was perplexed and asked . . . Sadat to convey to in his name his promise, which was an official undertaking, that the U.S. would not allow Israel to produce a bomb at any price, and would even use force if necessary . . . but Egypt, who knows the value of American promises, and especially when they deal with Israel, cannot trust them. Therefore the President [Nasser] made an open and clear warning when he spoke of a preventive war.

According to the official American "Memorandum of Conversation" between Sadat and Johnson, the conversation itself took place the day before:

> We were not as alarmist [said Johnson] as the Egyptians on the subject of possible acquisition of nuclear weapons by Israel. We were watching the situation closely. The U.S. would be against such a development because of our firm policy against the proliferation of nuclear weapons.[34]

Accordingly, Johnson promised Sadat nothing. In my view, the president demonstrated, rather clearly, an acceptance of Israel's actual—if not its open—adoption of a nuclear option. According to Ambassador Evron, the difference between Johnson and Kennedy and the Bundy group was Johnson's tacit understanding that Israel had no chance of survival without that option.

In the meantime, however, the Bundy group allowed Egypt to work together with the United States to publicly delegitimize Dimona on the one hand, while Cairo was making direct threats of waging war to eliminate it on the other. The Eshkol cabinet certainly seemed to be encouraging Nasser to make these threats: It had yielded to American pressures to declare Israel's deterrent illegal by making its "introduction" dependent on Arab nuclear acquisition; and it had rendered the deterrent ineffective by making concessions on the missile issue.

One may further argue, on the basis of Eshkol's own fears later during the crisis that preceded the 1967 war, that none of Eshkol's deals with Washington would prevent Arab preemptive strikes against Dimona itself—and the possible radioactive fallout resulting from it—except the Hawk SAMs, which were linked to American efforts to delegitimize Dimona. In retrospect, the motives of the Bundy group seem to be clear. The main goal was to prevent the proliferation—and, especially, the use—of nuclear weapons once they reached the Middle East (and elsewhere); conventional wars were by far preferable. Yet in the United States' own conventional entanglements, they adopted threats and signalling à la Schelling which, when combined with the fear of the bomb, may explain the conventional disaster in Vietnam in which members of the Bundy group were now more and more involved.

From Eshkol's actual behavior, one can infer that his argument would have been that he had secured the weapons—i.e., the Hawk—that could help defend the nuclear compound better than anything else. And that eventually he would also get conventional aid during a period in which Israel's nuclear options were not yet fully developed. The counterargument to this could be that by adopting his ambiguous posture and forfeiting the missiles he had "minimized" them to nothing, and was thereby encouraging a conventional war that might ruin the nuclear option itself and expose the Israeli population to its hazards (if Dimona was destroyed). Moreover, he allowed Rabin's High Command to undertake a variety of escalating, "deterrent," conventional military actions, mainly against Syria. This approach played into Arab hands, if they wanted a preemptive war of their own. Eshkol's "executive agreements" would not make the Americans help Israel in a war if the casus belli was Dimona—or indeed any of the other contested issues between

Washington and Jerusalem, such as the freedom of navigation in the Red Sea or even Israel's rights in Jerusalem. And even if the Marines did come, they might be too late. Moreover, Eshkol's and Meir's political allies, the Allon-Galili group, wanted territorial expansion in the West Bank for both ideological and strategic reasons. That alliance was dangerous by definition, because of its structure and the influence of a minority group over the ruling coalition, the contents of the Allon-Galili group expansionist ideology, and its conventional preemptive strike doctrine.

In trying to reconstruct Eshkol's strategy, one can conclude that Eshkol had achieved Ben-Gurion's own traditional goal: an American security guarantee. But this was done in secret and was conditioned by Israel's nuclear behavior. Ironically enough, he then followed Ben-Gurion's own advice against Mrs. Meir's stance "vis-à-vis the United States in regard to Dimona,"[35] refraining from giving that secret guarantee much significance, and pursued a policy of obtaining "an independent deterrent." Yet later he did give in to Washington on issues related to Israel's nuclear behavior, which prompted a quasi-open attack on Eshkol by both Dayan and Peres. As we have already seen, Ben-Gurion criticized Eshkol very sharply for his "security blunders." In fact, both sides conducted the whole debate using hints and indirect language. In this way Eshkol was able to benefit from the public's inability to follow the actual content of the arguments, and from some groups' rejection of Ben-Gurion's style, long rule, and possibly also his nuclear option. Privately, Ben-Gurion could have argued his side of what was a paradoxical situation. The U.S. pledge of protection was the result of the nuclear option; therefore it was a major asset and was necessary for maintaining U.S. support. And yet the nuclear option was also an obstacle to the fulfillment of U.S. pledges in the sense that Washington would hardly be willing to defend Israel if the Arabs started a war over Dimona, as in fact Ambassador Badeau was in advance justifying their doing, and then such a war further escalated.

If Eshkol continued to work on the nuclear option, but agreed to American demands to make it illegitimate and was ready to forfeit the missiles, what did he really want? Did he have any clear idea of what he was doing in this regard, or was he just continuing Ben-Gurion's policy without understanding the difference between nonexistent and possibly existent capabilities? Did he continue because the job had already been begun and paid for, or because he had some ambiguous idea that the option should somehow be around, at least to balance out similar Arab efforts? Was he primarily interested in conventional arms? Or was he primarily interested in continuing work on the nuclear option, but was ready to give up on the acquisition of the necessary delivery means in order to attain American tanks and jets? And was he succumbing to Washington's pressure in this? Or did he have a strategic concept in mind? When these things were happening, Ben-Gurion was asking himself, rather loudly, whether Eshkol was a statesman who had some guiding principles for the nuclear age, or whether he was simply a conventional wheeler-dealer. (And after his resignation, Ben-Gurion initiated a new probe into the Lavon Affair, the result of which showed Eshkol, at least in Ben-Gurion's eyes, to be a petty politician, indeed.) We must wonder whether Eshkol accepted Allon's and Ben-Aharon's view that the whole nuclear option had meaning only as a "last resort" option. And further, that it might have already lost even that meaning, with or without the French-built missiles, due to the "Soviet nuclear guarantee" given to Egypt. Following this line of thinking, Israel would do well to trade off the missiles for American conventional aid.

Since we do not know whether the missiles (MD 620s and 660s) were fully ready in some numbers when Eshkol "traded them off," we have no answers to these questions. He might have "delayed" something that was not, in fact, ready in any quantity; thus conceding nothing in reality (unless he was denied the missiles due to his deteriorated relations with the French, and his close relations with the Johnson Administration led him to make unnecessary concessions to the Bundy group). So, the ambiguous nature of the proceedings denies us the answers to any of these questions.

But based on Ben-Gurion's overall modus operandi, we can speculate that he would have insisted that Israel was better off making clear choices than involving itself in ambiguous situations, in crude lies, and in self-defeating intrigues with the Americans. An ambiguous atmosphere may have encouraged the Arabs to attack Dimona. And once a war was under way, they could have escalated it to a general offensive. Thus, Israel should acquire its own means of survival, and argue openly with the Bundys and the Rostows. Or, if this proved to be impossible, Israel should do what it had to do in regard to the missiles. There was no need for anyone to make the missile issue, in particular, public; Dimona itself had been exposed by Washington in 1960 in a rather crude way. Later they found ways to deal with the matter in a more subtle fashion that did not really interfere with Israel's primary goals. The main problem was the Russians: If they supplied the Arabs with countermeasures, Israel needed the French-built MD 660, to be ready in 1967, aimed at Soviet territory, a proposition first published abroad several years later.[36]

Eshkol, as far as Ben-Gurion was concerned, was caught in the web of his "wheeling-dealing" games, trying to please and bluff too many parties at the same time. He was finally driven to helping the Americans in their bid to obscure and delegitimize Israel's means of achieving coexistence with the Arabs, while endangering the means to do so effectively and alarming and provoking the Arabs at the same time.

Ben-Gurion's decision—following Eshkol's visit to the United States in 1964 and the approach of the 1965 national elections—to challenge Eshkol's leadership across the whole political board supports the above interpretation of his views.

Ben-Gurion's doubts about Eshkol could have been related, in practical terms, to a major American-Israeli deal concluded in early 1965 between Eshkol and the American delegation headed by W. Averell Harriman and Robert W. Komer. General Yitzhak Rabin, at the time chief of staff of the IDF, tells us in his memoirs[37] that Komer and Harriman sought a "strategic understanding" between the two countries, based on three points:

> (1) Israel would not initiate a preventive war against the Arabs.
> (2) Israel would not undertake a general military action against Arab water diversion efforts . . .[38] (3) Israel would pledge not to be a nuclear nation, in possession of nuclear weapons. If Israel accepted the conditions and limitations, an Israeli mission could leave for the United States to discuss her needs in planes, tanks and guns.

Rabin, a "conventionalist" by nature, quotes himself as having answered negatively in regard to the first two points. "Komer, and Harriman a little less," he adds,

> were rough and tough in regard to the nuclear weapon issue. They did not let go. They rejected our argument that Prime Minister Eshkol had said during his last visit to the United States that Israel would not be the first state to introduce nuclear weapons to the . . . Middle East.
> Komer asked for a personal conversation with me . . . and used rough language, not excluding a threat: "if Israel embarked in that direction, it might cause the most serious crisis she ever had in her relations with the U.S." I tried to allay his worry in that the Prime Minister's declaration was indeed our policy, and I added: "Your representatives visited our reactor in Dimona. You know exactly what is happening there."

Rabin was referring here to a visit by American inspectors to Dimona. This could have been regarded as an interim solution to the problem, especially when immediately leaked to the press. We do not know whether, in addition, Israel offered a pledge not to accept delivery of the missiles from the French, or possibly not to purchase more than the limited quantity already ordered. Whatever the reasons, a formal agreement was signed several days later regarding tank and Skyhawk jet supplies. According to the LBJ Library files, the jet supply agreement was concluded in March 1966. To some interested observers, such as Simcha Flapan, the agreements regarding both plane and tank supplies, Israel's tacit consent to U.S. tank deliveries to Jordan, and the American inspection visits to Dimona could have been a package—that is, Eshkol might have agreed to exchange the nuclear option for conventional weapons.

In a face-to-face meeting with Eshkol,[39] Ambassador Harriman assured him that "for one thing, the late President Kennedy had cured Khrushchev and Company of using the threat of nuclear war." This gave Israel reason to believe that it had some kind of an American guarantee should the Soviets resort to direct nuclear threats (without Israel having to make concessions). However, Komer, backed up by Bundy, made such a guarantee conditional on Israel's concessions regarding this very issue—its own nuclear behavior. In fact, Khrushchev had left office several months earlier, and the Bundy group was rather worried about Soviet behavior, especially if the "ideal" conditions of the Cuban missile crisis were not repeated, and Soviet missiles were deployed in a country like Egypt.

Komer, however, did his best to arrive at some kind of a deal with Eshkol. But the result was inconclusive, as we can see from a March 18, 1965, State Department telegram entitled "Talking Points for Presentation Letter from President to Nasser." In this document, the American ambassador in Cairo was told that

> Harriman/Komer talks have eased situation, but basic problems remain and are still a potential cause of war . . . USG [United States Government] will keep up pressure on Israel not to go nuclear. As Nasser undoubtedly aware fact of recent American visit to Dimona has been revealed by US press [italics added].[40]

The American visit caused Eshkol trouble in his election campaign of 1965 in which he faced Ben-Gurion, Moshe Dayan, and Shimon Peres. (Ben-Gurion had enlisted Dayan and Peres when he left Mapai and founded a new electoral party, Rafi, "The Workers' List of Israel.") Eshkol's troubles were even more serious when the inspection visit was leaked to the American press in order to please the Egyptians—who were not pleased at all.

According to a telegram dated April 18, 1965, regarding the meeting between Assistant Secretary Talbot and Ambassador Battle and President Nasser,

> Talbot stated question US inspections arose only in circumstances only [sic] when there no acceptance IAEA safeguards. US too would be concerned if Israeli reactor used for military purposes. This would be matter between US and Israel as well as between UAR and Israel. He could tell Nasser that in view of importance of issue we have satisfied our own curiosity on this issue.
>
> Nasser said he understood our concern, but Israel has influence in US and UAR does not. Talbot replied proliferation is a global problem, and Nasser could have confidence US is dealing with it in terms of global concerns . . .[41]

The spirit of Talbot's assertions, which hardly satisfied Nasser as we have seen, in turn angered the Israelis. On July 13, 1965, a conversation took place between William C. Foster, President Johnson's arms control chief, Arieh Dissentchik, editor-in-chief and part owner of the Israeli right-wing newspaper *Ma'ariv*, and Dissentchik's son Ido. Dissentchik was a major Israeli opinion-maker and an ally of Eshkol's in the 1965 election campaign; he had ties to General Dayan, to Shimon Peres, and to Mr. Begin, too. Foster was director of the U.S. Arms Control and Disarmament Agency (ACDA). Their conversation reflects the complications regarding the whole nuclear complex.

> Mr. Dissentchik expressed regret that there has been a leak on television in the US regarding US knowledge of what goes on at Dimona. Without pausing, he continued by saying that Israel does not want war with the Arabs, even a victorious one, because of its costliness in human life and property. What is important, he thinks, is the knowledge of the other side that Israel is four or five years ahead in know-how in the nuclear field and could quickly take the last steps to make the weapons. Under those circumstances they will think twice, he said, and therefore Israel has a vitally important deterrent.
>
> Mr. Foster strongly expressed the hope that Israel would go no further in a military direction than it has, stated our great concern over the threatening situation that would be created for the whole Middle East . . .[42]

This statement left Dissentchik unimpressed; on the contrary, he seemed to be more worried about the prospects of an NPT agreement, and India's advanced stage of covert proliferation.

Soon afterward, an ugly affair in France—the so-called Ben-Barka Affair—endangered Israel's ties with de Gaulle and added to Eshkol's troubles. Mehdi Ben-Barka, a Moroccan opposition leader, was kidnapped on French soil—without authorization from the French authorities—and was extradited to his enemies. The Mossad (Israel's foreign intelligence institution) was allegedly involved as a favor to the Moroccan security services. Apparently, Eshkol (as the minister in charge of the Mossad) could have prevented the Mossad's involvement but failed to do so because of ambiguous orders.[43] In response to this "affair," de Gaulle ordered a general survey of all interagency relations between his country and Israel, and then ordered that they be reduced to a minimum. This might have included the missile program itself. Thus, France might have cheated Israel twice: first, when de Gaulle took Israel's technical aid regarding his bomb but then refused to complete the 1957 agreement regarding the reprocessing plant, and second, when he perhaps used Israeli aid to develop his own missiles and then dropped Israel again.

The Ben-Barka Affair was used against Eshkol following the 1965 election campaign. Ben-Gurion had pressured a reluctant Shimon Peres and a vacillating Moshe Dayan to join him in his last campaign, as head of the newly created Rafi Party, which was known among the privileged few as "the atomic party."[44] The election campaign was an ugly, ambiguous battle in which Rafi vaguely tried to delegitimize Eshkol as "unqualified to lead the country." Later, they accused him of a "major security blunder" (possibly related to the missile issue), and a "less serious" one (related to the Dimona inspection or to the Ben-Barka Affair in France). The Israeli public had no idea what its leaders were talking about in regard to security blunders. Ben-Gurion's campaign went nowhere. Eshkol won a relative parliamentary majority, and Rafi remained in the opposition, against the ruling center-left coalition, from where it criticized the Eshkol government's overall strategic and military behavior.

Israel's defense policy on the ground grew more and more aggressive—in intervals—as time went on. This policy was due to Syrian challenges, to Israel's growing confidence in its conventional might, and to Rabin's conventional doctrine of controlled escalation aimed at deterring the enemy, which prompted a heavy attack against Jordanian territory used by Palestinian guerrillas operating from Syria and escalated to major operations against the new Ba'ath regime in Damascus. At first, Eshkol tried to restrain the IDF and secure public opinion, but personally he was inclined to tough responses to Fatah and Syrian attacks. He felt he had to demonstrate that he was no weaker than his formidable predecessor. All he managed to do, however, was to alternate between reprisals that were either too weak or too tough against the challenges in Syria and Jordan.

Things were coming to a head, and the 1967 war was only a matter of time. Soon enough, one of the many parties involved in the Middle East conflict would commit the initial mistake or play into the hands of the Palestinian organizations. Yassir Arafat's Fatah, based in Syria, or the PLO, then under Egyptian auspices, were interested in a general war before "Israel went fully nuclear." Indeed, in retrospect, it seems that since its inception in 1964, the policy of Arafat's outfit had been to inflame the nuclear scare among Arab leaders—in anticipation of a complete Arab desertion of the Palestinian cause once Israel went nuclear. The PLO then followed suit.[45] The escalation process that led to the war was a complicated combination of activities by many actors. We cannot analyze this process here in any detail, but it is worth noting a couple of points.[46]

Since 1964, the participants of the Arab summits had agreed on something like a division of labor to deal with the Israeli bomb-in-the-making, a bomb that could lead to Israel's establishment as a fait accompli. Egypt—with its conventional might, missile force, and political weight—was supposed to carry the burden of a regular, preventive war. Syria—and Egypt—also endorsed Palestinian guerrilla options, following the Algerian and Vietnam models, to fight Israel as best they could.

Yet Nasser's involvement in Yemen since 1962 had diverted his—and Israel's—attention elsewhere. Furthermore, it is doubtful whether Nasser felt ready for his declared preemptive war or was willing to take the risks involved. He publicly made such an enterprise conditional on protecting Egypt's position first. He was aware of the vulnerability of his forces in Sinai—a vast desert that his forces had to cross before they reached the Israeli boundary. He had fortified positions in the Sinai but left them unmanned. Air cover would be decisive here. Nasser might have believed that if he deployed enough forces forward and his armor well behind—under the sufficient protection of his modern air force—he could take limited risks. However, he needed access to Jordan in order to threaten Israel's heart. He might have believed that he had found a way out of a straightforward attack by forcing Israel to attack first (as long as he had sufficient Soviet backing to sustain the attack). Then he could, at least, use his air power to destroy Dimona.

It is less likely that the whole exercise was at first a limited demonstration of power in support of Syria. The most aggressive Arab power at the time, Syria was constantly involved in direct border clashes with Israel, and was indirectly supporting Arafat's guerrilla activities. Such a demonstration, when supported by air power, could secure the occupation of Eilat, the isolated Negev harbor, and create a land bridge between Egypt and the eastern Arab world—and possibly eradicate Dimona. But Israel would resist that with all its might. The Egyptian president was bound to Syria by virtue of a defense pact, but, in fact, the pact could make him a Syrian tool. He was aware of this, and his spokesman, Hassnein Heikal, warned the Syrians not to expect automatic Egyptian aid in each case of an Israeli attack against Syrian positions.[47]

Instead, Heikal, and Nasser himself, seem to have decided to wait, at least until the Soviets were drawn far enough to allow action against Israel. The issue of whether an Arab bomb would allow a "war of destruction" by conventional means against a nuclear Israel could be deferred, for the time being, if Israel's own nuclear option was gone. It is possible that on the eve of the Six-Day War the Egyptians were misled into believing that the Soviets would support some limited action.[48]

At the same time, Nasser may well have viewed Eshkol's cabinet as an uneasy, not very clever, coalition, due to its series of more and less reluctant military reprisals against poor Jordan and the aggressive Syria. While Nasser stood aside in several cases of Israeli-Syrian clashes and Israeli-Palestinian clashes in Jordan—which seemed counter to his desire for legendary influence among the Arab masses—he was involved in the frustrating intervention in Yemen, which in turn embroiled him in trouble with Saudi Arabia and its conservative ally Jordan. Late in 1966 and again in the spring of 1967, Israel exchanged heavy, escalating blows with Syria. This prompted Soviet warnings and behind-the-scenes activities to protect their Ba'ath clients in Damascus. Finally, in May 1967, Nasser deployed his troops in the Sinai, and soon afterward demanded the withdrawal of U.N. buffer troops from the positions in which they had been stationed following the 1956 war.

Eshkol realized that Rabin had stupidly threatened the Syrian regime shortly beforehand, although Allon and his friends were able to save Rabin from Eshkol's justified wrath.[49] Eshkol's cabinet did not want war with Syria, let alone with Egypt. But the prime minister had previously endorsed Rabin's reprisals, and, in fact, had given him the conventional means for a strategy of conventional deterrence-compellence, which the IDF high command had endorsed before and now demanded to pursue. The concentrations of Egyptian troops grew more serious daily, accompanied by a propaganda campaign that reminded many Israelis of the rhetoric of the "Final Solution." And, finally, when Nasser closed the Eilat straits to Israeli shipping, the IDF demanded to take action. Eshkol, meanwhile, was trying to get a sense of the attitudes of the Americans and the French. De Gaulle was furious because what he regarded as the unnecessary escalation with Syria had occurred without any consultation with him, and he feared Soviet involvement. Foreign Minister Abba Eban interpreted a vague assertion by President Johnson as meaning that the United States would move if Israel waited long enough.[50]

Eshkol's cabinet was evenly split and decided to wait instead of going to war. This decision prompted a nearly open rebellion among the generals, ruined Eshkol publicly, allowed Nasser to gain momentum among other Arabs (including King Hussein's complete submission to Egypt's policies), and triggered a major domestic coalition crisis that prompted far-reaching changes in its composition. However, the new coalition arrangement was destined not to prevent the IDF from occupying the whole West Bank once Hussein joined Nasser.

Nasser's gambit could have been the result of a calculated maneuver to end the war in Yemen without losing face, to gain some prestige in a limited move against Eshkol, to reestablish himself as the leader of the Arab nation, or, indeed, to attempt a limited war with Soviet backing before Israel "went nuclear" (knocking out Dimona at the same time).[51] We do not know which was the primary motive—nor did Rabin, who was not trained to speculate about the enemy's motives. When the alarming concentration of troops in the Sinai was followed by an Egyptian reconnaissance flight over Dimona, he strongly recommended an almost general mobilization.[52] Eshkol agreed, thereby presenting Nasser with the dilemma of whether to withdraw in the face of an open challenge or to push a mobilized Israel (which could not afford indefinite mobilization) to fire the first shot. If Israel fired the first shot Egypt would have the political conditions necessary to respond—without creating the impression that Egypt was the one to launch the shooting war. At that juncture, Dimona—and Israel's nuclear option—might have been destroyed.

One can discern here a certain pattern, which repeats itself in variations based on changing circumstances: an inter-Arab feud (the Yemen war) combined with the Israeli nuclear challenge, and with a radical Arab power's economic frustrations at home and its quest to assert itself vis-à-vis the United States in the name of pan-Arabism. Pushed by other

Arab powers—radical and conservative alike—such an Arab power might guard itself against becoming the tool of other Arabs (Palestinians included) but still be provoked to some action against Israel, if it felt sufficiently strong (due to Soviet backing, for example) or sufficiently endangered. If we look at this as a pattern, the Yemen war—not a victory for Egypt—could be compared to Saddam Hussein's futile attack on Iran twenty years later. Once the war was over, the large standing army would need to be refurbished or discharged, either way adding a burden on the civilian economy and possibly endangering political stability. Israeli or American "provocations" could be used by the Arab rivals of such a power to justify their own policies of nonaction, due to their relative weakness. Jordan did just this, while blaming Nasser for "hiding behind the U.N. troops in Gaza instead of fighting Israel," until Nasser ordered the U.N. troops to withdraw and finally forced King Hussein to join him in his challenge to Israel. Or Arab powers such as Syria, actively engaged in a constant military friction with Israel, could cite their own activities as a challenging proof of their rival's inactivity.

Once Egypt was pushed to action, the action itself was an act of limited aggression. Nasser's order for the U.N. troops to redeploy to camps inside Gaza was aggravated by U.N. Secretary General U Thant, who accepted the advice his deputy, Ralph Bunche, to call Nasser's bluff. The U.N. secretary general presented Nasser with a dilemma: the U.N. would accept no half-measures; either Nasser had to let them remain in their forward positions or they would be withdrawn altogether. U Thant believed that Nasser would back down, because he was not interested in having the troops withdrawn altogether. But when challenged, Nasser chose to ask for their complete withdrawal. Now no barrier remained between the Palestinians in Gaza—armed by Nasser and to whose cause he was officially obliged—and Israel. Furthermore, U.N. presence in the Straits of Tiran, another trouble spot, was eliminated. And Nasser would not allow Israeli shipping in "Arab waters" once the neutral barrier—which prevented him from exercising Arab sovereignty over the contested straits leading to Eilat—was gone. (In the eyes of many Israelis, this was one of the causes of the 1956 war.) But even Egypt's closing of the straits to Israeli and Israeli-bound shipping was a "limited" act of aggression, legally based on Nasser's own acceptance of the U.N. troops in 1957 and upon claims that the straits were "Arab," because they so narrowly separated Egypt from Saudi Arabia. Thus Arab use of legal arguments—to the point of denying Israel's very "legality"— is a factor that should be taken into account in observing the behavior of Arab leaders in general.

Further, this pattern showed a limited act of aggression, and then the immediate adoption of a defensive posture, so that the other side would have to start a full scale war, and thus—as Nasser hoped—create a united Arab front against the "aggressor," help mobilize Soviet and Third World support, and split the West. As we shall see, this pattern assumed somewhat different postures in 1973 and—in Saddam Hussein's case—1990.

CHAPTER SIX

The Road to the Yom Kippur War

In 1967, it took Eshkol several weeks to get the cabinet to agree to use the mobilized troops in a preventive war. The IDF had been pressuring the cabinet to undertake this move from the beginning of the crisis, when the issue was brought to a head as Nasser imposed a blockade on Israeli shipping to Eilat. In doing this, he unilaterally returned to the pre-1956 status quo and touched upon an explicit Israeli casus belli.

The cabinet that finally capitulated was not the same as that which had been stalling all along. It was composed of a new coalition put together solely for the purpose of conducting the preemptive 1967 war.

Faced with Nasser's serious challenge, Eshkol's original center-left coalition found itself in a quandary, vacillating between Allon's conventional preemptive strike doctrine and fears for Israel's very existence, related, as we were told by his military adjutant General Lior, to the safety of the Dimona facility. One may infer from this that the reactor itself—and Israel's cities in general—seemed to be vulnerable unless all Arab air forces could be neutralized. The cabinet tried at first to sense the attitude of the Americans and to consult General de Gaulle. Washington refused to perceive Nasser's gambit as a threat to Israel's survival, nor did the United States accept Israel's bleak estimate of Nasser's intentions. W. W. Rostow's May 25, 1967 letter to President Johnson sheds light on the conflicting Israeli and American intelligence estimates on the eve of the Six-Day War and the "highly disturbing estimate" submitted by Israeli intelligence to President Johnson's attention via the CIA. (Rostow was NSC chief at the time; archival sources tell us that he was later replaced by his predecessor, Bundy, because he and many others in Johnson's staff were Jewish.) Nasser is described in

Rostow's letter as "shrewd, but not mad." Washington expected the Egyptian president to seek U.N. intercession rather than to attack, and to push for heavy concessions such as grain supplies and financial assistance from the United States as his price for keeping the peace. Thus Egypt's gambit was perceived by Washington as a calculated move toward the United States no less than toward Israel. Nasser's confidence in this was backed by qualified Soviet support.[1]

One can, of course, judge from this that in Rostow's eyes Nasser would have been "mad" to directly attack an Israel whose nuclear potential had already been perceived by him as a cause for serious alarm. Although, according to Pean's dates and the quotes from the NSC files mentioned above, Israel might not have had delivery means yet and would have to rely on obsolete medium bombers. According to McGeorge Bundy, "Certainly there were no nuclear overtones for Washington in the war of 1967, when I found myself temporarily back in the White House as the responsible staff officer."[2] So, if it seemed that the Israeli nuclear deterrent was not ready yet and was an important factor here for Nasser, Rostow expected that the Arabs would at least fear American intervention on Israel's behalf.

But even in conventional terms, Israel was a formidable enemy. Nasser's intentions might have been political, rather than military, even though—at least as the Israelis saw it, according to General Lior—bombing Dimona could have been a rather limited and yet plausible goal for the Egyptians. Eilat, the isolated harbor in the south, and the sudden pact with Jordan, created direct threats to Israeli territory proper, especially with Iraqi troops in the process of joining the relatively small army of King Hussein. Still the Arabs had to command the air before they became a real menace. But Palestinian raids from Gaza threatened to harass Israel as before the 1956 war, and Syrian-backed raids and direct shelling from the Golan Heights would certainly continue.

However, the Americans' own game in regard to the validity and legality of Israel's nuclear option might well have greatly contributed both to Nasser's confidence and sense of alarm (although he would not move until he convinced himself that he had qualified Soviet support, and when he did move, his actions would be rather measured and short of any open act of war as he understood it). We can see here something like a "historical opacity": The refusal of the countries involved to admit to mistakes relating to nuclear matters, such as Dimona's role in generating the 1967 war (including the ensuing occupation of the West Bank) and their unwillingness to pay the political price related to the process leading to it. In other words, the main problem for Johnson's NSC was to illegalize Israel's nuclear option. And this might have encouraged Nasser, with a degree of Soviet support, to take the risks that later embroiled the whole region in an unnecessary war and resulted in the occupation of the West Bank. But for that matter, we must first return to Israel's conventional doctrine and to Eshkol's coalition and its crisis.

The Americans refused to solve the immediate problem for Israel. When Egypt closed the Straits of Tiran, the United States tried to mobilize some international support for keeping the straits open. However, Washington warned the Israelis not to move in the meantime, thereby creating the impression that its previous promises to come to Israel's aid were just so much empty talk—or that Washington would come to Israel's aid if it waited long enough.

In fact, no one in Washington remembered what President Eisenhower had promised Ben-Gurion about freedom of navigation in the Straits of Tiran when he forced Israel to evacuate them in 1957. And it was not an issue relating to Israel's boundaries, which had been covertly guaranteed by Kennedy. It was indeed a "borderline" case, as an unimpressed de Gaulle told Israeli Foreign Minister Abba Eban. General de Gaulle hinted that Israeli reprisals against Syria had given Nasser his opportunity to counter with a limited act of aggression while waiting for Israel to commit the first formal act of war. De Gaulle also hinted that Nasser's action was related to ambiguous and difficult issues, including: the status of the Straits of Tiran; or the fact that the Sinai was sovereign Egyptian territory, where he had the formal right to move troops anywhere; or U.N. presence in his territory or in Gaza, which depended on his consent. Nasser felt he had enough Soviet backing to finally bring himself to take the risk. Should Israel fire the first shot, Nasser would, of course, retaliate and probably even destroy Dimona. France's support would not be forthcoming, as France was not consulted and feared a superpower confrontation.

Ironically, this was, to some extent, Ben-Gurion's own conclusion when a depressed Rabin came to ask for his advice. Ben-Gurion blamed Eshkol for the general mobilization and previous escalation. But he did not expect further Egyptian attack or a superpower confrontation here—unless the Russians intervened directly and, for example, attacked Dimona. Soviet intervention was a proposition that, according to Minister Yosef Burg, haunted all Israeli decision makers.[3] But Ben-Gurion's conclusion about Nasser's further moves was pretty close to the American estimate of Nasser's limited goals.

After all, if the Egyptian leader had wanted a surprise attack, he would have undertaken it right away. But instead, his moves were rather cautious and limited in scope, with his armor deployed close to the Canal Zone, not to the Israeli border but in the Sinai and in a defensive formation. However, if Israel attacked him, he might retaliate and destroy Dimona.[4]

Ben-Gurion was basically in favor of preserving a status-quo, therefore would not attack; he was not bound to doctrines of conventional preemption and conventional compellence as a matter of course. His main concern, as I interpret his behavior at the time, was the final goal of nuclear deterrence. Thus he was not interested in preemption that would deteriorate to a conventional bloody war and even, possibly, endanger the nuclear option. He must have remained unimpressed by the Soviet guarantee to Egypt. The Soviets could hardly support an all-out Arab *attack* against Israel by using their own nuclear might. At least they never had used nuclear power to support other nations' aggressions that could lead to the eradication of a legitimate state. In ambiguous situations, they might have been drawn to do so; and they did threaten Israel directly in 1956, when it attacked Egypt openly. But, of course, they could support a limited attack against Dimona, carried out either by Arab air power, supplied by them, or even by means of a limited land offensive.

Ben-Gurion's own solution was to "dig in"—no preventive wars "against the wrong enemy, in the wrong place, and at the wrong time."[5] If any action was called for, then it should be a limited land operation to open the straits. His reasoning in regard to Dimona might have been threefold: first, to rely on the nuclear option as far as Israel's very survival was concerned, and refrain from linking it to a side (though important) issue like Tiran; second, to do nothing to endanger Dimona itself, until the missile issue had been resolved; and third, to keep his promise to consult de Gaulle. (His extreme sensitivity to de Gaulle's reaction could lead us to the conclusion that the general had agreed in 1960 to broaden the 1956-1957 agreement with Ben-Gurion to include some kind of mutual consultation in a crisis situation.) Ben-Gurion could tolerate Arab guerrilla attacks from Gaza, and even the closure of the straits, or respond to them by invoking reprisals. But he would not have risked a general war between 1955 and late 1956 unless foreign aid was secured and a decisive defense goal was pursued—the link to France in 1957, which had yielded Dimona. The centrality of the nuclear option here may seem like a deductive game on my part, but it is supported by circumstantial evidence about his behavior as prime minister in 1955-1956 and by his warnings against the forthcoming conflict in 1967.[6] He might also have calculated that if Eshkol took his advice and waited further without acting, his regime would collapse, and the crisis might bring about a long-overdue, far-reaching constitutional reform.

Ben-Gurion's strategic approach was incompatible with the public's understanding of what was happening. Thus the sense of alarm, humiliation, and desire to act (which Ben-Gurion had long since instilled in Israeli hearts) could hardly be ignored and be translated into cause for a frontal attack against Eshkol's regime. Eshkol, himself, disagreed with Ben-Gurion's defensive approach; Ben-Gurion was traditionally perceived as an "activist" leader who had responded vigorously to Arab challenges in the past; even though, in fact, his responses were limited and controlled compared to the impression they gave. But Eshkol was judged according to what was regarded in public as Ben-Gurion's decision to launch a preemptive attack against Egypt in 1956. He was even hard-pressed to appoint Ben-Gurion as defense minister in order to force a decision to act, a decision that, in fact, Eshkol wanted but Ben-Gurion did not. Eshkol finally picked Dayan to carry the decision out. He thus split Ben-Gurion's own camp by appointing Dayan to the Defense Ministry; this left Ben-Gurion alone, as Peres followed Dayan's decision to cooperate with Eshkol within a broadened parliamentary coalition.

Ben-Gurion's 1956 decision to join the French and the British in their war against Nasser was related to the acquisition of nuclear assistance from France in return for Israel's cooperation with the French against Nasser (although, in reality, according to Pean, it was the failure of the 1956 endeavor that clinched the promise). Ben-Gurion's decision was never intended to be a binding precedent for a preemptive conventional policy. Since that time, however, Allon's doctrine of conventional preemption had taken root. And—due among other things to the official ambiguity imposed on Dimona—the Israeli public had no basis for seeing things otherwise. As a result, Eshkol was losing public support daily by waiting at his cabinet's behest for Washington's response to his pleas. When other Arab states joined a seemingly unopposed Nasser, Eshkol faced a full-blown rebellion among members of his coalition, especially among junior representatives of the religious parties.

The press then interfered—after having been behind Eshkol in his battles with Ben-Gurion it now deserted him. A semi-independent army general headquarters, which would never have been allowed such a role under Ben-Gurion, was protesting loudly. Finally, Eshkol had to resign his defense job. But as he anticipated a bloody war requiring national unity, he not only appointed Dayan to succeed him as minister of defense but created a grand coalition that spanned the political spectrum and included Menachem Begin. Thus, Begin's nationalist views and commitment to an unpartitioned Palestine were given partial legitimization by Eshkol himself.

Allon, a close political ally who would have been Eshkol's natural successor in the Defense Ministry, was replaced by the popular Moshe Dayan; and Ben-Gurion was pushed aside as the leader of Rafi by Dayan, due to Ben-Gurion's defensive posture and Eshkol's stance. Ben-Gurion thus fell victim to his advanced age, to his defensive approach centered on Dimona, and to Dayan's willingness, once given access to real power, to join Eshkol against Ben-Gurion's explicit wishes. According to Lior, Dayan's view was that Israel was strong enough conventionally to take care of the Egyptian threat by invoking conventional offensive means.[8] Ben-Gurion's defensive posture would allow the Arabs to escalate their activities against Israel further, and the initiative would remain in their hands.[9]

Ben-Gurion was right about the reasons for the crisis. But as Dayan saw it, a defensive posture was not the answer to it. Dayan refused to accept his former mentor as an unofficial adviser. Ben-Gurion might have advised him to restrain the war to the necessary minimum, such as forcing the straits, in order to avoid any far-reaching changes in the regional status quo. A war might also spark an uncontrollable domestic debate; the occupation of the West Bank would immediately become a source for ideological-political disputes because of religious and nationalistic arguments and interests.

At any rate, Dayan soon gave the order and a preemptive strike was begun, targeted first against the Arab air forces. The ensuing victories went to Dayan's credit. A three-way rivalry between Eshkol, who remained prime minister, Dayan, a defense minister chosen by him due to pressure from the press and junior members of his multiparty coalition, and an extremely frustrated Allon (in addition to the army's direction by Rabin) may go some way to explaining the complete occupation of the West Bank, which was never authorized in advance by the cabinet. Instead, it resulted from the relative freedom of action given to IDF commanders in the field by the new coalition, and from the fear and distrust that existed among Eshkol, Dayan, and Allon—let alone Rabin.[10]

As planned, the Arab air forces were destroyed on the ground, the Egyptian front was pierced, and Nasser's armies routed. King Hussein's intervention was a problem, but he and the Iraqis who had joined him had no air cover. The Syrians, who helped trigger the war, actually stood aside, except for heavy shelling from the Golan Heights. We do not know whether they were interested only in guerrilla warfare and artillery attacks because of their "North Vietnamese" and "Algerian" concepts of fighting a nuclear Israel. (They probably believed that Israel was in possession of an assembled bomb.) They might also have calculated that, if they went too far, the Americans would intervene.

Was it necessary to occupy the West Bank as a whole? Not from a defensive military point of view. It was, however, an old element in Allon's strategic thinking and a dream of the veterans of the War of Independence (who were now generals) to occupy the West Bank, at least as far as Jerusalem, and several other parts of that region. Holding the West Bank gave Israel "strategic depth" in the area most vulnerable and most vital to its very survival, the area around Tel Aviv and Jerusalem. The Negev Desert had remained empty; no one had followed Ben-Gurion's call to settle there.

In an updated version of *A Curtain of Sand,* published after the 1967 victory, Allon argued in favor of the "strategic depth" gained by the occupation of the West Bank and against relying on the nuclear option, which might have remained for him the "last resort bomb in the basement."[11] That is, the nuclear option might have some value if faced with the prospect of losing a conventional war or if the Arabs gained access to nuclear weapons. Allon and company were not very concerned about Arabs gaining nuclear weapons. They felt that if Israel refrained from "introducing" the nuclear factor to the region, the Soviets would not supply nuclear aid to the Arabs. Therefore, for all practical purposes—especially as far as an open Israeli nuclear posture and the adoption of an Israeli nuclear strategy were concerned—the Arab-Israeli conflict should be kept conventional. Allon, and many like him among the younger IDF commanders, was confident that the territorial changes following 1967 plus the conventional performance of the Israeli army would further guarantee Israel's conventional superiority by giving it the necessary "strategic depth."[12]

Moreover, the West Bank, as well as the Sinai, would be Israel's trump cards for peace when partitioned in a way that would give Israel control over its most important strategic areas and return its Arab-populated areas to Arab rule.

Allon changed his traditional views in this direction rather early, when the hostilities began on June 6, 1967—according to the minutes of various government and party bodies, recently published in the Israeli press.[13] Once he realized the extent and the meaning of Israeli rule over so many alien Palestinians in the West Bank (and having no Ben-Gurion to fight on the issue of Israeli control there), Allon was contemplating the establishment of "an autonomous (Arab) region in the West Bank . . . subject to our policy," and the annexation of the rest to Israel. Dayan, at first, contemplated holding the West Bank in part only, mainly East Jerusalem (which was annexed de facto by a general consensus in the cabinet) through the hilly divide between both parts of Western Palestine. He then changed his mind in favor of holding the whole West

Bank, without legal annexation. Annexation would have made the West Bank's Arab population Israeli citizens eligible to vote. Without legal annexation, the Arab population could be given "independent rule" — i.e., self-rule but no access to matters of foreign policy and security. Or, if they refused this, they could be given some link to Jordan. The Cabinet's Defense Committee offered to Egypt and Syria a complete Israeli withdrawal from Sinai and the Golan Heights, in exchange for peace and security arrangements, such as demilitarization in the occupied territories.[14] But the Arabs were not ready to negotiate at all—let alone on the basis of Allon's partition plan.

Arab public posture was expressed at the Khartoum Conference of September 1, 1967. According to Hassnein Heikal:

> Nasser came to the conclusion that the only course was to leave the [post-1967] negotiations to the Russians . . . [reserving] his position on only two points—nobody could ask him to give up a square foot of Egyptian territory, nor could he surrender any of the rights of the Palestinians.[15]

Both issues, however, and especially the "rights of the Palestinians"—at the time a synonym for no rights for Israel—kept the Arab-Israeli conflict wide open. They prevented the use of occupied Arab territory as a trump card for peace and led to a political stalemate. Very soon Allon, still a senior minister in Eshkol's grand coalition, encouraged Israeli settlements in the West Bank, in and outside of his own designated plan. And Dayan could not afford to appear less patriotic. The Soviets replaced lost Arab equipment, and a war of attrition slowly developed along the Suez Canal.

In fact, the Arabs won something that was recognized everywhere, but especially in their own eyes, as a legitimate if limited war aim, in terms that allowed them more practical flexibility than before: the recovery of occupied Arab land and the end of Israeli rule over occupied Arabs. It probably took them some time to realize that for the moment they could hit Israeli-occupied territory, rather than Israel itself—thereby bypassing the issue of Israel's very existence, which was bound to Israel's nuclear option and to American guarantees. The nuclear option had been a major constraint for them when Israel's very existence was at stake. Any attack within the pre-June 1967 lines could be perceived by the Israelis as an attempt to wipe out Israel's very existence. And even a limited Arab challenge might have escalated, in spite of initial planning, to the official commitment to eradicate the Zionist entity, as seemed to be the case at the outbreak of the Six-Day War.

Now the Israelis felt "secured" in their new boundaries, in conventional terms. And this gave the Arabs more, not less, options to use their relatively larger conventional potential, if they played their cards right. For the time being, the Arabs were satisfied that de Gaulle was withdrawing his support from the Jewish state for not following his advice (or rather for not adhering to Ben-Gurion's agreements with him to maintain Israel's original boundaries and the structure of the sensitive Middle East). The MD 660 was gone, as we are told by Pean. And it is possible that in fighting to prevent the supply of the "25 experimental missiles ordered by Israel in France" the Americans were successful in preventing their delivery. Or perhaps de Gaulle refused to supply them before the 1967 war. Finally, following a big Israeli raid on the Beirut Airport in 1968, de Gaulle imposed a general embargo on weapons deliveries to Israel. The Arabs were temporarily in the clear until Israel could develop its own Jericho system or receive suitable aircraft from the United States.

Therefore, from a general Arab point of view, the issue of Israel's very existence could be deferred and the matter entrusted to the PLO, now recognized as an autonomous guerrilla outfit under a new chairman, Fatah's commander Yassir Arafat. The PLO would be able to fight Israel proper, when entrenched in Jordan, below Israel's conventional and nuclear threshold; and Egypt would concentrate on the canal war. Other nations had seemingly done the same: Algeria had won against a nuclear France, North Vietnam was beginning to wear out conventional American forces, and Mao had insisted that nuclear arms were not a serious consideration to mass guerrilla armies fighting foreign invaders. The Arab definition of Israel as a foreign base, an unnatural, imperialist plot, and/or the notion of Jewish betrayal of the Jewish Diaspora tradition itself, could provide an explanation for the whole Israeli phenomenon that would allow Arab leaders to create a strategy that followed the victories of the Chinese, the North Vietnamese, and the Algerians over Western nuclear powers. On the basis of Marxist-Leninist ideology—following Marx's own remark about war as the "locomotive of history" and Lenin's and Trotsky's teachings on war in the prenuclear world—one could construct a theory of war against "colonialist" phenomena in the Third World and apply it to Israel. Because of the close ties between Moscow and the Ba'ath Party, now ruling in Syria and Iraq, and the developing ties between the Soviets and the PLO since 1968, the Arabs could endorse this theory of mass guerrilla warfare in the nuclear age. (Although the Christian element among them was more prone to adopt Marxism-Leninism and Trotskyism, Arafat maintained a strong Islamic identity.) Or they could see that this theory did not work that easily in the nuclear age (based also on Moscow's example) and become eager to get their own bomb.

Yet the issue was not simple. When a general Arab mobilization to a popular war against Israel was called for by radical Arab states, such as Algeria, it was intertwined with the problem of Arab unity and the issue of leadership that was a pre-condition for such an enterprise. The radical Arab approach was for the abolition of Israel altogether, and thus required, for the Algerian military thinker who proposed it at the time, a counterbomb.[16] And this issue could serve as a basis for a joint Arab effort—which had, to a certain degree, always been missing. Arab cooperation raised the problem of how to control the Palestinians in order to avoid Israeli reprisals against Arab host states. Arafat was not really a trustworthy ally of anyone, except possibly President Nasser, who however would not allow him to operate from Egyptian territory. And the PLO did not have a united, orderly structure. Since 1967 other Arab states intervened in the exiled Palestinian scene and helped them to create their own outfits—along purely Palestinian lines—which competed with Arafat's Fatah. Arafat's initial military activities in the occupied territories soon ended, due to the effective control Israel imposed over the West Bank. It was sealed off from his bases in Jordan because of the topographic conditions in the Jordan Valley—not a Vietnamese-like jungle but a desert area that was easily controllable from the air. Arafat's aim was to maintain the struggle, as long as other Arabs were unable to fight, and to mobilize them, either as umbrellas for his guerrilla war or as regular forces for his cause. However, King Hussein, the calculating and cautious Saudis, and the Syrians —whose destiny had just fallen into the hands of a very careful, and yet radical-nationalist Hafez Assad—were all careful to pursue their own interests. They tried to control the Palestinian issue the best they could—sometimes because they wanted to use the Palestinian cause for their own hegemonic ambitions—while avoiding the danger of taking serious risks for Arafat's cause, whose only rationale was the abolition of Israel.

Nasser might now have divided the Arab-Israeli conflict in two: first, the recovery of Egyptian land, which was his direct responsibility; and second, the cause of the Palestinians, which could be entrusted to Arafat, releasing Nasser from his commitments to fight a "war of destruction" against Israel on his own. Other Arab leaders cultivated hegemonic ambitions in direct relation to the acquisition of the bomb, as we shall see below. They would be studying the development of East-West relations and possibly attach great importance to the forthcoming Non-Proliferation Treaty.

From the Israeli point of view, the occupation of the West Bank brought out several shared opinions between Dayan and Allon, despite their personal and political rivalry. Dayan was not impressed by Arab conventional power, nor did he fear it as the main challenge to Israel's very survival, as Ben-Gurion did. Before the 1967 war, he shared both Ben-Gurion's interest in nuclear affairs and—to a degree—his profound dislike of the idea of occupying the West Bank. However, now that territory was occupied. The occupation was due in part to King Hussein's intervention in the war, so now the king's previous signs of weakness and his difficulties in controlling the West Bank population could be cited against him. These were not the reasons for the initial occupation. The reasons could be found in the composition of the Israeli cabinet and in the IDF's own initiative. But now Dayan, like Allon, came to want "new boundaries and different relations" with the Arabs.[17] This meant Israeli control over most of the occupied territories and peace and cooperation with neighboring Arab nations. Yet Dayan would neither partition the West Bank nor annex parts of it. To him, the area was too sensitive, Hussein was too weak to rely on—even if a peace agreement with him was signed and the West Bank returned to Jordan— and a Palestinian state therein would seek to delegitimize and undermine both Jordan and Israel. Still, no other good solution for the West Bank problem was in sight, except perhaps for some kind of benign Israeli occupation for the foreseeable future in tacit cooperation with Jordan.

Dayan's primary interest was Egypt—as the most important of the Arab nations and the one whose collaboration with the Soviets seemed to allow Moscow a growing, dangerous role in the Middle East. Direct Soviet intervention in the canal war was a possibility that Dayan could not ignore; as patrons of Egypt, Soviet prestige and credibility in a vital region and in the Third World as a whole were at stake. Indeed, Soviet advisers, and later Soviet Air Force pilots, became more and more directly involved in the canal fighting.

American involvement was vital, not only for direct military aid but also to balance out the Russians. The Soviets could conceivably threaten Israel to force withdrawal from the occupied territories without any change in Arab behavior. In this case, the United States was needed to equalize the situation so that Israel would not be totally exposed to Soviet involvement for Egypt on the ground—or to Soviet nuclear threats (as had been the case in 1956).

Early in 1968, Dr. Henry A. Kissinger met a group of Israeli academics, of which I was a member, in Jerusalem. Kissinger was national security adviser to New York Governor Nelson Rockefeller at the time; he had arrived in Israel from a secret visit to Moscow. Kissinger warned this group that the "Soviets might go to the brink to help the Egyptians in their bid to liberate the Sinai." When asked what exactly he meant by "brinkmanship," Kissinger replied that the Russians might launch inter-mediate-range ballistic missiles (IRBMs) against Israeli Air Force bases in the peninsula. The action would be swift, an accomplished fact against which the United States would do nothing. "No American pres-ident would take the risk of World War III because of you," Kissinger said, in a way that made his listeners think he made no distinction between occupied territory and Israel proper. The theory behind this was the fear of an accomplished nuclear fact, which would leave the vic-tim with real results, not with the anticipated ones, thus avoiding the deterrence phase. The problem, rooted in deterrence-theoretical calcu-lations typical of the 1960s, seemed to be that once a party to a conflict had delivered a first strike—and thus moved from "deterrence" to the actual use of its nuclear power—the response would be of no actual meaning because the initial damage would be bad enough. And a sec-ond strike delivered by the enemy would be devastating. Thus for some Western thinkers, the issue of preventing first strikes and maintaining deterrence seemed critical as well as achievable, at least in the case of the superpowers themselves. But an American response to a Soviet mis-sile attack against Israel seemed inconceivable, once the missiles had landed. Kissinger seemed to play on the Soviet fear in order to make the Israelis more flexible vis-à-vis Egypt. But he might have encouraged them at the same time to get the Americans more involved in favor of Israel in spite of themselves. Kissinger's worries were published by the author the next day in Ha'aretz. But I have no idea whether the Israelis were pushed at the time to develop their own missiles. The motive to do so had been ascribed to them a decade before.

During the meeting with Kissinger, the Israelis argued that Soviet IRBMs would be detected by the United States first, and thus could trigger an American response (unless the Soviets warned Washington that Israel was the target, thereby losing the fait accompli effect). Kissinger deliberated, and then said that the Russians would deploy the missiles in Egypt. This, of course, was an entirely different proposi-tion: Soviet-made missiles launched not from Russia but from Egypt would expose Egypt, at least, to Israeli retaliation.[18] Dayan was well aware of such American arguments.

The French had left Israel all on its own, but Dayan felt that the Americans could be mobilized only if Nasser made enough mistakes to push Washington closer to Jerusalem. On the face of it, this maneuver seemed impossible to execute. Washington sided with the Arabs against Israel's bid for serious territorial changes and was not in favor of pushing the Arabs to make far-reaching political concessions to Israel, as Dayan's "new relations" required. Such new relations excluded the problem of the 1948 Arab refugees, and went beyond the incontestable Arab national consensus. The solution the Arabs proposed for the problem of the 1948 Arab refugees was for them to be allowed, in principle, to return to the pre-1967 territory of Israel. With such a solution, a deal regarding return of the territories occupied in 1967 would be made irrelevant to achieving a comprehensive peace.[19]

Moreover, Washington was supposed to be the superpower most interested in curbing nuclear proliferation and the use of nuclear threats. So, Israel could hardly hope to receive from the Americans aircraft suited to carry nuclear weapons (like the F-4 Phantom fighter bomber). Yet, as we are told by Bundy years later, having passed through the trials of creating its nuclear weapon infrastructure unopposed, Israel was in a position to benefit from several developments. In 1964, China had joined the nuclear club openly, and India was accordingly alarmed. A series of issues had been of concern to the superpowers in this regard. Would some kind of Indian-Egyptian cooperation emerge from this? And what role would China play as a "leader of the Third World" and as an ideological-political rival of Moscow? At the same time, the problem of nuclear sharing—some kind of West German access to American nuclear weapons—had constantly worried the Soviets. By then the *Bundeswehr* had nuclear-capable aircraft and missiles, made in America, at its disposal. But the earlier discussions of MLF and other forms of nuclear sharing ended with no actual transfer of American nuclear weapons to the West Germans, nor with German-developed ABC weapons, even if Bonn intended nuclear technology for a peaceful use. This seemed to have established rules acceptable to both superpowers—if not to India—and to West Germany, now under the Social-Democrats.[20]

Indeed, despite the bitter rivalry between the superpowers regarding the Vietnam war and the Middle East—as well as the ongoing trouble concerning Berlin and the issue of East German recognition by the West—the superpowers agreed on the Non-Proliferation Treaty. In 1968 NPT was implemented, officially outlawing nuclear proliferation. This step was understood by Third World nations to be mainly the outcome of an American concept, and less so of Soviet ideas.[21] NPT established mechanisms for safeguarding nuclear facilities and nuclear material by means of the IAEA's and the suppliers' own inspections. It allowed signatories to withdraw from the treaty with only a short notice, but this seemed to have been an unavoidable price to pay. Sovereign nations would be able to withdraw from the treaty anyway, or they could not sign the treaty to begin with. In any case, one of the main results of NPT was the establishment of a norm, and the official illegalization of nuclear weapon facilities and related material. This created the atmosphere of outlawing nuclear threats de jure—as far as internationally accepted norms were concerned—by third parties who might actually have nuclear capabilities. It further implied nuclear protection by the superpowers of third parties if threatened by other third parties; but this interpretation depended totally on superpower interests and on the relations between them, the treaty notwithstanding. It also contained a general nuclear disarmament clause, which would leave some nations with no protection, if the clause was invoked without making sure that everyone sufficiently disarmed at the same time. Here, Israel was a special case in various ways: it seemed to have joined the club beforehand, even if unofficially; Israel's unofficial status as a de facto but not de jure member of the club left it in a twilight zone, whereas Arabs were far from joining the club either way. Furthermore, NPT could lead to the interpretation by third parties that it had imposed serious restraint on Soviet behavior with regard to them (once they agreed to outlaw proliferation, they could hardly station nuclear weapons in countries beyond their previous rule without infringing upon the spirit of NPT). Thus NPT required restraint on the part of the superpowers themselves, to be followed as a norm by the other members of the club. At least NPT was the first move toward detente.

Israel was placed in a strange situation. It is possible that by 1967 the Arabs saw that something like NPT was forthcoming, and realized that a country that won the nuclear race beforehand would be treated as an established fact. Their motives in striking at Dimona in 1967—perhaps with a degree of Soviet backing—are thus clear enough. But once the Arabs perceived themselves as having missed the boat, they could argue that the United States was officially responsible for Dimona's publicly benign nature and could try to push the Russians to compensate them for America's behavior. (See Sadat's arguments vis-à-vis President Johnson quoted in the previous chapter.) In addition, they could—as Libya would soon do in a crude way and Iraq would begin to seriously implement—try and acquire their own bombs inside NPT or outside of it.

The Israeli issue became increasingly burdensome for Washington. Should the United States continue to carry public responsibility for Dimona because of its inspection of a facility supplied by the French to a nation that had some influence within the American political system—but with whom the United States had no other common interests? In fact, the Americans had more interests among Israel's enemies, who, in turn, made Washington accountable for Israel's behavior. The inspection was a political-strategic move aimed originally at stopping Dimona and, later, at outlawing open nuclear threats. If the Americans had had any doubts at the beginning of their inspections about whether plutonium separation could be achieved by Israel, these doubts were in the process of disappearing, according to Bundy: "There are reports that in 1968 he [President Johnson] learned of rising concern about Israeli [nuclear] progress among the estimators in the CIA, but my successor [as NSC chief] Walt Rostow, remembers no presidential concern on this question."[22] Yet by virtue of this useless inspection, the United States remained publicly responsible for Israel's nuclear activities. Thus, while Dimona was undoubtedly there to stay, and the effectiveness of the inspection proved nil, according to Bundy, it could still be used as a tool in Arab and Third World hands to embroil the superpowers. They could ask for Soviet compensation for Dimona in terms of guarantees and military backing.

As Bundy put it in the conclusion of the Israeli section of his book, the United States was primarily concerned by now with other nations. Israel's nuclear effort was a fact.[23] But, according to Jed Synder and Samuel Wells, U.S. treatment of the matter then and later seems to justify the presumption that Washington wanted to insure that Israel would not use open nuclear threats.[24] Theoretically, in the framework of arms control negotiations following or leading to peace, a nonpublic nuclear threat could be given up, without complicating the peace process. At this stage, however, such a process was far from realization. And forcing Israel to join NPT would mean either that Israel would become an open nuclear nation or would find ways and means to cheat on the IAEA, an obviously bad precedent. Yet Washington's direct responsibility for the Dimona reactor had to end in order for the United States to avoid possible Soviet charges, and ongoing Arab charges, that the United States "allowed" Israel to "go nuclear" under the curtain of—perhaps purposely—the ineffectual American inspection.[25]

Such issues had to be of some concern to Henry Kissinger, President Nixon's newly appointed NSC chief, and a nuclear strategist himself. We quoted his remarks above with regard to Soviet brinkmanship vis-à-vis Israel during the canal war. The horror scenarios he described, which were grounded in deterrence-theoretical games to begin with, did not materialize. Kissinger was in doubt about whether Israel would be able to stay afloat in the surrounding ocean of Arab hatred. Nuclear weapons might indeed be the only hope—provided Israel did not add insult to injury by ruling over too many hostile Arabs and occupying sovereign Arab land.[26] As an American politician, Kissinger was not primarily concerned with Israel's problems, and therefore we can only guess as to what extent his opinion influenced the Republican administration's actual decisions in regard to Israel. According to Helmut Sonnenfeldt, who would become Kissinger's counselor at the State Department, Nixon and Kissinger did not approve of McNamara's campaign against France's nuclear force to begin with; "they legitimized the *force de frappe* and integrated its operations (into their own planning) much more than overtly known. This is because *they believed in the benefit of having as many anti-Soviet nuclear powers as possible* [italics added]. On Israel, since the Arabs were Soviet clients, Kissinger could not be expected to come down on Israel's nuclear program."[27] Until recently, we had no Israeli sources to verify this, except Ambassador Dinitz's testimony, to be quoted below, which supports Sonnenfeldt's testimony well. Yet President Bush's May 1991 Middle East arms control initiative triggered a semi-official Israeli response in this very connection. Bush's initiative called upon Israel and its neighbors to ban the production of nuclear weapons, join NPT, and allow inspection in their nuclear facilities. A journalist close to Prime Minister Shamir, Moshe Zak, published the following on the behind-the-scenes agreement between the United States and Israel, pertaining to foreign inspection of Israel's nuclear facilities, in the larger strategic context: "There exists an American promise to maintain Israel's quality edge over its neighbors. The quality edge is aimed at balancing the quantity edge, which favors the Arabs in munitions and manpower. *This American commitment is included in a letter, unpublished until now, which was sent by President Ford to Yitzhak Rabin* (when he was prime minister) in 1975. *In fact it was given orally to Golda* [Meir, the prime minister in the period discussed in this chapter], *by Nixon and Kissinger* [italics added], and was made known to President Carter, when he took office. Its meaning—the administration is committed to freeze its demand that Israeli nuclear installations will be placed under international control."[28] In fact, the Nixon Administration ended its own inspection at Dimona.[29]

At the same time, we should be wary of linking the end of American inspection at Dimona in 1969 and the decision by the Nixon Administration to supply Israel with Phantom jets, which was announced after a particularly vicious Palestinian act of terror against Israel. The decision to end the inspection could have been the result of the Nixon-Kissinger basic philosophy that Moscow should be confronted with various, not just the American, nuclear threats (as Sonnenfeldt put it) and the Arabs were Soviet clients. The Nixon Administration had less of a problem with something that was an established fact anyway. The decision could further end American responsibility for Dimona, even if it was never made public; whereas the sale of Phantom jets was openly acknowledged. The Nixon Administration made the final decision to supply the jets following the failure of Soviet-American negotiations on the Middle East, while trying to push both Israel and Egypt to make mutual concessions toward negotiating a way out of the canal war.[30] Both decisions followed a series of secret Soviet-American negotiations on the Middle East conflict, which ended in Brezhnev's refusal to deviate from Egypt's position. Egypt's position was totally unacceptable to both Washington and Jerusalem because Nasser would not make any meaningful concessions at all in exchange for occupied territory.

The jets, of course, could be seen as conventional weapons, and had no real deterrent value as far as Soviet territory was concerned. As for the Arabs, if they wanted any territory back, the United States was ready to talk to them. The Americans pretty well agreed with their territorial demands in any case, and remained distant from Israel's demands for a peace that entailed something like an American-Canadian or Dutch-Belgian relationship between Arab and Jew.

Israel's refusal to join NPT—which indeed was signed by most nations—was Jerusalem's responsibility. The United States simply could not guarantee the behavior of a nonsignatory by means of a nominal inspection of its nuclear facilities. Although there is no access to primary sources in this regard, one may further speculate that any dialogue with the Soviets on further proliferation in the world could be separated from the Israeli case, at least as long as the Arab-Israeli conflict remained an issue of survival to Israel. The case of Israel was a sui generis situation and could not be compared to other cases of proliferation. In fact, though, America felt secure that Israel's behavior could still be controlled, thanks to American conventional supplies and growing economic aid. And so, all direct U.S.-Israeli discussion of Dimona was reportedly terminated in 1969 (as I was told in an interview with Mr. Gazit). Or rather, as Moshe Zak stated, the American commitment was passed from one administration to another; and was made in written form by Gerald Ford and Kissinger. Then President Bush reopened the case in 1991.

In these terms, the end of the inspections can be linked to American diplomatic activity in 1970. It is possible that in exchange for Israel's strategic gain in regard to the end of the inspections and the supply of conventional weapons, Israel was asked to make several concessions regarding a cease-fire at the canal front, accompanied by negotiations on the future of occupied territory—including the West Bank. The internal debate on this issue brought about the collapse of the Israeli across-the-board coalition that was originally created to fight the 1967 war but had remained in office ever since. Since Eshkol's death in early 1969, the coalition had been presided over by Golda Meir, following the merger of all center-left parties into Israel's Labor Alignment—a merger in which the previous political bodies remained alive and kicking. Menachem Begin's right-center Gachal bloc—which later became the Likud Party—left the cabinet, because of opposition to possible concessions in the West Bank.

In the Arab world, the American diplomatic initiative brought about Palestinian demonstrations of power and acts of international terror, committed from and in Jordanian territory, designed to demonstrate to the world that their claims were main issues in the Arab-Israeli conflict. The outcome of this was an uncontrolled threat to King Hussein's monarchy and to the governing non-Palestinian element in it. They fought back, crushing the Palestinians in "Black September" 1970, and pushed them out of the country, mainly to the weak Lebanon. President Nasser tried to extinguish this fire, but in the middle of his efforts he suddenly died. Still, Nasserism, itself, as a viable policy of mobilizing Soviet and American aid for Egypt's purposes, was not completely finished. But Nasser himself had learned that Cairo's maneuverability was painfully limited, due among other things to superpower restraint in regard to nuclear matters, which imposed obvious limits on the degree of aid that he could get from the Soviets. He could try to get them directly involved in the canal war—which, to a degree he did—and he could make the Americans than intervene to stop the war; but the following negotiating process required concessions from him as well. In the meantime NPT came into being and the Dimona inspection was lifted by the Americans. And the Soviets could hardly be relied on, if Nasser resorted to more than a limited war with limited Soviet aid. Yet Nasserism always entailed a bid for Arab independence and unity as a great power, and this must have included an interest in Arab nuclear weapons as a matter of course. With Nasser's death, following the economic disaster of the mid-1960s and the defeat of 1967, this bid for Arab great power was difficult to sustain in Egypt, but it never died. Even before Nasser's death, others were waiting to take the idea over, possibly even driven by NPT—which constrained their bid for sovereignty—to use the treaty for their own purposes.

Shortly before his death, President Nasser received Muammar Qaddafi, a young admirer who had just overthrown the old pro-Western regime in Libya. The Libyan offered all the resources at his disposal for the holy task of destroying Israel—Nasser's declared aim. He was astonished to hear from the grand master of pan-Arabism that a "war of destruction" against the Jewish state was not possible because it would entail a nuclear holocaust.[31] According to Hassnein Heikal, the open "nuclearist" among Arab politicians, Qaddafi at first believed that Nasser was referring to the fact that the superpowers might be drawn into the regional conflict and escalate it to a nuclear exchange between them. Indeed, this was the danger Moscow and Washington would openly try to avoid in their detente negotiations and agreements of 1972-1973.[32] Yet, even in 1969, Nasser warned the Libyan zealot that the issue was not a nuclear exchange between the superpowers; rather, it was the superpowers' intervention to avoid nuclear holocaust in the Middle East that the Arabs must not ignore, if they embarked on a war of destruction against Israel. "The superpowers would not allow this," quotes Heikal, as if only the superpowers were concerned about the Israeli nuclear option, and only they would prohibit a war of destruction against Israel on that account.

This is the only way to understand the second part of the Nasser-Qaddafi dialogue—as quoted by Heikal under the heading "Buying the Bomb." Qaddafi immediately asked whether the Arabs had an answer to the Israeli challenge. Nasser admitted that he had tried to find such an answer but had failed. Thereupon, concludes Heikal, the Libyan sent his close aide, Abd al-Salam Jallud, to China "to buy a bomb": "Not even a big one . . . a tactical one would do." But Jallud returned empty-handed. Beijing advised him that nuclear weapons were not for sale.

This brings us back to the Allon school's arguments a decade before that an Israeli bomb, when introduced, would immediately be countered by an Arab bomb. The result of this, as Allon wrote in his updated version of *A Curtain of Sand*, would be an unstable "balance of terror." Using American nuclear deterrence theory, Allon argued that the Arabs were irrational, emotional, and competitive among themselves to a degree that would make their nuclear threats much more credible than Israeli threats "due to our humanistic and rational tradition . . . With nuclear weapons the Arabs would carry the day, thanks to Arab irresponsibility."[33]

In the thirty years since Allon's warnings were initially made, the Arab bomb—delivered by the Soviets or the Chinese—has not materialized. The enormous Arab sensitivity on the issue would lead some of them to the long route of buying the whole necessary infrastructure abroad, a variation that we will look into later. However, the Israeli occupation of the West Bank and of sovereign Arab land like the Sinai Desert and the Golan Heights had come about—due, among other things, to Allon's own doctrine of conventional preemption followed by border changes and peace negotiations based upon conventional power and territorial assets—while no peace was yet in sight. This development, justified in terms of avoiding dependence on the nuclear option, complicated the situation in various ways. But Dayan never gave up the nuclear option—in addition to occupied territory and conventional power. Nor did various Arab leaders. It took a Qaddafi, in his simplistic fashion at first, and Iraq, to try to make an independent Arab bomb the cornerstone of Arab strategy for the destruction of Israel, as they sometimes openly described it. In this, they were seemingly in opposition to the experienced Nasser and his successor, Sadat, who realized that such an option was, first, not available and, second, would be highly problematic if it were. But in fact they might have had other reasons to pursue the bomb, in addition to the Israeli challenge. The basic idea could have been that nuclear weapons were the cornerstone of independent Arab power in the nuclear age in general. These weapons could give an Arab power a hegemonic position within the Arab world or in a given area therein, in addition to giving Arabs more leverage vis-à-vis Israel and the U.S. But this could mean that the Arabs must wait until the dream materialized, as if there were no other parties who would respond to the process of acquiring such an option. The Egyptians, instead, had opted for a limited war, with limited Soviet aid, to liberate Arab land.

In striving for a bomb, as in many things, there may have been some important differences between Nasser and his successor, Anwar el-Sadat. Israel was not necessarily the only target in this regard. Another goal was Arab quest for power in the modern age. Nasserism was aimed at Arab unity and transforming the Arabs into a regional, and later a world, power. Yet Egypt proved too weak to pursue this goal, especially in domestic economic terms. It could of course try to push the rich Arabs by invoking the Israeli threat. But if Egypt did finally acquire the bomb, it would have—as I see it—invested an enormous effort in something that might cause its own eradication. Yet the temptation to have it may have persisted, even in Egypt. It may well be that Nasser planned his limited war as an interim solution until Egypt could acquire its own bomb. Afterward, Egypt under Nasser might have pursued several more aggressive strategies, thanks to the balancing effect of the bomb vis-à-vis Israel and its impact on the regional and the international situation. This, at least, is how Nasser and Heikal understood the bomb's role in the rivalry between the superpowers. Soviet nuclear power gave Moscow—and later Soviet clients in the Third World if they repeated the model—more freedom of action, and thus could give Egypt and Egyptian clients a similar degree of maneuverability. Yet, Moscow and Washington never risked a war of destruction between each other. Thus the bomb was needed to achieve less than obliteration, while allowing more political freedom (as Heikal quoted the Russians to this effect) if supported by enough conventional might. The Arabs needed the bomb at least in order to count more—much more—in the Middle East and elsewhere. If the Arabs had no bomb, Israel was indeed indestructible; with the bomb, the Jews may lose their nerve in a proper game of chicken, as I interpret Heikal's nuclear crusade in the 1970s. At any rate, Heikal's advocacy—high risk, confrontational, nationalistic, and pan-Arabist—would have used Israel's own nuclear option to advance its pan-Arab goals and establish the Arabs under Nasser as a regional, and perhaps later a world, power. Therefore, Heikal publicly called upon Egypt to "get, buy, steal" or produce the bomb following the 1973 limited war and the Arab oil coup that allowed, in his view, a common Arab effort in this direction.[34] Sadat's growing rift and final break with Heikal and other Nasserites seems to indicate that this was one of their arguments in a political struggle paid for by Qaddafi or inspired by Heikal, and that Sadat disagreed. His problem was immediate: Israel's control over Egyptian territory in the Sinai, the problem of the West Bank and Gaza, held by a nuclear Israel that might, sooner or later, acquire missiles for its bomb. As long as Israel had no missiles, following de Gaulle's embargo, Sadat could still risk a limited confrontation with it.

Thus Sadat might have reached the conclusion that he did not need an atomic bomb at all for the time being if he resorted to a limited offensive; whereas Heikal would see the offensive and the ensuring oil boycott as a tool to get the bomb. Sadat seemed to concentrate on Israel and was constrained by its nuclear option, anticipating the introduction of Israeli missiles; whereas Heikal, reaching for greater horizons, concentrated on the bomb for its own sake. Both might have agreed that a limited war was possible now, and an independent Arab nuclear power should be sought later. Then Heikal pushed that vision too far and too quickly.

We have this window into Egypt's nuclear dilemmas of the time. It should be-emphasized that Israel's nonpublic nuclear posture allowed the Arabs to discuss the matter without open Israeli threats. The issue for the Arabs seemed to be superpower "collusion." After 1967, the Arab debate became much less public, too; they realized that the nuclear issue had pushed them to premature action. Also, a public Arab debate about a nuclear option might have given Israel's nuclear policy public credibility and pushed them to do something about it prematurely again. In fact, as we shall see, Dayan resorted to "opaque" threats.

Indeed, an open nuclear option and the adoption of a nuclear strategy seemed unnecessary from an Israeli point of view. After the 1967 war, a national consensus emerged that Israel was protected now by "defensible boundaries"—all that was required to fight a successful conventional war. If Israel needed a nuclear option at all, it was to address Moscow's challenges in a nonpublic fashion. The Arabs alone were not a serious threat; Arabs plus Russians were.[35]

This seems to have been General Dayan's view. And Egypt may have thought the same—that it had no chance of succeeding in a war of destruction against Israel without help from Moscow (which it was not likely to get for that purpose). But Egypt did not give up entirely and agree to border changes and peace, which is what the whole Israeli leadership hoped it might eventually do. Instead, Egypt opted for a major, but limited, offensive. It dropped the traditional Arab war aim—the war of destruction—which was Dayan's primary concern. Not that Dayan ruled out the possibility of a limited war entirely; he just seemed to be confident of Israel's ability to handle a scenario of this kind. At the same time, he adopted a policy of avoiding a war of any sort, seeking interim solutions that might circumvent the simple choice between war or comprehensive peace, as interpreted by both sides according to their opposite views and constraints. Dayan even went as far as to try to make concessions to Egypt in order to start a peace process, or at least to avoid war (although these concessions were short of Allon's proposed peace treaty).

Dayan's efforts, however, did not satisfy President Sadat, and they created trouble for him in the cabinet at home. As the 1973 Israeli general elections were quickly approaching, Dayan dropped his efforts, at least for the time being.

Publicly, of course, the Egyptians were obscure about their intentions for a limited war. This switch may well have been a logical continuation of Nasser's frame of mind when he met Qaddafi back in 1969. At that time he suspected that the superpowers would constrain far-reaching Arab military schemes in order to prevent a local nuclear holocaust, perhaps because he understood that NPT signified the beginning of detente. It could be that Sadat understood that if an Arab-initiated war required some kind of a credible Soviet nuclear guarantee such a guarantee and Soviet behavior in general might be affected by detente.

In his Arabic memoirs, Sadat described detente as an almost unmitigated disaster for the Arabs.[36] His arguments remained general, but they describe the very spirit of detente: the official, almost ceremonial, acknowledgement of nuclear parity and the desire to avoid first strike situations. It was this spirit that permitted SALT I and the prohibition of the use of nuclear threats or nuclear war in regard to regional conflicts.[37]

For the Arabs, detente rendered any Soviet nuclear guarantees given to them in the past meaningless, unless they were attacked by Israel—which at the time was a status-quo power. NPT had constrained Soviet nuclear aid to them, at least by implication, and NPT made it illegal for them to obtain their own nuclear option. The nuclear status of Israel, on the other hand, remained unaffected by either detente or NPT. In other words, since Israel's nuclear status had not been challenged by Moscow before the Russians signed their agreement with the Americans, Soviet hands were now tied. They could no longer make nuclear threats vis-à-vis Israel—let alone the United States, in the context of a regional conflict involving an American nuclear client—should the Arabs resort to a "war of destruction" or even to a major offensive against vital Israeli centers. This could lead, as we may interpret Arab fears, to the stabilization of the status quo. Israel was in a better position than the Arabs to influence the superpowers, due to the power of the Israeli lobby in America. Israel was not bound by either detente or NPT as far as its own nuclear behavior was concerned, unless the United States compelled Israel to abide by the rules. Such arguments could have been used by the Arabs in their bitter deliberations with the Soviets in order to get their support for an Arab limited war to liberate the occupied territories, a war which they had to fight against a supposedly nuclear client of the Americans.

It is significant that after 1966 the Egyptians learned to treat nuclear matters cautiously in public (possibly in an attempt not to make Israel's option salient and thus constrain their own freedom of action). Deterrence-theoretical notions regarding "credibility"—when nuclear threats are open and binding, attached to "red lines" and the like—and avoiding "credible" threats by at least publicly ignoring them might have played a conscious role here.[38] Because of the officially conventional nature of the Middle East conflict, and the issue of Israel's borders and occupation of Arab land in 1967, the problem of what Israel's "red lines" were was left rather open. But one couldn't totally ignore Israel's nuclear option. According to Heikal, the Soviets had "guaranteed" the Aswan High Dam, and by implication the very heart of Egypt, against Israeli nuclear attacks.[39]

This guarantee, of course, was nonpublic. And one could certainly doubt its value—not only because of the spirit of detente but also because of the very nature of such "guarantees." Would the Soviets be ready to use nuclear weapons against Israel once Egypt was almost destroyed? And what difference would it make to the Egyptians at that point? What power did the Egyptians have to make the Soviets implement their guarantees? As a deterrent, such a guarantee was literally "ambiguous"—not binding publicly and questionably valid according to the rules of detente. And, indeed, from the beginning of the detente negotiations the Soviets refused to supply Egypt with the equipment they needed to storm the Suez Canal or to deliver sufficient counter-measures to prevent Israel from bombing the heart of Egypt. Only in 1973 did the Soviet Union first supply Egypt with modern, if conventional, short-range missiles.

Detente seemed to have made Soviet nuclear threats against Israel impossible. The key to Israel's behavior, if there was one, was held by the United States—not Moscow, the patron of the Arabs—and Washington was in Israel's hands. Such an analysis permitted the strategy Sadat used to get out of this net: first, he put growing pressure on the Russians to supply Egypt with offensive conventional equipment, which indeed started to flow in early 1973; second, he fought, and he set to work to find some common ground with the Americans.[40]

These developments followed Sadat's decision in the summer of 1972 to end the Soviet military presence in Egypt.[41] Whereas Nasser and others like him might have believed that a growing Soviet presence on Egyptian soil constrained Israel's freedom of action, Sadat realized during the detente negotiations that Soviet military presence in Egypt constrained his own freedom of action more, and he asked the Soviets to leave. In statements relating to his ongoing talks with President Nixon, Leonid Brezhnev had always stressed his loyalty to the Arab cause. Once released of direct responsibility to Washington for Egypt's behavior, Moscow felt free to supply Egypt with the necessary equipment for a limited war.

It is not clear what Brezhnev's ultimate motives were. It could simply have been that the detente agreements were formulated in such a way that he could break them in spirit while still maintaining the letter of the law. On the other hand, he could have been expressing his annoyance at the Jackson-Vanik Amendment, which linked American aid and commercial agreements to the free immigration of Soviet Jews.[42] It is likely that he was under extreme pressure from the Third World and the Chinese to do something for the Arabs in order to avoid charges of a superpower "collusion" at the expense of the "southern world." And finally, he might have wanted to demonstrate that Kissinger's advertisement of detente at the time was not the real thing, as far as Soviet ties to the Third World were concerned.

The Israelis and the Americans interpreted the effects of the Soviet departure from Egypt wrongly; they welcomed it as a major shift in Egypt's military disfavor. Both were busy with their own domestic affairs when Egypt and Syria struck.

From this we can learn, however, that superpower "collusion"—
and much less than that, the difficult detente negotiations and agreements of the early 1970s—was bound to make Arab leaders feel
deserted or rather weakened. In their quest for autonomous power,
Arab leaders since President Nasser saw in the superpower rivalry a
source of Arab power—at least in the interim period, before Arabs
could create their own autonomous power in the nuclear age. The
involvement of a nuclear superpower on their side seemed to the Arabs
to be a source of power for them. (Soviet involvement had transformed
the 1956 Suez campaign against Nasser into a debacle—even the United
States had contributed the decisive blow against the French-British-
Israeli scheme.) Detente seemed to endanger this strategic advantage,
from an Arab point of view. And *perestroika* and the ensuing nuclear
arms control negotiations would be perceived by radical Arabs such
as Saddam Hussein and Muammar Qaddafi to be yet another reason to
seek independent Arab, including nuclear, power. In a way, the Suez
campaign, which strengthened Israel's decision to seek an autonomous
nuclear power, might have created in Arab eyes a sense of security.
This sense of security was now rapidly diminishing due to yet another,
but different by nature, superpower "collusion."

But the old Nasserite, pan-Arab approach was not endorsed by
Anwar el-Sadat. He carefully chose the middle of the road.

CHAPTER SEVEN

The Walls of Jericho

Israel's "defensible boundaries" proved to be the suitable ground for a conventional Arab attack. While conventional preemption remained the official defense doctrine, the "defensible boundaries" were supposed to have rendered it unnecessary. But according to several non-Israeli and Israeli sources, nonpublic nuclear threats were radiating from General Dayan.[1] Based on Dayan's previous behavior, according to Evron,[2] and Dayan's own post-1973 public statements, the defense minister seemed—between summer 1972 and the Yom Kippur War—to be the major supporter of the nuclear option among Israel's decision makers. According to his behavior, we could say that he believed that Israel's "ambiguous" nuclear options (in the sense that the components of a full-fledged nuclear arsenal, including missiles, were not fully in place) vis-à-vis the Arabs had lacked credibility because of Arab-Soviet cooperation and whatever nuclear guarantees had been given the Arabs by the Soviets. Therefore, when Egypt forced the Soviets out of the country in summer 1972 and such guarantees were decidedly weakened, Israel's implied nuclear options would finally gain credibility. (It had been six years since the Arabs first discussed Israel's implied nuclear option at their 1966 summit.)

If this was Dayan's view of the Egyptian-Soviet rift of 1972, it explains his confident prediction that there would be "no war in the next decade."[3] We have, of course, no further public statement to prove this, but Dayan's nuclear prism might have been fixed on an Arab war of destruction supported by the Soviets. His behavior at the time and later supports this speculation, since, otherwise, he was rather conventional (although he did believe that "no war"—i.e., no general offensive without Soviet aid to the Arabs—would only preserve the status quo for the time being and lead to political negotiations, not necessarily in Israel's favor, under American auspices, after the 1973 Israeli general elections were over). He assumed that once the Arabs realized that the United States held the trump cards for a political process, Washington would side more with them and less with his territorial and political demands. Thus he anticipated a political battle, rather than a war.

His personal rivals and political enemies, Allon and Galili, might have agreed with this, even if they were less flexible than he was in regard to territorial concessions to Egypt along the canal (negotiated within the framework of an interim Israeli-Egyptian agreement). They would not allow any further use of the nuclear option for political or strategic gains, fearing the Russians—and the Americans. When Sadat seemed to have brought Soviet-Egyptian cooperation to a major crisis, both the Americans and the Israeli decision makers—always preoccupied with a Soviet-supported major war that might endanger Israel's very survival—became more confident that no war at all was in the offing. The only Arab leader who publicly went along with this reasoning was Muammar Qaddafi, who pursued an Arab counterbomb as the precondition to any war. Primarily he alone—and to some extent the Iraqis—was devoted to such a war. And he feared that even a limited Arab offensive could not be launched against a supposedly nuclear Israel without an Arab bomb—or at least he said so, to get more support for his bomb procurement.[4]

To Israelis, a war of destruction meant an all-out, simultaneous Arab offensive from all sides, aimed at Israel's very heart. In October 1973, the Arabs attacked simultaneously from two sides, but not from the third and most vulnerable side: the Jordan Valley and the West Bank. But they did not penetrate deeply into Israeli-occupied territory. The Egyptians crossed the Suez Canal, overwhelmed the regular Israeli tank division which protected it, and then dug in within close range of their own artillery batteries and missile bases on their side of the canal. This bridgehead was made in anticipation of an Israeli counteroffensive, which, however, had to wait until armored reserves were called up and sent to the front. In the interval—at least twenty-four hours—the Egyptian army could have advanced further, still within the range of their SAMs, toward the Israeli sectorial headquarters, the ammunition and supply depots, and the strategic passes leading toward the depths of the Sinai. They could have tried to intercept the Israeli armored reserves on their way to the front; and they had the opportunity to launch aerial attacks against Israeli military targets beyond the immediate battle zone, especially into Israel's heart.

But they did almost none of this—except launching one subsonic air-to-ground KELT missile from a bomber over the Mediterranean in the general direction of Tel Aviv. And even this missile was duly, and not unexpectedly, intercepted by the Israeli Air Force and shot down over the sea.[5] This incident, which took place early upon opening hostilities, was isolated, and could be interpreted as a signal to Israel not to repeat the in-depth bombing of Egypt that had taken place during the canal war.

Syrian behavior was even more puzzling. The Syrians advanced across the occupied Golan Heights toward the 1949 armistice demarcation line (which was in fact the historical boundary of British Palestine) in the central and southern sectors of the heights. The whole distance was rather short, due to the proximity of the 1967 cease-fire line to the boundary. The main body of the Syrian attacking force remained well within the heights, and their advanced tanks were ordered to stop when they reached the vicinity of the international boundary. With regard to Syrian behavior, Charles Wakebridge raised several interesting points in his article "The Syrian Side of the Hill":

> The [Syrian] plan called for the bombing of [the main bridge leading to the heights from Israel proper] . . . to be immediately followed by insertion of commandos by helicopter to deny [this supply and reinforcement line] from the Israelis. General [Mustafa] Tlass [the Syrian Chief of Staff, in an interview with Wakebridge] admitted this omission, but would not discuss it except to say that he considered the Jordan River [i.e., the international boundary] to be the natural Syrian boundary. An initial seizure of the bridge would have severely hampered Israeli reinforcement tanks, vehicles and guns . . .
>
> One of the main unanswered questions of the war was why the Syrians halted at 1700 on the 7th, when some of their thrusts might well have succeeded in reaching the . . . River. There was little in the way of Israeli defense to stop them . . . Tlass . . . admitted such an order . . . hesitated, and said that "the time has not yet come to discuss the reasons for it."[6]

Israel was always fearful of the possibility that Syria and Egypt, and perhaps other Arab nations that would join them sooner or later, would present it with two other types of belligerency in addition to a war of destruction: a "war of attrition" and an "escalating limited war." The Israelis perceived the Arabs as nations that could easily be drawn into affairs against their original intentions. They feared that a successful but limited Arab offensive could escalate wildly due to Arab "emotionalism" and competition between the various members of the Arab coalition. A "limited war" could thus entail a "war of destruction" if not quickly stopped.

If, on the other hand, a "limited war" did, by chance, remain contained, it could entail a dangerous "war of attrition": a more or less static war, anchored in a front that is secured on both flanks. This type of offensive does not allow outflanking or penetration of the enemy's front and "fanning out" behind his line, which is what Israel's armored doctrine expects the IDF to do to win a war quickly. Such a war would assume the character of infantry clashes and artillery exchanges, in which the Arabs were numerically superior and could sustain heavier losses. Therefore, Israel could not allow the Arabs to start wars of attrition at will. Such wars would end with the Arabs achieving clear-cut gains on the ground, by slowly bleeding Israel to death. Therefore, Israel had to win all wars as quickly as possible.

The October 1973 surprise attack seemed to Dayan to be a candidate for both these types of offensives. Once he saw that the Egyptians, who had crossed the canal successfully, had not fanned out (as they should have if they planned an in-depth penetration) but instead adopted a defensive formation, he realized that their intention was a limited war at first.[7] They defeated a hasty Israeli counteroffensive, but allowed the main bulk of the Israeli army, the armored reserves, to reach the battle zone without serious interference. The problem at the canal was that there was a front whose flanks were anchored on the Mediterranean on one side and the Great Bitter Lake on the other. This looked set up to become a tremendous, very costly, war of attrition.[8] Later, after wearing out the Israeli army, the Egyptians could advance and penetrate into the depths of the Sinai. But a more immediate problem for Dayan was the Syrian front, which gave the impression of becoming an escalating limited war.[9]

Because of Arab open threats and public war aims, these real options were confused in the mind of the Israeli public with an all-out war of destruction. After a while, the limited character of the Arab offensive became clear to those who were able to follow it, especially Dayan. However, Menachem Begin, the leader of the nationalist opposition, accused the Labor coalition of a major "security blunder" that endangered Israel's very existence. Most Israelis agreed, and many of them would later help Begin win power on these and other false assumptions. Since Labor, and the Americans, hid the main reason for the Arabs' confining themselves to a limited war, they should not have been surprised that politics were later shaped by the perceptions of the war rather than the realities.[10]

These realities were quite blurred, it is true. Having caught the IDF off guard, the Syrians were able to fan out in the relatively narrow Golan Heights before the IDF's reserves were mobilized and thrown into the battle; yet strange as it was, Assad's tanks stopped wherever they came close to the international boundary.

One more point in Wakebridge's observations should be emphasized: The Syrians successfully used helicopter-mounted commandos to capture the Israeli intelligence-gathering outpost on Mount Hermon. The same tool could have been used to block both bridges leading to the heights, and thereby create confusion in the assembly areas of the Israeli reserve units. This never happened, but a short-range FROG missile was fired at an Israeli air base within Israel's pre-1967 heart, missed, and hit a nearby civilian target. In line with the Egyptian KELT missile firing, the Syrians aimed again at the base, missed again, and hit another civilian target; informed of their misses by the Israeli media, they then hit the residential area in the base itself. Israel mounted a series of major—and costly—air attacks against Syrian civilian and military targets (oil depots, electricity plants, military headquarters), with no effect on the conduct of the war.

The heights, captured in 1967 after some hesitation on Dayan's part, presented to the Syrians a legitimate and secure conventional war zone, at least in their own eyes, once Assad had replaced the doctrinaire Ba'ath regime that had contributed to Syria's defeat in 1967. He was Minister of Defense under this regime and had a seemingly coordinated war scheme with Sadat now. Relatively free of foreign concepts of "guerrilla warfare in the nuclear age" imported from Vietnam and Algeria, Assad was ready to risk a conventional offensive, provided it was limited and would not trigger, or justify, an Israeli nuclear response, which the Arabs had been deliberating since the late 1960s. Thus his forces were ordered to refrain from cutting even the few bridges leading from Israel to the heights, nor did they fan out into Israeli territory proper. Yet when the Israeli reserves arrived and started to push them back in the most endangered sectors of the occupied Golan front, the Syrians concentrated their offensive effort on the other sector, which had held successfully until then. But, now, no Israeli reserves were available to come to that sector's aid. Had the Syrians succeeded in breaking through the northern sector, they could have enveloped the others, with no strategic reserves left to stop them from invading Israel itself.

This threat escalated to a momentous crisis on October 8, 1973, when Dayan was reported to have issued an order, with Mrs. Meir's consent, to deploy Israeli nuclear missiles. The first allegation to this effect was published in *Time* magazine on April 12, 1976. In his book

Living by the Sword, American writer Stephen Green quotes William B. Quandt, the NSC's Middle East expert at the time. Green makes it seem that the Pentagon's METG (Middle East Task Group) was very worried about Dayan's mental condition in the early stages of the war. The CIA's representative in that group is quoted as having said that "Dayan went out of his mind." Green then cites Quandt to the effect that U.S. Intelligence learned from intercepted electronic communications that Israel was preparing to arm Jericho missiles should the Egyptians force the passes leading to Sinai. Green quotes the U.S. Air Attaché dispatch from Tel Aviv on March 3, 1965, regarding the Jericho testing on Ile de Levant; this testing had made the missile a top intelligence target for the Americans, who are reported to have detected at least one launching test since, but failed to gather enough information about missile quantities and storing places.[11]

According to military analyst Amir Oren of *Davar*, Green's 1988 book is biased and obscure as far as many of his sources are concerned. His treatment of the missile complex, of U.S. policy toward Israel, of French-Israeli relations, and of the Israeli domestic scene described in an earlier book is partially based on primary sources from the LBJ Library already mentioned here, censored and sanitized though they may be.[12] But Green has been highly selective, omitting sources that might cast a shadow on Arab behavior and dismissing arguments regarding Arab ideology and actual behavior in favor of his thesis concerning the militancy of Israel. Many other primary and secondary sources, which were available before his book was published, are missing, and as a result, the overall picture he offers is rather simplistic.

According to William B. Quandt, as cited by Green in *Living by the Sword*, the Nixon Administration was more worried about Israel's behavior at first, because it evaluated Arab goals as limited, and did not expect vital Israeli interests to be threatened.[13] In a conversation I had with Dr. Quandt in 1979, Quandt said that Sadat signalled to Kissinger on the third day of the war that he wanted negotiations toward a settlement: "This is a statesman, Kissinger is quoted as having said, who understands that diplomacy is the other side of the battlefield." According to Quandt, Sadat planned a limited war, probably the last before the final introduction of nuclear weapons to the area, or rather of missiles armed with nuclear warheads.[14] Since there were no means to intercept these missiles—the Soviets had given him means to intercept aircraft only—they must have been of great concern to him.

This leaves wide open the question of whether Israel indeed possessed missiles at the time. Or did Israel only possess aircraft, which were certainly not credible enough to prevent a limited war? Thus the issue of the "means" necessary to make nuclear threats credible seems to have remained of the utmost importance since 1967, when Israel was not perceived to have them at all. Another question remains wide open: Was superpower nuclear strategy (anchored in the deterrence-technical thinking of the Nitze school inspired by Wohlstetter and Kahn) adopted by the superpowers' clients, complicating a basic situation—that of the acceptance of the atomic bomb *from the beginning* of the process as a reason to make peace. In other words, nuclear "credibility" required means, which Israel did not possess (yet), and therefore, the high-level conflict could be maintained and prolonged the way it was maintained between the superpowers, until Gorbachev acknowledged its futility—thanks, among other things, to "Star Wars."

In my conversation with him, Quandt did not venture into the missile issue, which must be borne in mind as a major problem or challenge to Israel. But he said that Sadat indeed recognized the dangers inherent in an overall offensive, even a limited one, beyond the Sinai passes because of the anticipated Israeli nuclear response. "It is true," Quandt said in response to my assumption, "that the [Israeli] nuclear option has dictated his calculations ever since, and was the source of his controversy with Qaddafi." And yet, Sadat's early contacts with Kissinger, as described above by Quandt and later by McGeorge Bundy,[15] could have been a calculated move in the nuclear context. When he told the Americans that his war was limited, he, in fact, told them that Israel should be restrained in this regard. He thus did not trust Soviet guarantees or equipment alone. At the same time, it should not simply be taken for granted that Sadat's behavior meant that Egypt gave up its own nuclear ambitions for a more remote future. It is possible that Sadat was more realistic. He may have seen that the Israeli nuclear option had actual value in terms of Israel's very survival but that an Egyptian nuclear option would inherently endanger Egypt's very survival. But his actions, or the actions of any Egyptian government, are the sole judge of their intentions—if opacity permits a clear analysis of such actions.

Dayan's behavior vis-à-vis the Syrians, as reported by *Time* magazine in 1976, could be perceived as a case of actual opaque nuclear threats during a limited, conventional war. It does not seem to have been a case of either insanity or panic, but rather a logical continuation of his military thinking in which nuclear options were given some deterrent role against Arabs backed by the Soviets. Once the Arabs had proved themselves to be formidable foes using Soviet supplies even though Soviet direct involvement was over, he alerted his nuclear "basement" without admitting it in public. He thereby communicated to the Syrians—and to the superpowers—his anxiety about an escalating limited war, should the Syrians break through the front and fan out into Israel.

On the face of it, the Syrians were not given a chance to fan out, because the northern Golan sector held and managed to defeat the Syrian onslaught. The crisis was over, but not before President Nixon had warned Arab ambassadors in Washington not to cross Israel's international boundaries.[16] This seems to indicate that the administration was very concerned with Israel's response to an Arab violation of its pre-1967 boundaries, and possibly of its presence in the West Bank as well.

Nixon reportedly had previously given Israel some assurances with regard to its boundaries. He did this to make Israel agree to his new diplomatic initiatives (following the failure of his 1970 initiative), and possibly also to prevent Israel from "going nuclear" publicly. Such assurances entailed occupied Arab territory, too, and not just the pre-1967 boundaries. Possibly without admitting it, the Arabs honored Nixon's pledge to the Israelis, by limiting their offensive to the margins of the occupied territory—at least in terms of their military behavior, though not in terms of their politics and diplomacy.

According to Simcha Dinitz, a former Israeli ambassador in Washington, Mrs. Meir reached an agreement with the United States in 1971 which was closer to the Israeli quest for "secure boundaries," including occupied territory, and which entailed American recognition of Israel's nuclear potential. This meant the United States had dropped its demand that Israel should return to the pre-1967 lines "with small corrections," as contained in the 1969 Rogers plan (named after Secretary of State William P. Rogers). We have no documentation to substantiate this far-reaching statement Dinitz made to me on May 15, 1982; but the spirit of such an "understanding" was implied in a published source, Dan Margalit's *Message from the White House.*[17] As described by the ambassador, this arrangement gave Kissinger and Nixon "a place of honor in Jewish history." However, such arrangements are always open to new interpretations in changing situations, and the 1973 war might indeed have created such a new situation.

Moreover, the new situation could have inflamed the old, hidden debate in regard to the value of territory and conventional power vis-à-vis the nuclear option. Dayan could be blamed—in public—for carrying the ministerial responsibility for the initial setbacks and the many casualties suffered by the IDF in the October 1973 war.

Yigal Allon, Dayan's old enemy, whispered loudly behind the scenes (including in a conversation with me in 1976) that the minister of defense had indeed intended *to use nuclear weapons against Syria.* I asked

Dayan directly about it, and the former minister, whose public career was ruined by the initial "blunder" of the surprise attack on Yom Kippur 1973, absolutely denied that he had issued any such orders. His denial was strengthened by an interview given by Israel Galili, Allon's own political ally.[18] The issue was publicly raised by the author in the Israeli press in 1981, as I (and others) had been told by Allon about Dayan's alleged intention to use the bomb against Damascus in 1973. Mr. Galili volunteered to testify before a parliamentary committee of inquiry in this connection. Peres, at the time chairman of the Labor Party, probably had the issue "killed" during the 1981 election campaign (in which I was a candidate for the Knesset on Dayan's parliamentary ticket). Peres made an Israeli journalist, his biographer Matti Golan, publicly dismiss the issue in *Ha'aretz*. His claim was that it was an irrelevant episode related to the early stages of the 1973 war, when the cabinet did not know what the Egyptian war aims were and thus considered all kinds of options.

A similar description of the 1973 Israeli nuclear alert was published by Golan's colleague Dan Margalit in October 1990. Margalit compared the 1973 alert to Israel's dilemmas regarding the recent Iraqi threat: "An episode was published [*Time*'s version is dropped here altogether]—which is now 17 years old—that during the Yom Kippur War Israel had deployed nuclear missiles and targeted them against Syria. But even if this happened [here is the opaque formulation] they were not planned, but were an expression of panic. This is not the situation now."[19] My main point when I published Allon's accusations against Dayan in 1981 was that Allon had used the alleged nuclear threats of 1973 for domestic political purposes, to portray Dayan as a nuclear "madman." Such a reputation cast a shadow on the strategic, foreign-political context of Dayan's 1981 independent election campaign as well. Dayan endorsed a political plank that, compared with Begin's, was flexible in terms of the future of the West Bank—and in which nuclear deterrence played a role, as we shall see. Peres, whose Labor Alignment felt threatened by Dayan's party during the election, was also interested in cooperating with the Allon group, especially with its new leader, General Rabin, who had succeeded the late Allon shortly before.[20]

At any rate, the walls of Jericho did not fall in 1973. They were not even close to falling, because the Arabs were rather careful. They planned a limited war on the margins of the occupied territory, specifically not aimed at Israel's heartland and pre-1967 boundaries, in order to accomplish limited ends through a growing attrition and superpower intervention in their favor. McGeorge Bundy puts it this way: "The statesman here was Anwar Sadat, who had no nuclear weapons and no desire to test anyone to the point of nuclear danger. The war he was fighting was a war for the pride of Egypt, not for the extinction of Israel."[21] Bundy was ready to admit this in his book written fifteen years after the fact; on the next page he returned to criticizing all U.S. administrations for having done nothing about Israel's nuclear program after Kennedy—in line with his own attempts to curtail it—because "any American president must consider the domestic political cost of any choice that American friends of Israel will oppose" (as if Arab freedom of action, if not constrained by the Israeli nuclear option, was not the master variable here).

In the meantime, returning to the 1973 war on the ground, a war of attrition did occur, which Israel was only able to end several weeks later following a Soviet-American cease-fire agreement—and in defiance of the cease-fire's territorial clauses.[22] This development was preceded by an American airlift of military equipment to Israel. At this time, Meir reportedly used the nuclear option nonpublicly again, in anxiety over the IDF's belief that the rate of attrition of its own equipment exceeded that of the Arabs, who had received seaborne and airlifted supplies from the Soviets.[23] Seemingly in response to the American airlift, the Arabs proclaimed an oil embargo, which gave a strong political-economic slant to the struggle on the ground. (In reality, the oil embargo had been planned long before.) Under these circumstances, Kissinger negotiated a cease-fire in Moscow, which went into effect on October 22. The Russians were fully aware of the danger to the Egyptian army following the canal crossing operation the Israelis had begun a week before. The Israelis pressed farther and encircled the Third Egyptian Army Corps in the southern canal sector. This prompted Soviet threats of unilateral intervention, and Washington pressed the Israelis to lift the siege they had finally been able to lay around the southern half of the canal front. Moscow proposed joint American-Soviet intervention to reestablish the cease-fire lines, and threatened unilateral intervention if Washington refused.[24] At about that time, a Soviet vessel was detected on its way to Alexandria, Egypt, carrying "radioactive cargo."[25] Washington's reply to Brezhnev's threats was a worldwide nuclear alert.

DEFCON III (Defense Condition III) was a clear signal to the Soviets that they had violated detente,[26] even though they might have thought themselves entitled to use nuclear signals against Israel. They had already threatened to intervene on the ground against a nuclear power that might feel unable to respond conventionally to the combined Soviet-Egyptian challenge. Now that Israel had violated the cease-fire agreement sponsored by the superpowers, Moscow might have decided to respond with a "visible" nuclear presence on the ground. Due to the nonpublic nature of these threats, the "Soviet nuclear vessel"—which reportedly never unloaded its cargo at Alexandria[27]—became in some Israeli eyes an American bluff to force the IDF to lift its siege around the Third Egyptian Army Corps and thereby portray the United States to Egypt as the savior of the Egyptian Army.[28] In fact, Bundy's version, in which he quotes Kissinger, underlines U.S. obligations not only to the Soviets but to the Arabs in regard to the cease-fire, which was violated by the "Israeli provocation."[29] Accordingly, Kissinger saw a chance to deliver Israeli occupied goods, to begin with, to "moderate" Arabs, in order to replace the Soviets as their patron, while detente was basically maintained. This could well be an ex post facto description of a situation that at first seemed more alarming, at least until Sadat retreated from inviting the Soviets. And we can guess that he did this in return for some—still unpublished—American promises regarding his besieged troops, promises given to the Russians following the alert,[30] and probably to Sadat himself.

CHAPTER EIGHT

Sadat's Peace

The next logical step in Sadat's strategy would have been to accept and gain support from America—the superpower that had the most influence on Israel's behavior. Egypt had to work closely with Washington, despite the influence of the Jewish lobby in America, to avoid the limitations of the previous game—pushing the United States toward the Arabs via Moscow—as Nasser had tried to play it. In fact, Sadat recognized Egypt's failure in trying to push both superpowers toward meeting far-reaching Arab expectations, even if he seemed to be the political victor following the 1973 war. But, the fact remained: He had been able to maneuver to a limited degree between Moscow and Washington—and Israel had paid the price. The IDF had been prevented from finishing off the Third Egyptian Army Corps because of combined Soviet-American pressure, in which Washington held the trump card since it could deter the Russians and force Israel's hand. But Israel was still very much alive and even present on Egyptian soil proper.

In a world suddenly turned against Israel following the Yom Kippur War and the Arab oil squeeze, Israel was dependent on American conventional aid and political support. And Washington held the keys to Israel's behavior in other spheres as well. If Israel was to receive conventional military and financial aid to make good its Yom Kippur losses, and try to cope with Arab pressure in the U.N. and elsewhere, it would have to adjust to American demands. And these demands, in turn, could be conditioned by Egyptian maneuvers in cooperation with Saudi Arabia. Moreover, Washington could well be an important, if not the only, source of such aid to Egypt itself, aid that was free of the preconditions set by radical Arabs and other wealthier Arabs, such as the cautious Saudis, who had tried to maintain good relations with all Arabs, including radicals. Thus this game was far from being simple. Israel's nuclear option was its independent trump card, but it was not publicly recognized as such by Washington. True, it had proved to be irrelevant in the recent war during which the United States had intervened to save Sadat's Third Egyptian Army Corps, but this was the result of complex developments in which Russian involvement had proved very useful but also rather limited. Israel's own reliance on alleged conventional superiority and "defensible borders" had lured the country into a conventional-political trap.

By now, no one could promise Sadat that Israel would not be provoked to implement its nuclear option in the future should the Arabs try to destroy Israel or make it panic due to miscalculation. At least the Americans had more control over Israel's actions than anyone else. Soviet hands with regard to nuclear aid had been officially tied since detente and NPT. Even when the Soviets sent the "nuclear vessel" to Alexandria in violation of the spirit of detente, they did it when *their* agreement *with Washington* seemed to have been broken by Israel. When they were confronted with the worldwide nuclear alert—which might have been the reason for the vessel's nuclear cargo confinement to Alexandria Harbor—they withdrew several weeks later, in conjunction with the American pressure on Israel to partially lift the siege on the Egyptian troops. At least this how I—and probably also the Egyptians at the time—interpret Soviet behavior in this regard.

Of course, the issue was much more complicated, due to official and traditional Arab war aims. The Soviets never promised any aid—let alone nuclear aid—for an Arab-initiated war to *destroy* Israel. It proved difficult enough to obtain limited Soviet aid to fuel a "limited Arab war." Official Arab policy regarding a "war of destruction" had thus proved self-defeating. It became exactly that, something no one—outside the Arab world—would support. And yet Israel could either use that threat or accept it as genuine, in a way that would further justify efforts to develop, refine, and deploy the only weapon that could inflict death blows on the Arab nation and upon Egypt as its most dangerous adversary (in Israeli eyes and due to Egypt's self-proclamations). In fact, by administering a military-political blow upon Israel's conventional-territorial defense doctrine, the Arabs should not have been surprised when in 1974 (as Bundy tells us) Israeli president Efraim Katzir told Western journalists that "his country would be able to use nuclear weapons if it had to: 'Should we have need of such weapons, we could have them' . . . I agree with Bertrand Goldschmidt, who reads the statement of President Katzir as 'officially admitting that his country had the capacity to produce nuclear bombs, which no one doubted.'"[1]

The presidency in the Israeli parliamentary democracy is mostly a ceremonial office; but before he became president, Professor Katzir had been a major Israeli natural scientist. And his late brother, Aharon, had been a member of the Israeli Atomic Energy Commission. President Katzir was personally close to General Dayan, still a defense minister in 1974. Bundy, however, did not need Katzir's explanation, or that of what he refers to as "Israeli leaders [who] have said enough to make it clear that there is a major nuclear weapon program in Israel."[2] Bundy did not even need a CIA report made in 1974 which, according to him, confirmed that "Israel has already produced nuclear weapons."[3] What is important in Bundy's statements is the role of the Yom Kippur War, and the ensuing statement made by Professor Katzir—and by General Dayan after he was forced to resign as minister of defense later in 1974.[4] "One way or another [writes Bundy] . . . it does appear that the 1973 war, with its tumultuous aftermath, drew American attention to the Israeli nuclear program. It was only a year later that the CIA reached its firm conclusion that Israeli weapons existed, and it is reasonable to assume that this assessment responded to renewed interest among senior members of the administration. What is most remarkable about the CIA's conclusion, however, is that the United States does not appear to have acted on it."[5] We do not know whether things were really that simple. But how could the administration (which during Bundy's own time had tried arms control negotiations between Arab and Jew and failed) demand unilateral disarmament from Israel now? The Arabs were still bound to commitments implying or demanding the destruction of Israel—and in 1973 they had succeeded at first in bleeding the country quite seriously.

From an Arab point of view, the Soviets proved to be a difficult patron when it came to nuclear aid. Moreover, Soviet military aid to the Arabs was bound to prompt more American aid to Israel (even though Israel held occupied Arab territory). This was the logic of the superpower rivalry. The Arabs could try to assume a more conciliatory approach to Israel, and or at least a less friendly one toward Moscow, but this last measure would not be enough. Thus, the problem of Israel's very existence could not be solved, or at least not before the Arabs had their own bomb, if at all.

The 1973 war plus the ensuing oil crisis proved that the Arabs could not be ignored simply due to detente. Maybe, if enough American support could be mobilized, Israel could be pushed back to the 1967 lines. And finally, if the Arabs worked cleverly together with the United States, Israel could be left alone as a small, in fact meaningless, foreign enclave on Arab soil. The amount of risk to Egypt itself—with its peculiar concentration of population along the narrow strips of the Nile and in the delta, its dependence on the Aswan High Dam, and the desert which separated it from Israel—would be extremely high if Israel was destroyed. None of this was new. But if Heikal's cry to "get, buy or steal" the bomb, which he published in *Al-Aharam* immediately after the 1973 war, was heeded, Egypt would only gain a tool that could virtually lead to its destruction.

This did reflect, however, a new self-confidence and the old Nasserite quest for an independent, unified Arab power among powers, led by Egypt and free as far as possible from dependence on the superpowers. It should have given the Arabs the tool to play big games, and perhaps allow conventional war or brinkmanship games against Israel, breaking its spirit and will to exist under such circumstances. This might be attractive to pan-Arab hawks, and to Egyptian, Iraqi, or Libyan contenders for hegemony, and might combine their subjective rationality with low political motives such as personal, group, and national power. However, Israel's dependence on Washington made the United States the key to the recovery of the Sinai, the most pressing of Egyptian goals. The Americans could be helpful, if only Cairo played its cards carefully by lowering the level of the conflict and enhancing other Arab goals. And so, having saved his nation's honor on the battlefield, Sadat turned, first slowly and then abruptly, away from the Russians.

Henry Kissinger now stopped working on detente in order to extinguish fires in the Middle East, which stemmed, among other things, from detente. As Israel's "master" (as the Arabs saw him), he could neutralize the issue of the Israeli nuclear option by setting a new agenda. This, in fact, had been in General Dayan's mind since the early 1970s: the exchange of Egyptian political concessions to Israel for Israeli territorial concessions in the Sinai. Also, Kissinger could offer both Israel and Egypt American aid. These are plausible explanations for the peace process that took place beginning with the Geneva Conference of December 21, 1973.[6] Not everyone in the Arab world, however, was happy with the new agenda. And not everyone accepted Sadat's lower, pragmatic goals, or was ready to forgo the political game of opposing him and his realpolitik for domestic and inter-Arab purposes. Sadat's strategy meant virtually giving up Arab dreams for a great power status. His goals also meant American orientation—which he needed to feed his people, but Iraq or Syria did not necessarily need.

Two pieces of evidence in this puzzle that were indirect, partly because no one talked openly about the nuclear aspect, were Heikal's public cry for an Arab bomb published in *Al-Aharam* in November 1973 and the Iraqis' decision to start their own nuclear program (in the making even before the 1973 war).[7] Both can be interpreted as radical approaches to the Israeli question, the quest for Arab power in a world now dependent on Arab oil, and competition for leadership among the Arabs. Iran, however, might have been the main target.

Heikal and similar "nuclearists" in the Arab world argued in somewhat contradictory terms in favor of the bomb and Arab unification related to it.[8] His defensive argument—drawn directly from Schelling[9] and Gallois—painted Israel as a totally irrational creature that could not be trusted as a partner to any stable "balance of terror." In Heikal's eyes, this was due to Israel's very nature and to its two neurotic complexes: the "Massada complex" and the "Warsaw Ghetto complex." Having thus attributed enormous credibility to Israel's nuclear options, Heikal resorted to the old remedy, an Arab bomb that required Arab unification—that is, the financing of such an endeavor by the rich Arabs. He did not explain to his readers how an Arab bomb would neutralize the bomb held by the "mad" Israelis; rather, according to Heikal's reasoning, the Israelis would commit suicide as their brethren had done in Warsaw. But he didn't explain how that would help the Arabs, since this time the Jews had at their disposal, in his view, the only weapon that could inflict an unmitigated disaster on their enemies. Unless, of course, the Arabs used their bomb first in a preemptive strike as, indeed, Allon was expecting them to.

The only plausible strategy that Heikal might have had in mind involved a series of limited wars fought between Arab and Jew, where the nuclear factor would be neutralized thanks to its presence on both sides. This, as we have argued earlier, was a high-risk proposition that might have helped drive Nasser to forgo nuclear weapons altogether—or to seek the bomb for other purposes which would give him more political leeway. Thus, Heikal might have toyed with Nasser's dream of transforming the Arabs into the fourth superpower, a plan that required the bomb as a matter of course. Yet if this was his strategy, it was a long-term one that could involve Egypt immediately in unforeseeable trouble with a hostile, nuclear Israel, still holding on to the Sinai. This strategy would also require, eventually, good relations with the West, the only supplier of nuclear technology.

Heikal also made sure to mention Egypt's special destiny and added his view that the heart of the Arab-Israeli conflict was *not* the Palestinian issue or the recovery of occupied Arab land, but Egypt's hegemonic role in the Arab world, which was blocked by Israel's pre-1967 control over the Negev Desert and by its very existence. Sadat's allies in the Arab world, mainly Saudi Arabia, did not like this brand of old Nasserite hegemony. The Israelis, obviously, didn't either.

Such arguments led to Heikal's downfall in Sadat's Egypt, indicating that the new Egyptian president adopted a rather different strategy. In public, he dismissed the Israeli nuclear option as nonexistent or as something Egypt would be able to deal with. Sadat's interview with *Al-Ziad* in Beirut on January 12, 1976, is illuminating here:

> Question: It is absolutely clear now that Israel has more than ten nuclear bombs. Do you think she might use [them] if the political [negotiations] failed and a decisive war broke out? . . .
>
> Sadat: No doubt Israel would use such propaganda aimed at spreading a spirit of defeatism and despair which we have "imported" from them and which we now are "exporting" back to them. We are taking the possibility that Israel has atom bombs seriously, and this possibility is being studied . . . the possibility exists and it is a very serious matter. But does it mean that we shall surrender? Never! . . . Everything can be responded to and every act can be retaliated against by one similar or even greater. We have no atom bombs, and we shall not be the first to introduce nuclear weapons into the region, but if Israel does it, it will have to sustain the results.[10]

Sadat hints here of a response entailing the use of chemical or even conventional means of mass destruction, the damage from which to tiny Israel might be equal to the damage nuclear weapons could inflict on Egypt. At the same time, his statement suggests something entirely different. Since Egypt would have to attack, as Israel was the status quo power in the area, the issue is not that of his response to Israeli countermeasures. Rather the issue is this: Since Egypt has no nuclear weapons, Israel has no right to use nuclear weapons against Egypt; therefore, in practical terms, Israel will not use them, pending Cairo's own behavior. Thus, the renunciation by Egypt of the nuclear option could render the Israeli nuclear option useless, as long as Egypt either fought limited conventional wars against a nuclear Israel or did not fight at all. To this day, the conventional-chemical war-fighting strategy is officially maintained by Egyptian spokesmen, even though the formulation is rather opaque. For example, *Rooz al-Yusuf,* January 12, 1987, quotes retired Major General Tala'at Muslem, now active as a scholar at the Strategic Research Center of the *Al-Aharam* paper, as saying that Egypt

> does not need an atomic bomb to achieve a [strategic] balance with Israel. [It needs] conventional weapons such as surface-to-surface mis-

siles, warplanes, and nonnuclear means of mass destruction such as incendiaries, chemical [weapons] and bacteriological ones, which are real deterrents against nuclear weapons.[11]

Yet this posture is rather defensive, and takes Israel's very existence—Ben-Gurion's primary goal in regard to Dimona—for granted. In the meantime, a peace treaty was signed between Sadat and Israel.

The process leading to that treaty was complex. At first, obtaining a nuclear infrastructure for Egypt was one of Sadat's main aims immediately after the 1973 war. President Nixon promised both Egypt and Israel nuclear reactors for peaceful use during his visit to the Middle East in 1974. (But later, Egypt alone was eligible to purchase them, according to an agreement signed with the United States in 1981 when Cairo ratified NPT.) However, in terms of his overall foreign policy, between 1974 and 1975 Sadat was drawn more and more to Kissinger's "step by step" diplomacy, which slowly returned to Egypt territory in the Sinai in exchange for increasing political concessions to Israel, short of Israel's demands for a peace treaty. The Syrians and other Arab radicals watched this process with disgust. So did many Israelis.

In fact, Kissinger did not seem to believe that Egypt would be able to make peace without finding a comprehensive solution to the Arab-Israeli conflict, including the 1948 Palestinian refugee issue. Kissinger wanted Israel to place the crown on the moderate, pro-Western King Hussein, as the representative of the Palestinian cause, and to make concessions regarding the occupied West Bank in order to start some movement in the direction of solving that issue. But Israel refused, and Kissinger's diplomacy was stalled and remained at an impasse until Menachem Begin became prime minister in 1977. This followed Jimmy Carter's inauguration a few months earlier.

Begin made the disgraced Moshe Dayan his foreign minister, and General Ezer Weizmann, the architect of Israel's modern air force, his minister of defense. It appeared that this troika was very different from the previous Israeli cabinet, which had followed Dayan's personal disaster and the fall of Golda Meir in 1974, both due to the legacy of the Yom Kippur War. In that cabinet, Yitzhak Rabin had been made Israel's prime minister by the Labor Alignment's party bosses, and his old mentor, Yigal Allon, had been foreign minister. The minister of defense had been Shimon Peres. As prime minister, Rabin seemed to have quasi-openly opposed the nuclear option except as a last resort capability, according to published Israeli sources.[12] However, according to Vanunu and Barnaby, the power of the Dimona reactor was increased "from 26 to 70 MWt before 1976, and was again increased presumably to about

150 MWt," either during Peres' tenure as minister of defense, or following Begin's takeover in 1977 (the year Vanunu was hired as a technician at Dimona). This increase in power was made possibly to make good a presumed backlog in producing spent fuel and its enrichment, as Spector interprets it.[13] At the same time, Spector tells us that in 1974, before Rabin took office, "Israel [had] . . . developed a 260-mile nuclear-capable ballistic missile, known in Western intelligence circles as the Jericho. The missile is noted explicitly in a 1974 CIA analysis of the Israeli nuclear program."[14]

However, when asked in an American Broadcasting Corporation interview on April 15, 1975, whether Israel had tactical nuclear weapons, Prime Minister Rabin had answered, "No." Adding, "No doubt Israel is ready to do the ultimate for its defense, but we believe that we live in an era in which we can do it with conventional weapons." On September 30, 1975, Foreign Minister Allon proposed in a speech to the U.N. General Assembly that there be consultations with all states concerned in order to establish a nuclear-weapon-free zone (NWFZ) in the Middle East.[15] On April 14, 1976, Rabin was quoted as having reiterated that the official nuclear policy remained unchanged, and said further: "Conventional power suffices to guarantee Israel's security in the near future. Attempts to rely on mystical weapons are negative."

The philosophy which emerges here is that of relying on Israel's alleged conventional superiority (though during each conventional round the losses were always afforded better by the Arabs) as long as the Arabs did not obtain their own bomb. The Israeli nuclear option was used as an asset to obtain conventional and political aid from the United States, and as a last resort "bomb in the basement." This last resort had been rebuffed quasi-openly by Dayan and less so by Peres.[16] In a *Davar* interview on April 30, 1976, Peres was quoted as having said that Israel could support a conventional arms race for the next ten years, "though not without difficulty." He added that the nuclear option had "served us well until now"; so Israel should not relieve the Arabs of their anxiety about it, as Rabin seemed inclined to do, according to Inbar.[17]

The "hidden debate" between Rabin and Peres, two bitter rivals in Labor's leadership at the time, might have been personally motivated. Yet in terms of nuances, Rabin indeed seemed to minimize the nuclear option as far as possible. Dayan—and Peres—tended to at least give it more strategic and political weight, both vis-à-vis the Arabs and the superpowers—without, however, risking open trouble with them caused by using far-reaching statements. In the longer run, the question is what Peres had in mind when the ten years he mentioned was over. It is possible that he shared Dayan's view that, even in the next decade, Israel could not rely on its conventional force, as Ben-Gurion had recognized years before. According to various, published estimates of the impact of the 1973 war on Peres (some based upon Dayan's own public statements), he felt that Israel could not afford to be drawn into another Yom Kippur-like massacre.[18] This required that some action be initiated then. One can only guess whether the long-range solution for Peres was the neutron bomb—a low-yield battlefield nuclear weapon that was being developed in the United States at the time—or other kinds of "tactical nuclear weapons," which for decades had seemed to NATO planners to be the only answer to overwhelming Soviet conventional offensives.

PGMs—precision-guided munitions, or "smart" conventional bombs—had now been introduced to Western arsenals, and had played a limited role in the Yom-Kippur War. Rabin seems not to have liked nuclear "miracle weapons," as we have seen, because he expected them to trigger an Arab drive for similar weapons. This would transform the Middle East into a "push-button" battlefield, rather than allowing conventional warfare, which in his opinion (in the spirit of Allon's traditional arguments) was still Israel's better choice. Nuclear weapons remained, in this school's view, a last resort option, should Israel fail to win a conventional war or be threatened with similar weapons of mass destruction from the outset. Nixon's and Kissinger's commitments not to pursue international inspection at Dimona, and "to maintain her qualitative edge over the Arabs," had been formalized in a "hereto unpublished letter" by President Gerald Ford to Prime Minister Rabin, probably as a result of Israel's territorial concessions to Egypt in 1975, which crowned Kissinger's "shuttle diplomacy" in the Middle East at the time.[19]

But all this belonged to the past, or so it seemed, when Begin won the 1977 elections, and Labor found itself in the opposition for the first time since Israel's birth. Dayan switched horses and joined Begin's cabinet as foreign minister, alongside Weizmann, the minister of defense. A completely "mad" Israeli government seemed to have emerged in 1977, considering Begin's image as a terrorist, Dayan's unsettled accounts with Egypt and his nuclear stance, and Weizmann's extreme hawkish reputation.

We are told by Vanunu and Barnaby that "in 1977, the Israelis built a pilot plant to enrich lithium-6," which supposedly reached full production in 1984. Then, three years later, production was suspended. After succeeding in producing lithium-6, the Israelis produced tritium, both elements being necessary for constructing fusion (hydrogen) bombs—either large ones, or battlefield neutron bombs, or enhanced atomic bombs. According to Spector, both elements were likely to be used to produce "boosted" (40- to 50-kiloton) or "superboosted" (about 100-kiloton) atomic bombs rather than thermonuclear weapons.[20] If we believe these assessments of bomb production, it seems that the decision to produce them was made during Begin's two tenures as prime minister.[21]

At the same time, Sadat was closely tied to the United States, whose newly elected president adopted the Brookings Institution's comprehensive peace program for the Middle East, which demanded peace from the Arabs in exchange for occupied territory.[22] The more knowledgeable authors of the Brookings program were aware of the significance of the nuclear option in the hands of angry, frustrated Israelis, who had been forced by Kissinger to yield territory in the wake of a bloody war for less than peace.[23]

Sadat knew that radical Arabs wouldn't make peace, and that for the PLO under Arafat the struggle would have only begun if Israel withdrew to its pre-1967 boundaries. He understood that if Carter tried to woo the Syrians and the PLO—and even tried to make the Russians partners to comprehensive peace negotiations—the outcome would be a dangerous stalemate. This would be due not only to Israeli preconditions in regard to such negotiations, including the issue of PLO participation which Dayan was cleverly softening, but also due to Arab ideologies, different interests, Soviet backing, social and political structures, and Carter's naiveté in pursuing the other Arab states rather than concentrating on his main ally, Egypt. Sadat was afraid that Egypt would become trapped by its own pan-Arab duties and by its obligatory loyalty to the Syrians and Palestinians, two difficult allies who had made Egypt do their fighting for them in the past, while sticking very closely to their own interests and ideologies. Moreover, he calculated that if Israel resorted to war under Begin and his two formidable aides, their main target would be Egypt. Also Israel had received modern equipment from the Americans in exchange for concessions to Egypt, while Cairo had lost its Soviet connection and had just started to adopt Western armaments. In sum, he was concerned that Israel's primary strategic problem would not be Syria or the PLO, but the largest and now the most vulnerable Arab state.

Yet the new Israeli government had its own worries and priorities. At least generals Dayan and Weizmann were determined to remove Egypt, to begin with, from the fighting Arab front, taking into account its Arab obligations, and make territorial concessions to Cairo in the

Sinai. Documents captured in the U.S. Embassy in Tehran provide a primary source describing this, in the context of nuclear proliferation in the region. One of the documents contains the minutes of a meeting between General Weizmann and an Iranian emissary, General H. Toufanian, who visited Israel on behalf of the Shah.[24]

The meeting took place when Prime Minister Begin was in Washington, shortly before he met with President Carter. Weizmann hinted about peace feelers on the Israeli side, rather than belligerence: "If we could have—which is a highly wishful thinking—a separate talk with the Egyptians, I am sure we could go a long way with them . . . the Sinai from a territorial point of view is much more negotiable than other parts." The Iranian general remained skeptical about Arabs in general, and in his case, about Iraqis in particular. (The Shah had just negotiated with the Iraqis the settlement of a territorial dispute over the Shat-el-Arab river, which would be broken four years later by Saddam Hussein.) But his declared main concern was Soviet Russia, and for both reasons he wanted a "deterrent force." We do not know what was initiated by the Shah at the time in the nuclear field; but he did reveal his intentions to make some effort in this area. This might have been one of the arguments in favor of Iraq's own nuclear ambitions, which, however, had begun in some earnest much earlier, in 1968, and in connection with Arab perception of NPT as having left them out due to an early Soviet-American "collusion." The Iranian was interested in Israeli missiles, in connection with the "deterrent force" mentioned above. At this point, an Israeli official who was also present at the meeting mentioned the arrival of Soviet-made SCUDs in Iraq.

The Iranian guest was invited to a demonstration of an Israeli missile. About a particular "firing" the guest was invited to observe, Weizmann said: "It is a very impressive piece of machinery . . . it gives you a completely different environment. We have it . . . in various ways of launching, whether rigid or mobile, etc. We started working on it in 1962 . . . All missiles can carry atomic heads, all missiles can carry a conventional head . . . ours is 750 kg . . ." Having stressed what the Iranian could see as a source of Israel's strength and readiness to make concessions (at least to Egypt), Weizmann then added: "The worst thing that can happen to this area is when everyone starts playing with atomic weapons—the Iraqis, Gaddafi [sic], and the Egyptians—and this can be in less than ten years. And the French will sell anything to anybody." Thus Weizmann introduced his guest to one of the sources of his own flexibility vis-à-vis Egypt.

In a conversation with Foreign Minister Dayan,[25] a common Iranian-Israeli missile project was openly discussed—possibly to meet

Iraqi SCUD threats mentioned in the Weizmann-Toufanian meeting. Thus the issue was not necessarily Russia, but a common Arab enemy supplied by the Soviets with conventional missiles. Ironically enough, Khomeini's revolution soon ended such options, and in fact made it possible for Saddam Hussein eventually to win his war against Iran by launching SCUDs into Tehran in great numbers, while Iran had no missiles to counter them, due among other things to Khomeini's hostility toward Israel. But in the meantime, "Dayan raised the problem of the Americans' sensitivity to the introduction of the kind of missiles envisaged in the joint project," and remarked that at some stage this problem "will have to be raised with the Americans." Dayan reiterated "that Israel will seek peace with Egypt," adding Jordan and Syria to the list, and emphasizing that "every problem is negotiable with the exception of PLO and a Palestinian State." This formula was also acceptable to Begin. Syria was unlikely to negotiate at all, and anyway, Begin would never concede the Golan Heights to Damascus; whereas, weak Jordan could not negotiate without the PLO's tacit consent. In fact, Egypt alone was offered an important concession—large parts, if not all, of the Sinai.

And so, Sadat made his surprise visit to Jerusalem later in 1977, followed by the difficult but unavoidable peace negotiations that led to a peace treaty in 1979.[26] The Egyptians tried to neutralize the Israeli nuclear option as part of the negotiating process by making Israel join NPT.[27] They failed, and the issue was discussed then in public, though not by Sadat himself. The pro-Sadat press justified his November 1977 visit to Jerusalem by arguing that

> the alternative to peace is terrible: a holocaust that the modern state [modern nations] has never sustained . . . Should a fifth war break out, it will be more horrible than all the previous ones. It will be a war based on elements of fear and despair and such a campaign is the most criminal in the history of all peoples. Thus logic wins over emotion when we support peace.

This became one of the reasons for Arab and Egyptian domestic criticism of Sadat's peace as well.[28]

One of the reasons Egypt failed to force Israel to join NPT was the already existing, semipublic nature of the Israeli nuclear option. How could Cairo seriously expect Israel to forgo the option without some equally strong gesture from nonnuclear Egypt and the rest of the Arab world, which refused any negotiations whatsoever with Israel?

Neither President Carter nor President Sadat could pressure Israel to make concessions in regard to the nuclear option. How could they, when, in fact, this nuclear option was one of the main reasons Sadat was ready to negotiate in the first place—not in the sense that he feared a nuclear attack from Israel, but rather in the sense that he was involved now with the United States, Israel's patron, which demanded peace from the Arabs. And he could not afford to ignore this U.S. demand, even if the radical Arabs did. Ignoring this demand was dangerous by itself, but it was even more dangerous because of the record of the leading Israeli "troika." They were likely to be less responsive to American pressure, and—as he might have calculated—more conscious of Israel's own nuclear potential due to the 1973 debacle, especially after Israeli-made Jericho missiles were added to Israel's arsenal (as the above-quoted CIA report tells us happened in 1974). Israel's air force was now more capable of hitting Egyptian targets than before. Besides, as we discussed above, President Carter "was informed" about Gerald Ford's letter to Prime Minister Rabin, which promised no international inspection at Dimona—or, at least, the maintenance of Israel's "qualitative edge" over the Arabs—in exchange for returning Sinai territory to Egypt without peace in 1975.[29] Yet the nuclear factor was never mentioned publicly by Sadat as a main reason for peace. This was an Egyptian version of nuclear opacity. It was mentioned by the Egyptian delegation in Jerusalem and at the ensuing Camp David peace talks in private, and then dropped, to be raised later with the Americans, as we shall see. Egypt itself had to join NPT if it wanted Western reactors, which it did in order to begin on the long path toward creating a nuclear infrastructure of its own.

Israel's success in signing a peace treaty with the most important Arab nation without sacrificing its nuclear option was completely ignored at home. But it became a limited, yet sharp, public weapon against Sadat in Egypt and in other radical Arab quarters.[30] Very few Israelis paid attention to the details of the Sinai accord, which in fact had neutralized parts of the large peninsula, and thus infringed on Egyptian sovereignty therein. The partial demilitarization of the Sinai, and the stationing of U.N. and U.S. observation points in the area, in fact prevented a conventional surprise attack on Israel through the Sinai. This type of attack would have—in theory—prevented the use of tactical nuclear weapons, because attackers would have been mixed with defenders. A similar disengagement was pursued by Dayan in the Sinai when Israel agreed in 1974 to partially withdraw from occupied Egyptian territory. The same idea would later influence—in my view—Israel's views of Syrian presence in Lebanon, which would allow Damascus a direct "mixing" with Israeli troops without early warning systems that had been installed on the Golan Heights as a result of the

1973 war and the ensuing negotiations between Israel and Syria.

Menachem Begin was criticized by his own public for his willingness to give up the whole Sinai peninsula and to evacuate Israeli settlements there, and for his concessions on future Israeli settlements in the West Bank. Soon enough, he interpreted his West Bank commitments in favor of his rigid loyalty to the vision of Israel's control over Western Palestine "as a whole," and he pushed Dayan aside when Dayan tried to continue negotiations on Palestinian autonomy in the West Bank.

The American-Israeli-Egyptian negotiations on the West Bank that followed the 1979 accord—i.e., the Israeli-Egyptian peace treaty that was negotiated at Camp David in 1978 and signed in 1979—were stalled (and finally terminated following Israel's Lebanon war in 1982). This happened, as General Avraham Tamir—a former director-general of the prime minister's office and a close political friend of General Weizmann—put it, because "the Camp David Agreement did not provide for principals to [govern] the connection between [Palestinian] autonomy as an interim period [as agreed upon at Camp David] and the final status of the [occupied] territories afterwards."

Begin insisted on "autonomy to people," not to territory, and his cabinet pursued enhanced settlement policy in the West Bank and the Gaza Strip. This policy was pushed by Gush-Emunim, a militant religious group, and by a new rightist party, Tehia, which came into being following the Sinai accord and Camp David, which were too much for them. The main issues during the futile autonomy negotiations were the make-up of the autonomy authority and its powers—the source of legitimacy of such an authority. For Israel, any role played by the PLO in this connection would be unacceptable, and for West Bankers and Gaza dwellers the PLO, their "only representative," declared the whole idea of "autonomy" an anathema. Other issues that frustrated the autonomy talks between Israel, Egypt, the United States, and (unofficially) Jordan, according to Tamir, were the status of the water sources in the West Bank, which also feed Israel proper, and that of "government"— i.e., not private—property, which may be used for settlement activity, according to Begin's interpretation of "autonomy to people" but not to the land. Two other issues remained unresolved in the ensuing talks: Jewish settlements, which according to President Carter were supposed to be frozen soon after the signing of the peace treaty, and Israel's involvement with the judicial process and the domestic problems of the autonomy regime for the occupied territories. In 1982, the talks were suspended altogether.

Dayan's intention had been to prevent a wedge from being driven between the United States and Israel if Israel did not honor its Camp

David commitments in regard to autonomy. Therefore, he was not enthused by the enhanced settlement activity in densely populated Arab areas, although he would not sharply condemn it either. He had his own commitment to Israeli "rights" to settle in the historical homeland and he refused to withdraw from the West Bank. He wanted to withdraw from Arab populated parts of the occupied territory and allow its population to run its affairs in conjunction with Jordan, except for foreign affairs and security matters. This could be congruent with "autonomy," which required real changes on the ground, such as withdrawing the IDF from large Arab cities. He also aimed to win local Palestinian, Jordanian, and even latent Saudi support for Sadat's realistic approach, as opposed to the "Arab rejection front," which emerged after Camp David and was headed by Iraq and Syria. General Weizmann, who favored Dayan's approach, followed his colleague's steps off the stage, thus making room for a new high-level actor to enter the scene—General Ariel Sharon.

Instead of Jimmy Carter's "comprehensive peace," and despite Carter's renewed antiproliferation campaign, Begin was able to negotiate a separate peace treaty with Egypt while maintaining what is described by Spector as a growing nuclear arsenal, which he initially had inherited from the previous Labor governments. At least this is how Arab rejectionists saw it in numerous publications and academic journals. Begin plus the bomb, as implied above by the pro-Sadat press, was a combination with some initial advantages for Begin vis-à-vis Sadat—although the Egyptian president had no need to address himself publicly to that issue during the negotiating process. Neither did most of the Israeli public perceive Begin's ascendancy in such terms. The advantages of opacity in this situation seem to be obvious, though they are hardly justified by common democratic criteria. But only Sadat, the Israelis, and, of course, the Americans maintained silence in this regard. The Arab rejectionists objected, and some did it rather loudly.[31]

However, Begin now faced other problems. He had to address himself to what appeared to be the beginning of an Arab bomb. Pakistan's "Islamic bomb," which was meant to be a follow-up to India's "atomic test for peaceful use" in 1974, had actually been financed by eager Arabs.[32] And Sharon was waiting just around the corner.

CHAPTER NINE

The Doctrine of Opaque Nuclear Monopoly

Shortly before the 1981 elections, the Israeli Air Force attacked and destroyed the Iraqi nuclear reactor Tammuz 1 near Baghdad. Several months later, Begin became prime minister for the second time, thanks, among other things, to the successful attack, and to the unpopular counterarguments presented by Shimon Peres, the new chairman of the Labor Party. The election victory was narrow, though, and Begin needed every vote he could muster in the Knesset, including that of Ariel Sharon, a general-turned-politician who had joined Begin's nationalist-populist Likud bloc, but had retained his independence within it at the same time. Soon General Sharon, who had publicly advocated such an attack without being specific, became the new minister of defense.

According to Begin's cabinet secretary, Arieh Naor, in about October 1980 (about a year before the attack), the prime minister had brought a motion before the cabinet that was linked to the attack. Later on, the initial decision was formulated in public to the effect that "Israel would not allow an enemy state to develop or acquire means of mass destruction."[1] According to Naor, this "Begin Doctrine" was linked by the prime minister directly to the Iraqi nuclear effort: "Begin argued that three . . . Hiroshima . . . type bombs would suffice to destroy Israel. Iraq, he said, might be tempted to use this weapon, once she had succeeded in developing it." Thus the motion, endorsed as it was, gave Begin, his future defense minister Sharon, and chief of staff General Rafael Eitan the formal base on which to act.

When he took office in the autumn of 1981, Sharon made several public announcements that could have been interpreted as a new defense doctrine. The most important was a speech about Israel's strategic agenda, which was printed in *Ma'ariv* on December 18, 1981, under the title "An Undelivered Speech." The speech was scheduled to be presented a few days before its publication as the opening address at a symposium at the Tel Aviv University Strategic Center, but it was never delivered, because at the time the Knesset was embroiled in a debate on the annexation by Israel of the Golan Heights. The annexation itself was meant to be one of the Begin-Sharon cabinet's responses to American displeasure with Likud's nationalist policy.[2] Sharon's speech was described in the Arab world as something like "an opaque nuclear monopoly." And it was closely tied up with Sharon's self-image and his domestic political calculations.

Sharon's manners and behavior in the past—a mixture of aggressive, sometimes unscrupulous and opportunistic outbursts—could lead one to underestimate him. Yet he was able to think in a strategic and political "grand" fashion, though the same approach was grand enough to be shallow as well. His habit of ignoring details every now and again proved disastrous several times during his career. His new doctrine must have been founded on his analysis of the four forms of war-making mentioned in Chapter 7: (1) a war of destruction (for example, Israel's War of Independence); (2) an escalating limited war (which could become a war of destruction and was the common Israeli perception of the events leading up to the Six-Day War); (3) a limited war on Israel's margins or a war of attrition (aimed at limited territorial gains, at killing as many Israeli soldiers as possible, and at gaining superpower intervention—Sharon's public definition of the 1973 war)[3]; and (4) a guerrilla or a terrorist campaign. This last form of warfare was meant to describe activities emanating from Lebanon of various Palestinian organizations in Israel and abroad after 1970.

Sharon's new doctrine was supposed to address all four possibilities "without buying one more airplane or tank" to boost Israel's conventional power. Despite the growing conventional might of all of the Arab states—including Egypt, but especially Syria—Sharon publicly promised something close to absolute security without further procurement of conventional weapons.[4] One reason for the disparity between Arab and Israeli "might" was that Israel's manpower seemed to have been exhausted in the large conventional efforts since 1973, while Arab manpower was just beginning to mobilize. And shortly before he died in 1982, General Dayan had protested against further Israeli conventional efforts, in line with his older nuclear stance coupled with his peace strategy (which had led him to Camp David and to the peace treaty with Egypt in 1979).

Dayan's official stance was publicly formulated when he stood as an independent candidate during the 1981 elections:

> Israel should invest in defense within the limits of her ability. Our goal is not a conventional balance of power with all the Arab states. We should emphasize the IDF's quality and avoid an arms race which could destroy our economy without necessarily guaranteeing our security.[5]

Dayan's election campaign was a failure; and shortly afterward, he died. However, Sharon—very much alive—was working at that time on the possible bombing of Tammuz 1. It seems that, in his eyes, the bombing was a precondition for the implementation of the rest of his plan.

"Osiraq," the French name given to a large "Osiris" research reactor, purchased by the Ba'ath regime in Baghdad (and renamed "Tammuz" by the Iraqis after the ancient Assyrian-Babylonian god of fertility), was close to completion. Iraq was a signatory of NPT, and the reactor was subjected to IAEA and French inspection. Yet, according to a recent American proliferation survey:

> despite signing the 1968 Treaty . . . and acceptance of full-scope safeguards as prescribed and monitored by the . . . IAEA, Iraq had nearly reached the point where it had . . . both the accumulated fissile material and technical support to explode a small nuclear device . . .[6]

We do not know for certain whether the Iraqis, whose reactor was not yet operational when bombed, were really that advanced, but the main point made by the American scholars quoted above is that Iraq demonstrated that "working within IAEA constraints, a nation can acquire the fissile material and the technical training necessary for a nuclear weapon program." The question is: how and why?

The Iraqi-French agreement was signed in November 1975 and completed by an exchange of letters on September 11, 1976. French and Italian supplies and technical know-how were secured (according to the above-mentioned study) because of the dependence of both countries on Iraqi crude oil. This explanation, while basically true, is not enough: American behavior vis-à-vis the French after the 1973 oil crisis—when Washington took charge and prevented any political deals between the Europeans and the oil-rich Arabs—and NPT itself, as the framework allowing "legal" French and Italian supplies of nuclear equipment to Iraq, were also factors. About a year after the agreement was signed, Arab newspapers maintained that the agreement would be implemented despite American intervention with the French to prevent it.[7] Ignoring U.S. displeasure, the regime, under the effective control of Saddam Hussein,[8] had already made several ambiguous threats against Israel. In September 1975, the first nonambiguous news about Iraq's declared intentions was published in the ever-eager Lebanese press, specifically the weekly *Al-Usbua al-Arabi*:

> IRAQ PURCHASES NUCLEAR REACTORS FROM FRANCE—A FIRST STEP TOWARD THE PRODUCTION OF ARAB NUCLEAR WEAPONS . . .
> [Saddam Hussein's visit to Paris] is the answer to Israel's nuclear arms and a first step toward the production of Arab nuclear armaments, even if the declared aim of the construction of that reactor is not the production of nuclear weapons.[9]

The ascendancy of the first Begin cabinet following the 1977 Israeli elections prompted a memorandum submitted by Saddam's government to the Arab league "in which it warned . . . that Israel would very probably use nuclear weapons in a fifth war with the Arabs. The memorandum was brought before the Arab foreign ministers in order to agree on a practical Arab stance . . ."[10] Saddam himself was quoted by the Iraqi ambassador in Kuwait to the effect that: "We shall get the atom, and Israel won't be able to interfere with our effort; the power of Iraq is the power of the Arabs, and the power of the Arabs is the power of Iraq."[11] Saddam's regime was a sworn enemy of the Jewish state. And Iraq had refused to conclude armistice agreements with Israel, even after Iraqi expeditionary forces returned home from engagements with Israel. Saddam had played a central role in cementing the anti-Sadat "rejection front." Therefore, he appeared to be a new contender for Arab leadership, following the spirit of Heikal's teachings, but at Cairo's expense.

Saddam had tried to establish Arab—and his own—hegemony in the Persian Gulf when he invaded Iran in 1980, having first "settled" the latent, and sometimes open, border dispute in the Shat-el-Arab river with the Shah in 1975. Then came Khomeini, who of course perceived in Saddam and his regime a secular dictatorship of a Sunni clique. Khomeini tried to export his revolution to the Shi'ite majority in Iraq, though Arab not Persian, and at the same time his regime seemed to have weakened Iran significantly and isolated it politically and militarily. Iran was thus an easy pray, in Saddam's eyes. It was a religious-political threat to his own regime; and Khuzistan, the oil-rich province served by the port of Abadan, was a lucrative price for war, and its occupation could be justified because of the Arab majority living there. Also, Iraq sought control over the contested border areas. Saddam's Ba'ath regime could be defined—if we follow A. James Gregor—as a semi-Fascist, secular, or rather pagan doctrinaire outfit, based on mystical, pre-Islamic notions of Assyrian and Babylonian imperial might coupled with aspirations to both pan-Arabism and regional hegemony.[12] The semi-Fascist traits of Saddam's state were further manifested by many factors. It employed indoctrination, secret police terror, and the unscrupulous use of power at home. The state derived its power by invoking a personal cult of the leader, based on a single, exclusive party machine. It mobilized the masses, without giving them any real influence on the political process, by invoking a secular, modern political religion based on remote images of ancient glory, mixed—when necessary—with Islamic elements. In this way, it used extreme emotional nationalism and the military to cement national unity in a rather mixed population lacking an established, traditional elite and "public rules of the game." And it invoked ethnic and sometimes racial postulates— such as discriminating against Iraqi women who married foreigners— within this mixed population. Saddam's regime blamed others—i.e., foreign powers—for the nation's troubles and the leader's own mistakes. This regime also jumped at the throat of what it saw as weak but annoying neighbors—a process that involved the leader with escalating foreign wars. But he would not admit mistakes, thanks to the mysticism of power—his source of legitimacy.

Saddam's hegemonic ambitions got the regime into trouble with Syria in addition to Iran. The rivalry between the Ba'ath regimes in Syria and Iraq goes beyond the premises of this book, but one could argue that both regimes claimed a "greater," i.e., a hegemonic, status for their countries at home and the Arab world. A strong Syria would endanger Iraq and vice-versa.

For Iraq, the bomb had a mystical attraction, but more important, it was the incarnation of modern power, and was "absolutely necessary to balance out Israel." In this way, Israel served hegemonic Iraqi claims, a precedent not unknown to us since Nasser's days. An interview with Tarak Aziz, at the time the (Christian) vice-president of Iraq, with *Al-Huweidath*, Beirut, on July 31, 1981, is illuminating here:

> Q: The world, as you see it, always supports the aggressor and the strong. Why, then, are you always talking about peace and justice and why has Iraq no atomic bomb?
> A: The world supports the strong but not necessarily the aggressor. We have means and we shall exploit all the means at our disposal to strengthen Arab power for the sake of the whole Arab nation. The creation of an independent power is the foundation of all Arab states to withstand Zionist aggression. As far as the acquisition of an atomic

bomb is concerned, our aim is to exploit the atom for peaceful purposes . . .

When we were asked by foreign powers about the possibility of a
solution to the Arab-Israeli conflict, we always said that an absolute
precondition is a balance of power between Israel and the Arab
states . . .

It is true that the destruction of the reactor is a blow to the Iraqi
revolution, because the reactor was one of its achievements, but Iraq
will build another one . . .

But before proceeding, we will return to the destruction of the old one.

Its designs were clear, and although the French did not deliver a
separation plant for the illegal plutonium the Iraqis might have produced in such a reactor once activated, they did, however, deliver the
first shipment of highly enriched uranium to operate it. The French
ignored American and Israeli protests, as well as sabotage directed
against delivery of the reactor, which was committed on French soil by
unknown agents.[14] The French worked carefully within the rules of
NPT, and Italian sources independently supplied the Iraqis with "hot
cells" that could be used to start illegal plutonium separation.[15] As stated
above, both France and Italy were in dire need of Arab oil following the
two oil crises of 1973 and 1979. De Gaulle had been gone for more than
a decade, but some of his successors reminded the suspicious Israelis of
Frenchmen they had known thirty years before, people who had had
the knack of rationalizing whatever served their own idea of French
interests. General de Gaulle, who had had a sense of responsibility and
extreme sensitivity to everything nuclear, could have stopped them
from selling a nuclear infrastructure to Iraq; but de Gaulle's successors
seemed not to be antagonistic in principle to the spread of nuclear
weapons as long as remote nations were concerned. After all, the "balance of terror" was a French concept, and maybe "regional balances of
terror" were not impossible. This principle could have been used to
justify French behavior to Gaullists of the new generation—such as
France's cynical prime minister of the time, Jacques Chirac.[16] At any
rate, he, or President Giscard d'Estaing himself, advanced French interests by hiding behind NPT, and left the final results for the Americans—and the Israelis—to deal with.

In fact, the Iraqis were far from being able to separate plutonium, let
alone produce it illegally. They were, however, on the verge of legally
operating a large research reactor whose sole purpose was the production of plutonium. Once the Iraqis learned production techniques, they
could continue to separate plutonium illegally, although if they
remained signatories of NPT, they would not be able to threaten Israel

openly. At first, they had to secure natural uranium from foreign sources, such as Niger and Portugal, or buy slightly enriched uranium in the world market.[17] But by the late 1980s, they were reportedly working on developing their own uranium supplies near the Turkish border and installing gas centrifuges to enrich it.[18] Only much later, after the Gulf War, was a third route they used—probably the most important one—discovered: electromagnetic separation by means of devices known as calutrons. But at this stage, Iraq's efforts were concentrated on "Osiraq," which was not even ready when the regime tried to justify its strategy by invoking anti-Israeli slogans and arguments. In accordance with the General Assembly equation of Zionism with racism of November 10, 1975, the Iraqis launched a high-intensity anti-Israeli and anti-Zionist campaign before they had actually acquired any meaningful ways to implement their open and implicit rejection of Israel within any boundaries at all. In this sense, they created in Begin's mind a clear link between Tammuz 1 and Ba'ath Party ideology.[19] It could be that through their paradoxical behavior they were staying within one of the purposes behind NPT: if a signatory nation violated the spirit but not the letter of the law, their nuclear efforts remained within some kind of manageable, restricted framework because they were "nonopen" efforts. On the other hand, signatories could simply withdraw from the treaty once ready—and for the Iraqis, Israel, a pre-NPT nonsignatory, could be seen as a ready excuse.

As Shimon Peres cautioned Begin: whatever the Iraqis decided to do, it would take time. And Israel could afford to wait since the "deadlines reported by our people are not the real ones." In a letter to Begin dated May 10, 1981, Peres argued that "material could be replaced by [harmless] material."[20] In other words, Peres' Socialist friend Francois Mitterand, just elected president of France, could somehow recover the enriched uranium that had been supplied to the Iraqis (which could be used to produce plutonium) and replace it with another sort of safeguarded uranium to operate the reactor, maybe without the Iraqis noticing. Or Peres might have calculated that the 12.5 kilograms of highly enriched uranium already supplied by the French to operate the reactor was not enough to produce a bomb. So, the immediate problem was to prevent the French from supplying 12.5 kilograms more, which would suffice to make a bomb (and was part of the original Iraqi agreement with the French).[21] Peres further warned that "what is intended to prevent may encourage" the Iraqis to seek the bomb without restraint. And if Israel attacked the Iraqi reactor, there could be an Arab counterattack on Dimona. And he finally argued that Israel might isolate itself totally as a result of the attack.

As stated above, the 12.5 kilograms of enriched uranium supplied by the French was not enough to produce a bomb by itself. According to old textbooks, about 19 kilograms are needed—if uranium reflector is added to the bomb's core—to produce an atomic bomb, and about 50 kilograms are needed to produce one without the reflector.

According to Leonard S. Spector, in the 1990s even the 12.5 kilograms of highly enriched uranium was enough to produce one Hiroshima-type bomb.[22] The French shipment was needed to operate the reactor, and it could have been used—with some difficulty—to produce illegal plutonium from the legal natural uranium Iraq was openly acquiring in countries such as Portugal. This would mean moving along the route toward an arsenal of plutonium bombs. The plutonium route required years of acquiring knowledge and the illegal plutonium itself, then more time for its weaponization and the acquisition of delivery means; it also required cheating within the rules adopted by Iraq when it joined NPT.

The second route available to the Iraqis was to use the full quantity of highly enriched uranium supplied by the French to build at least one uranium bomb, whose triggering mechanism required additional equipment. But if they did this and were caught red handed, they would be exposed as having broken the NPT rules and would be forced to forgo Western aid for operating the reactor. And the French would be forced to stop their cooperation; thus the plutonium route would be closed. That route was more promising in terms of quantity. It was also more promising in terms of the needed to acquire a sizable arsenal while obtaining delivery means for miniaturized bombs, which could be adapted to Soviet-made SCUD-B missiles or any of the fighter bombers already in Iraq's air force. Only later, it seems, and in conjunction with their war with Iran, did Iraq embark with Egypt on the production of the Argentinian Condor 2, or Condor 2000, missile.

In November 1980, the Iraqis refused to allow IAEA inspection of the highly enriched uranium already supplied by France, arguing that the war with Iran interfered with such activities.

Israel was in a difficult position. According to Shlomo Nakdimon, Peres believed that the quantity of uranium supplied already was just about half of the amount necessary to build a bomb, and that the plutonium separation facilities supplied by the Italians were far from being a real reprocessing plant.[23] He failed to convince the prime minister that the Iraqis could either be persuaded to return the uranium to the French or could be cheated into doing so. As we have already seen, Peres was worried that if attacked, the Iraqis would be driven even more intently to acquire the bomb, and that they might retaliate against Dimona. Ezer

Weizmann, one of the architects of the peace treaty with Egypt, was dead against an Israeli raid on Tammuz, due among other reasons to the possible ramifications on Israeli-Egyptian relations. And he tried to mobilize everyone he could persuade behind the scenes.[24] Other ministers were very much concerned about a possible Soviet reaction to an Israeli attack against a client state. Regarding Peres' hidden motives, we can add an entirely different proposition than those cited above: He feared that the enriched uranium already in Saddam's hands could somehow be used as a bomb, in retaliation to the attack.

Yet Peres' fears seemed not to have been well thought out. Osiraq was not yet a "hot"—that is, nuclear—target as Dimona was; no radioactivity would escape from a "cold" reactor if attacked. At the time, the Iraqis had no other means at their disposal for a counterattack. Moreover, an attack on "hot" Dimona would justify a much more formidable nuclear counterattack by the Israelis than would an attack on a "cold" reactor still short of being fueled and operated. Only if Israel allowed the Iraqi reactor to become a real nuclear target would it risk a nuclearlike attack against Dimona, or against civilian targets in Israel.

One may speculate (and published evidence indicates) that Mr. Peres was following the doctrine of a nuclear "balance of terror" on the assumption that the Arabs were bound to acquire a bomb one day. He might even have seen some benefit in such a situation, following Kenneth Waltz's arguments that "more might be better," provided clear-cut "red lines" were drawn and other deterrence-theoretical tools were added to the nuclear arsenal itself while Israel worked toward settlement of the conflict by means of a territorial compromise.[25] The strategic problem was how to overcome the deterrence practical-theoretical arguments that Israel had no credible nuclear threat because it had no second strike capability, due to the country's original, pre-June 1967 size. In theory, a "credible second strike" required more territory, including West Bank territory. Even the superpowers had developed nuclear submarines on top of their fixed launching sites, scattered over a vast territory, and had diversified their arsenals no end to ensure a "second strike capability." Further, Israel, if bordered with open deserts while holding many Arabs as virtual hostages, could threaten Arabs more effectively than if it returned to pre-1967 lines. Arab targets would be separated from Israel by these empty territories; whereas if the Arabs used the bomb against Israel, they would expose many Palestinians, possibly Jordanians, and even Syrians, to the hazards of such an attack. Here "strategy" seems to have been a much better solution to Israel's security problem than a political process entailing territorial concessions (or rather each contradicted the other), and this strategy could become Likud's political tool to justify its West Bank militancy.

At the time, the prevailing official opacity in nuclear matters prevented open arguments in this respect, but Likud argued that any territorial concession in the West Bank was ideologically unacceptable and would allow a Palestinian guerrilla war to be launched against Israel's vital centers. And thus Israel's strategic advantage vis-à-vis the Arab states (who were already the main problem despite well-protected post-1967 Israeli boundaries) would vanish with a return to "indefensible boundaries" based on pre-1967 divisions, in favor of independent Palestinians who were supported by Arab states.

Any political process seemed to entail either evacuation or continued occupation. Labor has never discussed the nuclear aspects of West Bank withdrawals in public, but maintained a more flexible view of its future. Either the West Bank should be divided between Israel and Jordan, with Israel sticking to the Jordan River itself as its security boundary, or some interim solution must be found—without annexation—to begin satisfying local Palestinian expectations without allowing a PLO state to emerge in the West Bank and Gaza.

Peres alone mentioned nuclear options in public, but his public stances were at first dictated by domestic calculations—how to recover the votes Labor had lost in 1977 when many upper-class Israelis voted against Labor because of the aggregated results of the 1973 war, Labor's long and rather corrupt rule, and Rabin's amateur party leadership. Most of these voters were "doves," and one needed to adopt a positive, peace-oriented plank to keep them and maintain a political bloc with the left-wing Mapam party. On the other hand, votes lost directly to Begin's Likud, and many right-wing Laborites as well, were rather "hawkish," and less inclined to territorial concessions in the West Bank and Gaza, even if most of them were interested in the conventional, historical, or economic aspects of the issue. Rabin would become their natural leader, and threaten Peres' position if he miscalculated.

A nuclear option aimed at peace and a territorial compromise in the West Bank could not be spelled out fully in domestic terms, due to psychological-political reasons. Israelis would hardly perceive in nuclear weapons anything real and probably would be inclined to believe that the other side would acquire the bomb immediately; such fears would combine with deterrence theory as a negative model. Waltz's arguments could help, and if someone—such as Shai Feldman—could somehow prove that clear "red lines" plus a "launch upon warning" posture plus territorial concessions would lead to stable deterrence, the Peres-inspired press would give that someone the due publicity, leaving Peres himself in the background, and allowing him to appear less ready to make territorial concessions. The Peres-inspired press did just this, especially Dan Margalit of *Ha'aretz*, but no serious discussion of Feldman's "massive retaliation" doctrine was offered to the readers. In this situation "massive retaliation" seemed not only obsolete in terms of modern nuclear strategy but indeed impractical, as Israel's enemies were numerous and Israel could be threatened from various directions. The pursuit of a deterrence-theoretical solution to Israel's problems by Feldman could be easily defeated by deterrence-theoretical counterarguments, especially because one could argue that Arabs were "irrational."

Thus the premises of the debate, which should have been cultural-historical, were defined by nonexperts in abstract terms, forcing Feldman—a nonexpert himself—to argue that Arabs were "rational," a historical-psychological argument that was far from his actual expertise. Peres did not endorse Feldman's 1967 withdrawal scheme, but it appears that he did accept Arab nuclearization as inevitable, and one can speculate that he was withholding an open Israeli nuclear posture until at least one Arab state went nuclear. If he were at all influenced by Mr. Feldman, and beforehand by the author,[26] or by Waltz via Feldman (who claims influence over Waltz himself), still his emphasis would not have been on our recommendation to go nuclear publicly. It might have been Feldman's presupposition that nuclear proliferation in the Middle East is indeed inevitable—a concept Peres might have harbored since Gallois' day—and could stabilize the region if some kind of a carrot were added to the nuclear option while Israel still held the option of a nuclear monopoly. Yet a public nuclear posture, among the other advocacies offered by Feldman, did not seem to Peres to be necessary to bridge the "credibility gap." Even such an option seemed to have left this gap open; one could cite the 1973 war as a precedent for Arab refusal to be deterred. But in return, Peres could have argued that the 1973 experience should have taught the Israelis to attach less importance to occupied territory and seek peace instead of continuing to be involved in a protracted conflict. He, of course, was cautious not to cite an unpopular war for that purpose, but returned every now and again to the nuclear issue. Yet he refrained from advocating open nuclear deterrence plus territorial concessions as his strategy for peace. Strategically, for him, opacity sufficed, while Waltz's general arguments in favor of regional nuclear proliferation were in line with Peres' traditional views. Waltz's main argument in favor of nuclear proliferation is that nuclear weapons "socialize" elites, minimize uncertainties, and create clear-cut choices right from the beginning of armed conflicts under conditions of mutual deadly threats. The bomb does work that way when it is actually acquired *by both sides* and its enormous power is understood, as happened with the Soviets. According to this argument, by the time one or more Arab countries acquires nuclear weapons, Israel must be seen as a "peace-oriented party" and not as an abrasive and possibly dangerous enemy, and therefore be ready to make concessions regarding occupied territory.

Peres' public opinions on the issue of the nuclear option remained rather vague during the 1981 election campaign. Keeping them vague also avoided trouble with Rabin, who stressed conventional doctrines and didn't trust Peres' strategic judgment in general, and with the left-ists, not to mention the Americans. But Peres assumed a more explicit posture in the 1984 campaign when his leadership of the Labor Party was firmly established. During the 1988 campaign, however, which he ran almost alone as the main Labor leader, he hardly mentioned the nuclear issue at all. Back in 1981, in conjunction with elections that were meant to reestablish Likud as the legitimate alternative to Labor's long supremacy in Israel's politics, Peres' stance in regard to the bombing of Iraq's reactor played straight into Begin's hands. Peres' approach was rejected by the Begin cabinet, which had developed what Arab observers interpreted as a doctrine of nuclear monopoly as a solution to the threatening Arab bomb. Begin and Sharon carried the whole coali-tion government with them, and its nuclear doctrine was publicly repeated again and again by other government spokesmen.[27] Deter-rence theory was mobilized here, again, as a negative model. The argu-ment was that Israel could not afford a "balance of terror." Due to its small size (even in the post-June 1967 lines) it was deprived of any cred-ible second strike capability. Thus, Israel needed a preventive first strike strategy—and the necessary tools to deliver it—against the enemy's nuclear infrastructure, before Iraq developed a first strike capability. Chief of Staff Raphael Eitan, now a politician and a radical hardliner, spelled this out publicly in April 1990 when the Iraqi threat seemed to have revived. "Small states would be destroyed by a first strike," and thus we can't afford a "balance of terror," said Eitan.[28] Begin's own pub-lic stance was aimed mainly at justifying the Tammuz raid in terms of the enemy's intentions, emotions, and indeed of Israel's territorial vul-nerability, which would combine to trigger the actual use of the bomb by the Iraqis the moment they had it. Since he had to prove all this—as Tammuz was under IAEA inspection—he published a rather clumsy, and inaccurate, description of Saddam Hussein's stance based on one of the Iraqi leader's speeches, which supposedly drew a direct link between the Iraqi reactor and Ba'ath official anti-Israeli policy. Begin quoted an Israeli intelligence translation that he was later unable to produce.[29] In Israel itself, there was no serious discussion in public of either the issue as a whole or of the strategic concept behind it.

Once Tammuz 1 was destroyed, the Begin-Sharon cabinet ignored vehement IAEA—and less vehement American—protests and limited punitive action.[30] They impressed the lesson of Tammuz 1 on the rest of the Arab world—leaving Egypt, which was officially at peace with Israel and a fresh signatory of NPT, somewhat aside. Israel repeatedly proclaimed that any nuclear potential in the hostile Arab world would be viewed as a target for similar attacks. As Sharon put it in his "Unde-livered Speech":

> . . . The third element in our defense policy for the 1980s is our decision to prevent access to nuclear weapons from both confrontation states and potential ones. Israel cannot allow the introduction of nuclear weapons. For us it is not an issue of a balance of terror, but a question of our continued survival. Therefore we shall have to prevent this danger from the outset.

The argument against the balance of terror might have been aimed against Peres' approach. Moreover, it was then, in 1981, when Begin won his second election, that he appointed Yuval Ne'eman, a renowned Israeli physicist and an extreme hawk, to be minister of science and technology.

If Vanunu's information and its interpretation by Barnaby and Theodore Taylor (the American bomb designer who was also consulted by the London *Sunday Times* in regard to Vanunu's information) are correct—that the Israeli nuclear option was boosted by Begin in 1977—then in 1981 we have a combination of two or three elements. The first was the liquidation of the beginnings of an Arab bomb. This assured an optional Israeli monopoly, rather than allowing a surreptitious balance of terror to emerge slowly. Such a "balance" would have provided Arab conventional and guerrilla forces with a nuclear umbrella that could be perceived by Arab leaders as similar to that given to North Vietnam by the Soviet Union and China. At least, whether this umbrella was given or not, it could not be ignored by the Americans. This threat seems to me to be the only way open to Iraq, or any Arab country, to effectively use nuclear threats without taking incredible risks to them-selves. No analyst could prove such risk-taking in their previous behav-ior—i.e., the historical experience could not substantiate direct risk-tak-ing in Arab behavior, except for the risks created by the theory of nuclear strategy itself. Arab cruelty to other Arabs, including the use of poison gas by Nasser in Yemen, Assad's order to almost wipe out the city of Hama, or Iraq's later use of missiles and gas against Iran (when gas was used against Iranian soldiers on Iraqi soil and against Iraqi Kurds) could, of course, be interpreted as deviations from established norms of warfare. And yet, none of those entailed a very high risk-taking. On the contrary, some such actions were administered against weak, domestic elements threatening to grow if unchecked, and others were limited to Iraq's own territory or to a rather helpless Yemenite enemy. (Iraq's August 1990 invasion of Kuwait will be dealt with separately later.)

The boosting of Israel's nuclear options, as described by Vanunu and Barnaby and recently evaluated by Spector,[31] may be related to other Arab calculations, as perceived by Israeli decision makers at the time, which were based for years on the estimation of a relatively small number of Israeli Hiroshima-type bombs that would be targeted at Arab cities. The Arabs might have convinced themselves that such a threat was tolerable.[32] Israel would be politically constrained when considering a nuclear attack against an Arab metropolis (a view supported by Egypt's Butrus Butrus A'ali, as we have seen). And at the same time, Israel's arsenal was too small to threaten the vast Arab spaces. This had allowed some Arabs, those who were convinced that they were less vulnerable than Egypt with its Aswan High Dam, a degree of confidence that they could survive an Israeli atomic attack if necessary. Here, Arab self-image as a huge, proud nation and the political ambitions of some Arab leaders could combine with the overemphasis the theory and praxis of nuclear strategic thinking placed on the "means"—i.e., calculations related to the relative strength and credibility of nuclear weapons. This kind of thinking had led to a mad nuclear race in terms of sizes, numbers, and weapons systems in West and East alike. Israel herself would suffer from the fallout effects of Hiroshima bombs dropped on Arab targets close enough to its heartland.[33] Moreover, Israel was so small that it could not sustain the impact of one bomb, "even a tactical one," such as Qaddafi had been eager to obtain since his meeting with Nasser in 1969.

Arab obsession with Arab capitals as the "logical" targets of an Israeli nuclear attack ("countervalue" targeting), and their belief that such an attack would be neither practical nor mortal to the Arab nation, might have been seen, by radical Arabs such as the former Egyptian chief of staff, General Shazli, as an important limitation because of the composition and size of the Israeli arsenal.[34] Shazli argued that Israel had about twenty to twenty-five Hiroshima-type atomic bombs. He went on to say that "five such bombs would obliterate Israel, whereas ten such bombs won't do much harm to the Arab World . . . So I do not think that Israel would be the party to gain an advantage from using atomic bombs." Even Shazli was careful to distinguish between an Arab "war of destruction" (in which the Israelis—having nothing to lose—would use the twenty to twenty-five bombs they supposedly had) and what he called a "conventional war" (in which Arab war aims would be limited and thus no no-way-out situation would be created for Israel, which would allow enough freedom of action to the Arabs). This argument, as I interpret it—when combined with the lessons of the 1973 war—was the most dangerous from the Israeli point of view. It ignored what the Arabs feared most, but allowed them to use what they could afford more, much more than the post-1973 Israel: a conventional, if limited, war of attrition, or limited offensives, casualty-rich and economically expensive. Shazli—if not Sadat, or Heikal, or Saddam Hussein—would risk such wars.

In particular, Syria, probably in cooperation with Libya, had openly adopted such a posture, although President Assad himself seldom talked in these terms in public. Abdalla al-Achmar, the deputy secretary general of the Syrian Ba'ath Party, published a typical discourse of this kind in his party organ *Al-Thawra*, arguing that the "genial Vietnamese leadership has already shown us how to neutralize the American nuclear factor: by mixing their forces with the superior American forces in the same battlezone."[35] In other words, Syria was too close to Israel to allow the latter to effectively use nuclear weapons, and in pitched battles such weapons would be valueless.

This may explain why Barnaby estimated that Israel had developed thermonuclear weapons—as a solution to this and other problems, such as Soviet nuclear threats—or at least the possibility that Israel had boosted the Hiroshima bombs from 20 to about 100 kiloton yields (which is how Vanunu's pictures were interpreted by Spector).[36]

If properly targeted, multimegaton monsters would indeed be able to destroy the whole Arab world, including Qaddafi, Syria, and the Palestinians in exile, along with oil targets along the coasts and in the deserts. This would be a real doomsday, comparable in a sense to the biblical act of the blind Samson. Moreover, thermonuclear weapons of that caliber, mounted on advanced Jericho missiles, would be a real threat to the Soviet Union and could obliterate Pakistan.

But according to Spector's most recent research,[37] "Presumably, the manufacture of full-fledged, multi-stage thermonuclear 'hydrogen' bombs with megaton yield would require an extensive nuclear testing program and thus remains beyond Israel's abilities, since Israel is not known to have conducted such tests," except for the common interpretation of the flash that occurred near the coast of South Africa in 1979.

This "flash" was perceived abroad as a nuclear test conducted by Israel and South Africa together.[38] The Carter Administration officially investigated the affair. But no conclusive evidence was ever published, either because none was found or because of the stronger desire to refrain from officially acknowledging Israel as a nuclear weapon nation to avoid risking trouble with Congress and its antitest legislation—and in order to maintain the game of opacity. Still, the "boosted" atomic bomb, if produced by the Israelis by means of adding tritium or lithium 6 to the plutonium or uranium cores,[39] could give Israel—according to American bomb designer Theodore Taylor—"the size of some warheads on the U.S. strategic missiles."[40] It was not necessary, however, to wait for Vanunu's revelations (as interpreted by Theodore Taylor), if one followed General Sharon's speeches closely enough and understood his opaque language. Also, according to the credible *Aerospace Daily*,[41] Israel in 1985 had deployed a large number of Jericho missiles in the Negev and on the Golan Heights, which were described as "greatly improved," with the range of 400 miles. Later on, the test flight of a missile described as the Jericho 2 was detected at almost the same time as Vanunu's information was disclosed.[42] And yet, everyone, including foreign experts, was surprised by the magnitude and the alleged diversification of the Israeli arsenal following Vanunu's information.[43] Of course one of the prices of opacity is the problem of demonstrating capabilities, which became synonymous with credibility and had fueled the nuclear arms race between the great powers to its mad heights. In Vanunu's case, some foreign analysts were led to believe that the man was in fact an Israeli government tool; that he was used to spread the real facts about Israel's nuclear might. In fact, when we later discuss his verdict as finally released by the Israeli Supreme Court in summer 1990, we will see that Vanunu acted out of vengeance; and his disclosures included technical data that could invite attack and an enhanced Arab nuclear effort.

Here the opacity dilemma assumes its other, older aspect: that open nuclearization would push Arabs to obtain their own nuclear option, and thus opacity, even if less "credible" in deterrence theoretical and established nuclear strategic terms, is the better choice. Still, the shock wave in the Arab world in the wake of the publication of Vanunu's information reduced opacity almost to a minimal, verbal-diplomatic game, as far as Arabs were concerned. And soon they dropped it almost altogether, at least in foreign-related forums, even if the conclusions drawn by various Arab governments were different.

As far as Israel's initial decision to enhance and diversify its nuclear efforts, we could speculate, as Barnaby did on the basis of Vanunu's information, that one of the main lessons learned from the Yom Kippur

War was the neutron bomb battlefield option. According to Sam Cohen, its "father," neutron bombs enable strikes at concentrations of enemy infantry carrying antitank missiles, enemy armor, and artillery.[44] Their use could spare Israel the attrition it had suffered in 1973 when the enemy was met by garrisons taken—possibly inevitably—by surprise, and when the hastily called up reserves had to fight too long and too hard for what amounted to too little in terms of the ensuing political process. Here again, the "means" (neutron bombs) could impose themselves on a conflict that would remain high level despite what was perceived by Arabs as the introduction of the bomb.

At the least, this was one of the lessons Sharon chose to learn from that war. He viewed its outcome as a result, primarily, of the enemy's having taken the initiative and having been able to determine the political results by pushing reluctant superpowers, including the United States, over to its side.

Our analysis above suggests that a more complicated process led to that war and affected the negotiating process that accompanied it. However, it does seem plausible that in Sharon's view the nuclear option played a role in those events, and that he saw it as having constrained Egyptian and Syrian freedom of action. The nuclear option dictated the limited war that otherwise might have escalated, and which he felt could escalate in the future if Israel's credibility in this and other respects was undermined. The destruction of the Iraqi reactor was thus a first step toward the establishment of rules of behavior supported by credible threats, as opposed to the unclear concepts of previous governments. Sharon perceived all the territory held by Israel to be part of a "deterrent posture" (whereas his predecessors had perceived in it only conventional belts of safety), and he saw Arab territory such as Jordan, southern Syria, and Lebanon as part of the same strategy; The terminology he chose seemed to mix deterrence with the actual use of force if "deterrence" failed ("compellence"); but in fact his argument was aimed at credible "deterrence":

> We shall have . . . to prevent war by assuming a deterrent posture against the threats to our survival. Should deterrence fail and a war break out [we must] secure a military capability to maintain the integrity of Israel's territory against all possible cases of the opening of hostilities, including a surprise . . . attack, and we shall have to undermine the fighting coalition by striking at the very heart of its offensive power.[45]

This could mean not only the abandonment of the last resort concept but also the extension of Israel's nuclear option to its territorial margins,

occupied or not, by preventing "limited wars on the territorial margins," and achieving the credibility necessary to make such a doctrine
workable—with or without Washington's blessing. If this was Sharon's
view, the Americans could not accept it. The very well informed Israeli
columnist Moshe Zak recently put it just this way:

> After the bombing of the reactor in Baghdad, President Reagan sent a
> special envoy to Begin and asked for rules to be agreed upon regard-
> ing ahead of time coordination between Israel and the United States
> pertaining to Israeli responses. Begin convinced the envoy that in coor-
> dination there was a degree of accepting responsibility for Israel's
> actions. The United States should be careful not to accept such respon-
> sibility, whereas Israel could not bind her own hands in matters of
> self-defense."[46]

Zack further quoted a book by the late CIA director William Casey,
according to which the United States had supplied Israel with the satellite photos of the Iraqi reactor, in response to Israeli "restraint" regarding the supplies of AWACs early-warning systems to Saudi-Arabia.
But American "complicity" in the Osiraq bombing never became publicly known; Washington even punished Jerusalem for the attack by
suspending warplane supplies and by supporting a strong motion
against it in the U.N. Security Council. Begin might have been satisfied with the overall results of the raid, but not so Sharon.

Paradoxically enough, one of the opaque "languages" used by
Sharon to enhance the credibility he thought necessary was his conventional incursion into Lebanon.

CHAPTER TEN

Lebanon and the Demise of the Begin-Sharon Cabinet

Sharon now used a new language of opacity, clearly understood by Washington, Moscow, and some Arab leaders—but not by the Israeli and Arab peoples. In opaque language, he extended Israel's nuclear threat over the occupied territories as a whole, and gave up the last resort option. His forceful—and highly controversial—personality played a role as an important constant. Sharon believed that his new language had a fair degree of credibility, and he hoped that the combination would establish him firmly as Begin's successor.

As he saw it, Israel needed to strengthen its credibility immediately by way of an Israeli-initiated limited war to destroy the PLO's "state within a state" in Lebanon, in the framework of his "grand" strategy. His ultimate goal was to establish a friendly regime in Beirut which could control the Palestinians in Lebanon, and under certain circumstances even send troublesome Palestinians back to Jordan. He saw this as a way to eliminate the risks and damages emanating from Palestinian guerrilla warfare and Syrian "under the threshold" war-fighting doctrine. In fact, he argued that Jordan itself could be turned into a Palestinian, rather than a Hashemite, state, thus solving the problem of the Palestinian quest for self-determination. Palestinians under Israeli rule in the West Bank and Gaza, territories that Likud believed belonged to Israel, would be asked to leave for their independent state if they did not like Israeli rule. Or they would be provoked to leave by an enhanced Israeli settlement effort in these areas, an effort made possible thanks to the changed strategic position of Israel in the region and vis-à-vis the Americans.[1] Otherwise they could stay as loyal subjects.

At the same time, Soviet-American rivalry could be mobilized within the context of President Ronald Reagan's efforts against the "Evil Empire," by inflicting a strike against pro-Soviet Syria. In this vein, a limited but public "memorandum on strategic cooperation," which mentioned the Russians by name as the common opponent, was signed by Washington and Jerusalem in November 1981 and was leaked to the Israeli press in December.[2]

This "grand design"—as its Lebanese element was later nicknamed by the Israeli press—required a direct military effort to push the Syrians out of Lebanon while inflicting a severe military blow on Assad's troops there.[3] American Secretary of Defense Caspar Weinberger, who at first had endorsed the strategic memorandum, rejected it later, when Sharon's "grand" and rather autonomous design became more clear to Washington. But this only made the general even more ready to attack. According to Yosef Harif's February 1982 article in *Ma'ariv*, Sharon was explicit about a future action in Lebanon in a meeting with Senator John Glenn in mid-February 1982.[4]

According to the well-informed Harif, Sharon's plans for Lebanon were much in defiance of what he termed "Weinberger's policy" in the Middle East. The main argument was directed against American weapon supplies to Saudi Arabia and Jordan; Syria was receiving modern weaponry from the Soviets, and Iraq was getting materiel from all sides (even if Saddam's war against Iran seemed to be mired in the marshes of the gulf). A pattern had been established: one radical regime in the region—Saddam's—should be strengthened against the more radical one—Khomeini's—in order to help defeat the totally uncompromising fanaticism of the latter. In general, the United States was responsible for growing Arab conventional power, which in turn upset Israel's own priorities, and at least indirectly protected the PLO in Lebanon. That torn country, lacking a central authority since the outbreak of a civil war in 1975, was controlled by competing non-Lebanese entities — the Palestinians and the Syrians, who were both competing with each other and committed to each other (in the sense that, under certain circumstances, one could involve the other against Israel). Thus the weak Lebanese state allowed the Palestinians almost complete freedom of action unless checked; the Palestinians could be used by—or in turn use—the Syrians, by attacking the Israelis from Palestinian bases in Lebanon. Israeli retaliations, on the ground or from the air, were usually censured by the United States. Thus Washington, in Sharon's view, allowed Lebanon to become a protected guerrilla base or the trigger for a new war under conditions favoring one of the other interested parties—the Syrians or the PLO.

The invasion was timed both to ensure no interference from Egypt and to undercut domestic political criticism from the extreme nationalists. Israeli nationalists were inflamed by the Israeli withdrawal from the Sinai—and the destruction of Israeli settlements there—by Sharon himself in his capacity as defense minister after the 1979 Israeli-Egyptian peace treaty. By acting while the Sinai withdrawal, a major concession to Egypt, was still fresh, Sharon reasoned that Cairo would stick to the peace treaty, and would not be militarily ready to move into the Sinai and threaten Israel from the south. Besides, Egypt was being denounced by the other Arabs as a traitor to the common cause by having signed a peace treaty with Israel and would not be so willing to rush to the aid of the most vocal critic among them.

Egypt could not be completely forgotten though. A number of events that could endanger the Israeli-Egyptian accord were in the offing: e.g., the assassination of President Sadat by Moslem fanatics; the ascendance of a lesser-known personality, Hosni Mubarak; Egypt's loud intentions to create a nuclear infrastructure "for peaceful use"; the angry reaction among Egyptian opinion-makers to the Osiraq raid; and the stalled West Bank autonomy talks, which were supposed to follow the Sinai withdrawal.

Egypt's nuclear program had hit several snags. The highly ambitious Egyptian nuclear program to build eight nuclear reactors for peaceful use was conceived following President Nixon's visit to the Middle East in 1974; the Egyptians planned to use nuclear explosives to blast a link between the Mediterranean and the Qatara Depression in the Western Desert. The program in general, though, had enormous planning and infrastructure problems: the lack of trained personnel, the question of the location of the proper sights, the disposal of nuclear waste, and so on. These problems were further complicated by the financial burden and by Cairo's deliberations on whether or not to join NPT fully (while Israel refrained from doing so). The Egyptian press dealt openly with these issues, reflecting various conflicting views. Once Egypt ratified NPT in the early 1980s, the initial enthusiasm over nuclear issues seemed to have vanished, but the destruction of Osiraq by Israel triggered a wave of criticism and sense of humiliation. *Al-Da'awa*, Cairo, gave a religious Moslem accent to the raid, linking Israel with the Crusaders—a persistent argument among Arabs—and justifying a counterraid against Dimona.[5] And opposition leaders such as Haled Muhi al-Din called upon the Arabs to acquire nuclear weapons of their own.[6]

President Sadat refrained from addressing Begin's nuclear doctrine directly, but he called it a retreat by Israel to the old psychological barrier that the peace process had removed for the Egyptians. By the same token, he criticized his Arab opponents, who had rejected Egypt's peace treaty with Israel, by remarking on their failure to intercept the Israeli Air Force jets that raided Baghdad.[7]

Soon Sadat was dead. A friend of the late president, Anis Mansur, the weekly editor of *October*, reminded his readers of the Israeli nuclear threat during the siege laid by Sharon around Beirut not long afterward:

> *If [the Arab state] would have panicked in a moment of confusion, it would have been a major mistake. Israel would have used the nuclear bomb* [italics added] . . . Israel would have argued that the Arabs had united to destroy [her]. [She] still has this option—the nuclear option—to solve conflicts in the future. These conflicts were created by Israel herself due to her very existence and aggravated by her violent behavior.[8]

The opposition's arguments in Egypt could be perceived by Sharon as a withdrawal from Sadat's peace strategy, and they were bound to influence Mubarak. Moreover, Mansur's argument might have been perceived by Sharon as a sort of tacit Arab acceptance of an Israeli last resort option (as described earlier by General Shazli), making Israel's very existence no longer the goal of regular warfare—at least as long as the Jewish state held what both Mansur and Shazli perceived to be a nuclear monopoly. "[Israel] would argue that *the Arabs had united to destroy her*," as Mansur, a mainstream Egyptian opinion-maker, and not just the exiled General Shazli, put it. Only under such conditions would the Arabs honor the bomb. And thus they were given, as had occurred in 1973, the chance to choose any other kind of belligerency that might suit them—short of a sheer "war of destruction"—such as highly costly conventional wars, which could yield the same, though aggregated, results. Therefore Sharon's strategy was aimed at depriving them of freedom of action through changes in doctrine, "opaque" as they were, that would signify the end of the "last resort" option by using geostrategic activities such as the Lebanon war. Other components of Sharon's strategy must have included the support of a large-scale effort to diversify Israel's nuclear arsenal and efforts to construct theater nuclear weapons and strategic ones (as one may interpret Spector's 1988 and 1990 reports) while Israel's regional hegemony was, for the time being, assured. The deterrence practical-theoretical arguments behind such developments could have been drawn from NATO's own deliberations and decisions in the late 1970s regarding theater nuclear weapons. These weapons had seemed necessary to create a regional nuclear deterrent to counter such Soviet weapons—combined with the Soviet conventional advantage—which might have given the Soviets a "first strike" option in Europe (although NATO countries rested on a geostrategic status quo, whereas Sharon was aiming at changing it).

This brings us back to the problem of Israel's optional "second strike," and the technical viability of its nuclear options, as criticized years before by Allon and Galili. Israel had started its missile program with the "purchase of 25 missiles" from France, as mentioned earlier, and the Jericho was a short- to medium-range missile with a range of about 400 miles, according to Spector's most recent research.[9] If this was true, it was a "theater nuclear weapon" to begin with. If it was deployed, it could have been placed in fixed positions, or—as Spector quotes from a U.S. Defense Intelligence Agency document entitled "Surface-to-Surface Missile Handbook—Free World"[10]—the system was "deployed on a wheeled TEL [transporter/erector/launcher] vehicle." This (if true) gave Israel a higher degree of protection for its Jericho 1s from "first strikes" aimed at fixed positions. The "Jericho follow-on"— which according to Spector's 1990 book had been "tested" but not necessarily "deployed"[11]—had a 900-mile range, making it more than a theater nuclear weapon. Since the testing of such "follow-ons" took place in the second half of the 1980s, according to a variety of foreign sources, one could imagine that the decision to produce them was made at the beginning of that decade, even if the basic idea could be traced to Pean's MD 660 and to Ben-Gurion's times. Cruise missiles and submarine-fired warheads could also serve as "second strike" tools, and thus reduce Israel's dependence on fixed, vulnerable land bases. They could, in fact, make Israel less dependent on occupied territory as well—a complex issue to be discussed later. But none of this was publicly discussed, maybe because—among other reasons—it was politically more supportive of Likud's position to argue that conventional security reasons dictated Israel's rule over the whole West Bank and the Golan Heights. Also—as Sharon could have argued—the present danger in conventional and unconventional terms required action now, while Israel's conventional might was at its peak and at least Egypt's conventional power was at its lowest and Cairo's future course was uncertain.

Egypt's growing cooperation with the United States, and the enormous conventional military aid given to it by Washington, lent room for uneasy speculation in Israel. Egypt, indirectly, and later in direct cooperation with oil-rich Arabs, could build a modern conventional army. Also, thanks to the support of Secretary Weinberger and others in the Reagan Administration, the oil-rich Arabs would acquire modern aircraft such as F-15's and AWACS early-warning systems. Once all was ready and Israel's Sinai withdrawal was forgotten, President Mubarak could rejoin the Arab camp at will and push Israel into making concessions in the West Bank and Gaza. He would be backed by American-supplied military power, and would be able to act from a position of political strength as a U.S. ally, supported by the oil lobby and sustained by constant American disapproval of the Israeli occupation of at least the Arab-populated parts of the territories. Although peace with Israel neutralized Egypt in the short run, the resultant American connection gave the country quite an advantage in the long run.

And, of course, the Heikal option was still open. But now it could be implemented in a much more clever way: thanks to the peace treaty with Israel, Egypt would obtain a nuclear infrastructure from the West, even if it required in the meantime the signing of NPT. Begin's doctrine to destroy Arab reactors could hardly be implemented as long as peace with Egypt was maintained. What was more disconcerting was that one of Mubarak's initial acts upon taking office was to release Heikal from jail—where Sadat had sent him, following, among other things, the publication of his nuclear treatises abroad.

Thus the setting for the Lebanon invasion was ready, except that the Israeli public was not given any in-depth analysis. They were presented only with vague, misleading, and wrong information, including blurred war aims and false remarks about the extent of the operation. We do not know whether the cabinet, too, was misled by Sharon into believing that the operation would be much more limited than he actually planned.[12]

Very soon, however, Sharon was confronted with some of those hated details that always hampered his grand strategy: a large Shi'ite element in Lebanon, which was divided into more and less pro-Iranian elements, rejected Sharon's idea of crowning the divided Maronites as the rulers of the country. They started a guerrilla war against the invading Israelis, while trying to assert themselves against rival communities. The fighting Druze community, tiny but tough, would not accept Christian hegemony; moreover, it would not take Israel's part because it had a large Druze community in Syria to worry about. And the Sunni Moslems felt even more threatened by the Israeli invasion. All this was in the making while the actual target, the PLO, was under siege in Beirut. Soon the PLO was evacuated and Israel's Maronite ally Bashir Gemayel, was assassinated. Then Israel took control of the Palestinian quarters of the city, and Gemayel's compatriots took their revenge on Palestinian refugee camps.

This massacre of Palestinian civilians committed by Christian troops, the protracted siege of Beirut which preceded it, the long casualty list, and the apparent contradiction between Sharon's initial war aims and the length of the operation, brought about a domestic explosion in Israel. Mass rallies followed American protests and the landing of the Marines in Beirut on a "peace keeping" mission, which in fact drove the Israelis away from its Moslem quarters. Elsewhere in Lebanon there was no apparent solution. The armored Israeli columns were not trained to fight a prolonged guerrilla war in a foreign country.

In Israel, there were also serious signs of opposition among junior members of the parliamentary coalition and among members of the cabinet from Begin's own Likud bloc, due to Sharon's high-handedness toward his cabinet colleagues, their own fears of public wrath, and partisan calculations. The prime minister needed them all to maintain his parliamentary majority, and thus he was forced to agree to a judicial inquiry into the Beirut massacre. Sharon had to resign the Defense Ministry following the inquiry, and Begin followed suit shortly afterward, ill and unable to regroup his followers and strengthen his parliamentary base. Upon leaving, Sharon asserted to stupefied Israelis, who still did not know what he was talking about, that by his departure Israel "had lost half of her credibility."

Yitzhak Shamir, who succeeded Begin as prime minister and as leader of the Likud bloc, vacillated between his own rather "hawkish" convictions, his bloc's investment in Lebanon, and his tendency to deal with larger strategic-political issues in a less spectacular fashion than Sharon. Once Sharon left the Defense Ministry and the aeronautical engineer Moshe Arens succeeded him, the nuclear option was handled more cautiously.[13]

In the meantime the Syrians had recovered, thanks to Soviet aid supplied after the initial setbacks in the Lebanon war, and were now talking again about a "strategic balance" that would allow them to go to war against Israel. This was the first time they publicly declared Dimona itself to be a target.[14] Syrian defense minister Mustafa Tlass quoted a Soviet "nuclear guarantee" given to his country against Israel's nuclear option without specifying details. There is no known public Soviet confirmation, however, to substantiate this claim.[15] Both these threats—of attacking Dimona when necessary and the alleged Soviet guarantee—seem to have been belatedly used by Syria to play on earlier Israeli sensitivities. But these sensitivities were by now reduced, or gone altogether, in a Likud government, once (according to *Aerospace Daily* in 1985, and Spector in 1988 and 1990) Israel had a larger missile force and a diversified nuclear arsenal at its disposal. Soviet-supplied missiles, such as the not-so-accurate SCUD-B, which is reported to have a 300-kilometer radius, actually gave Syria a conventional capability to strike into Israel's depth. Yet it was already reported several years earlier that the SCUD-Bs were armed with Syrian chemical warheads. To Syria, and to several other Arab states such as Iraq and Libya, chemical weapons were seen as the "poor man's deterrent" and more: their actual use against Israeli targets such as Tel Aviv would hardly endanger—in terms of fall-out, for example—the neighboring Arab communities. Should the Iraqis resume their nuclear efforts, chemical missiles may give them better protection for their nuclear installations as deterrents. Chemical weapons may also help limit a war to conventional warfare—in which Saddam would hope to prevail due to his numbers, equipment, and the experience gained in the Iran conflict—if they were positioned at the H2, H3 area (named after two old British oil pumping stations) in western Iraq, the closest site to Israel on the Jordanian boundary. Technically, the issue was not quite so simple: the SCUDs' payload was reduced to about 150 to 250 kilograms when their range was extended in order to reach Israel, and the construction of chemical warheads was not a simple matter. By 1990—when the Kuwait crisis broke out—it was estimated that Iraq had a limited number of chemical missiles at its disposal. Information about the gas itself—whether it was more or less lethal, whether it was the nerve gas Sarin or the Soviet-made, sticky and persistent, highly lethal nerve gas called Soman—remained unknown. But the chemical threat was yet to come.

At first, Shamir's objective was to signal to the Americans, and to the Russians as well, that he had not changed Begin's doctrine of preventing the Arabs from going nuclear, but his version of opaque warnings was less provocative than Sharon's and closer to the norm of striving to prohibit nuclear proliferation altogether.[16] Sharon's semi-Gaullism and his apparent vision of extending Israel's nuclear options to the very edges of the occupied territories, plus something like a "first strike" doctrine, were not necessarily Shamir's view, at least in public. As foreign minister, and as prime minister, Shamir was ready to play the game by seemingly returning to Eshkol's old formula.

Then came the 1984 national elections, in which the issues of grand strategy seemed irrelevant to the battling politicians. During the domestic political campaign they were hardly mentioned; the economy and the political show governed the scene. The puzzling result was a tie—a clear-cut division of Israel along ethnic and class lines, with the Labor Party representing the upper and more pragmatic classes and the Likud finding deep loyalties among the non-European members of the working and lower-middle classes.

Since its defeat in 1977, Labor seemed to have managed to conceal the differences between its historical factions; Peres, as chairman and candidate for the premiership, and Rabin, as the candidate for the defense ministry, had adopted a partition plan for the West Bank in cooperation with Jordan along the lines of the old Allon plan, which postulated Israel's "defense boundary" along the Jordan River. Shimon Peres whispered loudly to editors of the daily *Ma'ariv* that

> he was deeply worried about the future of the region, when nuclear weapons would be introduced into the Middle East in 10-15 years. Therefore, we must work for peace with Egypt, Jordan, and Syria.[17]

He further "disclosed" that "the late President Sadat had entered into peace negotiations thanks to the atomic reactor in Dimona." Peres added, however, that Likud under Shamir would encourage the Arabs to fight another round. His reasoning was phrased in the following terms in an interview given to a rather elitist Israeli monthly with a rather small circulation:

> *I am worried that in about 10-15 years nuclear weapons will reach the Arabs . . . today we have what we have, and they have not what they have not, and the truth is, that there is no technological answer* [italics added]—there is only a political answer, and regarding the latter I am ready to be steadfast.[18]

In the interview quoted from above with the more hawkish newspaper, *Ma'ariv*, Peres had elaborated the last point:

> Labor, in contradiction to Likud, will be verbally generous, and only around the negotiation table shall we be tough . . . one should be generous with words, not with territories.

These opaque statements could be interpreted as follows: Israel had a nuclear monopoly option, which indeed had played a role in bringing Egypt to the peace process. However, this process was stalled due to Likud's refusal either to implement its own commitments to Palestinian autonomy—as per the 1979 Israeli-Egyptian peace treaty— or to try to negotiate a final peace with Jordan—a peace that, however, should not return the West Bank as a whole to King Hussein. Furthermore, Likud was provocative in its behavior with Arabs by humiliating them, adding insult to injury, and killing diplomacy. Therefore, Israel's nuclear monopoly option, which was bound to disappear in any case within ten to fifteen years, was being wasted, since it could be used to work toward peace. Finally, if peace were not in sight when the nuclear monopoly was gone, or at the very least, if some kind of diplomatic process had not been added to the military-political conflict, the future of the region as a whole could be affected. Israel would not be able to maintain its monopoly option by introducing any technological solutions to Arab nuclear threats.

Whether Peres was that pessimistic about modern technological developments, such as anti-missile missiles, one can only guess. He might have chosen this formulation to avoid foreign interest in such developments. Or he might have been out of touch with them, or ready to trade some of them off for a form of conflict resolution, in which the Soviets would play a positive role. Such speculations are unavoidable when we have only opaque public expressions at our disposal. On the one hand, such statements may sound doubtful as deterrents; but they are "opaque" rather than "ambiguous" in the sense that they reflect an Israeli nuclear monopoly option and threats to the enemy, as indeed the Arabs understood it. But at the same time, however, such statements are designed for domestic and foreign use in order to enhance the peace process without seriously discussing the issue in public.

In response to Peres' statements, Likud could have argued, opaquely, that the real reason the peace process was stalled was because the Jordanians and Palestinians in the occupied territories (let alone the PLO, Syria and Iraq) had rejected it from the beginning, and that Syria, Iraq, Libya, Algeria, and the Yemens were still dead against it. In fact this description of the Arab position, in the wake of the Iran-Iraq War, was not accurate, at least on the face of it. If anyone were likely to negotiate at all it would be King Hussein, but only to recover the whole West Bank including East Jerusalem, which Mr. Peres was not ready to give up, due in part to the strategic depth necessary in the nuclear age. Also, Likud would insist that its approach was not to toy with words, but rather that its stance was loud and clear: If the Arabs were ready to negotiate, Likud would honor its commitment and enter into negotiations based on both their own and the Arabs' planks, barring any dealings with the PLO, which was not accepted as a partner for negotiations by either Likud or Labor. Likud, of course, would insist on its claim over the West Bank and Gaza, and demand its annexation to Israel. Since no Arab party would accept that, Likud would be ready to drop annexation and agree to Palestinian autonomy of sorts therein, but not to any other changes in the status quo.

As for Peres' assumption that nuclear weapons would reach the Arabs anyway and that therefore Israel should make concessions, Likud under Shamir would have dismissed Peres' approach as self-defeating and would not discuss nuclear issues in public at all. If the Arabs listened to him, they would wait until they had the weapons to negotiate—or fight—from a position of strength; they could only be encouraged to do so by Shimon Peres' public arguments. Peres' desire to disengage from occupied Arab lands by means of territorial concessions was dangerous in terms of Arab nuclear attacks aimed at the Jewish populated area, once it was defined and segregated from Arabs. And the matter of whether a technological solution to the Arab threat could or would not be developed in the meantime should be pursued. Perhaps a technological solution, such as antiballistic missiles, could be pursued now, thanks to the more practical and limited "strategic agreement" with the United States that had been concluded in 1983 to replace Sharon's December 1981 memorandum of strategic understanding that had been suspended.[19]

Both Likud and the more militant Tehiya Party under Minister of Science Ne'eman could also have argued against Peres that occupation, and the territorial depth that went along with it, was less dangerous in the nuclear age than giving up Israel's direct control over the parts of the West Bank. Withdrawal would entail exposing Israel to even short-range rocket attacks close to its pre-1967 heart, which could then trigger a general war in a nuclearized environment.

However, rather than discuss any of this in public, both Likud and Tehiya used conventional arguments in their respective 1984 election campaigns, probably due in part to their fear that some voters might accept the argument that Israel's nuclear option rendered control over the West Bank unnecessary. Without exception, Israel's leaders also anticipated that if they gave up the existing level of opacity, there would be repercussions on Israel's relations with the United States, and possible Soviet reactions in public. Besides the few statements mentioned above, most of Mr. Peres' own arguments in the 1984 campaign were economic—he even refrained from criticizing Likud's war in Lebanon—and his nuclear statements were sporadic and isolated. He never mentioned nuclear options as a reason to decrease investment in across-the-board conventional deterrence and conventional war-winning capabilities, so dear to Mr. Rabin, his partner for Labor's leadership, whether he wanted it or not. Nor did he reduce the possibility of concentrating in specific conventional areas to win "limited wars," the challenge that Israel seemed more likely to face since 1973. Thus, both Likud and Labor argued around one of the nation's most important points.

In 1984 none of the major parties won a working parliamentary majority, and a similar result was achieved in 1988, with more power given by the voters to smaller parties, mainly religious ones. In 1984 the larger parties finally had to agree to a grand coalition in which both parties were given equal representation, with the premiership rotating between Shamir and Peres.

CHAPTER ELEVEN

From Lebanon to the Intifada

Prime Minister Shimon Peres seemed not to be interested in foreign affairs as a top priority, but rather in economic problems and in the endless Lebanon war, which became a major domestic source of concern. However, in May 1985, under Peres as prime minister and Shamir as his senior deputy and foreign minister, the usually well-informed *Aerospace Daily* reported that Israel had *deployed* a large number of Jericho missiles in the Negev and in the Golan Heights, as discussed in the previous chapter.[1] The deployment of the 400-mile Jericho system was confirmed in Spector's 1990 book.[2] If these reports were true, the stage had been reached when a mass deployment of at least short-medium range, homemade missiles was possible and agreeable to both coalition partners, despite their political differences. The ensuing testing of Jericho "follow-ups," which according to foreign sources took place later in the 1980s, must have also been the result of an agreement between Likud and Labor.[3] The difference between Likud and Labor may be sought in terms of Peres' use of opaque, but more and more visible, nuclear options as a tool to promote a political process entailing some territorial concessions.

One could learn here from Helmut Schmidt's 1979 "double track decision" to deploy modern "theater nuclear weapons" in Germany and negotiate with the Soviets at the same time.[4] However, once again most Israelis were unable to follow this line of thought, even after the publicity given to the alleged missile deployment and missile testing. Moreover, in Israel's case no American ICBMs or submarine-fired missiles were part of the superstructure of such a "double track decision," as they were in the German case. We can thereby explain foreign sources' claims that Israeli-made IRBMs, possibly ICBMs, were added to the shorter-range "theater weapons" mentioned above. By now they could be interpreted as a tool to encourage the Soviets to enter the peace process. We do not know whether Peres perceived in such weapons a trump card that could be fully or partially traded off when Moscow responded positively, because the game was played by implication.

When Mordechai Vanunu, the nuclear technician employed at Dimona, was fired and got himself into spiritual and financial trouble, he published information in which he tried to stress that Israel was doing illegal things in the most sensitive sphere of international affairs, instead of making peace. Yet the impact of Vanunu's disclosures on the Arab world, at least as far as its press and official statements were concerned, could be seen as divided: Arab radicals such as Qaddafi, and those in Egyptian opposition circles, reacted with anger and dismay, doubling their demands for an Arab bomb. Others, such as Iraq and Syria, responded by invoking chemical weapons as an interim solution until they got their own bombs. Whereas Egypt repeatedly argued that chemical weapons, mounted on missiles, were enough as a counterthreat, due to Israel's known sensitivity to any meaningful losses, especially among civilians. Of course, such a threat was not enough to cover an Arab war of destruction against Israel. But it could cover limited wars, and Arab efforts to produce their own bomb.

On the other hand, the Syrian press used Vanunu's revelations, the missile disclosures, and Israel's refusal to join the NPT to portray Israel as a "pirate" state.[5] And it tried to transmit these Israeli threats to the Soviet Union, inferring that the Israeli program was relevant to East-West rivalry, because (as Arabs saw it) the United States was interested in Israeli nuclear threats vis-à-vis the Soviet Union. This argument, aimed at getting the Soviets more involved on the Arab side, could, of course, make them become less involved, especially after Gorbachev's takeover. It could make the Soviets seek some kind of a conflict resolution, and *not* a "strategic balance." The Syrians—and the Iraqis—had been talking about such a balance since 1973, arguing that they were confronted with the Israeli nuclear option in its various opaque patterns. Like many others, the Syrians failed at first to comprehend the deep changes in the Soviet Union, which were soon to be manifested by an entirely new and unknown quantity, Mikhail Gorbachev, and which were only partially related to foreign and defense issues and the enormous costs of a futile nuclear arms race. Only later would President Assad draw his own conclusions from these changes.

Arab policymakers like President Mubarak must have analyzed the relatively large Israeli arsenal, as disclosed by the experts who verified Vanunu's information, on its merits. It could have helped Egypt adhere to the peace treaty despite domestic outcries about Israel's behavior since 1979 and other, older arguments against any dealings with the Jewish state. Whether the peace strategy could be maintained until an Arab bomb entered the picture remains an open question that must be studied on the basis of various public actions taken by various Arab leaders, then and since—such as Saddam Hussein's political activity, which culminated in the 1990 invasion of Kuwait. Such developments, in turn, must be analyzed within the context of their time, including the outbreak of the bitter struggle between Iraq and Iran in the early 1980s, and its conclusion.

Still, a new meaning could be given here to the distinction between "moderate" Arabs and "radical" Arabs, in the sense that "moderates" could have endorsed, in the course of time, a stance that refused to allow the Arab-Israeli conflict to lead the region to a nuclear holocaust. When both sides had the bomb, such a holocaust would be much closer to becoming a reality. This would be especially true if "radical" Arabs had access to the bomb and thereby tried to influence the Arab scene at first, and then involve the region in a nuclear conflict. Certainly, some basic differences—economic, temperamental, ideological, and historical—would prevail here, when one remembers Egypt's population explosion and its complete dependence upon American economic aid, which was not the case with Iraq or Libya. Arms control on both sides—which Nasser's Egypt might have negotiated in the 1960s—would be the final target of the "moderate" Arabs. And Soviet-American cooperation would be a precondition to achieving it (as Israel's stance remained opaque at all times), provided of course that all Arabs, including at least the most involved "radicals," played the same game vis-à-vis the great powers and demonstrated moderation. The result could be, at the very least, the isolation of Israel.

One can argue that in the meantime the Israeli nuclear option contributed heavily to Egypt's peace strategy, because war—maybe any kind of war—against Israel could develop into a nuclear war, that is, to the only kind of threat that was deadly to the Arabs at large and to Egypt in particular. Other Arab leaders might have thought differently—that the bomb would give them more freedom of conventional action, prestige, and hegemonic roles to play among themselves, mostly low political goals. But for the time being none of them had the tool to play those games, although Iraq, Libya, and possibly Syria were trying to acquire it in the long run, while absorbed—in various and opposing ways—in the Iraq-Iran War.

In the meantime, while these political-strategic premises prevailed, a series of Arab summits were convened at Fez, Morocco, in November 1981 and September 1982. At the first summit, a peace strategy vis-à-vis Israel was discussed, but no decision was reached. At the second Fez Summit, such a strategy was endorsed and combined with the rights of the Palestinians for self-determination, with the reiteration that the PLO was the sole representative of the Palestinian people. For Israelis this could readily be seen as the old contradiction in terms, since the PLO was committed to its own "National Covenant" of 1964. This covenant denied any political rights to Jews in Palestine; it was committed to the return of Jews to the countries of their origin, and to the concept of a "secular Palestinian state in Palestine" as a whole, once all exiled Palestinians returned home. Yet the second Fez Summit could be interpreted as something like the Soviet peace campaign vis-à-vis the West in the 1950s, in which the negative, hostile, seemingly unbridgeable terminology of earlier Stalinism was abandoned. When "coexistence" with the West was added to this, and the Soviets themselves stressed the role of nuclear weapons as a reason for "coexistence"—without entirely giving up the cold war or their hopes to win it—the struggle between East and West adopted a more positive character based on the nuclear scare.

In the case of the Arabs, a peace strategy was officially adopted, but no public reasoning—in nuclear terms—was given for it (except that given by several Egyptian commentators quoted above). But the "nuclear aspect" of this strategy might have been the main reason, following the Soviet example and American inputs, for the softened Arab position, when combined with the Iran-Iraq War, the declining impact of oil as a weapon since 1979, and the lessons learned from the adverse effect of open, belligerent statements calling for the destruction of Israel (which in fact played into Israel's hands and justified its unconventional options). The peace strategy gave the Saudis, who openly endorsed it, a more positive image in the West. And, if pursued, it could make Israel seem to be the less flexible party, whose main interest was sheer occupation. Even Iraq seemed to fall in line with this, while Libya and Syria—who supported Iran as well—remained isolated.

Israel's Labor Party was always more sensitive to international public opinion and more open to American and European arguments than Likud, aiming to soften Israel's own position. Peres had to pursue a strategy of "openness" abroad, without losing public opinion—mostly hawkish—at home. His problem was how to use the nuclear option politically without admitting it publicly; or rather use it in an opaque, implied, or behind-the-scenes fashion, in order not to get a boomerang effect from the sensitive Arabs or an unpleasant reminder from Washington that this game must be played very carefully.

When Peres became prime minister, and Vanunu intervened in the game in his crude way, Peres must have been furious, especially because Arab rejectionists such as Qaddafi and the Egyptian opposition used it to the utmost to spoil the peace prospects. Those who played the game of peace after the Fez summits could argue vis-à-vis Washington that because of its nuclear option Israel was too arrogant to make peace with—although, as far as Peres was concerned, this very option was needed to make peace.

Peres, then, in agreement with Foreign Minister Shamir, had Vanunu brought to Israel and jailed as a traitor. When he rotated the premiership with Shamir and became foreign minister, the grand coalition would have had to agree to the running of what Spector calls detectable test flights of the Jericho "follow-ons." One of the reasons for this might have been American pressure on Israel to disengage from South Africa. Thus, instead of running missile tests from a South African range at Overberg and on the Prince Edward Islands, Israel might have decided to move the testing site to its own shores.[6] In addition, for Peres, the value of the testing would be to encourage an understanding between Israel and the Soviets, based on the perception of Israel as a "mini-nuclear power" having missiles whose range exceeded the radius agreed upon in the framework of the Intermediate Range Nuclear Forces Treaty (INF). INF itself, by barring missiles with a radius of 500 kilometers or less, would prohibit the Soviets from supplying more advanced SS-23 missiles (with a radius of 500 kilometers, and highly accurate) to Syria and to Saddam Hussein's Iraq. The hope would be to make the Soviets partners in a restrained and manageable Middle East, in the context of the new Reagan-Gorbachev detente and the INF treaty, while denying any targeting of Soviet territory.[7] Shamir might have agreed to parts of such a concept, but he would not agree to any territorial concessions that would most likely be included in a larger package involving the Soviets. He would have had serious concerns about whether the Russians, with their commitments to the PLO, might turn around right after an international Middle East conference—a diplomatic umbrella demanded by King Hussein for a renewed peace process and accepted with reservations by Peres—and help transform any territory ceded to Jordan into a PLO state.

So Likud and Labor agreed on at least some missile testing, as we can interpret their behavior when the tests were disclosed abroad. After the launching, Israel was publicly warned—first in Soviet broadcasts in Hebrew beamed to Israel alone, and then in Russian on Russian television—not to deploy the new missiles, which allegedly could reach the southern parts of the Soviet Union.

First, Moscow Radio Peace and Progress in Hebrew addressed itself to both the Israeli nuclear option and the Jericho missiles.[8] Then, late in October 1987, Gennadi Gerassimov, the spokesman of the Soviet Foreign Ministry, addressed the issue in a rather restrained fashion, saying that the situation in the Middle East would seriously deteriorate "should Israel develop nuclear missiles." This was quoted in *Al-Hamishmar* on October 31, 1987. Gerassimov repeated the old Soviet argument that "some day the Arabs, too, would have the bomb," thus trying to limit the issue to the regional conflict itself, and leaving Moscow out of it.

Later, Moscow Television in Russian addressed itself to both issues in a remarkably open manner, and reported on Israeli combat tests of a medium-range missile.[9] According to commentator Yuri Rostow, the tested missile had a range of 1,500 kilometers; because it was not very accurate, it could be used as a nuclear missile only; and it could reach most Arab capitals. Soviet targets, well within this range, were not mentioned. The obvious tactic chosen here was to expose the testing in its initial stage to prevent further development and deployment by means of international—especially American—pressure on Israel in this regard, and to limit the Israeli nuclear option to the Arab-Israeli dispute and remove Moscow from it. (On other occasions, Moscow attacked Israel for its involvement in the—conventional—aspects of President Reagan's "Star Wars.") The first warnings were opaque, due both to the formulations used and to the language chosen in which to make them. But while later formulations and threats were open, they were soon followed by much more friendly Soviet and Eastern bloc diplomacy toward Israel, and toward Shimon Peres personally. Peres probably hoped that if Labor won the 1988 election and providing Israel would be able to satisfy some Soviet reservations, he might be able to use the new missiles to bring Gorbachev into the Middle East peace process.[10]

As a restraining power, the Soviet leadership could push the Syrians away from Assad's traditional rejectionist position and at the very least, stop supplying Damascus with more dangerous chemical warheads for its missiles, or any other unconventional equipment. One can imagine that the Israelis were not unaware of the significance of INF; they later noted to their satisfaction that the much dreaded SS-23 Spider, which they feared would be supplied next to Syria, belonged to the category of missiles the Soviets were supposed to completely destroy during the three-year period beginning on June 1, 1988, specified by INF.[11]

Iraq, we should remember, was still mired in the Iran-Iraq War. However at that time, Saddam Hussein had started to use Soviet-improved SCUD-B's against Iranian targets.[12] Armed with a relatively small conventional warhead that gave them a longer range, about two hundred SCUD's reached Teheran and administered a serious blow to Iranian morale, even if the actual damage caused by them was small. In the battlefield itself, but not inside Iranian territory, Saddam used poison gas in various ways, mainly dropped from his French- and Soviet-supplied planes, against the Iranians and Kurdish rebels. The Kurds—many civilians included—suffered heavily. Soon enough Iran, unable to break through Iraqi defenses, would sue for an armistice, leaving Saddam with three dangerous and contradictory results of his eight-year war against them: (1) a sense of victory without any meaningful results (on the contrary, according to Israeli estimates published in 1991, Iran reversed Khomeini's initial rejection of nuclear weapons and in 1987 revitalized the Shah's nuclear program*); (2) a giant standing army; and (3) an enormous debt (to the Gulf states, including Kuwait) in a modernizing society—still deeply divided and ruled by a military, minority sect—that was completely dependent on oil revenues.

Returning to Peres' policy, his attention was not focused on the Gulf at the time—and no one else calculated in advance Saddam's future moves. Peres' main problem was the superpowers, and a possible positive role to be played by the Soviets now that Israel was reported to have tested something that was understood abroad as IRBMs, to be followed soon by the official display of a powerful booster made of three stages. (The first two stages of the booster could have made up the shorter-range IRBM[13]—and the whole could be perceived as an ICBM, "whose most obvious assumed target [was] Soviet territory," according to Spector.)[14] The main issue was Soviet strategic aid to radical Arabs, which—thanks to the changing climate between the great powers—was limited to a considerable degree. As far as the PLO was concerned, the Soviets might learn—from their own experience as active partners—that the ideology, interests, and inner structure of the exiled Palestinians made them a hopeless case, a nonpartner to a constructive deal entailing peace for territories. Or else, perhaps, the Soviets could push the PLO to make far-reaching concessions that might destroy Arafat's outfit. In any case, the PLO—exiled from Lebanon and pushed to the edges of the Arab world—did not seem to bother Shimon Peres seriously at that stage.

But having agreed on the test flight of an advanced Jericho missile, and later on the launching of the satellite Ofek 1 (to which we shall

---

* See Ron Ben-Yishai, "Iran on the Road to the Bomb," *Yediot Aharonot*, November 15, 1991.

return), the grand coalition was unable to endorse Peres' initiative to open negotiations with King Hussein regarding the West Bank. In April 1987, as foreign minister, Peres had reached an agreement with the king regarding both the form and some principles pertaining to substance that could serve as a framework for an international conference on the Middle East in which Jordan would not have to start bilateral negotiations with the Jewish state. However, because of its commitment to Israel's presence in the West Bank, Likud would accept neither the procedure—especially when Peres arranged it on his own—nor the substance of these negotiations. It is possible also that Likud had a genuine fear that such a diplomatic process would assume its own momentum, and either make King Hussein a surrogate for the PLO from the outset, or later, once the West Bank territory was given to him, make him yield to the pressure of other Arabs. Likud was also apprehensive that the whole conference would simply be used by most participants to isolate Israel and serve their own interests.

The grand coalition was stalled. All that was accomplished in its four years in office—other than the possible deployment of Jericho missiles and the testing of new, improved ones from home bases—was the withdrawal of the IDF from most of Lebanon after three years of a massive presence. This unilateral withdrawal, short of Israel's original war aims, seemed to have been forced upon Israel by constant guerrilla warfare. Other acts of the grand coalition—such as the release from Israeli jails, and into the occupied territories, of 1,500 sentenced Palestinian guerrillas and terrorists in exchange for three Israeli POWs—could only have encouraged trouble.

The Peres-Hussein agreement, which ignored the Palestinians, and the public relations lessons of Lebanon, combined with the influx of the liberated guerrillas into the occupied territories, the rise of a new generation of local Palestinian leaders there, and the accumulated impact of the occupation, all culminated in the spontaneous West Bank-Gaza popular uprising that began in 1987—the Intifada.

The PLO tried to control this spontaneous uprising and transform it into a political tool, merging the interests of the occupied and exiled Palestinians. At first, the PLO leadership was so inspired by what seemed to be a breakthrough for their cause that they declared Palestinian independence in the occupied territories. But then, Yassir Arafat convened a meeting of the PLO's Palestine National Council in Algiers. At this meeting, the official ideological plank of the PLO was softened, boosting the PLO's international standing. Speaking before a special U.N. General Assembly meeting in Geneva early in December 1988, Arafat seemed to reduce his previous claims and to accept the idea of a

Palestinian state in the West Bank and Gaza, alongside an acceptable Israel. It was at this point that the United States started official talks with the PLO.

In Israel, an even more restrained strategy in regard to the nuclear complex was proposed by Labor at the outset of the 1988 elections. The grand coalition had decided shortly before to launch an Israeli satellite, Ofek 1, mounted on what was described by the Israeli and foreign press as a boosted version of the Jericho 2 missile. Officially named "Shavit" ("Comet"), the rocket was fired against the movement of the earth, ostensibly to prevent debris from falling on Arab territory in case of failure. Even if it carried a harmless first-generation satellite, the radius of the missile plus its payload gave room to far-reaching speculations in Israel and abroad, when combined with the previous testing of what was described as Jericho "follow-ons."[15] An authoritative American source, Steven Gray, of the U.S. Lawrence Livermore Laboratories, was quoted in mid-May 1989 in *Aviation Week*; he interpreted the launching as an "Israeli missile capability which could hit Moscow."

According to Spector, the Jericho "follow-ons" comprised the first two stages of the three-stage "Shavit" booster, which carried the Ofek 1 satellite into its orbit on September 19, 1988.[16] If true, both had a "range that is far greater than indicated" by separate "tests of the system." Shavit's booster "was unusually powerful . . . Any rocket that can be used as a space launcher can be adapted for use as a surface-to-surface ballistic missile, if its payload and trajectory are suitably modified and a re-entry vehicle is added." Yet for Spector this was a "public demonstration" of Israel's "rocket capabilities."[17] The demonstration was followed by several analyses, which Spector quoted. According to one analysis, Shavit could carry a one-ton (900-kilogram) payload just over 3,000 miles, or a half-ton payload nearly 4,700 miles, "in effect making the missile an intercontinental system . . ." According to Spector's interpretation, if the components of Shavit's booster were indeed Jericho "follow-ons," their range would be far longer than previous tests had indicated. "This would mean that the system was intended, at least in part, to reach targets outside the Middle East—the most obvious assumed target being Soviet territory."

Peres declared that Israel was "strong" and, therefore, could make territorial concessions for peace. On the Likud side, earlier in Summer 1988 sources close to Shamir published accounts revealing Syrian preparations to build an underground nuclear reactor to protect it from Israeli strikes. In the July 1, 1988 issue of *Ma'ariv*, Yosef Harif quoted the following from a "Kuwaiti newspaper," which in turn quoted "Western reports" based on an unspecified American investigation:

five Arab states met to acquire a nuclear option by the mid-1990s. These states are Algeria, Egypt, Libya, Iraq and Syria. According to the [American committee report] Syria has built a nuclear reactor in a mountain to protect it from a possible Israeli air attack.

An earlier article, "Assad in Damascus: The Day Is Not Far Off When We Shall Have Our Own Nuclear Capability" in the March 10, 1988 issue of *Ma'ariv*, followed the same theme. Arab efforts to acquire missiles and arm them with chemical warheads, and Iraq's actual use of chemical weapons against Iran and against its own Kurdish population (even if Saddam Hussein did not use chemical weapons outside of his own territory), were stressed by Likud strategists and acknowledged by Labor. Some Likud-oriented columnists saw the chemical-weapons stage as an interim phase before the Arabs went nuclear.[18]

Late in December 1988, President Reagan exposed Libya as having built a huge chemical weapons complex. Shortly afterward, the United States convened an international conference in Paris to introduce more strictly defined international norms to ban chemical weapons. The radical Arab states, led by Syria, openly linked their chemical weapons acquisition to the Israeli bomb. It is also possible that chemical missiles were developed by Syria to deter Israel from using any smaller weapons assumed to be in its unconventional arsenal, such as low-yield A-bombs or neutron weapons.

The Saudi acquisition of Chinese-made medium-range missiles, which China had agreed to sell in 1985, plus reports in Israel of Syrian efforts in the same direction and the Iraqi-Egyptian-Argentinian effort to build the medium-range Condor missile, all happened to coincide with Likud's ideological and political commitment not to withdraw from the West Bank. Military commentators close to Likud added a strategic argument that a "small Israel" would be an ideal target for such weapons, and with the Palestinian uprising in the occupied territories, one could argue that no territorial concessions in the West Bank could be made in the age of nuclear, chemical missiles, and popular-guerrilla war. A "reduced Israel" would be hopelessly vulnerable to strategic threats—nuclear threats included—combined with actual guerrilla warfare,[19] whereas a "larger Israel," including its Arab population, would be secure from conventional surprise attacks on its borders. Moreover, if nuclear weapons were used by Israel's enemies on a larger rather than on a smaller Israel, Arabs in Israel and in Arab centers close to Israel could be just as threatened as Israelis. (And, of course, this form of "nuclear hostage taking" was usually mentioned by Arab commentators.)

The main point to reiterate here is the sporadic use of deterrence-theoretical arguments—both Right and Left—to discredit Israel's nuclear option. One side was interested in maintaining the West Bank and argued that without it Israel's defense would become impossible and its nuclear option would have no credibility—even if behind the scenes contemporary nuclear deterrence thinking led to the diversification and to the enhancement of Israel's nuclear option. The other pole argued in favor of "peace," and that nuclear disarmament and even a Nuclear-Weapon-Free Zone, must be attained before peace could be agreed upon. The more extreme antibomb posture was assumed by some scholars such as Evron, Inbar, Yaniv, and several Leftist politicians, in whose doctrinaire thinking deterrence theory played a major role as a negative model.[20] Labor leaders fell between the two poles. But all these debates remained in fact tacit; the politicians seldom argued the point in public. They could cite the United States and "damage to the American-Israeli relations" as reasons not to argue publicly; and yet one of the reasons they avoided public debate was to avoid domestic political damage (any opinion on nuclear matters could have been persuasively attacked) and maybe also to avoid undesirable Arab reactions.

Since no one addressed the real strategic issues directly or even in a comprehensible indirect fashion, Israeli election campaigns did not reflect the real strategic debate between Shimon Peres and Likud. Peres seemed to believe, but never argued openly, that nuclear options gave Israel the basic security needed to justify withdrawal from parts of the West Bank in King Hussein's favor. Moreover, he was reluctant to publicly support the idea that the enormous investments in conventional deterrence and war-winning capabilities since 1973 had ruined the economy, as Dayan had indicated in his 1981 election campaign. This argument was politically dangerous. Peres also refrained from adding that nuclear options had been conceived by Ben-Gurion as a tool or some kind of coexistence, not for ruling over Arabs in the West Bank.[21] The reason for his reluctance was domestic-political no less than foreign-political: Mr. Peres wouldn't give up all of the West Bank to King Hussein, but only parts of it, and he wouldn't renounce the Jordan River line. This concept of "defensible boundaries"—even if in the West Bank itself Arab populated territory could have been ceded to Jordan—had been enshrined in Labor's political platform since 1968. Peres—who in the 1970s had even successfully fought Prime Minister Rabin to allow Israeli settlements in the middle of a purely Arab populated region of the West Bank—now became a "dove." But if he wanted to survive in his own party and avoid Rabin's immediate ascendance, he could not afford to give up the Jordan line or return to the 1967 boundaries (even when he might have wanted to do so). When he talked about Israel's "strength" and "power" allowing "concessions," he might have sounded flexible. But most Israelis saw little link here to the nuclear option—because they were unwilling to or were not interested enough to be informed. And no one could determine why he was talking about Israeli strength in conditions that seemed to have worsened because of the Intifada and reports of Arab unconventional efforts. Peres appeared to be tricky and untrustworthy. So, the majority of the Israeli public continued to support the opposing view, conventional deterrence and war-fighting doctrines, in which "territorial depth" seemed essential, unless the Arabs were offering "real peace," even though Likud's position entailed occupation and its obvious ramifications. Thus, the Left's emphasis on conventional deterrence entailed continued occupation.

One of the few plausible explanations for Likud's confidence in Israel's political-strategic maneuverability vis-à-vis Washington—even while holding on to the West Bank—was that they were relying on division in the Arab camp, on the influence of radical Arab states in it, on the PLO's ideology (its interests and inner divisions despite changes in the PLO's public position), and on America's own fear of a PLO state in the fragile Middle East. This fear would persist until the United States was convinced that the PLO would thoroughly change. Likud hoped that it would be able to convince Washington this would never happen or to use this fear to force the United States (with help from the Jewish influence within the American political system) to ask the PLO to make concessions that might destroy it from within. Also, Likud could be counting on their own high credibility, and on America's basic interest in preventing Israel from going openly nuclear, which could follow a serious American-Likud rift.

East-West rivalry could have been relied on to do the rest to sustain the status quo, that is until *perestroika* and INF changed the picture. Once they did, Soviet support of the PLO could still serve Israeli interests in Washington, along the lines described above. And Soviet military involvement in Syria, including alleged Soviet aid to sustain Assad's chemical warfare threats, and the supply by the Chinese of medium-range missile technology to Saudi Arabia would enhance U.S.-Israeli cooperation on the development of the Arrow antimissile missile.[22] This was what was hoped for, rather than what the Soviets were calling for now—to "demilitarize" missiles in the region in the spirit of INF, in combination with a broader peace process in which the Russians could play a positive role, while demanding a Palestinian state in the West Bank.

Soviet maneuvering in regard to the PLO could serve several purposes. The first would be purely political, as a measure to maintain friends among Arabs, that is, the continuation of Moscow's own influence among a dynamic Arab factor. Yet another consideration could have been a genuine desire to "localize" the Arab-Israeli conflict and transform it, once a Palestinian state was created, to a Palestinian-Israeli solution or to an ongoing but controllable dispute. Controllable how? Through Soviet—and American and maybe European—guarantees to the parties involved, which would legitimize Soviet presence in the area as an equal partner. Arms control was an official part of the Soviet vision in this package, but in fact it could be interpreted as unilateral Israeli nuclear disarmament. The Soviets might have hoped that some kind of regional peace, or "security system," would trade off Arab missiles and chemical weapons for at least the more dangerous elements in Israel's nuclear option, such as long-range missiles, and fully delegitimize Israel's nuclear option by making it join NPT. Further, Arab claims for nuclear weapons could become illegitimate; at least the incentives for Arabs to "buy, steal or get" the bomb would be minimized. It is possible that the Soviets envisioned the unconventional issue as the true basis for beginning negotiations between Arabs and Jews, as it was in Soviet dealings with the Americans. The so-called confidence building measures (CBMs) could be the removal of unconventional weapons (weapons that might have been aimed at the Soviet Union itself). But at the same time, the Russians never dropped their quest for an independent Palestinian state in the occupied territories.

According to Soviet estimates, the Palestinian question required a solution to the problem of the 1948 refugees, whose foremost spokesman was Yassir Arafat. And another element here was the Palestinian majority in Jordan. And so, a sovereign Palestinian state, if created in the West Bank and Gaza, could give some satisfaction to Palestinian national aspirations, and also enable Palestinians to live in peace, if under protest, between the two stronger states surrounding it, Israel and Jordan, in a framework of a Jordanian-Palestinian federation. Yet another possibility could be the release of the PLO from Arab restraint once sovereignty, meager as it may be, was achieved, and Jordan was transformed into a much larger Palestinian entity. Both new entities could, theoretically, give the Palestinians a framework in which to develop their own identity and be absorbed in their own affairs. Both may require guarantees from the superpower and other foreign powers, and thus involve the Soviets in something like a "regional peace structure" that could include arms control talks and an ongoing political process instead of a high-level, nuclear-colored conflict. In fact later, in

1989 and 1990, the Soviets tried to initiate arms control talks as a preliminary step toward a general international conference to end the Middle East conflict and were repeatedly talking about a Middle East "regional security system."[23] We do not know for sure whether this became an integral part of the East-West arms control talks that took place in this period. However, it was not an accident that the Americans, too, started talking about a "new order for the Middle East" early in 1990, and agreed, in private and in public, to involve the new Soviet leadership in such an agreement, now that the cold war was over.[24]

On the other hand a Palestinian state, once it took over Jordan by virtue of "self determination" rights for the Palestinians there, could behave very differently if given enough room to maneuver. (This could have been the case, at least, before Saddam's coup in August 1990 and the ensuing turmoil in the region.) This new Palestinian state, which would be relatively large in terms of the population, including exiled Palestinians with no sound economic base, could try to make Saudi Arabia, the rich but weak next-door neighbor, eager to ransom itself, as Ryad had done in the past in its relations with other Arab brethren such as Syria. The Soviets might see in this a better chance to involve Israel locally, to preoccupy it with a nation equally capable, in the long run—even with a possible "local" nuclear threat, self-developed or acquired, which might create a "regional balance of terror" à la Gallois. But such a regional balance would be very fragile. Thus, in order to prevent disaster, extraregional involvement, including Soviet involvement, would be necessary—perhaps, by means of arms control talks and foreign guarantees, possibly supervised by a revived U.N. Another theoretical possibility, of course, could be "regional mutual destruction," if these scenarios, anticipated by Gallois himself, remained local and free of any Soviet involvement.

In other words, whereas Israel's dispute with the Arab states entailed only a degree of Soviet involvement, a peace structure allowing a Palestinian state to emerge as a sovereign nation might calm down the area, and entail active Soviet involvement. Or, if this did not happen, the two real rivals, Israel and the Palestinians, would be preoccupied with their own troubles, either by learning to coexist or trying to destroy each other. The doomsday option, however, could be prevented if the Palestinians were given some kind of satisfaction. Of course, the Palestinians might ask for Soviet support once they gained independence, along the same lines as the Arab states did. This support might be granted, but in a positive, rather than negative, framework; and it would create a state that was friendly to the Soviets between Israel and Jordan (two American clients) or, if the Palestinians succeeded in taking over Jordan, next to Saudi Arabia. In sum, the prospect of a grand Palestine would involve the Russians, but also give them important trump cards in the heart of the Middle East. With or without a grand Palestine both sides would be forced to learn to live with each other, thanks, among other things, to Soviet influence. At the same time, they would be preoccupied with themselves, rather than involving Moscow as the patron power—with the nuclear ramifications that would entail—of one side alone. The Soviets would thus appear as positive patrons of a peaceful regime for the region as a whole, instead of being a nuclear-targeted arms supplier and political backer of radical Arabs only.

It was impossible, however, for the Israeli public to follow Soviet logic; Israelis had no comprehensive explanation of Israel's real dilemmas, mainly those in the nuclear field. Nor was the public able to decode Israel's opaque warnings vis-à-vis Syria, in response to Damascus' chemical weapon threat. And even if the Israeli public was halfway conscious of Peres' apparent bids for some kind of an understanding with the Russians in the context of Israel's apparently advanced nuclear option, they still could not understand why Peres was doing what he was. The reasons for all of this "lack of understanding" can be understood by looking at Israel's rather apolitical heritage.

Israelis are very much interested in politics, and obviously in military matters. Israel's press is usually well informed and fairly aggressive. True, the nuclear issue was always subject to military and self-imposed censorship, but Vanunu's case, the missile testing (both reported in detail in the Israeli press) and the launching of Shavit, are all activities that could not escape the attention of at least the better educated public.

The lack of any comprehensive view of the nuclear issue and the missing public debate were thus the result, among other reasons, of some passivity and of a general reluctance, among the rank and file, even among most scholars, to touch upon a sensitive, highly dangerous, complicated matter. It belonged to "qualified people" such as the politicians and security experts, who, in turn, used opaque language in this regard. Israelis tend to accept the views of the establishment—sometimes without criticism—especially when it comes to security matters, despite their rather anarchic habits. They tend to accept being told what is going on and what to do from above, or they follow established—Left or Right, Likud or Labor—political networks (unless things "go wrong" as they did at the outset of the 1973 war or in Lebanon). In regard to nuclear options, almost everyone was bluffed all the time, and most liked it, especially when nuclear weapons were perceived as related to a new, unmeasurable holocaust.

For the time being, in the period between 1988 and 1989, the Arabs were not ready to accept Labor's partition of the West Bank in Hussein's favor. And Shamir's endorsement of the Camp David Palestinian autonomy concept in the wake of the uprising in the occupied territories and Israel's deteriorating international standing could seem to foreign observers—though not to many Israelis—to be by now too little and too late. Shamir had reservations about the 1979 peace treaty with Egypt, but now Camp David was viewed by him as a legitimate international agreement, which bound at least the Americans and Egyptians. For Israel to abandon it in favor of negotiations with King Hussein seemed at the least to be unwise. The king was too weak to endorse Camp David or to negotiate with Israel within the framework of an international conference on far-reaching territorial concessions from his side—and the framework itself had not been demanded from Israel at Camp David. But in the meantime, in late 1988, King Hussein decided to disengage himself from the West Bank, at least for the time being, due to the impact of the Intifada, which seemed to have unified everyone behind the PLO. He had done the same thing in the past when the PLO seemed to have carried the day. In doing this, he left Peres practically hanging in the air. Ironically, Labor was forced to fight for the idea of the international conference with an unwilling Hussein, while Likud was able to argue as a result of it that Peres' peace plank for the 1988 campaign did not hold water.

Shimon Peres seemed unconvincing and even less sincere when he refused to explain the true strategic calculations leading to the problematic interim diplomacy of an international conference. Through the conference Peres aimed for a real deal with Hussein. One of the reasons was his desire to at least get rid of the Arab populated parts of the occupied territory as long as Israel maintained its nuclear monopoly option, and start a process of opening the boundaries with Jordan toward a general relaxation of the conflict in the whole region. If that was unattainable, at least Israel would be shown to be positively involved in the diplomatic process rather than being accused of delaying the only hope for peace. This would justify Israel's nuclear monopoly option, and isolate the Arabs—rather than Israel—in the eyes of the world. Likud would have argued that the Arabs were too numerous to be isolated, and the Arab states—the PLO, of course, remained an anathema to Shamir—must be drawn, through Israeli persistence, to making concessions by negotiating peace directly and bilaterally with Israel. The center-left bloc lost several crucial parliamentary seats, which in turn forced Peres to accept Shamir's premiership in a continued grand coalition, and vacate the foreign ministry in favor of Moshe Arens. The only winners in all this seemed to be Shamir and Arafat.

Labor's reluctance to discuss the nuclear element during the 1988 campaign may have emanated—if one can isolate one domestic factor—from the expected outcry from leftist groups, and from a possible lack of understanding between Peres and Rabin. Peres was inclined to stress the nuclear option's vital importance as a deterrent and as a reason to enter into peace negotiations soon, while the Soviets were willing to contribute their share; whereas Rabin remained primarily conventional, despite his having threatened the Syrians and the Iraqis with some kind of "massive retaliation" should they resort to chemical warfare.[25] And Rabin was much less confident about quick results in the peace process.

Rabin's role was important, in part because he remained Labor's acknowledged number two, the heir to Allon's conventional heritage, and a potential contender for the number-one position in the party. In 1984, when Shamir and Peres agreed upon the rotation of the premiership, Rabin became defense minister, and remained in office until the 1988 elections; he again became defense minister late in 1988, following the election tie. Therefore, even if he resigned from Shamir's cabinet in spring 1990—with all Labor ministers—his contribution to Israel's strategy and foreign policy had already been quite significant. In 1984, when Rabin assumed office, Vanunu and Barnaby tell us, the lithium-tritium program at Dimona was "suspended." Whether this meant forgoing battlefield nuclear options or the "boosted" atomic warhead program as described earlier by Spector, we do not know. What we do know is that, during Rabin's tenure, a conventional preemptive doctrine was publicly reemphasized. Yet four years later, while Rabin stayed in the same office, the grand coalition agreed to launch the Israeli satellite Ofek 1 by means of the powerful booster Shavit described above.

If Rabin thus paid tribute to Peres' strategy and to Likud's own version of nuclear options, his real concern still seemed to be Israel's conventional deterrent, and its ability to fight—and win—conventional wars and even to preempt them by using conventional means. He appeared to still perceive the nuclear option as a semi-open "last resort"; one that had been well known to the Arabs for decades as such and that still had not prevented them from resorting to a variety of conventional challenges. These challenges, in Rabin's view, were and are the main Israeli problem. Moreover, he would not break the rules of the NPT world and lose the advantages of staying within the context of America's nonproliferation policy and U.S.-Israeli relations, which were based among other things on Israel's nonopen treatment of the nuclear option. In this way, Israel had secured priceless conventional and political aid.

In 1991, during the Gulf War, Rabin became more explicit about his defense doctrine.[26] In a Labor parliamentary meeting, he said in his time as defense minister he had been preparing for an Arab-Israeli war in which the enemy (mainly Syria, but possibly also Iraq and even Saudi Arabia) would use missiles to hit Israeli cities. Therefore the Gulf War was a rather positive development from Israel's point of view. Yet as far as his planning for an Arab-Israeli—not an Iraqi-Allied Coalition war, in which Israel played a subordinate role—was concerned, Rabin distinguished between "deterrence" and "compellence." Deterrence had proved successful within the Arab-Israeli framework; Syria "did not dare to attack us, in spite of the fact that she has SCUD missiles or SS-21s, because she knew that Israel could respond several times more and compel." On the other hand, Rabin understood compellence mainly in conventional terms; traditionally this strategy was seen in terms of conventional preemption. In a press interview on February 22, 1991, Rabin said that "our initial emphasis was laid on developing [our] deterrent power. Therefore *we have made it clear, using clandestine but also open methods that our response to [enemy] hits on [our] home front will be the destruction of Arab capitals* [italics added]."[27]

He further emphasized "defense" and mentioned that it was during his tenure as defense minister that the initial decision to produce the Arrow antimissile missile was made. Thus "defense," especially against missiles, could be coupled with preemptive strikes against their sites—and in the future by using the new Arrow, being developed in cooperation with the United States.

Mr. Peres might have rejected the logic of this argument, according to which Israel had to get ready for war, conventional war included, in which the main effort would be to compel the enemy to stop belligerence and eventually make peace. For him—and for some important political friends and aides, such as General Weizmann, who had objected to the bombing of the Iraqi reactor Tammuz 1, and General Avraham Tamir, who had served as Peres' director-general—the time for peace had come.[28] Peace must be based on respect for Arab demands, including, possibly, in the nuclear field, since no one could prevent Iraq from gaining access to the nuclear option. This position could be backed up by Tamir's initial criticism of the Gulf War,[29] two years after he had met in secret with high-ranking Iraqi representatives, Foreign Minister Tarak Aziz included, according to his own revelations in *Yediot Aharonot*, February 15, 1991.[30] Tamir, and General Weizmann, his political mentor, hoped for a breakthrough with Arab rejectionists if Israel showed that it understood their grievances and worked for the solution of the Palestinian problem. One such grievance could be Israel's nuclear monopoly, as perceived by Iraq. According to his own testimony, Tamir had heard from Tarak Aziz that the issue was not only Israel's occupation of Arab land, but (Aziz was quoted as having said)

> "Israel—this we know—has also nuclear weapons. And therefore, in our military build-up, we must ensure deterrence on our side on both [the Iranian and the Israeli] fronts . . . in order to safeguard our existence . . . In both fronts there is a territorial conflict. With Iran, the conflict focuses on the sea routes in the Shat-el-Arab, and with Israel on the occupied territories. We have also some problems with Kuwait, but I believe that it would be possible to solve these problems in an Arab framework."
>
> Question: "What makes you acquire 'unconventional weapons'? It is known that you have used chemical weapons in the war against Iran."
>
> The Iraqi Foreign Minister: "Iraq will not accept a situation, allowing Israel to be the 'nuclear policeman of the region.' Iraq must find solutions to this situation . . . each state having security problems, such as the dangers threatening Iraq's existence, with everything she has at its disposal if it felt that its existence was at stake."[31]

Aziz cleverly linked the occupation of the West Bank to Iraq's nuclear claims, and this linkage—which had nothing to do with Iraq's "existence"—was accepted by Tamir, possibly Weizmann and Peres, as a legitimate source of concern for Israel, according to Tamir in the above interview. Israeli intelligence, too, according to a press report in March 1990, was worried that the "Begin Doctrine" might push the Iraqis to launch a preemptive attack against Israel once they feared one on their own installations.[32]

Peres, whose political quest was to offer a "peaceful" alternative to Likud and an alternative to Rabin's cautious strategy, could hardly afford to openly challenge Rabin; that is, until mid-1989, when he did so publicly as minister of finance, in a programmatic *Ha'aretz* essay.[33] In this essay, Peres vaguely and indirectly criticized official doctrine of conventional preemption as a viable option in Middle Eastern politics, calculating that its price would be intolerable and arguing against occupation of territory as a trump card for peace. His focus was on economic development in the spirit of *perestroika* and Francis Fukuyama's "End of History" essay. The idea seemed to have been an agreement with all Arab states on a Nuclear-Weapon-Free Zone that would open all nuclear facilities—but not existing arsenals—to international inspection in exchange for peace, foreign guarantees, economic cooperation, and either an agreement with Jordan on a territorial compromise in the West Bank or a peace process with elected Palestinians (involving a combination of some form of Palestinian statehood in the territories, Israeli presence along the Jordan river, and demilitarization). This might have earned him points in Washington and in Moscow, but due to the opaque terms, his position was hardly understood in public. Peres was credited abroad with a major improvement of ties with the Soviet Union; but hardly at home, since this "improvement" seemed to be aiming at an Israeli-PLO negotiating process that might lead to the establishment of a Palestinian state in the West Bank and Gaza. Soon afterward Peres believed he had a parliamentary majority for a coalition without Likud, due to the growing tension between the Bush Administration and Likud over progress in the stalled Middle East peace process. He then maneuvered his own ouster from the cabinet, bringing about the resignation of all other Labor ministers. Peres tried a coalition coup within the recently elected parliamentary set-up, since he realized that general elections, at least when he tried to win them, always brought about a tie, or a near-tie that prevented Labor from assuming power as the principal coalition party.

It is possible that the total absence or at least "blurring" of a major, if not the most vital, issue during both public and closed-door debates among the elites was one of the most important factors influencing the final election results in 1969, 1973, 1977, 1981, 1984, and 1988. But this is, of course, an open question. One could interpret the nuclear issue either way. Likud indeed had succeeded in creating deep loyalties among its followers and had a simple formula to defend its commitment to the whole of Western Palestine plus negotiations in which the Arabs would make concessions first. But Labor's leadership and foreign political as well as its strategic planks were complicated, polemical, or reduced to meaninglessness in 1988.

In the nuclear sense, the reconstitution of the grand coalition in December 1988 did not essentially change the picture, except for Peres' public posture in mid-1989 regarding the "borderless Middle East," which he published in Ha'aretz as finance minister in the grand coalition, and which has remained hanging. There were, of course, domestic political differences between the new and old government coalitions, but they go beyond the scope of this book.

In the meantime, the American dialogue with the PLO, which started after Arafat's December 1988 statements, had not solved the problem of Palestinian sovereignty to which the Americans remained officially opposed. In mid-1990 the U.S.-PLO dialogue was suspended, when Abul-Abbas, a member of the PLO council, launched a terrorist attack against Israel from a base in Libya. The PLO's leadership had committed itself to stopping acts of terrorism in order to allow dialogue with the United States. But it had difficulty censuring Abul Abbas, due to its fragile structure and its commitments—in the inner-Arab context—to go on fighting Israel until at least the Intifada yielded some results for the Palestinians in the occupied territories. During the whole period, the United States, in spite of the developing diplomatic process which, as we shall see, would soon involve Egypt, repeated that its goal was *not* the creation of a Palestinian state. It is not clear whether this American opposition had a nuclear dimension. For a Palestinian entity, unlike the Arab states, may be ready to take on nuclear risks because the desire to undo Israel was so dominant in Palestinian tradition, and they had imitated Israel's behavior in the past. The Americans might have been aware of the centrality of the nuclear issue in PLO eyes since the 1960s, when the Palestinians had tried to mobilize Arab states to fight Israel before it went nuclear. After all, the only national group among Arabs that perceived itself as wholly uprooted, completely victimized, and thus as fighting a battle of life and death with Israel, were the 1948 refugees and their political organizations. Among the Arab states the perception of Israel as an enormous threat and as a cause of deep humiliation took root, after 1948 and before, due to the perception of Zionism as illegal in principle and as an expansionist, cancerous phenomenon striving to control more and more Arab lands. But this was never the whole story. Israel was used to enhance various Arab interests and create various political platforms among Arabs or sustain others.

Moreover, viewed in retrospect, Sadat's peace in 1979, which entailed the recovery of Sinai, a huge Arab territory, could signal to the Arab states that Israel's "expansion" had been stopped: when coupled with Israel's nuclear option, a "reduced" Israel was acceptable to Sadat, if not to Heikal. But even a reduced Israel within its 1949 lines "occupied" *Palestinian* land and kept its inhabitants in exile.

The difference between Palestinians, especially 1948 refugees, and the Arab states in accepting Israel's very existence as a given fact becomes clear here. The destabilizing factor was now the Palestinians; since 1964, when Fatah and the PLO were established, they had taken this role over from the Zionists, who prior to Israel's 1948-1949 War of Independence could have been perceived as destabilizers. The occupation of the West Bank in 1967 gave the population thereof a recognized quest for freedom; however, that claim was tied to the broader issue of the 1948 refugees who were organized within the PLO. And the PLO had managed to become the spokesman of most West Bankers and the

dwellers of Gaza. Yet this role was challenged after a while by fundamentalist groups, such as the Hamas and other offsprings of the
"Moslem Brethren" tradition, coupled with the impact of Khomeini's
revolution, which officially endorsed a total rejection of Israel. By
accepting a "West Bank state" alongside Israel, now that the Intifada
generated sympathy and growing worldwide support for the Palestinian cause, Arafat's PLO seemed to have renounced its previous
demands for a "secular Palestinian state" in Palestine as a whole in
which the Arab majority would, of course, rule the Jews according to
their preferences. Yet the Americans, in cooperation with Egypt's
Mubarak, tried at first to get a Palestinian-Israeli dialogue going, in the
wake of the Intifada and Arafat's mellowed public stances, without yet
committing themselves to the final outcome.

It could be that the ironic result of Sharon's war in Lebanon, which
deprived the PLO of any military option, and of the IDF's forced withdrawal from Lebanon later on, was to help spark the Intifada. But the
public relations damage to Israel, especially on Western TV screens,
was a political fact. (And maybe Eastern Europeans learned their own
lessons from the "stone kids" who stood against fully armed, modern
troops in the occupied territories.) This public relations damage combined with the changing of the guard in Washington. The Bush Administration might have learned from past experience that the first year of a
new administration was crucial if it wanted movement in the Middle
East. It felt that American Jewry was badly shaken by the Intifada. And
the administration was under permanent pressure by close allies such as
the Egyptians and the Saudis, who might have feared Moslem fundamentalism cloaked in pan-Arab, anti-Western, and anti-Israeli terms.
But Arab-Arab relations remained quite complicated. One must distinguish here between separate interests, common causes, and domestic
calculations among all Arab entities concerned.

Saudi Arabia, for example, could be endangered by a sovereign
Palestinian entity supported or even provoked by radical Arab states
and by Iran, combined with the possible destabilization of Jordan—
with its large Palestinian population—and its ensuing disintegration
in favor of an aggressive, irredentist Palestinian state. And one day it
might acquire its own bomb. At least the Israeli grand coalition of 1988
would do its best to avoid any dealings with the PLO. And it would
maintain control over the occupied territories, even if its motives for
doing so were only emotional-conventional and, of course "low political," as the grand coalition partners were tied to each other due to the
1988 election results.

In other words, with its typical political-ideological policy to stick to the "whole of Eretz Israel," Likud would use strategic arguments, even if mostly conventional, for its initial purposes. Only after that would the grand strategic arguments themselves play their roles. Labor's arguments in favor of an enhanced peace process, with the Egyptians and the Americans as go-betweens, following Secretary of State's James Baker III initiative, were carried by both Labor leaders, Peres and Rabin; both invoked a variety of political-ideological arguments, including moral ones. Rabin emphasized the U.S.-Israeli connection as an asset that should not be jeopardized if Israel wanted to maintain its military options—he was anxious to sustain Israel's conventional power and to develop the Arrow. Peres also emphasized the economic necessity to maintain American support, but he was more impressed by arguments that he heard from Washington, Europe, and Moscow, that this was a period of peace, of negotiations, and of concessions; his main argument was that Israel could not maintain the status-quo much longer in the face of foreign, mainly American, pressure and that the country might find itself totally isolated.

The changed international political climate, combined with American demands that Israel give the diplomatic process a fair chance, drove Rabin, a former ambassador in Washington and a pragmatic "hawk," to devise a formula to get Israel out of the diplomatic stalemate: free elections should be held in the West Bank and Gaza, then Israel, together with Egypt, would begin negotiations with the elected Palestinian leadership. Those elected would be West Bankers and Gaza dwellers, not 1948 refugees living in exile. Thus, a process would begin in which occupied Palestinians, who never left the country, could assert themselves against the PLO, who had left; the elected Palestinian delegation would be asked to finally give up impossible demands such as the "Right of Return" of all 1948 refugees to the West Bank state and to Israel proper. Shamir agreed, and named the proposal "Israel's Peace Initiative" of May, 1989, although the prime minister seemed to have endorsed Rabin's initiative rather reluctantly, hoping that the other side would decline it.

And yet, the "grand strategy," especially in the missile field, would further play its autonomous role—due also to a low common denominator between Likud and Labor—which allowed yet another missile launching, this time a warhead that landed 400 kilometers from Qaddafi's Libyan shore late in September 1989.[34] The political-strategic timing could have been dictated by Israel's desire to demonstrate some kind of missile fait accompli "beyond INF capabilities" on the eve of President Mubarak's visit to the United States early in October. American sources were quoted as saying that Egypt had renounced its cooperation with Argentina and Iraq in developing the IRBM Condor 2000. In other words, President Mubarak might have been ready to give up the Condor 2000, but would argue vis-à-vis the Americans that if Egypt gave up a strategic asset while facing a militant Israel armed with publicly tested Jericho missiles, then Cairo was entitled to American compensation: either in regard to Israel's unchecked nuclear missile program, and/or some movement toward a solution of the Palestinian question, in coordination with PLO chief Arafat. This could have been one of the reasons for the proximity between Mubarak's "ten points" and Secretary of State Baker's "five points" regarding elections in the West Bank, which was the source of much diplomatic activity in the autumn of 1989. There were, of course, many other reasons for both parties to endorse a peace program for the Middle East, and to give the PLO some role to play in it.

The peace program had started under Secretary of State George Shultz before Baker took office. The Bush Administration decided to pursue an active, and leading, role in solving the Middle East's problems, among other reasons because that region was the most dangerous, and least controllable, and it was of vital importance to the Western World as the most important source of oil. In this regard one could have divided it into the "Western Middle East," which has little or no oil, and the Gulf region, which has a lot. And indeed the American Central Command, under General Norman Schwarzkopf, with headquarters in Florida, had forged plans to meet Soviet aggression in that region. Central Command had no dealings with Israel, while Bush was taking over from an administration that had suddenly faced the decline of Soviet power—in terms of sudden Soviet concessions in the bilateral arms control talks and the disintegration of the Soviet Empire in Europe. The Bush Administration watched these developments without intervening. Then the unification of Germany fell like a bombshell due to its swiftness, and was not fully welcomed, at first, by the president. But he allowed the process of liberation to unfold on its own, under the mottos of "self- determination," market economy, and human and individual rights. No public American initiative was necessary here, and in fact one would have complicated a process that the involved peoples were pursuing on their own. Very few, if any, saw in the 1989 events and in German unification the beginning of the end of the Soviet Union itself, for this and many other reasons. The only arena that was dangerous and vital enough to dictate active American involvement was the Middle East, and its unconventional dangers. Pursuing a comprehensive Middle East solution based on abstract principles would not only be a politically difficult exercise but a practically frustrating matter—trying to get all parties to agree when they each had their own historical, domestic political, economic, and inter-Arab reasons to pursue very different goals. Still, recognizing linkages between Arabs in the Gulf and in the Western basin and eager to contain or to reform Islamic fundamentalism the Bush Administration made the Middle East a top foreign policy priority—"having in fact no other foreign policy priority," as Professor Robert W. Tucker put it.

Of course, Bush and Baker were Texas oil men who had never entertained close ties to American Jews or to Israel. Thus they must have been exposed to the traditional, enshrined Arab consensus pertaining to the cause of the Palestinians. As a peculiar conservative phenomenon, Bush was resolved—in principle—to maintain a status-quo ante, as Saddam Hussein would soon learn, and Bush must have seen in Israeli occupation of Arab land and in the Jewish settlement efforts therein an unacceptable change in the status-quo ante. As a professional politician, he tended to personal behind-the-scenes dealings with individual counterparts, aimed at politically tangible, when possible spectacular, results at home—such as a Middle East peace conference that would later be pursued by bilateral or multilateral negotiations related to his dealings with the Soviets (concerning START).

Arafat's outfit was recognized by all Arabs, Egypt included, as the sole representative of the Palestinian people, whose cause gathered political momentum since the outbreak of the Intifada. The PLO may not have actually initiated the Intifada—which seems to have been sparked by the occupied Palestinians due to their own grievances and to foreign sensitivities and actual intervention on their behalf. But Moscow, China, the whole Third World, and the European Community linked the Intifada to the PLO. In spite of Arafat's violent past and the unstable structure of the PLO, he was perceived as being ready to accept higher political risks toward Israel and become socialized through negotiations. At least Arafat's Fatah, the largest element in the PLO, seemed now to be both more important and a better alternative to the fundamentalist alternative, which could endanger moderate or secular and pro-Western Arab regimes. Arafat could be brought into the negotiating process without being forced on Israel as a direct partner—an option that the PLO itself and Arab states such as Syria tried to counter by invoking the concept of an "International Peace Conference for the Middle East." In fact, Shamir was taken at his word regarding his own proposals for elections in the territories, but following his "initiative," a long discussion began about the PLO's participation in the preparatory talks leading to the elections and other thorny issues, mainly the participation of exiled West Bankers and Palestinians from

East Jerusalem in the elections and/or in the ensuing negotiations. East Jerusalem was officially annexed to Israel in the early 1980s, and thus, in Likud's view, its Arab population was not eligible to vote or send representatives to the West Bank delegation when elected. At the same time, Mubarak ended the long, official rift with Qaddafi when the Libyan ruler visited Egypt in mid-October 1989. Thus he might have gained some freedom from the United States now that he seemed to be pushing Egypt back from its isolation to the center of the Arab world, following its peace treaty with Israel.

Soon afterward, the CIA or the Pentagon leaked reports through NBC news about Israeli-South African cooperation in regard to missile testing and development.[35] Congressional hearings, mostly secret, followed the public revelations.

Since such reports could hardly have been leaked without endorsement from higher authorities, the reasons behind the leak could have been the following:

1. An angry American response to the very launching of Ofek 1 by means of something like an Israeli ICBM, as described earlier by Spector; Israel might have been justified in retrospect in developing theater nuclear options and missiles, but not IRBMs and ICBMs, which remained a superpower monopoly and responsibility.

2. A genuine American desire to at least stop Israel's continued cooperation with South Africa once more evidence to this effect was made available to the Bush Administration, despite the reported launching of Israeli missiles from Israeli territory since 1987.[36]

3. A combined effort to compensate Mubarak for his alleged withdrawal from the Condor program and to put pressure on Shamir to get moving on the Palestinian issue, after he had agreed to hold elections in the West Bank and Gaza.

We have no space here to discuss other relevant issues such as the enormous growth in Jewish immigration from the Soviet Union to Israel late in 1989. The numbers of Soviet Jews who wished to emigrate exceeded American immigration quotas, possibly because of an explicit American decision not to allow the immigrants to enter the United States. The resulting enormous increase in immigration to Israel required that the Bush Administration offer a variety of gestures—open and less open—in favor of several Arab states and in favor of the Palestinians.

The Iran-Iraq War drew the United States closer to Baghdad, and early in 1990 it was disclosed that Washington had given Saddam's regime credits to buy food and equipment in the United States and had guaranteed loans given to Iraq by foreign banks for this purpose.[37] Saddam's—and Egypt's—efforts with regard to missiles and chemical weapons could have been perceived as being mainly a psychological strategy directed against Iran and Israel. By now, following the termination of Saddam's war with Iran, Khomeini's death, and possible political progress in the Arab-Israeli dispute itself, this required attention.

Soon enough, however, Iraq proved to have renewed its effort to acquire nuclear weapons. There may have been a degree of Iraqi-Egyptian cooperation here as well; Egyptian agents, directly under the command of Defense Minister Abu A'zala, were caught red-handed in the United States shortly before Mubarak's visit, trying to smuggle out sensitive strategic materials. Reportedly, if not publicly, Washington forced Mubarak to renounce the Egyptian Condor project, and A'zala resigned his army position in 1989. However, the general soon reappeared as Mubarak's defense adviser. In the meantime, the United States seemed to have moved Egypt away from Saddam's most dangerous projects, while trying to compensate Iraq in other fields, such as food supplies and conventional weapon production, civilian development projects, and the like. According to the Wisconsin Project on Nuclear Arms Control, quoted in the *New York Times*, June 25, 1991, the administration had difficulty in pursuing a coordinated export control policy toward Iraq; to ensure diplomatic gains, the State Department overruled many of the Commerce Department's objections to specific export licenses.

Egypt might have responded positively to the American anti-Condor efforts without giving up future options. Without the United States, Mubarak's economic situation was hopeless, and he was ready in principal to assume Sadat's "moderate" approach to the Arab-Israeli conflict, now that the Iran-Iraq War was over and his obligations to the besieged brethren in Baghdad could be relaxed. Behind the scenes, Mubarak could have complained to the Americans, again and again, that Israel was given almost a "free hand" in regard to nuclear matters and missiles, something Mubarak would hardly be able to accept. Saddam's response to this, among other challenges, was yet to come.

The occupation of the West Bank and the plight of the Palestinians remained a big issue on the international agenda. True, Iraq was caught red-handed, late in March 1990, when it tried to import American-made nuclear bomb triggers, and later it was publicly reported that Saddam Hussein had deployed chemical missiles on his border with Jordan, close enough to hit Israel—and thus protect his future ambitions.[38] The Israeli chief of staff, General Dan Shomron, publicly disclosed Israel's assumption that Iraq was working on a new solution to its nuclear dilemma—a bomb without a reactor.[39] The idea seemed to be to import slightly enriched uranium from any possible source, or even use self-produced natural uranium and enrich it by using centrifuges, which were easier to buy abroad than reactors. Several suppliers were named in this connection—China, West German firms, South American nations such as Brazil, North Korea—it not being known yet that in fact Saddam Hussein had also chosen a third route, calutrons. At any rate Saddam's nuclear ambitions had become clear to those who cared to notice. The Middle East had thus devised its own solution to the nonproliferation problem. In due course Iraq could have an open nuclear posture; in the absence of a reactor, there would be no evidence of a nuclear option, allowing Saddam to play the usual opaque game. We shall return to this development in the next chapter. It was exposed mainly by the United States and Great Britain and denied by Saddam—who, however, admitted after Shamir's grand coalition collapsed in March 1990 that he had the largest arsenal of chemical weapons "after the superpowers."[40]

Reports that Egypt was working on its own bomb and had reached a rather advanced stage remained hanging in the air, or were dismissed by commentators in the Israeli press, but not officially. Sharon's pressure on the right wing of Likud, when combined with the personal interest of some other Likud politicians, forced Shamir in the preparatory talks leading to the West Bank elections to adopt a less flexible stance toward Secretary Baker's diplomatic efforts, especially in regard to the participation of exiled Palestinians from the West Bank and Palestinians from Israeli-annexed East Jerusalem. Labor demanded a more flexible response; it accepted the idea of a meeting in Cairo with Egyptian and PLO-confirmed Palestinian representatives to discuss the promised West Bank elections and was ready to be flexible about the East Jerusalem issue as well. The main thing was to get the negotiations going, even if Rabin, on the "hawkish" side of Labor, might have hoped that in future talks about a possible settlement an elected West Bank representation would develop its own separate spirit and interest, whether confirmed by the PLO or not.

Peres was maneuvering to topple Shamir as prime minister and create a "narrow coalition" that he himself would head, with the help of smaller party leaders to avoid an open rift with the United States. Shamir responded by firing Peres from the government, whereupon all Labor ministers resigned, and a mad race to build a "narrow coalition" took place between Shamir and Peres.

The ensuing political process in Israel in early summer 1990 led to the creation of such a "narrow coalition" under Likud's exclusive control. Peres was pushing the cabinet to accept Baker's proposals—and indirect PLO involvement in the proposed Cairo talks concerning West Bank elections. He was misled to believe that several small coalition parties would join him and help topple Shamir, if he risked a coalition crisis on that issue. Instead, under heavy pressure from their own rather nationalistic and religious rank and file, those same parties joined Shamir. Soon afterward Rabin tried to force Peres out of his office as party chairman and candidate for the premiership, but failed in a ballot vote in the party's governing body. Instead, the party's central committee decided to hold the issue until 1991, when Labor will hold primaries toward the 1992 general elections.

Yet as a caretaker prime minister, Shamir decided to launch yet another Israeli satellite in early April 1990, "Ofek 2." As with Ofek 1, the main point of interest here was the launcher, according to Spector's 1990 report.[41] The issue of hydrogen warheads and reentry vehicles was discussed in this connection in the American press. Israel was described as working on both but in need of U.S.-made supercomputers to complete the job. A supercomputer was ordered by Israel in America, causing concern among Pentagon officials; yet such a computer was promised to India in April.

At this point, I would like to return to the beginning of our story. Has our narrative brought us to an "Algerization" of the Arab-Israeli conflict (something feared greatly by Ben-Gurion, something he wanted to avoid by, among other things, adopting the nuclear option)? Did the angry domestic and pro-American reaction to Ben-Gurion's views (in favor of American intervention and the benefits derived from yielding to it, at least in an ambiguous fashion) combine with Arab politics and Soviet input to make the 1967 war and the occupation of the West Bank and Gaza inevitable?

Is the ensuing development of the Palestinian problem, especially Israel's rule over unwilling aliens, at the heart of the Arab-Israeli conflict? Or are the Arab armies and future modern weaponry the main problems? What would be the effect of those armies, armed with modern weaponry, in combination with the possible emergence of a Palestinian state between Israel and Jordan with claims against both? With such enemy proximity to Israel's vital centers would Israel be able to use nuclear threats successfully to maintain its reduced status and long borders against Arab limited attacks, similar to the one initiated by Egypt and Syria in 1973? Would there be any hope for peace with a Palestinian state manipulated by foreign Arab agents and exiled Palestinians who would never accept it as the solution to their problems? And as the PLO has already imitated Israeli nationalism in many respects, would a Palestinian political entity also be influenced by this mirror effect to acquire their own bomb sooner or later as a matter of course?

Were the Arabs able to launch a limited attack in 1973 because Israel's nuclear stance was too ambiguous? Has Israel found a less ambiguous solution to its problem with the regular Arab armies? Does Israel have any answer to under-the-threshold guerrilla war and civil disobedience? And would Assad's Syria, with its own claims to Palestine as "Southern Syria," agree to forgo denying Palestinian nationalism every now and again while cultivating its own Palestinian alternative to Arafat's Fatah and allow the establishment of an independent Palestinian entity? Would Syria try to undermine Arafat's control over the PLO and assume power over the Palestinians by itself (while working on its own bomb), as it was doing in Lebanon? Is Syria at all capable of such ambitions when its traditional patron, the Soviet Union, seems unable and unwilling even to sustain Assad's conventional arms race, let alone back him in a new war that may occur before he acquires his bomb but as a result of its looming threat? Would Assad try a similar game with the help of the United States, with or without a bomb?

Would Iraq, then, assume such a role? Has the second detente between the superpowers affected regional conflicts, as it was supposed to do between 1970 and 1973, and if so, how? Would this second detente push the Arabs once again to at least limited cooperation among themselves, as Saddam Hussein reacted to it in public?[42] Or would the decline of Soviet power and support to the Arabs cause Arabs to develop a doctrine of self-reliance that would entail pursuing Arab nuclearization as a matter of the utmost urgency? Or did most Arab leaders realize that an "Arab bomb" might trigger the only kind of war in which the Arab nation itself might perish; and thus Israel's option dictated under-the-threshold tactics for good vis-à-vis Israel, but the bomb would remain a necessary tool to establish the Arabs as a power in a period in which the superpowers declined?

Have the Palestinians given up their aspirations to return to pre-1967 Israel proper, aspirations that first required the destruction of Israel, because they realize that a nuclear Israel cannot be destroyed? Or are they just holding off until at least one Arab state acquires the bomb? A sovereign Palestinian territory is no doubt one of the preconditions to achieving such a goal one day, because Arab nations that host the PLO are, in fact, Israel's hostages if they allow the PLO any activity that might endanger the Jewish state seriously, and Palestinians have been outspoken in their quest for an Arab bomb. The HDCI summary of January 27, 1988 (based on eight major Egyptian newspapers and the Kuwaiti *Al-Watan*) of the international conference held in Cairo between December 11 and 13, 1987, on the demilitarization of the Middle East and the Mediterranean Basin of nuclear weapons can shed some light here. Dr. Nafa al-Hussein, the PLO representative, addressed the possibility that Egypt might exploit its peace treaty with Israel and develop nuclear weapons, which were a supreme national requirement for the Arabs in any case.

In this regard, it is also interesting to look at an interview with Rageb Gibril, an exiled Palestinian leader who had been forced to leave the West Bank by the Israeli authorities:

> Question: Do you mean nuclear weapons?
>
> Answer: Qaddafi is around, Iraq too . . . Qaddafi has advanced preconditions, which we have rejected. But if we reach a point of despair—we might accept them . . . Now we are getting killed for nothing! Should we reach a point of despair, we shall accept Qaddafi's demands, and drop a nuclear weapon on Tel Aviv! Thus the chance should be sought in peace . . .[43]

Should the Palestinians have accepted Israel as an indestructible entity, due to the nuclear options that concerned not only themselves but all the Arab states? What can Israel offer them when it is divided between those who aspire to retain what was won in 1967 to avoid being dependent almost solely on nuclear options and those who want to retain less and still avoid open nuclearization?

Was the Soviet proposal, as originally suggested by high-level Soviet visitors in the region,[44] meant indeed as a "regional security system" based on superpower guarantees and their deep involvement to keep the peace, while satisfying their various clients as far as possible? Did they have the power to achieve such a goal? At least one can say that for the Soviets the period of opacity was almost over; they may have even used the Israeli option to impress upon their Arab friends that the time to make peace with Israel had finally arrived. This coincided with *perestroika* and the most liberal phase in Gorbachev's policy—and with the fact that the Russians found that they might be exposed to Israeli missiles, although they wouldn't necessarily admit this. At the same time, Moscow was interested in arms control. And thus the question remains, who would guarantee Israel's survival if one of the reasons—a very important one—for Soviet and Arab moderation toward Israel was indeed its nuclear option? A pro-Arab stance was further maintained, in the meantime, by Soviet endorsement of a Palestinian state. Such a pro-Arab stance would give the declining Soviet superpower a degree of influence in a sensitive region vis-à-vis the West, and help contain trouble in the Soviet Moslem republics. The final outcome of a peace process would depend upon the parties involved, and the degree of superpower effort applied to make them talk and accept each other, possibly under U.N. auspices. Thus peace and economic cooperation should be emphasized in a partitioned Palestine. This is what Ben-Gurion wanted from the beginning, with the nuclear option, and without the added burden of the 1967 war, its domestic complications, and the rise of the Palestinians as an occupied people. So the nuclear issue remains both as an incentive for and an obstacle to peace: "Radical" Arabs will stress their demand to disarm Israel, while pursuing their own aims, which in turn would justify Israel's quest for a nuclear monopoly and may justify Likud's uncompromising territorial stance, born as it was before Mr. Begin and Mr. Shamir had even heard about Enrico Fermi and Robert Oppenheimer.

As far as Washington was concerned, the Palestinian quest for independence and separate statehood was officially unacceptable due to the risks involved for both Israel and Jordan, and for economic reasons that make it impractical.

However, the American spokesman, Dennis Ross, in mid-June 1989 urged the parties to enter into peace negotiations, because otherwise the region might face another war fought this time with "unconventional means." Did Ross acknowledge the nuclear factor and the chemical weapons in Arab hands in order to impress upon the parties not only to accept Israel but to give the Palestinians less than they wanted? What the Americans might have had in mind was a socialization process in which the dangers of unconventional war would play a positive role, with no clear-cut, final objectives defined at this stage.

This aspect of Palestinian statehood was given its due public exposure when Qaddafi jumped on the issue, saying publicly in June 1989 that the "Palestinian state must have the right to possess nuclear and chemical weapons."[46] But the Israeli rank and file did not see the significance here, since its attention was not focused on the nuclear issue because of its apolitical habits and opacity—and for ideological-emotional reasons. Even an Iraqi message to Israel—published in the Israeli press, following the end of the Iran-Iraq War—to leave their new nuclear efforts alone "because they had no intention of attacking Israel" remained hanging in the dense Israeli summer air, as far as the general public was concerned.[47] And soon this message was replaced by

Saddam's more recent chemical-nuclear threats, even if he repeated his defensive intentions at the same time.

Even if we were not primarily interested in East-West relations here as a strategic-political framework and as a strategic-ideological source of influence on Middle Eastern actors, we could not conclude this chapter without reflecting on the issues of "sovereignty" and "self-determination" in what Francis Fukuyama called "the End of History." In fact, both Arabs and Jews struggle for both in an age in which such issues seem to be more problematic than ever. Yet the Jews succeeded before the Arabs were able to get a hold on the nuclear option, and Israel seems to have established itself not only as a military power but also as an acceptable version of Jewish history.

To Churchill, whose influence on Western political thinking and strategy was mentioned at the opening of this book, the issues of sovereignty and self-determination were the source of trouble in post-World War I Europe. In my view, they must be seen as a subject for fresh thinking at this stage of the nuclear age; not just because Fukuyama declared them to be less challenging than during the nineteenth century, but because of the much more down-to-earth meaning of the decline and fall—as it may now be seen—of the Soviet Empire; and not only because of the victory of Western ideas in a two-hundred-year struggle, as Fukuyama interpreted the final acceptance of Hegel's idealistic analysis, but mainly because of the nuclear age—as Pierre Hassner politely argued in response to Fukuyama's "End of History."[48]

In other words, if nationalism, Fascism, and Communism proved to be failures, and the "universal, homogeneous state" based on the ideas of the French Revolution has won the battle of ideas, and hence would shape the material world, the outcome could be the decline of the Soviet Empire to such a degree that full sovereignty and self-determination might be claimed not only by Hungary and Poland but by the Ukraine, by the Azars and Uzbeks, and by the Slovenes and Croats in Yugoslavia, as it directly affected the reunification of Germany. Is anybody interested in granting all of them full sovereignty in the nuclear age? Was NPT not an agreement aimed at limiting the sovereignty of third parties in the nuclear age? Has anyone the power to impose nuclear restraint on sovereign nations following the decline and fall of the Soviet superpower? Was not Marxism-Leninism, the materialistic ideology, capable of grasping the meaning of the nuclear age to a degree that imposed "peaceful coexistence" on the Soviet Union, which finally allowed Western liberal democracy the freedom to survive and to penetrate the Soviet Empire to a degree that might endanger its very survival and thus create new instability in the heart of Europe itself?

Fukuyama's answer to this would be that supranational arrangements should replace nation-states, following the example of the EEC. Did he speak in de Gaulle's terms, namely those of "Europe from the Atlantic to the Urals"? De Gaulle also spoke in terms of "Europe of the nations," whose basic structure was supported by a nuclear, almost hegemonical France. One can further argue that Fukuyama's acclaim of the EEC was in fact based upon military and political arrangements that preceded the building of the community, and which are still anchored in World War II realities and results, including Hiroshima. European reality was based on compromising the Wilsonian principle of self-determination for Germans, especially-East Germans, and it denied West Germany full sovereignty in terms of access to ABC weapons since Bonn's remilitarization in the mid-1950s.

Supranationalism was thus the result, not the source, of European developments for very contemporary, historical-materialistic reasons; it was not the result of the triumph of Hegelian idealism or of economic necessities alone. Yet can such supranationalism survive the collapse of the Soviet Empire and the speedy process of the reunification of Germany, which was dictated by East Germans and Chancellor Kohl? Could it be brought into, maybe imposed upon, the rival Middle Eastern nations? Will Israel, like France, be able to maintain a nuclear monopoly that would guarantee its survival and interests in a nonnuclear environment such as the one that forbids German nuclear weapons? Would such an arrangement, which must give Palestinians political rights, at the same time deny them full sovereignty in the framework of a supranational, regional arrangement? Is it possible to work toward such an arrangement in accord with Washington and Moscow?

Is opacity a serious obstacle in discussing such options because it makes them nonissues publicly? Or is it the precondition for seriously discussing them? At least in terms of the public debate in Israel, the answer to the first question is "yes, indeed."

The above questions were formulated in April 1990. In the meantime, Saddam Hussein invaded Kuwait.

CHAPTER TWELVE

The Rebirth of Pan-Arabism?

As we saw in Chapter 11, Palestinian nationalism has been one of the main problems of the Middle East. The "high political" goal of exiled Palestinians was proclaimed to be the regaining of their homeland, in its entirety or at least by establishing sovereignty in a part of it; and for local Palestinians it was freedom from foreign—i.e., Israeli—rule. We saw that both issues were intertwined. We discussed Syrian claims to Palestine as a part of Syria's own sense of sovereignty or statehood, even though this Syrian claim was not the centerpiece of Assad's foreign policy. Yet the Ba'ath Party—still ruling in Syria, and in Iraq—had always emphasized pan-Arabism, and thus rejected any form of non-Arab presence in a united (when the time comes) Arab world.

From this we can discern three forms of Arab nationalism. The first form is the search for sovereignty for a certain group or groups of people, such as the Palestinians. The second form is the search for extended sovereignty of an Arab state over other Arab entities, which is grounded in historical, economic, and strategic reasons, some "low political" in the sense of serving hegemonical and personal interests of some Arab leaders. This was demonstrated in the case of Syrian claims for Palestine. It was also demonstrated in the case of Iraqi claims for Kuwait, which could be seen as being cloaked in "high political" terms—as if the issue was of the highest significance to Baghdad, almost an issue of Iraq's very history, its rights and survival—even though the occupation of Kuwait could have saved the Iraqi regime from collapsing as a result of its previous adventures against Iran, which were basically "low political" at first. Still, this form of hegemony could mobilize pan-Arab sentiments and pretend to spearhead a general trend toward Arab unity.

The third form of Arab nationalism is pan-Arabism, the Ba'ath Party's main goal and a "high political" issue of the utmost importance to other Arab leaders such as Nasser and Qaddafi, even though it was not a precondition for the very survival of their countries—unless economic reasons and "low political" quests for personal and national hegemony leading to Arab unity could be combined with domestic and foreign challenges, with various dangers to the stability of a developing Arab nation, and with the growing gap between rich and poor in the Arab world. Thus, pan-Arabism could assume a social color—and a modern anti-Western one—as if the rich Arabs deprived the poor Arabs of wealth because of Western interest in keeping the price of oil as low as possible. Of course, whether this was the case recently—rather than that Arab *and* Western oil interests calculated that high oil prices would lead to the successful development of substitutes—is an issue that is outside the scope of this book. However, some Arabs were doubtless in dire need of more revenues.

For example, Saddam Hussein's Iraq needed revenue following his war with Iran, when he had an ambitious weapons production effort at home based on foreign procurement and had to maintain the costly civilian economy. A solution for him was to contest oil-rich border areas owned by neighbors, such as Kuwait, and demand higher oil prices regardless of the possible boomerang effect described above. The Kuwaitis and the Saudis would be very conscious of this reasoning and would refuse to comply, also because they would constantly fear that a larger and stronger Arab entity financed by them might endanger them. In Iraq's case, the Arab-Iranian rivalry in the Persian Gulf added to the Arab-Arab cooperation, once Iraq perceived itself as the "Eastern Gate" of the Arab world, resisting Iran, at least while the Shah of Iran was trying to control the whole Persian Gulf by seizing two islands in the mouth of the Shat-el-Arab River and by enticing the Kurdish population of northern Iraq to cede from the main body. This indirect encounter was settled in 1975, when the river was divided between the Shah's Iran and Saddam's Iraq, and the Kurds were abandoned by Teheran (and by the United States and Israel, who supported them via Iran).

The 1980 invasion of Arab-populated Khuzistan by Saddam Hussein could have been seen, in Arab eyes, as an opportunity to change the balance in their favor. And when it proved a bloody and prolonged, endless confrontation between Arabs and Persians, a general Arab front to support Saddam Hussein was established, which, to a degree, legitimized his efforts to procure weapons abroad. The Iraqis could have developed a sense of fighting for the "other Arabs," who at best helped finance their unsuccessful adventure against Iran and thus should have supported Saddam Hussein's ambitions elsewhere when the war ended in 1989 without any meaningful gains for the belligerents.

The three forms of Arab nationalism entailed religious-cultural elements from the beginning. The "Moslem Brothers" were an earlier form of fundamentalist pan-Arabism which threatened the more secular regimes of Egypt and Syria and were duly crushed. Khomeini's revolution in the non-Arab, Shi'ite Iran encouraged the rebirth of fundamentalism in mostly Sunni Arab nations and took root among some Shi'ite groups therein—although the main reason for this phenomenon could be sought in the crisis of traditional societies undergoing changes under secular regimes, some corrupt and oppressive and some unable to overcome the crisis of modernization by creating a viable secular ideology and identity for their divided elites and members of their growing masses.

These various contradictory and yet sometimes interchangeable and supplementary forms of Arab nationalism must be studied within the historical context of their birth. Some of the entities involved were not exactly historical nation-states, nor were they European-like, independent nation-states in the modern sense, but were Ottoman principalities, empires, ancient civilizations, and states created by the British, older regional powers, and weaker entities tied to each other and struggling with each other, while trying to maintain autonomy and enhance their own interests.

The Iraqi nation-state, in the modern sense, was born after World War I, under British control, and brought together three elements in the territory of former Ottoman provinces: a large Shi'ite element, a Sunni element, which has ruled the country ever since, and an oppressed and rebellious Kurdish element.

Kuwait was settled by Arab tribes in the early eighteenth century. The ruling dynasty was founded by Sabbah abu Abdulla (who ruled from 1756 to 1772). In the late eighteenth and early nineteenth centuries the sheikdom, nominally a part of an Ottoman province, was frequently threatened by the Wahabbis, a fighting sect from Hejaz, now ruling Saudi Arabia. Nominally, Kuwait was sometimes ruled by the Ottoman governor of the Shi'ite province of Basra in modern southern Iraq, but in fact it was left alone to conduct its business under the local sheiks, who always flew their own flags on their own ships.[1] In 1899 the sheik, fearing that the Turks intended to make their nominal authority effective, made Kuwait a British protectorate. In assuming that responsibility, the British were primarily interested in preventing Kuwait from becoming linked to the German Berlin-Baghdad railroad. Thus Kuwait had a definite history of its own, and British interest in its separate existence was primarily linked to the German threat in the Middle East before modern Iraq was born, when the British took over those parts of the Ottoman Empire following World War I and in fact created Iraq itself.

The oil-rich Mosul region of Iraq was not even occupied by the British Army when the armistice agreement with Turkey was signed late in October 1918. When someone in the British War Office realized that, the order was given to the troops to march north and take Mosul. For years afterward, Turkey claimed that region, and regarded its occupation by the British, and hence by Iraq, as utterly illegal.[2] (This, among other reasons, may explain Turkey's interest in the Gulf War.) But modern Iraq claimed Kuwait due to the former Ottoman suzerainty in Kuwait in the early 1930s, when the British granted Iraq almost full sovereignty—although British presence in both countries prevented the annexation of the small sheikdom by its larger neighbor. And this signified to nationalist Iraqis their helplessness vis-à-vis the Western great power, while they took it for granted that the Mosul region, a real part of the Turkish Empire, given to Iraq by the British, was an integral part of a country that in fact was created by the British one hundred and fifty years after Kuwait was born as a separate entity. In 1940, some Iraqi nationalists tried to establish a pro-Nazi regime in Iraq under Rashid Ali-el Keilani, with a degree of cooperation with the exiled Palestinian leader Amin al-Husseini, the Mufti of Jerusalem.[3]

Syrian claims for Palestine were also grounded in the Ottoman past, when Palestine was nominally a province ruled by the Turkish governor of Syria and was not—at least legally—a main Ottoman province such as Syria itself.

The pro-Nazi elements in the Arab world were subdued by the British during World War II by means of force and by giving Arabs some concessions in regard to the Zionist question to calm Arab public opinion. The Ba'ath Party was the post-World War II carrier of something like Arab Fascism (if we follow A. James Gregor's comparative research), which postulated ethnicity, pan-Arabism, a popular, socialist dictatorship, and Arab regional supremacy coupled with economic and technological modernization.[4] The Iraqi monarchy, left behind by the British after World War II, was deposed by General Abd al-Karim Kassem in 1958. Kassem himself was a target of Ba'ath assassination attempts, in which young Saddam Hussein al-Takriti (Takrit was his birthplace and remained his source of personal and network power) was involved. Saddam had to flee his country to Nasser's Egypt in 1959, when such an attempt on Kassem's life had failed. But he later followed Kassem enthusiastically, when Kassem laid public claim on Kuwait, after the British withdrew from the protectorate in June 1961 and

Kuwait became a fully sovereign, separate Arab state. Nasser himself, and all other Arab states, rejected Iraq's claim, due not only to Kuwait's oil richness, which the sheiks used to maintain their separate statehood, but indeed to the acceptance, even by pan-Arabs such as Nasser, of the separate sovereignty of Arab entities—unless, of course, they united with Egypt, or with each other, by their own choice (sometimes enhanced by subversion from within). Saddam was ready to defy Nasser on this, due to the emphasis of Iraqi nationalists, led by him, on Iraqi regional power and historical claims. These same nationalists postulated pan-Arabism as well.

This short history is necessary to make a general point—that Arabs, as well as many Jews, live in the past, including the ancient past, and derive most of their subjective rationality from it, including from the discrepancies between the myths of the past and the realities of the present. Arab power and glory of the past can be a source of enormous frustration to some, even if the nuclear age has revolutionized the meaning of power. Moderate Arabs, such as President Sadat, might have grasped this very well. Others may have combined all kinds of subjective rationalities with the quest for the only tool with which they could play the game of chicken with the West, and with Israel (once they had lost the Soviet backing that at least had given them a sense of greater power, if not the kind of autonomous power they wanted).

This frame of mind is complex, and therefore the term "subjective rationality" is inadequate to analyze it. The term itself exposes the inadequacy of Schelling's theory, when dealing with alien cultures. For example, Saddam Hussein's rationale, which by itself could be understood as perfectly rational, is shaped by exactly those variables the theory had deliberately tried to ignore, such as the Arab cultural-psychological focus on themselves as the main framework of their attention. This does not mean that moderate Arabs—and maybe even some radicals—could not understand the meaning of nuclear threats. But on the other hand, their focus on Arab affairs and on the role of specific leaders among Arabs, their view of others as aliens, and their views of Arab compatriots who refused to comply with their changing priorities could drive them to behave in terms that the theory was unable to cope with other than by invoking the term "subjective rationality." Thus, within Schelling's theory one might conclude, under some circumstances, that they were even "irrational." In this way the theory could lead to action based on an inappropriate supposition—"irrationality." An example of this type of action could be a campaign—short of the use of power—to force nonproliferation on Arabs, or to suddenly see in the behavior of a given Arab leader more "rational" facets and support him against seemingly "irrational" foes, who were in reality his victims. We can see this in U.S. "aid" to help Iraq against Iran.

East-West rivalry was also a primary consideration in American behavior, mainly because the Soviet nuclear superpower was perceived to be the main challenge. Weapons were developed to fight the Russians, and intellectual tools were forged to deal with them. So when they declined and refused to play the old game, a vacuum was created, declared to be the "End of History." True, Stanley Hoffmann called it "a silly notion based on mistaken assumptions,"[5] but at first Francis Fukuyama's metaphor was widely circulated through the mass media and helped create a sense of victory for Western ideas, added to the general relaxation of tension between the East—which stopped being the old "East"—and the West—which never had been fully united. The feeling that the world had entered a new era spilled over to other regions, and Saddam Hussein—once he had concluded his truce with Iran, and Iran lost Khomeini's leadership—was treated accordingly.

In fact, President Mubarak of Egypt was quoted by well-informed Israeli sources[6] as saying that Saddam had learned his lesson from his war with Iran and adopted a moderate posture. Mubarak was "the main source" used to convey optimistic suggestions of this kind to Israel. As prime minister, Shimon Peres reportedly created a special task group, chaired by Professor Emanual Sivan, a noted specialist in North African Arab history, under General Avraham Tamir, Peres' director-general. According to these sources, Saddam was trying to "tranquilize" Israel, while pursuing his nuclear and conventional ambitions. In fact he tried to legitimize his ambitions as a matter of "survival"—a terminology used by Israel itself. The idea seems to have been that no one could prevent him from going nuclear or from maintaining an enormous, modern army, and that both were needed to defend Iraq against Iran and even Israel itself. Saddam was reported to have signalled to Israel that he was not in fundamental conflict with it. And reportedly, Peres, Tamir, Member of Knesset Yossi Beilin (an important aide of Peres'), Minister of Energy Moshe Shahal, and General Ezer Weizmann all adopted a "pro-Iraqi" stance: Once Saddam's basic approach toward Israel had changed, due among other things to lessons learned in the Iran War, his obvious grievances—like Israel's nuclear monopoly option and the Palestinian issue—should be taken into consideration in a world that had changed beyond recognition since Gorbachev's *perestroika*. According to these sources and an interview published in the Israeli press late in February 1991, Defense Minister Rabin had remained skeptical at the time, but was ready to listen to Iraqi overtures aimed at him personally, which did not materialize; while Yitzhak

Shamir, Peres' successor as prime minister, reportedly promised Saddam that Israel would not pursue Begin's Doctrine and preempt his own "defensive" efforts, as described by Mubarak.

But in fact the West had already received some warnings that the end of the cold war was not the end of history. As we have argued above, detente had contributed to the outbreak of the 1973 Yom Kippur War. The second, and much more serious, change in East-West relations was bound to lead to some reaction in the Arab world as well, now that the Soviets, a friendly superpower, were a nonpartner to any radical Arab designs even by implication. Following the 1989 upheavals in Eastern Europe, Saddam Hussein publicly warned the Arabs that they must now rely on themselves. But this might be seen against the background of his own domestic problems: higher inflation, an enormous army standing idle following the armistice with Iran, and a foreign debt accumulated during the eight-year struggle with the Iranians—all of which threatened not only his ambitious plans for the future but in his view were coupled with Iran's future strength.

We do not know what role was played here by Western governments' 1989 exposure of Saddam's purchases abroad of equipment related to unconventional weaponry,[7] which followed the seizure of nuclear weapon triggers by Western authorities on their way to Baghdad, or by the 1990 exposure in the West of an Iraqi-bound, enormous gun, capable—in theory—of giving Saddam a tool that could do the job of IRBMs, and do it much better due to the theoretical accuracy of such a gun in comparison to first-generation ballistic missiles. We can only guess whether this was his way out of the Condor 2000 problem, after the United States had succeeded in torpedoing that venture by preventing Egypt from cooperating with Iraq and Argentina. According to the Summer 1990 issue of the *Programme for Promoting Nuclear Nonproliferation [PPNN] Newsbrief*, the development of the missile in Argentina "was suspended." The reason is said to be lack of funds, although it is also known that the U.S. government has exerted pressure on Argentina to halt the project, which was supposedly carried out in cooperation with Egypt and Iraq."[8] Shortly beforehand the devices described as "nuclear weapon triggers" were intercepted in London on their way to Iraq and were confiscated. This resulted in a vehement Iraqi denial that the devices were meant to be used for triggering nuclear weapons, but in this connection the Iraqi government confirmed that it had chemical capability it would use, if necessary, against Israel.[9] The supergun purchase seemed to have been torpedoed as well, although several barrels had been produced in Britain, shipped to Iraq, and possibly installed, according to press reports. Then came foreign and Israeli reports about Saddam's purchases of uranium enrichment equipment—seemingly for centrifuges—that would allow him to build bombs by importing low-grade or medium-grade enriched uranium and then producing the necessary high-grade uranium for his bomb. Later, the mining facility in Kurdistan's mountains was exposed, where Saddam was digging natural uranium for the same purpose. After the Gulf War, in the summer of 1991, a third avenue was exposed. An article in the *New York Times* identified a New York electric equipment company that had supplied Saddam with the tools necessary to implement magnetic isotope separation,[10] following the reported desertion of an Iraqi nuclear technician who exposed Saddam's calutron program.

In the meantime, an angry Saddam Hussein was facing the rich Kuwaitis and Saudis, to whom he owed about $40 billion after the Iran War, in which he—as the Arab "Eastern Gate"—had defended them against the Iranian onslaught for eight years, regardless of the fact that he had attacked Iran to begin with. He might have believed that he won that war, thanks to his missile attacks against Iranian cities. But in his fury, Saddam had a sense of self-confidence in military terms, for many reasons: the missile force, acquired from the Soviet Union and modernized thanks to Western—especially German—firms;[11] the enormous tank force built since the outbreak of the Iranian conflict; the digging-in tactics used in that war to defeat enemy land offensives; Soviet-built Sukhoy 24 fighter bombers and MiG-29 fighters; chemical weapons, used against invading Iranian troops and against the Kurds in northern Iraq; an enhanced effort to dig shelters for the command and control posts in Baghdad and elsewhere; possibly also the deployment of "smaller" caliber superguns; and the availability of a variety of communication routes.

Saddam's fuse is short, and like many military dictators pushing toward the status of a regional or even a world power, he might have convinced himself that he was in trouble anyway and thus must take a risk and invade Kuwait. The "jumping forward" mentality is nothing new. In fact the Japanese did something similar in 1941; the Germans did it their way in 1914, and in 1939. But in the nuclear age, facing a nuclear superpower—equipped with the most modern military gear to avoid nuclear war—Saddam's decision to invade Kuwait seemed to justify the "madman" scare that Schelling and others feared so much. Soon enough, Saddam used a whole array of threats vis-à-vis his potential adversaries, took thousands of foreigners as hostages, and broke old rules of diplomatic behavior to a degree that seemed to justify the worst fears. Only later did American experts start to blame the Bush

Administration for not having warned Saddam clearly enough, and even for misleading him to believe that the United States would not intervene to save Kuwait.

In my view, Saddam did not dismiss the possibility of a negative American response because Assistant Secretary John Kelly or Ambassador April Glaspie misled him. He knew, in my view, that they did not anticipate a full-scale invasion, and thus he expected some trouble. Not even a very friendly visit by Senate Minority Leader Bob Dole, during which Saddam's wrath over the 1981 Tammuz bombing was almost justified, could signify American acceptance of the annexation of Kuwait. But maybe the rapid unification of Germany did, since no one prevented something that Germany's old enemies were hardly happy with, in the face of the a popular German resolve to undo the results of World War II. At least, Qaddafi proclaimed World War II to be over (and hence Israel's right to exist) with the fall of the Berlin Wall.

But Saddam's basic motives for invading Kuwait must have been a combination of "last resort" measures to maintain and use his existent conventional and chemical weapon arsenal and biological weapons before his large army lost its spirit and became less modern. (And his growing foreign debt would make modernization more difficult.) East-West detente might have further frightened him in terms of future Soviet supplies and strategic aid, now that Iran was a target of Soviet interest because of the end of its war with Iraq and the Iranian fundamentalist threat to the Soviet Moslem republics, which could make the Russians pursue a policy of growing cooperation with Teheran. At the same time, the atomic venture, especially the Condor project, was being ruptured—but not fully destroyed, let alone fully uncovered—by the Americans (perhaps with some Israeli help), with Mubarak's consent; this might have made him feel humiliated and pushed into a corner. Yet Saddam might have considered threatening to use the existing quantity of enriched uranium he had received from the French, plus some he was able to produce himself by using calutrons or by purchasing it abroad, in addition to threatening to use his chemical and biological weapons.

But at least he did invoke far-reaching verbal threats that made his potential enemies hesitate long enough. He used the typical "I have nothing to lose" posture that dictators—Hitler included—assume in such situations, although Saddam lacked the Darwinian-racist infrastructure of Hitler's ideology, nor could he rely on Germans to fight his wars.[12] But he could hope to be able to use Kuwait's booty to bribe those elements in the Arab world who would accept the bribery—such as the PLO and maybe even Egypt[13]—and he used two different hostage-taking techniques: he picked up many foreigners, mainly Westerners, most of whom were originally hired to help him rebuild his country or worked in Kuwait; then he threatened to attack Saudi Arabia and Israel if the United States attacked him—since, as he said publicly in late August 1990, "he could not hit Washington." And on the other hand—like other radical Arab leaders—Saddam was influenced by the American defeat in Vietnam, by the role of the American media in this regard, and by the American hostage drama in Iran. He was also influenced by the hasty withdrawal of the American peace-keeping force from Lebanon, after it was subjected to terrorist attacks in 1982, and by Reagan's very limited military action against Syria in this connection, which was terminated when two carrier-based planes were lost. He might have hoped to be able to threaten to repeat such scenarios if the Americans tried to attack him, while invoking an enthusiastic wave of support in the Arab world. Saddam's conversation with Ambassador Glaspie, in which he said that "the U.S. could not take ten thousand dead," whereas he could, reflects this calculation and in fact was quite a problem for the Americans. But it is difficult to say whether this behavior could fully fit Schelling's definition of "irrationality," because the rates of risk for both sides were hardly similar from Saddam's point of view.

Saddam Hussein took the higher risk, and therefore the West could afford to leave him alone. Or, put the other way around: the West took the higher risk, and therefore should leave him alone. Their regimes, their standing, even their way of life were much less endangered in comparison to the kind of suffocating frustration he felt, supplemented by the Ba'ath Party's quest for Arab power and Arab unification under Saddam's influence. This describes what we have called the Arab sense of "victimization"; indeed the very word was used by the Iraqi ambassador to the U.N. following the initial Security Council decisions against Iraq early in August—and by Foreign Minister Aziz when he met with Secretary Baker in January before the war started. Finally, once he had invaded Kuwait and later annexed it, Saddam would not renounce his actions unless forced to; the logic of Arab politics dictated this—that withdrawal by force would be appreciated more than capitulation. This state of mind can be described as a combination of wounded pride, vanity, domestic interest and inter-Arab politics, of rationalizing his desires vis-à-vis the proud and cautious Kuwaitis, and of his awareness of the fragility of the whole modern Arab state known as Iraq — in fact a rather divided, nonhistorical entity that had to assert itself in its own eyes vis-à-vis Iran. All of this combined to make Saddam Hussein take the high-risk option. Aziz explicitly referred to "broken agreements" related to equipment supplies, meaning thereby the relatively late action taken by President Bush to prevent export of unconventional weapon production facilities to Iraq, as mentioned above.

Using theoretical terms, Saddam Hussein might have felt more credible than his opponents, and that his motive was "high political," a matter of life and death for his nation regardless of his wasteful wars and the bloodshed that had brought him to this point; whereas Western interests in the area were "low political," mainly economic, and related to their unjustified, as he saw it, standard of living, to their materialism and corruption. But, in fact, they were hated aliens, "crusaders" in modern nationalistic Arab jargon, if they dared to impose themselves on him. Thus the divide here was indeed cultural-political. Saddam was not acquainted with Western habits of accountability, public and self-imposed, for one's own previous criminal mistakes. For while ethnic and political values—coupled with the personality cult of the leader—commanded public attention, terror and secret police methods imposed his rule. But in theoretical conflict terms, the Americans had to calculate the higher risk Saddam would present to them if he succeeded in his adventure (on the basis of his high-risk behavior and the threats he was using) and thus preempt him then.

What he did—without Soviet support and amidst the beginning of the "End of History"—seemed to the Americans so absurd that they seriously took him for a madman. But, in fact, Saddam behaved exactly within the limits of American conflict theory, due to the peculiar nature of Arab history, culture, and politics, which the theory dismisses as "subjective rationality" or as "irrational" behavior. Saddam Hussein used what we may call terroristic methods, aimed both at his own people and at the "enemy." He used lies as official policy, and broke some international agreements while demanding that others honor them.

Many non-Western cultures, such as Saddam's, perceive themselves to be victimized by the West, or at least use this argument for political reasons. They have complicated relationships with their own masses that are not regulated by the democratic process, and sometimes they must be subdued not because they are "irrational" but precisely because they are rational within their cultural-historical spectrum and their political habits, in which naked power is not only legitimate but desirable and the source of pride and self-respect for millions of people. In some cases, this "naked power" is also the only source of stability in an otherwise ethnically divided and religiously problematic society.

But their culture has no historical-cultural answer to a full-scale defeat, or to a complete devastation of one's own nation and the adversary's, as could be the case with Arab and Jew in the nuclear age. No doubt, the rate of risk to both parties would be higher, and thus the bomb helped create modern "moderate" Arabs such as Sadat. Even when Saddam behaved in a fashion that seemed to be "mad," and at least highly emotional and cruel, he did not in fact exceed the limits of risk taking that could have destroyed Iraq completely.

Indeed, at first the United States reacted to the invasion of Kuwait and to Saddam's threats and hostage-taking by invoking the "madman" image—as if Saddam could not be deterred and therefore had to be crushed, later rather than sooner. Then the man proved himself to be a curious "madman" when he immediately gave up all his assets vis-à-vis Iran, assets won by sacrificing tens of thousands of his own people, which proved to some members of the Bush Administration that Saddam was capable of making concessions—which was not, as one may suggest, the case with Hitler. Thus Saddam could be made to make further concessions, and if he "jumped forward" again, against the assembling international forces in Saudi Arabia and in the Gulf, he would create a clear-cut casus belli that would cement American public opinion against him beyond any doubt. The Americans certainly wanted to avoid a repetition of the dubious Tonkin Gulf incident, which had driven President Johnson to his fateful decision to intervene in Vietnam en masse.

The question at this stage was, of course, whether Saddam Hussein could be made to give up Kuwait and his nuclear option directly or indirectly—by being pushed back into his initial financial problems without Kuwait's fortune to relieve him of his debt and open sources of foreign technology to him to help overcome the setbacks in regard to the supergun and the Condor 2000.[14] And yet these aspects of the Kuwait invasion—i.e., the dangers inherent in Saddam's regime if allowed to swallow Kuwait and be in possession of 20 percent of the world oil reserves plus the bomb—were not fully spelled out by American and other Western governments at the outset of the crisis in August 1990. The oil aspect was very much mentioned by President Bush, as were commitments to friends; and the whole conventional and chemical array were of course stressed by the Bush Administration to justify the blockade against Iraq. But the oil aspect was bound to raise questions about American misuse of the world's oil, about Bush's refusal to face the energy problem by imposing taxes on imported oil, and about Republican economic policy in general. If President Bush had said in public, "We fear Saddam, plus the oil, plus the bomb," he might have solidified his domestic base. But he may have believed that his domestic base was solid enough when he resorted to the blockade rather than to initiating hostilities, and that the nuclear aspect of the danger inherent in Iraq would be carried to the public by the media rather than by the government. This form of opacity in regard to nuclear matters, despite the fact that Saddam created a chemical weapon "scare" from the outset of the crisis—which might have justified a discussion of the unconventional threat inherent in his regime in general, not to mention unconventional counterthreats by the Americans—was maintained by the United States until early in September. The reasons for at first maintaining official silence in regard to Saddam's nuclear ambitions, and the possibility that a pan-Arab regime would in due course play the game of chicken with the West—and with Israel—could be explained by the following reasoning, while Saddam's fears of the revitalized Iranian nuclear program seemed to be totally ignored.

First, public attack on Arab nuclear research and development— when officially conducted within IAEA rules—could be politically harmful in terms of Arab pride and Third World sensitivities, and make IAEA involvement in maintaining the nonproliferation regime difficult. Before the outbreak of the Kuwait crisis, the IAEA issued a document at the request of the Iraqi authorities confirming that all materials under safeguard had been accounted for, which means that the 12.5 kilograms of uranium missing since the outbreak of the Iran-Iraq War[15] had been located by the international agency. On the other hand, after the invasion it was reported in the Western press that Saddam Hussein had invested a fortune in a uranium mine of his own, although sometimes the same site was described as a "nuclear reactor," close to the Turkish boundary. It was also reported by the Brazilian press that Saddam had purchased—from Brazil—more enriched uranium; and he was caught, red-handed, trying to import nuclear weapon triggers. His main illegal nuclear effort—whether using centrifuges to enrich low-grade uranium or his efforts to assemble a bomb from the enriched uranium at his disposal, the two routes then known—seems to have remained centered in a compound close to Baghdad. Exposing that effort and providing the evidence that would have been necessary to prove that it existed, without destroying it, might have been seen by the United States as too complicated to do outright. The blockade itself could halt or slow down Saddam's efforts in the unconventional field without breaking the existing rules of the nonproliferation game by using force as Israel did in 1981. In fact, in regard to Saddam's uranium-enrichment facilities it was "generally acknowledged that it would probably need up to ten years to acquire a substantial enrichment capacity."[16]

The problem here is what is "substantial," and whether Qaddafi's old desire to get "just one bomb . . . even a tactical one" to push Israel and acquire a major trump card vis-à-vis the moderate Arabs could be achieved by using enrichment equipment that Saddam had already acquired, or the old French uranium plus the Brazilian uranium and similar imported quantities that might suffice to build a primitive or a less primitive bomb. This bomb could then be mounted on a SCUD-B or carried by one of Saddam's newly acquired Sukhoy-24s, which are capable of all-weather, night and day, accurate low-flying bombing. What would Saddam do when he acquired a little more, and succeeded in buying modern missile technology from Europeans or South Americans with his new fortune and great political achievement, if he managed to swallow Kuwait? No Western government touched upon these options in public, at first. Of course, mere possession of the capabilities does not suggest that Saddam would use them except for political-psychological and economic purposes, because dropping a bomb on Israel, in due course, would bring about a holocaust in Iraq. But with a bomb in his arsenal, the rate of risk for his adversaries would increase and Saddam's standing among radical Arabs grow in direct proportion to his nuclear arsenal. Paradoxically enough, "just one bomb" had little meaning unless he indeed dropped it, and took the risk of wholesale devastation. Whether he had reliable delivery means became an important question here, and surface-to-air missiles such as the Israeli Arrow (and much less so the American Patriot) were important possible answers.

The real breakthrough, from Saddam's viewpoint, would be an Iraqi arsenal that might establish Saddam as the future of the Arab nation—a prospect that Egypt and Syria, each for different reasons, dreaded, especially after Saddam broke all the existing rules among Arab states and invaded an Arab neighbor.[17] In this sense, all of the Arab states suddenly became moderate. And yet, the implication of open talk in the West about knocking off Saddam's nuclear infrastructure at the beginning of the crisis—which would maintain Israel's regional nuclear monopoly option, and therefore could be used by radical Arabs to enhance their own cause—probably did not escape the attention of Western diplomatic planners and politicians. Early in September 1990, however, U.S. Secretary of Defense Richard Cheney, if not President Bush himself, openly addressed Saddam and his regime in terms of Iraq's nuclear ambitions.[18] The secretary reiterated that Saddam might have been much more dangerous if he had been allowed to produce nuclear weapons in the past, and would become dangerous indeed if allowed to do so in the future. Thus reports about weariness among the assembled American troops in the Saudi desert and doubts among Americans at home whether one should fight for "corrupt sheiks" in a god-forsaken place might have pushed the administration to finally drop opacity and formulate clear "war aims" in spite of the foreign political constraints mentioned above. Israeli deputy foreign minister Binyamin Natanyahu immediately said that the United States "should lead a system of denying nuclear weapons from dictators," echoing the language used by the Argentinian minister of foreign affairs when, upon arriving in Israel, he announced his country's decision to terminate its cooperation with Iraq in the development the Condor missile.

Thus, before we return to the Arabs in this drama, and to the seemingly astonishing support Egypt and Syria—but not the PLO or Jordan—gave to the American anti-Saddam campaign, let us briefly examine Israel's behavior in this crisis. From the outset it could be said that Saddam Hussein's behavior made it difficult for Israel to publicly maintain Begin's nuclear monopoly doctrine, and finally pushed Israel to the very edge of giving up its opaque nuclear posture and making the Israeli public aware, at last, of the fact that their national security depended to a high degree on the option of nuclear deterrence. In spring 1990 Saddam suddenly referred to Israel in public as his main objective and threatened to "set half of Israel ablaze" by invoking his "binary chemical weapons." Then he publicly deployed some SCUD-Bs, allegedly armed with chemical warheads, close to his border with Jordan, aimed at Israel. The president of Israel, Chaim Herzog, a former general and a close ally of Mr. Peres, even wrote to a British member of Parliament, who had complained to him about Vanunu's severe punishment, that *"the developments in and around Kuweit [sic] clearly present Israel's atomic potential in a defensive perspective,* different from the demonic suspicions of Mr. Vanunu [italics added]."[19] Herzog justified the Vanunu verdict, as we shall see below, in terms of guarding the state security, as "no government accepts the disclosure of classified information by a citizen." The commentary in the paper that published Herzog's statement read, "Now it is official: We, too, have atomic weapons, or as it was formulated in a letter sent by the President's Office. Now we can stop whispering." The Israeli press even mentioned names—Bergmann's, Ben-Gurion's, and Peres' (who in the past had himself taken the main credit for Dimona)—after Shamir responded publicly to Saddam's threats by invoking a "terrible, horrible" Israeli response if the Iraqi leader implemented his threats.

This process had entailed several stages, according to a well-informed source close to Shamir.[20] At first, when Saddam started his moves toward Kuwait by resuming a sharp—even if defensive—anti-Israel stance, quoting his "binary-chemical weapons" as deterrents, and later, when he deployed his SCUDs not far from the Jordanian border with Israel and farther west at al-Qiam close to the Syrian border (as proved to be the case during the war), President Mubarak of Egypt had tried to mediate between Iraq and Israel. The impression was that Saddam was responding to the Begin Doctrine by publicly refusing to go along with Israel's doctrine of opaque nuclear monopoly now that he had his "poor man's deterrent." His motives in so doing could have been, as interpreted by Mubarak and Shamir, the exposure of his supergun project and the demise of the Egyptian-Iraqi Condor project. It could be argued that the practical steps against Saddam's nuclear ambitions—including a possible Israeli contribution in the uncovering of the supergun project—made him verbally aggressive. In order to prevent Israel from preempting his chemical threat by possibly using nuclear weapons, as Mubarak interpreted the Begin Doctrine,[21] the Egyptian president told Shamir that Saddam's intentions were purely defensive in spite of his aggressive public statements. In fact, Mubarak said that Saddam himself had promised him that this was true. In exchange, Mubarak asked for, and received, Shamir's promise not to attack Saddam. Begin's doctrine was ruptured somewhat when Saddam was assured that Israel would leave alone Iraq's chemical missiles—the shield Iraq was in fact using to rebuild its nuclear potential. As I interpret it, the Israelis preferred not to try to repeat the 1981 strike against the centrifuges (which they perceived to be the main problem, even though Iraq was a long way from producing enriched uranium thereby) and against the missiles, because Iraq seemed to them to have learned its lessons from the war with Iran, and serious technical and political problems were involved in such attacks. Only later did the Israelis feel rather uneasy about Saddam's intentions.

When the Iraqi ruler broke his promise to Mubarak not to invade Kuwait,[22] Israel could feel and argue that his other promises were just as worthless. In other words, Saddam was always aiming at the independent, hegemonical, pan-Arab, nuclear, anti-Israel plank, for which he needed Kuwait's money now that he was unable to acquire such a status by other means. The PLO's immediate support of Saddam's invasion played into Likud's hands; Arafat's outfit had never given up its terroristic character and wholly anti-Israel intentions. This split the Israeli Left in regard to future negotiations with the PLO, which had seemed to the Left to be unavoidable. In fact, several years earlier, the PLO had developed close relations with Saddam's Iraq, due to the PLO's difficult relations with Syria and uneasy relations with the moderate Egyptians. Butrus A'ali, the number-two man in the Egyptian Foreign Ministry, formulated the problem in terms of "the PLO's weakness," in the sense that Arafat feared the Palestinian masses, who automatically supported the Iraqi strongman and hailed him as a hero who challenged the West and endorsed their cause. Also, the PLO would use every possible tool to gain a degree of autonomy by capitalizing on Arab-Arab differences at Israel's expense, just as Saddam himself "rebelled" against his dependence on the rich Kuwaitis, even though it was the result of his own wasteful war against Iran. For the time being, Arafat opted for Saddam's success, even if Saddam's annexation of Kuwait destroyed an Arab state and thus directly contradicted the claims of any smaller Arab entity for statehood: a stronger Arab state could simply annex a smaller Arab entity by arguing that it "belonged" to the former in the Ottoman past.

The annexation itself angered Mubarak, who was exposed as a fool because he had mediated between Saddam and the Kuwaitis just before the invasion; thus Mubarak helped bring about the creation of an Arab-American coalition to formally defend Saudi Arabia against Iraq and force Saddam's withdrawal from Kuwait.

As mentioned above, Saddam's threats against Israel and against the United States (the power who had in fact helped him to conclude his war with Iran honorably), and his use of force to maintain his power and gain more in explicit unconventional terms, brought about an end to the period of uncertainty in regard to nuclear deterrence in Israel, at least in domestic-psychological terms (although no serious public-political debate on the merits of the nuclear issue has followed, at least for the time being).

The Israeli government must have asked itself why it became Saddam's target, at least verbally, and must have concluded—and rather late warned Washington—that the Iraqi ruler may have wanted in fact to invade Kuwait, and by pushing Israel was diverting attention from his real goal, while trying to unify the Arabs behind the Kuwaiti action by invoking pan-Arab and anti-Israel slogans. By itself such use of force in the region was quite alarming, but its results (in terms mentioned above) would threaten Israel very seriously. Israel's previous doctrine of preemption was highly problematic against centrifuges and missile technology that could be purchased abroad when Saddam had the money to do so. Moshe Arens, reinstituted by Shamir as defense minister earlier in 1990, visited Washington shortly before the invasion. He said in an Israeli Television broadcast that he had informed the Americans about Saddam's intentions. Arens said that his warnings were not "taken seriously . . . there were illusions in Washington in this regard."[23] But they were appreciated later when Saddam proved himself to be the kind of bully the Israelis expected him to be, or knew that he would become at least in regard to Kuwait.

On his side, Saddam skillfully played the Israeli card—seldom, however, mentioning its nuclear option—by arguing that Israel did not comply with U.N. Security Council resolutions to withdraw from the occupied territories. (He grossly misrepresented Security Council resolution 242 of 1967, which called upon Israeli withdrawal from "occupied territories" in exchange for Arab political concessions, which at the time were not forthcoming.) He then created another propaganda linkage between Israel, the United States, and his Arab adversaries. He claimed that Israeli pilots in U.S.-made planes were deployed in "American-occupied" Saudi Arabia. So Shamir's government had to calculate the possible emergence of a "Jew's War" argument in the United States, i.e., that Israel was pushing the Americans to an unnecessary, risky war far away to achieve the goal of eliminating Saddam's war machine and mainly Saddam's bomb, which in fact was not an American but an Israeli problem. Saddam's crimes against his own people, against Iran, and against an Arab sister state would be easily forgotten or blurred in the typical media handling of such complicated and remote matters if Israel assumed a high profile in this crisis.

For the Bush Administration, the issue had to remain that of international law, of rules of behavior broken by Saddam, of America's commitment to its allies in a sensitive region, and of oil. The fact that the Americans transferred too much power to the Security Council, and to its new coalition partners, was at first not an Israeli problem. This course of action was understood to be necessary if Bush wanted to carry domestic public opinion and persuade Congress to make war.

Thus Shamir's government had done three things since the outbreak of the crisis. First, the prime minister warned Saddam that should Israel be dragged into the whirlpool and attacked, "[Iraq] will pay a terrible and a horrible price."[24] All Israeli print media interpreted this for the first time to be a nuclear threat, and repeatedly mentioned David Ben-Gurion, Mr. Peres, and the completely forgotten Ernst Bergmann as those who had given Shamir that option; some praised Begin for the 1981 Tammuz raid and criticized Peres for having tried at the time to prevent the raid. Second, Israel drew a "red line" in regard to Jordan, whose king was very worried about Saddam and about his own pro-Saddam population and was therefore inclined to support him to a degree. Thus the Israeli government declared that Iraqi military presence in Jordan would be a casus belli. Third, Israel approached the United States for more military aid, such as advanced anti-aircraft Patriot missiles, which could also be used, though not very effectively, to intercept various missiles. While President Bush was trying in public to separate the Israelis from the Gulf crisis as far as possible, reiterating

Israel's ability to "fully defend herself," the Israelis proceeded with their own defense.

Later, when war broke out, the Israeli military maintained that it had a capability to strike at the Iraqi missile sites. However, in order to keep the Israelis out of the action—to avoid alienating the Arab members of the anti-Saddam coalition, such as Egypt and Syria, who had joined Saudi Arabia in the multinational force—the Americans made something of a commitment to make "a decisive American response" should "Saddam turn his missiles against Israel," according to a source close to Shamir, the *Ma'ariv* columnist Moshe Zack. "Israel," he wrote, "is not obliged to advise Saddam about the degree of American commitment to Israel, whether it entails the obligation to strike at the Iraqi launchers that will be aimed at Israel."[25] Yet this formulation could be accepted as an American measure to avoid an Israeli "triggering" action that could give way to a general war—although "Israeli defense circles" were quoted, every now and again, as saying that if the United States hesitated long enough, Israel would strike Saddam on its own, because he would attack Israel in a "two-year period" if not defeated now. The "two-year period" must be connected here to BBC and "60 Minutes" reports about Saddam's centrifuge project, which would have given him some nuclear capability by 1992. The calutrons had not yet been discovered as the more primitive but much more immediate nuclear threat, nor was it known that the regular power stations Saddam had had built were intended to supply the calutrons with electricity. The whole calutron project, as I was informed by authoritative sources in Washington in July 1991, cost Saddam about $8 billion.

As the crisis remained unresolved, "high-placed Iraqi sources" were quoted in the Israeli press to the effect that Saddam would use a "Samson strategy," when necessary, and if attacked he would indeed "take Israel with him, and the oil wells."[26] Here we can determine an "Israeli-like Samson threat," as it was ascribed to Israel by Heikal, even if unconventional weapons, including biological ones, were used as deterrents for the first time to support a change in the status quo from the beginning, and not to defend the status quo. Continued Iraqi threats in regard to some "surprise" that the Americans would encounter if they resorted to the use of force also raised the question of whether Saddam had acquired—from a West German firm—the conventional capability of using gasoline-air bombs, which create tremendous heat in a given area, while consuming the hydrogen from the air in the vicinity of the explosion.

In the meantime, Israel had publicly tested early in August the first stage of the Arrow antimissile missile, although the system—largely

American-financed within the framework of "Star Wars" and American-Israeli strategic cooperation—would require seven or more years to be fully developed, according to Defense Minister Arens. The system itself, and especially its costs (even though about 80 percent financed by the United States), was criticized by military circles in Israel. However, the questions of whether such defensive measures could tackle enemy MIRVed missiles could be put aside for now, if Saddam's adventure failed and his missile capabilities were eliminated or remained rather limited, with no nuclear warheads.

A curious supplement to the Arrow test was a press conference given in Tel Aviv on September 3, 1990, by Dr. Edward Teller, the "father of the hydrogen bomb," with Professor Yuval Ne'eman, Mr. Begin's former minister of science and technology, as a host. By now Ne'eman was again a member of the cabinet, as minister of energy and of science in Prime Minister Shamir's new "narrow" coalition. Israel Television, which broadcasted parts of Teller's press conference, disclosed that the father of SDI, in fact, visited Israel "often" and was a "friend" of Mr. Ne'eman. When he suddenly appeared in public with his "friend," Teller offered an explicit opaque nuclear statement on Israel's behalf vis-à-vis Iraq. He said that Saddam Hussein's nuclear technologies were "ten years old," and that in that time the United States, in cooperation with Israel, had introduced "defensive measures" that could render Iraq's capabilities ineffective. He reiterated his well-known nuclear defensive—rather than deterrent—posture, and argued that science and technology remained vital in achieving security in the nuclear age. Teller refused to elaborate, however; we do not know whether he meant the Arrow or other American-Israeli ventures. Teller further said that Israel was "capable of developing small, underground energy reactors that will be clean and safe, and could be exported one day."[27]

In the meantime, the Israeli Supreme Court decided to release large parts of its verdict in Vanunu's case in response to Vanunu's own request.[28] The verdict itself—confirming the Jerusalem District Court's original condemnation of Vanunu as a traitor, and his eighteen-year jail sentence—remained at first classified, except for the operative part. But now—possibly due to a campaign abroad that portrayed Vanunu as an idealist who had exposed Israel's illegal nuclear effort for high moral reasons—the Supreme Court decided to lift the veil of secrecy on most of the verdict, even if in doing so it had to confirm the facts Vanunu had brought to light.[29] Typical of Israel's lack of established "public rules of the game," the Supreme Court felt that it had to teach Vanunu's attorney, radical political lawyer Avigdor Feldman, that the law could not accept breaches of its norms, even if the breaches were ideologically motivated, as Feldman chose to portray his client's actions.

In fact the ideological motivation itself was rejected by the court. Instead of confirming Feldman's portrayal, the court exposed Vanunu as a loner, an egotistical and troubled man on whom the socialization process did not work. The released verdict stated that Vanunu's frustration at work in the Dimona compound, his inability to build a family, and his sense of personal "failure"—in spite of his tremendous efforts and his poor social background—finally drove him to the radical left and closer to the Arab cause. In fact, according to the verdict, the Ashkenzi-Sephardi (European-non-European) tension in Israeli society gave birth here to an act of revenge. When Vanunu politicized his frustration during the Lebanon War, was warned by security officials, and almost fired, he must have felt mistreated by the establishment, which he felt was "white" and in fact pursuing illegal activities of a sort at Dimona. Unable, himself, to clarify the actual significance of these "activities," he filmed the underground facility before resigning his job as a technical operator, and left the country. He later even converted to Christianity—a far-reaching step for the son of an orthodox Sephardi rabbi—and tried to open a new chapter in his life in Australia. The conversion, itself a random decision made when he bumped into a missionary, and then a random meeting with a dubious journalist, affected Vanunu's behavior to a degree that made his idealistic motivation look doubtful. Instead, according to the court, the man gave vent to his frustrations and hate, while knowing very well that

> the State keeps the subjects which he picked up in secret . . . [censored] from her enemies. That enemy states were trying to . . . [censored] and that . . . [censored] what one's adversary does and which level he reached were of great importance. . . . [censored] The details . . . [censored] were not necessary to make a political case, and on the other hand, every marking of a target and its particulars, its internal structure and its arrangement on the ground, are categorized as giving an advantage to the enemy which he could not otherwise obtain.

In these key sentences the court confirmed the validity of Vanunu's disclosures, because it said indirectly that they were true, and hence the great damage—in terms of a possible air strike against the compound, for example, and in terms of "a possible push . . . [censored] to the enemy for serious and much more dangerous preparations of . . . [censored] fighting capabilities against Israel." In other words, the official opacity was supposed, among other things, to lower Arab motivation to acquire their own bomb. In judicial, but not in historical, terms neither Qaddafi nor Heikal nor Saddam were motivated by Vanunu's disclosures, and in fact they might have had a deterrent value in spite of Vanunu's alleged motives. Also, the court found the disclosures in a foreign newspaper, which was not widely read in Israel. This provided more evidence that Vanunu was not interested in a political fight in Israel itself, but in taking revenge on Israel abroad. Indeed, Attorney Feldman was the fighter here, representing a radical antibomb ideology that questioned whether a nation-state had the moral right to obtain, use, and perhaps survive because of, nuclear weapons.

A friend of the philosopher Avner Cohen, Feldman assumed the role of the defunct Israeli Anti-Nuclear Committee of the 1960s and invoked deterrence theory to support his case, including Schelling and Kissinger.[30] Whereas Cohen had learned enough about Arab intentions, dilemmas, and preparations to suggest some kind of talks, or even reaching a tacit understanding with Saddam to achieve a "mutual no-use" situation between a nuclear Iraq and Israel before the Kuwaiti crisis, Feldman chose to blame his country, Shamir and Peres alike, for endorsing "the language of the bomb" since the outbreak of the Kuwaiti crisis. Ignoring Saddam's unconventional threats altogether, Feldman compared deterrence theory to the "language of wooing and betrayal used by those who specialize in seducing" women, or to children's games in which ostentation and "showing off" give the balance of terror a fantastic dimension in which the "winner gets everything and the loser returns home to dinner and mother." Feldman's poor understanding of game theory and of Schelling's tremendous fear of the dangers inherent in the balance of terror, even when children were not involved, was combined with his hatred of the Israeli establishment, "those lonely, bitter, childless, and lustless" leaders, who used the new language of the bomb to warm their bodies, and thus create the cultural-political niche that would legitimize the monster of "preemptive strike," "universal deterrence," and the like. This is a good demonstration of Israeli radical leftist opacity, which argues that if you do not talk about something, it will not exist as an actual option. Once you do, and invoke the terminology of strategic nuclear deterrence, you won't be able to avoid nuclear war.

In the meantime, the Brazilian press disclosed that in 1980, before the Tammuz raid, the ruling military junta concluded a secret deal with Saddam Hussein to produce nuclear weapons.[31] Brazil supplied enriched uranium and other tools, which would have to be added to the French-supplied uranium. At the same time, the United States Navy was following an Iraqi ship in the Mediterranean that was carrying "nuclear materials [and] traveling in circles" to avoid interception and a search, according to the news agencies .

The previous, complete opacity was thus difficult, and unwise, to maintain. Yet the formulation chosen by the U.S. government remained at least partially opaque, and related to the concept of "a new order for the Middle East," as mentioned in the previous chapter. Early in September 1990, Secretary of State James Baker III added one more official goal to American policy vis-à-vis Saddam Hussein.[32] He said that the resolution of the Gulf crisis must become a "springboard to resolve the conflicts" rooted in the proliferation of weapons of mass destruction in the Middle East, nuclear weapons included. He mentioned Israel's relations with its Palestinian neighbors and with the Arab states as one such conflict, and suggested a long-range American presence in the region plus some kind of a permanent body that would guarantee stability in the Middle East.

At the same time, the administration reported technical difficulties in effectively attacking Saddam's unconventional installations from the air, not to mention the problems caused by the positioning of Western hostages in Saddam's vital installations and the threat of terrorist attacks abroad by Abu-Nidal, Abul Abbas, and George Habash, the Palestinian terror leaders assembled in Baghdad. According to Leonard Spector, Saddam's technological capabilities prohibited the use of the enriched uranium to build a bomb, and his nuclear potential, centrifuges and the like, remained meager, as yet.[33] In this respect, "there was not much to bomb," he asserted. But the chemical installations and the uranium mine, the mobile and fixed-base missiles, the new missile projects, and the Iraqi-manned warplanes remained the obvious primary targets for aerial attack. (In his 1990 report, Spector mentioned "missile systems" code-named "Tammuz-1," which apparently were related to the solid-fuel Condor 2000 and to a new missile, allegedly with a longer range.)[34] Saddam's answer to such an attack, as he publicly threatened, would be "to strike at Saudi Arabia and Israel," in addition to threatening the American forces themselves. By now President Bush had decided that the official target of the American-led expedition—Kuwait—would have to be dislodged from him whether his threats proved baseless or not. If the president himself remained undeterred by Saddam's unconventional threats, others—especially people close to the nonproliferation lobby did not. One of them told me privately, "had we been assured that Iraq had assembled a nuclear bomb or two, we would not have attacked Saddam." This remark suggests our concept of American nuclear "self-deterrence," once an adversary acquires nuclear weapons, which was common among Kennedy's aides in the 1960s but not necessarily acceptable to Bush. Yet the president and the nonproliferation lobby could agree among themselves that Saddam needed Kuwait in order to acquire the bomb, among other things, and thus had to be forced to evacuate the sheikdom.

Dislodging Saddam now required the transfer of large army units to the Gulf, to join the naval and air forces already assembled. And this process required time. Thus the blockade, the actual option chosen by the administration to cope with the immediate crisis, remained for the time being. True, Baker identified the problem before the House's Foreign Relations Committee as American refusal to allow the combination of force, weapons of mass destruction, and oil to shape the Middle East, but the actual build-up of American forces in the Gulf continued during the autumn. As far as American public opinion was concerned, a decline in the support given to Mr. Bush in his initial anti-Saddam campaign was registered in late October, when a dangerous link could have been emerging between the growing U.S. economic recession, the criticism of the Republicans as having "enriched the rich," Bush's own reputation as an American-style oil prince, and the stalemate in the Gulf, which for some threatened to deteriorate into an "oil war." Thus some of the reasons people saw the conflict as purely an "oil war" were: the semi-opaque treatment of Saddam's threat in terms of radical and barbaric behavior, a far-reaching control over the international oil market if he retained Kuwait, his nuclear ambitions in terms of future threats vis-à-vis the United States itself, and his threats against Israel.

The Israeli connection, created by Saddam, was followed at first by Soviet ideas of linking the Palestinian question to the Gulf crisis. This linkage was, at times, halfway endorsed by the Bush Administration, but never fully endorsed, since Baker and his experts might have seen that radical Arab behavior, including Palestinian support of pan-Arabism advanced by a remote leader who tried to establish Iraqi hegemony in his neighborhood is just as much "the root" of the Middle East conflict as the Palestinian issue itself. We can add that Arab weakness and frustration in the modern world had been demonstrated, and used as political tools in the case of Israel, to achieve Arab goals, both "high" and "low" political, since Nasser's time. The moderate option, challenged by Sadat's enemies after the Camp David peace treaty, was in danger again, but the early use of direct American force might also jeopardize it.

The issue was that of priorities: how to at least dislodge Saddam from Kuwait, and thereby bring about—if possible—his downfall; thus the radical Arab option inherent in his behavior, including his unconventional ambitions, would become irrelevant to the well-being of the

Iraqi people. If this could be achieved, there could be a return to the bigger scheme of a "new order" for the Middle East, which would include arms control talks, under Soviet and American, maybe European auspices, with an American presence in the Gulf—and maybe elsewhere in the region—or or perhaps U.N. forces, to guarantee the "new order." United Nations involvement would sanction this arrangement, which would place all nuclear facilities of the parties involved under IAEA controls. "Put the bombs aside, since you already have them," said Dr. Quandt, "and open your facilities to international inspection."[35] In other words, keep what you already have separately and allow inspection of your installations, in order to permit the peace process to substitute for future nuclear weapons production, in the framework of a pacified Middle East, in which the boundaries will be opened, Israeli occupation ended, and no Palestinian state established, since the regional structure—not the sovereignty of any particular state—would be the framework. "Indeed, sovereignty in the nuclear age is dangerous," said Quandt in response to my question, "but you will have to give up your sovereignty in regard to nuclear matters as well," at least in regard to future agreements. This means that opacity would remain a necessary tool in the Middle East game until—and when—the "new order" was established in the Middle East and Saddam's radical option proved to be a failure.

Things can become complicated in the meantime, though, as was proved when Arab demonstrators stoned Israeli worshipers along Jerusalem's Wailing Wall in mid-October 1990. The riot began on the Temple Mount, originally the site of the Jewish holy shrine that for that reason had been transformed by Moslems into their own holy places many centuries ago. The Israeli police stormed that highly sensitive area, whose control had in fact been declined by Ben-Gurion in 1948, and killed eighteen Arabs, with ensuing diplomatic damage and trouble for the United States. There were further complications of an Arab-Arab nature. While President Mubarak joined the Saudis and the Americans in the anti-Saddam coalition, hundreds of thousands of Egyptian workers, among other foreigners, left Kuwait (many Egyptians had left Iraq earlier, when subjected to mistreatment by demobilized Iraqi soldiers following the armistice with Iran) and added to Mubarak's domestic economic difficulties. Washington compensated Egypt by forgoing a $7 billion debt to the United States, when Egyptian complaints about the growing domestic pressure and fundamentalist danger were made loudly enough.

Another complication arose from King Hussein's typical dance between Saddam, the United States, and the Saudis, which he chose to do rather close to the Iraqi ruler. He feared his own pro-Saddam, mainly Palestinian, population, and he had been humiliated by the Kuwaitis when he had asked them repeatedly for financial assistance. As a result, the king found himself in trouble mainly with the Saudis, who cut off even gasoline supplies to Jordan, while Jordan was struggling to recover from the economic effects of absorbing the many foreign workers who had left Kuwait—and Iraq itself—after the invasion. Many thousands of Jordanians and Yemenites (Yemen was the only Arab state, other than the Sudan, which drew close to Qaddafi, who supported Saddam openly) were in fact deported from Saudi Arabia. Indeed, Saddam brought havoc to the Middle East.

Strangely enough, Qaddafi did not join Saddam Hussein openly. He might have believed that the Iraqi leader had endangered the main thing—his nuclear option—prematurely. Qaddafi would not make such a mistake.

And finally, Hafez al-Assad joined the anti-Saddam coalition for a number of reasons. One reason was the traditional Syrian fear of an Iraq that would grow too strong, and that had already broken the rules of behavior among Arab states; another reason was Baghdad's open enmity toward Damascus's much more pragmatic version of Ba'athist ideology, which took the form of personal enmity between Saddam Hussein and Hafez al-Assad. Assad was welcomed as an important asset in isolating Iraq, and possibly as a future partner for some pragmatic arrangement with Israel in return for badly needed economic aid.

At first, Assad proceeded in mid-October to eliminate the autonomous Christian enclave in Beirut, under General Michel Aoun, who was supported, among others, by the Iraqis to prevent a complete Syrian predominance in Lebanon. The ensuing massacres were treated by the international media as a matter of routine, an internal Arab affair, as Aoun had no oil and his nuisance value was nil. American diplomatic reaction might have been less cynical, and some degree of doubt was later raised in the American press about whether the honeymoon between Washington and Damascus would resemble the one between Saddam and the Americans regarding Khomeini's Iran. Syria, sometimes, argued in public that it would hardly be ready to eliminate Saddam's war machine, because this would leave Syria alone facing the enemy—i.e., Israel. Assad did send some troops to Saudi Arabia, however, and tried to convince the Iranians—who hardly needed him for that—not to come to Iraq's aid. At the same time, he was reported in the London *Telegraph* to have purchased missiles from China, and once conservatives raised their heads again in the Soviet Union, Defense Minister Mustafa Tlass went to Moscow to purchase more weapons, asking for compensation against the American Patriots sent to Israel. Officials in Damascus saw their country, once Iraq's power was eliminated, as becoming "the strongest confrontation" state vis-à-vis Israel, a position of power and benefit; this may explain Assad's cool maneuvering against Iraq in the Israeli context.

Yet Saddam Hussein was moving his own way. Iraq tried to fuel the Intifada as best it could, among other things by channeling money to the West Bank and Gaza, and transformed its secular Ba'ath regime into the protector of all Moslem holy places. Shamir's cabinet added to the complications when it categorically refused to accept a delegation of the U.N. Secretary General, voted by the Security Council to inquire into the killings on Temple Mount, as an infringement on Israel's sovereignty in the united city. The unification of Jerusalem was also one of the legal-political results of the Six-Day War, which Likud pushed through parliament as a barrier against any future negotiations on Jerusalem's status. Sharon, now minister of housing, fueled the fire by announcing large settlements for Soviet immigrants in East Jerusalem, and yet Shamir and the Bush Administration tried to avoid an open rift, until the "new order" for the Middle East was indeed closer to becoming a reality. Saddam, and President Bush's budget and economic problems at home, were too problematic to risk a domestic American complication prematurely.

While no American action was taking place in mid-November, the Middle East was boiling in several trouble spots. The most dangerous, in my view, was Jordan, if Saddam succeeded, even to a degree, in humiliating Washington. Jordan's weak structure, King Hussein's compromises with pro-Iraqi Palestinians and Moslem fundamentalists—at least in terms of allowing them public activities—and the ensuing deterioration of his army's control over the Jordan Valley, when combined with the recent developments in the holy places in Jerusalem, endangered the de facto peace between Israel and Jordan. If King Hussein fell, and Saddam remained in power, Jordan could become the next collision point between Saddam, Israel, Syria, and Saudi Arabia. The conventional burden and the political ramifications of such a development added to Israel's strategic dilemmas at the time.

The strategic dilemma had produced something like "reduced opacity," which was reflected in somewhat confused press reports. The October 22, 1990, edition of *Ha'aretz* contained a short notice that Professor Shalhevet Frier, a former chairman of the Israeli Atomic Energy Commission, would "present Israel's nuclear policy to the heads of the foreign diplomatic missions in Israel today, in a meeting described as closed, and [he would further present to them] several suggestions which were formulated in Israel to denuclearize the Middle East. The presentation of Israel's stance came as a result of an unpleasant development from an Israeli point of view in this area, toward the conclusion of the process [that would bring] South Africa to accept NPT. Israel did not join, and when South Africa does, she [Israel] may remain in the less honorable society of the countries who rejected [the Treaty]."

On October 23, 1990, *Ha'aretz* published a report of the meeting between Professor Frier and the foreign diplomats. According to it, the meeting was held by the Israeli Council on Foreign Relations, and the diplomats were invited guests. Frier was quoted to the effect that joining NPT "not only does not prevent wars, but the related safeguards are frozen [by the signatory nation such as Iraq] during the hostilities." The paper further quoted a current report by the U.N. Secretary General to the U.N. General Assembly, which "showed much understanding of Israel's needs." The U.N. report said that there were indications that Israel's conventional power was reduced.

> In this connection it should be mentioned that her potential adversaries obtain relatively long-range and rather accurate ballistic missiles. Since its population is relatively small in comparison to other nations in the region, Israel becomes more vulnerable to a prolonged war . . . Israel's security is characterized by three factors, which determine her stance toward the proposition of [making the Middle East] a NWFZ. Her territory is relatively small; there is an ongoing enmity between her and most states around her; and she has no military allies in the region.

Thus, the conclusion of the U.N. report was that "progress toward the resolution of the basic confrontations in the Middle East must be made, otherwise we could not develop the means to prevent war."

The very publicity given to Mr. Frier's meeting with his local and foreign audience, combined with the publication of the more positive parts of the U.N. report, indicated reduced opacity as an official line, following Saddam Hussein's recent public threats to "burn all that they build" in Palestine, even if sometimes he left the "burning" itself to the Palestinians, supported by a "strong" Iraq.

But which countries were referred to in *Ha'aretz* as those whose "unpleasant company" Israel would join by refusing to join NPT, other than the seemingly more willing South Africa? Mainly India, Pakistan, and possibly North Korea, which had signed NPT in 1985 but not the follow-up safeguarding agreements with the IAEA.

CHAPTER THIRTEEN

India, Pakistan, North Korea, Algeria, Iran, and the Rest

Up to this point, we have focused on nuclear proliferation as it applies to countries in the Middle East: Israel, Egypt, Libya, Iraq, and Syria.

We have not mentioned Algeria yet, because the news about its Chinese-acquired reactor was published worldwide only in mid-1991.[1] This reactor is described as a heavy-water research reactor, "too small to produce electricity economically" and "too large for research." Our source is not sure whether it could be used for research, but its potential as a plutonium producer remains. The timetable for its completion is not known; but the construction site was reported to be defended by surface-to-air missiles. When the construction became known, Algeria was reportedly ready to join NPT and to provide for IAEA inspection. We shall return to the Algerian reactor in the Epilogue.

The scope and the timing of the revitalized Iranian nuclear program became publicly known in Israel only late in 1991—in fact when this book was already in production. According to Ron Ben-Yishai, a well-informed Israeli military correspondent, who published his information in *Yediot Aharonot* on November 11, 1991, under the title "Iran on Its Way to the Bomb," the new regime under Khomeini was at first opposed to the Shah's ambitious nuclear program and ordered its suspension as a "satanic" matter. However, in 1985 the regime seemed to have had second thoughts, and as a result Saddam repeatedly attacked the already-existing nuclear infrastructure in Iran—mainly German-supplied—until it was finally destroyed. In 1987 the Iraqis launched their chemical weapons and missiles against Iran, whereas the Iranians were stalled on the ground. At that juncture Ayatolla Rafsanjani, now president of Iran, obtained Khomeini's permission to revitalize the nuclear program, and the expert who was invited to assess the Iraqi bombing damage was none other than Dr. Abdul Khader Khan, "the father of the Pakistani Atomic Bomb." Following the armistice between Iran and Iraq, Pakistan, China, Argentina, the Soviet Union—the latter pledging to sell two 440 MWt power reactors each—and India were reported to be the main suppliers; uranium mines were developed in the meantime, and missiles were to be purchased from North Korea and possibly from China. The official rationale for an Iranian or—as it was proclaimed publicly to be—"Islamic" bomb was the Israeli bomb, whereas the real threat was Iraq's enhanced nuclear program. Saddam's efforts to gain his own bomb should be, therefore, seen within the context of the revitalized Iranian program, which Rafsanjani was trying to pursue without antagonizing the West, while Syria could hope to gain strategically from Damascus' close relations with Teheran.

In the meantime we are interested in creating a comparative basis to examine Middle East proliferators' behavior. Therefore, in order to put their ambiguous and opaque nuclear policies into a global perspective, we will now make some comparisons with other countries not of the region. We will also examine possible ties between these extraregional countries and the Middle East in the nuclear context. We will begin with India.

India's behavior, mentioned briefly earlier, seemed similar to Israel's behavior, except that India's case was based on direct breaches of nonproliferation obligations made to its main suppliers—mainly Canada and the United States. However, in the final stage of their effort, the "opaque" stage, the behavior of these two nations has differed greatly: The Indians brought their project to the surface in 1974 with the detonation of a nuclear device, naming it a "peaceful nuclear explosion" (PNE). Although this device was described as being too heavy to be used as a nuclear weapon, it was nonetheless a nuclear explosion. With this description of a peaceful nuclear explosion, the semantics of the nonproliferation regime reached a climax, even though India had refused to join NPT in 1968 and thus was not obliged to follow the letter of the treaty. Ben-Gurion called Dimona a "nuclear reactor for peaceful use" for the "development of the Negev" following Eisenhower's and Kennedy's intervention, as described earlier by Mr. Gazit. When the vast, proud, and independent Indian nation was faced with NPT in 1968, it used the very vocabulary of the nonproliferation regime in order to circumvent it.

Besides its fear of the Chinese, India's main motives in acquiring nuclear weapons, and the method it used to make their acquisition known to the world, are anchored in its self-image as a great, moral nation, in contrast to Western values and especially to Western behavior in the past. On the other hand, Western ideologies such as Marxism, which were adopted by the Russians and the Chinese, have not appealed to India either. The country has, however, maintained closer ties with the Russians in order to neutralize a possible Pakistani-Chinese tie and to provide for the dismemberment of Pakistan.[2] Thus India's opacity is that of a great power in the making which is adhering to its own moral legacy. On the face of it, India adheres to the rules of non-proliferation, while making it clear to anyone who is not totally blind that it will not be a victim of "nuclear apartheid." Supplier restraint, though hampering Indian activities, has failed to prevent the country from finally launching its own ICBM without admitting the purpose.[3] We do not know of any serious opposition in India to its nuclear program, and therefore we must conclude that India's opacity, though reinforced by a sense of morality, is basically made for export.

As far as India's ties to the Middle East are concerned, one can cite early reports about Indian-Egyptian cooperation in nuclear research and development, or at least speculation that the two leading "non-aligned" nations would cooperate in this field following the 1955 meeting at Bandung that catapulted President Nasser to international prominence. No evidence has emerged yet to prove Indian-Egyptian cooperation. But according to a story published in April 1990 in the *Washington Post* India and Israel "considered cooperation among them" in the early 1980s to meet the Pakistani nuclear challenge.[4] Indeed, at the time, General Sharon offered some public threats vis-à-vis Islamabad that could combine with the raid on Tammuz 1 to threaten the Pakistanis to a degree that required their attention. As for India, Delhi did not adopt a "Tammuz" strategy, and India's—and Israel's own—alleged ties with Pakistan in the nuclear context will be mentioned briefly later.

Pakistan's case is much more recent. When Pakistan began its effort, it was well within the rules of a world seemingly governed by NPT.[5] In contrast, no international rules had been in existence when India and Israel began their efforts. India broke its promise to its suppliers only, and Israel received or obtained its nuclear infrastructure from the French, and had some complicated relations with them; in the process Israel became half-bound directly to America's nonproliferation effort, though not NPT, which came too late for Israel. In Pakistan's case, the final decision to acquire an "Islamic Bomb" had been made within the context of the country's defeat and dismemberment at the hands of India in the early 1970s. It was only later that Pakistan became indirectly involved in the Middle East, usually by backing moderate Arab regimes.[6] In the 1990 Gulf crisis, Pakistan supported the United States and Saudi Arabia, and even sent troops to the international forces facing Saddam Hussein, in spite of some uproar at home.

Pakistan's method of acquiring a nuclear infrastructure was a combination of theft, a supplier's irresponsibility, and services rendered to the United States. Pakistan aided America's opening to its ally, China, and also assisted the United States in the context of the American-sponsored effort against the Soviet presence in Afghanistan.[7] Islamabad itself and some American observers tended, however, to cite the Israeli, pre-NPT case as a role model for Pakistan and even to legitimize it that way.[8] The fact that Pakistan has not joined NPT, and that the Israeli case has been used to justify its nuclear program, sounds like a political excuse. This emanated partly from a genuine American focus on Israel's and India's proliferation, but mostly from what we must judge as real American doubts about whether a determined proliferator such as Pakistan could be stopped, especially when its services were badly needed in other areas. In other such cases, the only thing the United States had been able to do was to delay and delegitimize proliferators' nuclear efforts, and prevent both open nuclear threats and "red lines" as publicly defined deterrents, fearing situations that might be uncontrollable. This contradicted the open rules of the game of chicken played by the superpowers themselves, and seemed to maintain the perception that the nuclear club remained closed. By supplying proliferators with the necessary conventional weapons for their real conventional wars, and offering growing economic aid and various political moves in their favor, Washington could tie proliferators to it and to some extent control them. Further, if there is no way out of proliferation in real terms, not in terms of (mis)perceptions, proliferators could be balanced against each other, preferably within the opaque sphere.

Pakistan has had little reason to complain. Its opaque posture surfaced recently in several statements and denials made by Dr. Abdul Khader Khan, the "father of the Pakistani bomb."[9] Islamabad is, of course, a shadow member of the nuclear club, even though as yet it has neither a sizable arsenal nor modern delivery means such as IRBMs and ICBMs. According to an April 8, 1990, *Washington Post* story, in the early 1980s Pakistan even promised Israel that it would not use its nuclear capability in terms of an "Islamic Bomb" aimed at Israel's destruction, despite Qaddafi's offers to the contrary. According to the same story, Islamabad went even further to calm Israel's fears, as they were discussed, suddenly around that point in time, by Herbert Krosney and Steve Weissman in their above-mentioned book *The Islamic*

Bomb. The book disclosed a number of details, which we have already examined, regarding Israel's own nuclear program, probably in order to expose Pakistan's nuclear efforts by comparing them to Israel's nuclear program, even though in Israel itself it had received very little attention.

This form of opacity might have worked, according to the *Washington Post* story: Sharon's threats in regard to the Pakistani reactor might have made some impression if we believe the *Post's* report that Pakistan suggested to Israel some forms of bilateral cooperation—a sort of "covert diplomatic relations." According to the report, General Avraham Tamir—Ariel Sharon's chief of planning and later director-general of the prime minister's office under Peres—allegedly visited Pakistan and concluded some military and conventional deals with the Pakistani regime under General Zia ul Hak. We have no way of verifying this story, which sounds fantastic indeed, but only offer an opinion that, if true, it could have been inspired by Pakistan's real interest in staying out of the Middle East conflict itself, while securing its own bomb in an ambiguous fashion. Whether Islamabad hoped that such ties would ease American Congressional pressure on Pakistan to stop its nuclear program is anybody's guess. And yet, Pakistan, Saudi Arabia, and China might have embarked upon an innovative enterprise. In early March 1988 it was reported that after three years of negotiations, China had agreed in 1985 to sell Saudi Arabia an unspecified number (probably between twelve and twenty-four)[10] of its DF-3 East Winds, known in the West as CSS-2 intermediate-range ballistic missiles.

The Pakistani connection here seems rather obvious, for the following reasons. First, Pakistan and China are old friends; General Zia, the late Pakistani ruler, played an important role as a go-between in relations between China and the United States. Second, Saudi Arabia is a traditional, major American asset, and yet Riyadh wanted to diversify its arms supplies and become more autonomous of America, especially due to Israeli influence in the U.S. Congress. The missile deal with China was concluded long before Iraq and Iran started to use missiles against each other, but Saudi Arabia felt seriously threatened by Khomeini's Iran, which—after his death in 1989—remained officially at least bound to the exportation of the hated Shi'ite tradition. Pakistan, under Zia, cultivated its relations with Saudi Arabia for many years rather than with Qaddafi's Libya, which was reported to have financed the "Islamic Bomb" at first. Pakistan could not afford to obtain strategic missiles directly from China, nor could China afford to supply them to Pakistan without getting into serious trouble with both the United States and India.

The solution was thought to have been found by supplying Chinese strategic missiles to non-nuclear Saudi Arabia—whose standing with the United States is sufficiently strong, and who had legitimate defense requirements, some of which were turned down by the United States because of Israeli fears—while Pakistan had the nuclear warheads. This could create a viable "Islamic Bomb plus delivery means," even if it is hard to say which brand of Islam would be served here, except the Saudi regime and Pakistan, both in a peculiar, opaque fashion. Indeed, some observers were duly alarmed,[11] and America promised action to curb the missile race in the Middle East. It was difficult to follow the ensuing American-Saudi and American-Chinese negotiations by relying on media reports, but they entailed the U.S. granting most-favored nation status to the Chinese, without a firm commitment from the Chinese, in return for China not supplying missiles to the Middle East, according to an Israeli analyst.[12] This could have played into Israeli hands when the decision to launch Ofek 1 was made, as one may infer from the proximity of the dates. As described by Spector, earlier, the satellite was carried by a powerful missile and could reach Pakistan. The American reaction to this game of opacity was described earlier in the context of U.S.-Egyptian relations and the Middle East peace process, which the Bush Administration was trying to revive in 1989-1990.

After Zia's sudden departure from the scene, Pakistan's own nuclear program seemed to go on as before. And the same seemed to be the case when Mrs. Bhutto was deposed by the Pakistani army in summer 1990. But suddenly, in October 1990, the U.S. Congress voted to stop aid to Pakistan due to its atomic program. The sudden change may reflect the changed East-West climate, which was demonstrated at first when the Soviets withdrew from Afghanistan, and Islamabad's role in opposing them in that country was over. Also, the decision might have been the result of Congressional disapproval of the Pakistani-Chinese-Saudi connection, or even of a Soviet-American agreement to curb proliferation more energetically, now that they had decided to curb their own nuclear race. Another reason could have been a serious flare-up of Moslem agitation in Kashmir, which seemed to be leading India and Pakistan—two nuclear nations by now—toward a collision course.

There was no domestic opposition to Pakistan's nuclear program; rather, the program was welcomed enthusiastically, making Islamabad's opacity for export purposes only. It did not entail any strategic debate with regard to the country's boundaries, although it may touch upon contested territory such as Kashmir. It had no other serious purpose but to preserve the nation in its existing borders—except, again, for the touchy Kashmir issue—while at the same time boosting its own, rather than "Islamic," power and prestige. The case of Pakistan is, of course, a precedent—an important one—because, except for the preservation of official opacity, NPT norms were broken here almost openly.

Pakistan obtained F-16 fighter bombers from the Reagan Administration, just as Israel received its Phantoms at the time, and later more advanced American aircraft potentially capable of delivering nuclear weapons. F-16s are capable of carrying the bomb, although they can also be used for conventional purposes. Late in June 1991 it was reported that China had supplied Islamabad with short-range M-11 missiles.

Yet, what did Pakistan need the bomb for? In truth, Pakistan may believe that its survival is at stake, as Indian nationalists have never accepted the idea of a separate Moslem entity in the Subcontinent. But this conflict does not entail a priori a war of destruction against Pakistanis, or the forced evacuation of the remnants of the Moslem population from the country, as may be the case with Israel's Jews. On the contrary, the bomb—rather than anything else—could endanger the whole subcontinent. As in the case of the superpowers, nothing but the bomb may endanger the survival of both Hindi and Moslems; whereas for Israel conventional wars were equally dangerous both at the beginning and in the long run.

Upon her election in late 1988, Mrs. Benazir Bhutto publicly stated, first, that her father's demise had prevented Pakistan from becoming "a nuclear power as early as 1977,"[13] and second, that despite her bitterness toward General Zia's regime, which had had her father executed, she was ready to negotiate an agreement with India that neither country would attack the other's nuclear installations. In this and other respects, the Indian-Pakistani dispute, when compared with the Arab-Israeli conflict, seems simply to be less serious. In fact, the introduction of nuclear weapons in the Subcontinent may result in a nuclear doomsday. Opacity helped to mitigate this danger, as long as the parties did not use open threats, but the growing tension around Kashmir might have prompted more serious American action vis-à-vis Islamabad, when the Afghan war was over.

It may seem that the case of South Africa is closer to that of Israel due to the country's presence in an alien environment that is determined to abolish it, plus the historical injustices committed by its apartheid regime. Yet one cannot help but see that Israel's historical and religious ties to the ancient Jewish homeland are different from Boer settlement in Africa. Besides, Israel's handling of the Arabs is not the result of an apartheid-based ideology. Instead it is the complex outcome, as described earlier, of Israel's own behavior, of Arab behavior, and of the input of foreign powers. While Pretoria has also become a shadow member of the nuclear club, its only real problem is not outside military pressure but domestic unrest, which perhaps could be solved if the white minority was willing to give up most of the country and concentrate in a relatively small section, refraining from ruling over blacks. Then an opaque threat would have meaning: to preserve the survival of this "mini" South Africa. Pretoria's recent flirtation with NPT may signify a general relaxation of South Africa's domestic and foreign policy combined, even if it could try to follow the North Korean example and refrain from signing the necessary safeguarding agreements with the IAEA,[14] or try other methods such as opening its facilities to inspection while at least retaining the weapons-grade uranium already produced since the early 1980s.[15]

As far as the Israeli-South African connection is concerned, it is described in Spector's most recent report as follows: "Although the allegations of nuclear links between the two nations remain to be substantiated, they would be consistent with the pattern of bilateral security collaboration and should be taken seriously."[16] However, Spector cites an Israeli statement in March 1987 that "no further agreements would be concluded with South Africa" and that "existing contracts" would expire.[17] However, the above-described Jericho missile tests in 1987, launched from Israeli territory, and the launching of the satellite Ofek 1 from an Israeli-based pad, could be seen as evidence against reports of Israeli-South African missile cooperation. Such reports, quoted above from Spector as well, about Israeli involvement in South African missile ranges on Pretoria's territory proper, on Marion Island, and halfway between South Africa and Antarctica were reflected in the Arab press in its way, and were published in the Paris-based *Al-Wattan Al-Arabi* to the effect that Israel had its own missile-testing facilities in Antarctica.[18]

This story coincided with another story presented on NBC's "Today" show on October 26, 1989, about far-reaching, ongoing nuclear cooperation between Jerusalem and Pretoria.[19] The network repeated a claim first made by the writer Peter Pry that the American-supplied and -controlled research reactor at Nahal Soreq was in fact a bomb production facility, contrary to Israel's description of its functions.[20] NBC maintained that its source was a "Pentagon paper," and further that Israel "fully allows South Africa access" to its nuclear programs. They also reported that enriched South African uranium reaches an American reactor, e.g., Nahal Soreq, whereas Dimona is not American and has not been under any U.S. controls since 1969. The South African-Israeli nuclear deal, according to NBC, was based on Israeli technological support of Pretoria's own nuclear program in exchange for enriched uranium supplies and access to South African testing sites.

Soon afterward, Congress, mostly in secret sessions, began to look into the matter; as of June 1991, no public recommendations had been made, except for warnings even from Israel's best friends on the Hill to stop cooperation with Pretoria. In fact, the South African connection seemed to be one of two contested issues—the other was longer-range missiles launched from Israeli territory, according to authoritative American sources quoted earlier—as far as the relatively friendly Congress was concerned. But even an October 1989 *New York Times* editorial justified Israel's nuclear option, in the face of Arab hostility. Israel's own nuclear program was thus known and seemed to have been finally accepted as an established fact until Bush's 1991 initiative. McGeorge Bundy in his *Danger and Survival*, published in 1988, was the first American public figure of much weight who, by using public data, acknowledged Israel's bomb as a fact. And even though as National Security Adviser in the 1960s he had done his best to curb the bomb, in his book he, albeit reluctantly, justified its acquisition.[21]

One could calculate, therefore, that a public campaign in the U.S. against Israel's nuclear program could thus generate support *for* it in Congress, at least as a justified last resort option; not so the South African-Israeli connection.

Domestic changes within South Africa during 1990-1991, especially the release by the white minority regime of the African National Congress leader Nelson Mandela from prison, and the beginning of the end of official apartheid might have justified a Congressional debate in order to encourage further progress in South Africa. General Sharon, who had protested loudly in 1977, when Israel announced its decision to "freeze" its military ties with Pretoria, has not repeated his stance since, especially after Yuval Ne'eman, a new-old actor whose activity will be described later, became the spokesman of the extreme hawks in nuclear matters. On June 24, 1991, however, Pretoria announced that it was ready to forgo the possession of nuclear weapons and join NPT; whether this was an honest promise we do not know.

The cases of Taiwan and South Korea are similar to that of Pakistan. There may be a threat of these nations being swallowed up by their own people, but whole communities are not at risk of being wiped out. The issue here is political and ideological, not political-existential, and the antiproliferation influence of the United States is much higher here than in the case of Israel due, in part, to the lack of domestic American factors such as the Jewish lobby. Even so, both nations may join the nuclear club in an opaque fashion by using NPT rules, which seem to favor nonpublic proliferation over the open kind. In this way NPT emphasizes—in fact, far from its original goal—that public threat is the main issue to be prevented, when preventive measures prove insufficient to prevent proliferation itself.

However, early in 1990, the Southeast Asian scene was suddenly clouded by American- and South Korean-originated reports that North Korea was on the verge of producing its own bomb. The ways and means used by Kim-Il-Sung's regime to acquire a nuclear infrastructure remain in the dark at this stage, except for some West German involvement and for the technical assistance given by the IAEA to educate nuclear experts.[22] The ramifications may, however, go beyond Piongiang's possible effort to balance Seoul, and undisclosed American nuclear weapons deployed in South Korea. The North Korean bomb, if real, could be motivated, as Spector suggests, by the assumption that "nuclear backed American presence in South Korea was likely to remain indefinitely and that, even if American forces withdrew, South Korea might choose to develop nuclear weapons of its own."

> To pursue its policy of reunification through force, the North would need to neutralize this opposing nuclear capability. The ability of North Korea to threaten Southern cities with nuclear devastation could impose unacceptable costs on the use of nuclear weapons by the United States and South Korea, raising the prospects that the North could prevail in a future conflict by gaining a preponderance of conventional forces.[23]

Such a mode of thinking was typical of radical Arabs, influenced by what we have described as "American self-deterrence" in nuclear matters. If it dictated Kim's priorities, among other reasons, it demonstrated the independence of Communist regimes like Kim's from Moscow's effective nonproliferation controls, as compared with the Soviet satellites in Eastern Europe even before the demise of Soviet influence in Europe in 1989-1990. Also, North Korea was a traditional ally of radical Arabs, starting with President Nasser and continuing with President Assad of Syria. According to Spector's most recent report, Kim's regime cooperates with Iran—Syria's ally—in developing nuclear-capable missiles.[24] Whether North Korea could help a radical Arab state build its own nuclear infrastructure is an open question that is hard to answer due to the insistence of Kim's regime on arms control talks with South Korea, and his possible focus on Korean affairs. Yet the relative independence of North Korea despite, and in addition to, its ties with both Moscow and Beijing could have served radical Arabs as yet another incentive to rely on themselves as far as possible—especially since the Soviet Union under Gorbachev has almost fully abandoned its traditional foreign policy and agreed to far-reaching changes in the very heart of Europe itself, changes to Moscow's disfavor in a traditional sense.

Acquiring North Korean Scud-C missiles, however, would require better Arab relations with the West, since the missiles need sophisticated, Western-supplied guidance systems and command and control facilities. This may explain why President Assad of Syria was reported to have acquired Scud-Cs from North Korea but at the same time was ready to listen to American pleas regarding peace in the Middle East in July 1991. Better relations with Washington and with the West in general could be useful to Syria's military ambitions, by enabling it to obtain equipment both from the East and the West without sacrificing any of Assad's principles.

The reasons for Gorbachev to go his own way, the economic disaster, and the futility of arms races in the nuclear age seem, at the same time, to be clear to Egypt's President Mubarak as relevant to Egypt as well; whereas the richer Arabs, such as Iraq's Saddam Hussein and Qaddafi, might have followed the North Korean model, and in fact had tried to continue Nasser's early and Heikal's continued policy. North Korea may, therefore, serve them as an example of a successful proliferation effort by a determined Third World country.

Foreign examples of nuclear independence, of mastering Western technology by non-Western nations such as China and North Korea, are powerful incentives for Arab proliferation and for obtaining missile technology, in addition to the incentive provided by the Israeli challenge. But to obtain the goals of these incentives may require political concessions.

EPILOGUE

The End of Opacity?

Several weeks after I finished writing the previous chapters, war broke out in the Gulf. Since then the war seems to have been won, and the "new order" for the Middle East, including the end of the previous nuclear game in that region, was proclaimed by President Bush.

But before we discuss this new order, let us first examine the use—and the nonuse—of unconventional threats and unconventional weapons in the war. Afterward we can examine the unconventional aspects of the post-war period.

On the face of it, several parties used unconventional threats of a strategic nature before the war and during the first stages of the hostilities. One was Saddam Hussein, who told Peter Arnet of CNN at the outset of the air offensive on January 16, 1991, that he had nuclear, chemical, and bacteriological weapons, and threatened to use "everything at his disposal" to defend his country. In fact there was no use of ABC weapons, except for the very limited use of land mines filled with poison gas. Saddam further appealed to the Arab masses to topple his Arab adversaries, King Fahd of Saudi Arabia, President Mubarak of Egypt, and President Assad of Syria, by arguing that if Iraq prevailed, "a strategic balance between the Arabs and Israel will endanger Israel's very existence."[1]

Another party that openly mentioned weapons of mass destruction for its own purposes was the Soviet Union. Mikhail Gorbachev, apparently tilting between conservatives and liberals, facing the possible rupture of the whole Soviet system, warned after the first phase of the ground war was over that the Soviet Union could not remain idle if weapons of mass destruction were used in close proximity to the southern Soviet provinces. He blamed the United States for in fact triggering such a development by pursuing the land war. Thus Saddam's threats became Soviet threats, at least verbally. Whether this demonstration of Soviet impatience contributed to the early cease-fire, which left Saddam with a considerable part of his army intact, is not known. Other considerations, such as the possible dismemberment of Iraq, might have heavily contributed to the early cease-fire, as apparently no one among the members of the anti-Saddam coalition wanted a Shi'ite entity to emerge in the south, or a Kurdish entity in the north.

Professor Elie Kedourie, an Iraqi Jew and noted Arab expert, pointed out in an Israeli press interview that the Iraqi Sh'ites were Arabs, not Iranians, and that fears that they might fall under Iran's control were unfounded.[2] The fate of the Kurds—an entirely non-Arab but mostly Sunni nation spread over Turkey, Iran, Syria, and parts of the Soviet Union—seemed at first to be the same as that of the southern Shi'ites, whose rebellion against Saddam in the wake of the war was mercilessly crushed by Saddam's troops. Yet when many Kurds were forced to flee the country, following a short-lived rebellion of their own, their problem gained humanitarian attention and forced the Allies, and Turkey, to at least supply them with food and protect them from Saddam's wrath inside Iraq itself. The Kurdish north became a foreign-controlled enclave—U.N. troops took over from the Americans and the British later in 1991—while Saddam seemed ready to grant the Kurds far-reaching autonomy. It is not clear as yet whether he will honor his promises, which would deprive him of absolute control over uranium mines and nuclear facilities built in Kurdistan; he broke all promises before when unopposed. But Saddam's rule seemed to be unshaken thanks to the identification between the ruling Sunni Arab element and his regime, in the face of the Shi'ite and Kurdish challenges. The "Right of Self-Determination," so naturally accepted for Palestinians among the Israeli Left and others abroad, proved too complicated to be implemented in the case of the Kurds, as indeed if implemented it might have dismembered several existing states.

The third and fourth parties to mention unconventional weapons before and during the hostilities were the Americans and the British. Indirectly—the British openly—they threatened Saddam with "terrible punishment" if he resorted to using unconventional weapons. In a TV interview U.S. Secretary of Defense Cheney was asked whether Saddam did not make good his threats to launch chemical missiles against Israel because he feared that "Israeli tactical nuclear weapons" might be used against Iraq in response.[3] The secretary did not respond directly to the question, but maintained a degree of "reduced opacity" by responding that Saddam should indeed be careful.[4]

On Israel's side, the government—if not most of the Israeli media—refrained from going beyond "reduced opacity" in regard to Israel's possible response in face of Saddam's threats and actual launching of conventional missiles against Israel. In fact Israel refrained—and was publicly encouraged to do so by the United States and other Allied governments—from any response at all. Shamir's cabinet, in spite of some public verbal opposition to its passive role by General Sharon and Minister Ne'eman, was very careful not to stress Saddam's possible nuclear potential, even if it might have feared the use of this material by the Iraqis—if not as a bomb perhaps as a nuclear mass contamination device. The main concern was publicly directed at Saddam's threats to use chemical weapons.

The use of such threats by Saddam himself vis-à-vis the Allies could be explained in terms of deterring them from opening hostilities at all, or limiting their scope. These threats of chemical warfare could also be explained as a means to deter Saddam's opponents from using unconventional weapons while Saddam conducted the conventional land war he had planned, which was aimed at inflicting enough casualties on the enemy to succeed in reviving a Soviet-sponsored peace initiative that would allow him to survive and transform defeat into political victory. Saddam's models here, as in other cases, were Egypt's Nasser, who had survived defeats both in 1956 and in 1967; Mao Tse-tung during the Korean War; the Algerian FLN; and Ho Chi Minh. And the weapons necessary to win or survive a defeat would be mainly conventional rather than unconventional. Nonexistent or unused unconventional weapons, such as nuclear capabilities or chemical weapons, could be mobilized as political-psychological measures to help win, or at least avoid losing, a conventional war against a superpower equipped with the whole array of weaponry, unconventional included. They could be used to push the Soviets to intervene and to spread doubts and disarray among the enemies while gaining support among Arabs and Moslems abroad. The final goal was to survive and maintain a nuclear potential until it became operational.

Here we arrive at several paradoxes of the nuclear age, the subject of this book from the beginning. In order to go nuclear, a Third World nation such as Iraq needed money, imported technology, enough local know-how to deal with such technology, and what it believed was a sufficient conventional edge vis-à-vis the declining West and Israel. The name of the game was to allow such a Third World nation to achieve its goals by securing its ability to use conventional forces without risking a nuclear war. In the final account, the emphasis was on a conventional advantage, in Saddam's eyes, that would prevail once supported by unconventional means—ultimately nuclear, but in the interim stage, chemical weapons plus missiles. The fact that the chemical weapons remained unused could be explained by a variety of reasons, among them the fear of nuclear retaliation and the fear of mass casualties among the civilian population, which might endanger the regime. Thus Saddam's Iraq was not behaving "irrationally," in the sense of risking its vital centers. It tried, unsuccessfully, to threaten using unconventional weapons in order to allow a conventional war it hoped to be able to win or to prevail in long enough.

Thus the main problem for Israel remained Arab conventional power, especially when supported by unconventional means—when one compares the smart and regular weapons used by the Allies (let alone the logistics required to sustain the war and the political circumstances that isolated the Kuwaiti-southern Iraqi theater of operation) to Israel's capabilities. Instead, the only choice for Israel could be a further emphasis on its nuclear option, combined with security arrangements with the United States, which remained interested in avoiding nuclear war, and with a positive political process. In order to avoid the risks of a "last resort" nuclear option, which allows conventional wars to happen, and stretched to the utmost limit of tolerance in its opaque nuclear policy, Israel could develop neutron bombs that would be used from the outset of a major war. This would transform a war from the beginning to a nuclear one, while in fact inflicting losses on the enemy's armored and infantry concentrations. The creation of a large tactical force that could defeat all-around massive conventional assaults without necessarily invoking countervalue threats or actions (threats or actions against cities)—thus avoiding very serious issues of ethics, credibility, and the utility of making Arab civilians hostages to the behavior of their leaders—was publicly recommended by the present writer several years ago as a better strategic tool. It would allow the political level more flexibility and diminish the value of occupied territory. This has remained, in my view, an open option, though I could not verify either that it was acceptable to the IDF or that it was supported by the production of enough tritium—the element necessary to make fusion bombs, large or small. In fact during the Gulf War an Israeli newspaper speculated that since the 1960s Israel had concentrated on developing "clean" nuclear devices of that kind.[5]

At any rate, opacity should remain imperative, in the traditional Israeli view, to avoid Arab counterefforts and counterarguments that are not necessarily related to Israel's option, and to allow Israel to maintain such an option, once the post-war order calls for arms control in the whole area, including a disarmed Iraq—in unconventional terms—as demanded by Israel.[6] At the same time Israel could enhance the development and deployment of the Arrow antimissile missile system, which could intercept enemy missiles far away from Israeli territory, and maintain a conventional option based on its homemade Chariot tank and modern air force. The other choice would be to rely on "smart" conventional weapons, and reorganize the IDF around a new tactical doctrine to allow their effective use, while leaving the nuclear option in the background either as a "last resort option" or as an "intermediate solution," if PGMs proved ineffective at the outset of a ground war. The issue of protecting Israel's home front, which might be threatened from the outset of a war in which unconventional or even conventional weapons were used, seems to have become, since the Gulf War, a serious matter. Another serious matter is how to finance all these options in a nation suddenly faced with enormous waves of Soviet and Ethiopian immigrants. Conventional defense and the possible growing role of the nuclear option could be seen as justified by Israel's Likud government, whose stance regarding territorial concessions has remained unchanged—and is unacceptable in principle to the United States, the main source of Israel's economic and conventional military aid, whose view of Israel's missiles and its nuclear option is not necessarily the same as the Israeli government's.

On the face of it, Israel's deterrent power suffered during the war. Saddam Hussein used conventional missiles against Israel to achieve obvious strategic-political goals to incite an Israeli response that would eventually break the coalition that had joined forces against him; and Israel failed to respond at all. Saddam could have tried to use his modern, low-flying Sukhoy-24 bombers, armed with chemical bombs—a serious threat, in terms of the potential of such warplanes—but he preferred to fly them all, along with the rest of his first-line jets, to safety in Iran. As a result of his missile attacks, Israel suffered very little in terms of human losses, and some serious damage to property and to the economy. Politically Israel gained by refusing to respond when Saddam attacked it— a third party—and hit civilians. Iraq also resorted to conventional missile attacks against Dimona, which missed. By doing this Saddam came closer to an unconventional complication: If the reactor had been hit, it could have released dangerous radioactivity. Yet these and other conventional missile attacks aimed at strategic targets were conventional indeed; they were inaccurate, and were made within the framework of a multination war against Iraq in which Israel could have torpedoed the alliance. Thus Israel's primary interest was to keep the much more powerful alliance intact in order to allow it to finish Saddam off rather than to complicate the matter by adding a unilateral—Iraqi-Israeli—dimension to a conflict that served Israel's interests.

In practical terms, Israel had to reckon with severe complications if it resorted to any action to silence Saddam's SCUDs. A land operation, or even a combined air-land operation, against the launching sites in western Iraq would have triggered Jordanian response, since Israel's forces would have violated Jordan's airspace or marched through Jordanian territory in order to reach the launching areas. The ramifications of such an Israeli action for King Hussein's regime—which found itself tilted toward Saddam because of his popularity among Palestinians and fundamentalists—would have been serious, and both sides would have suffered casualties.

To destroy all of the SCUD-launching sites would also have meant venturing farther away to sites identified along the Syrian-Iraqi border. Also a longer-range version of the missile was reportedly launched against Israel from a region north of Baghdad—and thus a costly venture in western Iraq to end the launching of SCUDs against Israel would have ended with a new salvo of missiles from the Baghdad area. According to a report in *Ma'ariv* on May 2, 1991, such a base was located in Ramadi, about 60 kilometers west of Baghdad, from which the longer-range al-Abbas missiles (further-improved SCUD-Bs) were launched against Israel before the cease-fire.

According to a *Newsweek* report, instead of an Israeli action the Americans had to use commando units on the last day of the war to destroy twenty-six SCUD launchers aimed at Israel as a result of Israeli missile testing shortly before.[7] The Israeli missile tested was "nuclear capable," and its alleged testing was aimed at "hinting to the administration that Israel would be ready to use nuclear weapons to stop the SCUD offensive." We have no evidence to verify this story, but the "testing" could have been intended—this time successfully—to push the United States to do more than aerial bombing to stop the SCUDs, especially when Jerusalem publicly announced that a SCUD attack had been aimed at Dimona. This could have been seen as a justification for a possible Israeli response in the same direction—coupled with a growing public pressure to "do something" to stop the missiles and the considerable psychological effect of the missile attacks on the home front.

The main point was, it seemed, that the Allies, even though the relevant U.N. Security Council resolutions stressed the liberation of Kuwait, tried their best to destroy Saddam's unconventional infrastructure, and were empowered, legally, to do so by Security Council Resolution 678. On the face of it, the Allies were pursuing Israel's own policy since 1981: to deny a sovereign nation (Iraq) its "natural" right to possess whatever weapons it deemed necessary to obtain, once it had developed such weapons, under the cover of NPT. In July 1991, it is still unclear how the United States, the only remaining superpower and the victor in the Gulf War, will successfully enforce the ban on Iraqi nuclear weapons, a declared war aim, as specified in Security Council resolution 687, the legal framework of the war. In the words of that resolution, the denial of nuclear and chemical, biological, and missile capabilities from Iraq were steps toward the transformation of the Middle East into a region free of weapons of mass destruction.

It seems that the Iraqi case created both a legal mechanism—Security Council resolutions—and a practical mechanism—IAEA inspections on the ground—to enforce Iraq's unconventional disarmament. And these were coupled with further means: the ongoing economic sanctions against Iraq, ordered by the Council, which Saddam was eager to have lifted after the war. He then seemed ready to allow inspection on the ground, and answered—seemingly seriously, following some initial bluffing—all IAEA questions, to be followed by painful searches of his facilities by IAEA inspectors,[8] aimed at removing his enriched uranium and placing it in IAEA custody. However, late in June 1991, it became clear that the Iraqis had tried to conceal a whole dimension of their nuclear program unknown before the war—that of uranium isotope separation through the use of devices known as calutrons. When questioned by a special Security Council committee working with the IAEA, Iraq responded only to questions related to known activities and uranium purchases.[9] But slowly—after an Iraqi defector disclosed the dimensions of the huge calutron program—Saddam was forced to release more information, which was not accepted as sincere or sufficient. Late in July 1991, more inspectors were sent to Iraq, and on the eve of the Gorbachev-Bush summit meeting, the Soviet Union, mired in its own problems, demanded that Saddam disclose all his nuclear facilities and related products and hand them over to the IAEA inspectors.

This was a previously unheard of international act of nuclear arms control, which remains to be enforced, even by invoking military means again to finish the job. Yet the Soviets and the Chinese were opposed to such military measures, and President Bush seemed to be interested in securing a U.N. consensus before he resorted to using force again. Such an act of arms control became possible only due to Saddam's own mistakes, which were partially triggered by arms control restrictions imposed on him by the United States and others, and partially by other motives that had led him into Kuwait and to the "Mother of all Wars."[10] Yet Saddam had just lost a war, and he had to accept the victor's demands in order to survive and perhaps try again. Other Middle East countries were not in the same position. Still, the victor could perceive itself as working within an international framework, in cooperation with the Soviets, the British, possibly with the French, and hopefully with the Chinese, which would allow major steps toward unconventional arms control in the Middle East, Israel included. It is also possible that it was necessary to proclaim a general arms control framework for the whole Middle East to justify action against Iraq in this regard.

The American options with regard to unconventional arms control in the Middle East could be described in the following terms. Since the Soviet threat to the United States and her allies, and to the region itself, had markedly declined, Israel's possession of longer-range missiles was no more acceptable now than it ever had been. In fact, this must have been the subject of Soviet conversations with the United States since the late 1980s, with the Soviets asking the U.S. to remove the threat of Israeli missiles aimed at them. Israel could have been told that its air force, American-supplied and self-improved, would be able to take care of its security needs rather than missiles, which could be obtained by the other side as well and proliferate to a dangerous degree. Israel may have been further compensated by American aid to develop the Arrow—indeed an agreement in this regard was signed late in May 1991.[11] However, the development of the Arrow to meet the threat of improved Arab missiles could be regarded as strategic, rather than as a theater antiballistic missile, which would be problematic in view of the Anti-Ballistic Missile Agreement of 1972.[12]

The Israeli response would be that airplanes could not operate under severe weather conditions (which proved true during the Gulf War), whereas missiles could. Besides, the issue of verification of a general ban on missiles in the whole Arab world and in Iran, and possibly Pakistan, was a very serious obstacle that the United States always acknowledged in its dealings with the Soviets, and this was also true of the unconventional materials themselves. In this connection, the Israeli press quoted reports from the *New York Times* in mid-May 1991 that Argentinian president Carlos Saúl Menem was having "difficulties" stopping his own air force Condor missile development, which was largely financed by Iraq. Other reports followed about China's military's refusal to give up its own missile export deals with Syria and possibly Iran.

However, due among other things to Arab complaints, Israel's nuclear option could be perceived by Washington, even before the Gulf War, as a source of further proliferation (the Egyptian lingo was "source of destabilization") that could get out of hand due to foreign aid and supplies. This required, possibly, a "specific arms control regime" for the region, in conjunction with and on top of NPT, which should remain as a tool of international control and illegalization of nuclear threats and the use of nuclear weapons. Even if the administration recognized that Israel's option was just an excuse for Arab proliferators (maybe for Pakistan's bomb and Iranian efforts in this field), and even if this option had been justified in the past, an Israeli nuclear monopoly was impossible to maintain while a "specific arms control regime for the Middle East" was sought by the United States. A process of phased arms control could serve all the parties involved better than an uncontrolled, unconventional race in which there was no longer Soviet self-restraint to impose limitations on greedy suppliers from South America to Europe. Phased arms control could take into consideration the existing Israeli option but require the opening of the Dimona facility to international control, thus "freezing" Israel's nuclear arsenal at the existing level, without building on the life span of the reactor, which is usually thirty years and could soon be over.[13] Any further reactor construction in the region could be banned, "freezing" those that are being built. This could be linked to the peace process itself, or precede it, as Soviet emissaries used to approach the parties in this regard, if the peace process could not yet yield satisfactory results, and serve instead as a confidence-building measure,[14] or even used by Washington to enhance the latter, touching upon a very sensitive Israeli nerve.

Thus, President Bush publicly initiated on May 30, 1991, a "specific arms control regime" for the Middle East, although his official language was rather brief, general, and to an extent opaque indeed: He never mentioned any nuclear or nuclear-to-be nations by name (which suggested that the "undeclared" status of the bomb was possibly an asset for Israel). But he warned against unchecked proliferation of weapons of mass destruction by the end of the century and stressed that the Middle East was the most dangerous region in this regard. However, the speech itself was followed by several briefings and public announcements by key administration officials, such as Assistant Secretary of Defense Paul Wolfowitz. According to these briefings we could sum up the president's main points as follows:

• Guidelines should be agreed upon by the five permanent members of the Security Council regarding conventional weapons sales to the Middle East.

• Obstacles should be created to prevent the export of items that could be used to produce weapons of mass destruction.

• Surface-to-surface missiles in the region will be "frozen," and later a complete ban on such missiles beyond a minimal range will be agreed upon.

• Materials produced for the purpose of making nuclear weapons (enriched uranium, separated plutonium) will be forbidden.

• All the countries in the region—Iraq, Iran, Libya, Syria, and the Maghreb states—were included, but not Pakistan. And all of them, Israel included, which did not join NPT would be called upon to do so.

• All the nuclear installations in the region (including Dimona) should be placed under IAEA controls.

• The administration would further support the transformation of the region into a NWFZ.

• Biological and chemical weapons should be completely forbidden; the regional parties were called upon to take steps toward mutual security, such as nonsignatory nations' implementation of clauses in the Chemical Weapon Ban Treaty.

With these points, especially the first point, Bush acknowledged to a degree Israel's fears of Arab conventional threats as its main problem. A couple of days before, Western insistence on a significant conventional weapons agreement—CFE (Conventional Forces Europe)—had led to an accord signed in Lisbon between Secretary Baker and Soviet Foreign Minister Alexandr Besmertnich, paving the way for a START (Strategic Arms Limitation Talks) agreement.

The public announcement and the briefings that followed were preceded by reports, in Israel and abroad, about Iraq's real nuclear potential and by reports on missile and nuclear efforts in the Arab world and in Iran. One report, leaked from the Israeli Knesset's Foreign Relations and Security Committee following a military intelligence briefing, estimated that Saddam Hussein's enriched uranium before the war was around 50 kilograms.[15] Knesset member Yitzhak Rabin, the former minister of defense, was quoted in the Israeli press as saying that the president's initiative could hardly be taken seriously:[16] "An impressive array [650 tons] of chemical war materials remained in Iraq. The Iraqis further admitted to have enriched uranium . . . doubly as much as estimated by Western intelligence. Rumors are still circulating, not verified as yet, about a nuclear centrifuge in an underground facility somewhere in Iraq."[17] Soon afterward, on June 6, 1991, the Cable Network News Pentagon correspondent disclosed a revised estimate that Saddam's days were "numbered," and added that in the unconventional field he retained two assets: experts ready to work and his covert procurement network abroad (operating now through Amman, Jordan, to bypass the Allied blockade and economic sanctions, the only long-range weapons that could remove Saddam). The Nasser precedent of surviving major military defeats did work, to an extent, after all. In the Arab world the post-war period brought about interesting developments, coupled with the American peace and arms control initiatives.

The war coalition, an asymmetrical combination of moderate and radical Arab entities—the Gulf states, Egypt, and Syria, with a reluctant Libya trailing behind, and a domestically crippled Morocco—was fighting under American leadership with strong British support and French aid against Iraq, which was supported as much as possible by a weak Jordan. Yemen and to a degree Algeria were also sympathetic to Iraq, as was the PLO. When the war was over, Egypt and Syria were interested in maintaining military presence in the Gulf, to protect the Arab states therein by "Arab" means and be compensated accordingly, on top of the direct payments given them by those countries and a far-reaching arrangement by the Western nations to forgo Egypt's debts. At the same time, President Mubarak, always in some cooperation with his Syrian colleague Assad, moved back to the central Arab arena by again making Cairo the headquarters of the Arab League and making an Egyptian— his former foreign minister, Dr. Abdel Maguid—secretary general of the League. Egypt freed itself completely from the isolation imposed on it by its peace treaty with Israel, and this must have required concessions to the more radical states. Since May 1991, it seems that Egypt has sought better relations with Iraq and its ally, the PLO, without sacrificing its excellent relations with the United States. Domestically, the Egyptian leadership was always interested in demonstrating sympathy to the Palestinian cause.[18] All of this must be examined within the larger Arab context.

Egypt seemed very much on the offensive, trying to get its ally the U.S. to push Israel to make concessions in the missile and nuclear area and in the peace process as well, while taking into account unpleasant developments in the Gulf. Until the Gulf War, the leading Arab states had divided their power between military capabilities and economic might. Egypt and Syria belonged to the first category; the Gulf states to the second;[19] and Iraq and Libya to both. The unofficial division of labor among them allowed oil revenues to finance military efforts and cover parts of other requirements of Egypt and Syria in exchange for protection. The assumption was that the Gulf states could not defend themselves, nor could they allow foreign, non-Moslem troops to come and stay in their territories. The Gulf War created an important precedent: foreign troops, along with Arab forces, came (and some stayed) and could come again. Egyptian-Syrian protection had proved unnecessary, and indeed Mubarak and Assad called their forces home shortly after the cease-fire, when they felt that King Fahd wanted them to leave.

Enormous American weapons supplies promised to Saudi Arabia, and its insistence—publicly announced early in June 1991—on procuring elsewhere whatever Riyadh deemed necessary for its defense in spite of Bush's arms control initiative, only underlined Saudi Arabia's new strength. The name of the game was to seek American support to enhance the interest of each Arab entity separately, while maintaining a degree of Arab consensus vis-à-vis Israel, with some important variations. When Secretary Baker renewed his peace efforts after the war, all Arabs were speaking peace (at least on the face of it) and most seemed to have followed Sadat's precedent. That is, some kind of direct talks with Israel must take place—although for some time Damascus's willingness to open direct negotiations leading to formal peace remained vague. The continuation of the political status quo did not endanger any Arab regime. On the contrary, Assad cashed in on his partnership in the coalition by making Lebanon more dependent on him, while at first rejecting Bush's arms control initiative.[20]

Thus the results of Saddam Hussein's adventure could be contradictory, and mixed with the "low political" interests of the Arab regimes concerned. They were interested in their immediate gains and their quest to maintain their power and enhance their longer-range interests, while responding in their various ways to the challenge of a changed international environment, to the Israeli challenge, and to the fundamentalist challenge from within. We can distinguish a "low political" issue for the Arab entities involved — allowing Assad an aggressive, activist role to play, and Mubarak a low-risk field of activity— and a variety of "high political" problems, related to deep sentiments and to a quest for a required Arab consensus. These "high political" goals are inseparable from the "low political" interests, ambitions, and military requirements typical of Arab leaders and Arab states led by military professionals.

One of the results of Iraq's humiliating conventional defeat at the hands of the Allies could be an obsession, on the Arab side—Libya, possibly Syria, even Egypt—in spite of and due to their participation in the coalition, to obtain unconventional weapons. Egypt's ambitions with regard to missiles have already been mentioned. Early in June 1991, the Egyptian government reportedly asked for Soviet, Chinese, and North Korean aid in the production and sales of SCUD missiles,[21] possibly in conjunction with its own campaign to curb Israel's missile and nuclear programs. Cairo had tried unsuccessfully to link these programs to the Camp David peace negotiations, and use them to justify its own unconventional intentions—in competition with Syria—while preempting Bush's initiative. According to an official Egyptian newspaper, *Mayo*, quoted in the Israeli media as late as May 7, 1991, the Arabs would create "an inter-Arab deterrent force," if Israel was allowed to retain its nuclear monopoly and no progress toward arms control talks was made.

Syria, on the other hand, reportedly received from North Korea a new shipment of SCUDs—probably twenty-five SCUD-Cs in March 1991—and then reportedly signed a deal with North Korea to produce its own SCUDs.[22] Damascus was reported to have agreed on a further missile deal, to purchase M-9, solid-fueled, 600-kilometer missiles from China, capable of carrying chemical, or any other, warheads.[23] Thus President Assad was maintaining his military power—while profiting from the Gulf states' aid for his support during the war and taking steps to liberalize his economy and open it to Western investments. Assad also forced his lebanese allies to diminish independent PLO presence in souther Lebanon, which would make the Palestinians there dependent on him as well, without however renouncing his past claims on Palestine or allowing Arafat to dictate his priorities and interests. For the time being, Arafat—isolated to a large extent among the Arab members of the anti-Saddam coalition, and a persona non grata to Assad—had no other choice but to comply.

At that stage, the United States, faced with Saddam's continued nuclear cat and mouse game, left the Bush arms control initiative aside and turned to Hafez al-Assad in order to at least revive the Israeli-Arab peace process. But first, before turning to Assad, the U.S. had to renew efforts with the Egyptians, the Jordanians, and the Saudis. Then Assad was asked to participate in a Middle East peace conference. After praising Bush and Baker for their more evenhanded approach, Assad announced his decision, in late July 1991, to attend such a conference, based on U.N. Security Council Resolutions 242 and 338—which he could interpret as demanding Israeli withdrawal from occupied territory (especially the Golan Heights).

Now that Moscow has returned to its pre-war pattern, Soviet behavior during the crisis requires a short description here. Gorbachev was not the same man during the Gulf crisis as he had been during most of our narrative. Facing the dismemberment of the Soviet Union from within and tilted toward those who would prefer to concentrate on foreign conflicts rather than address the difficult problems at home, and having lost his liberal foreign minister Edward Shevardnadze, the Soviet leader tried his best to save Saddam, was ignored to a large extent, and assumed an uneasy course between the coalition and Saddam. Immediately upon President Bush's declaration of the suspension of hostilities on February 28, 1991, Soviet officials revived the linkage between the Gulf crisis and the Palestinian issue. Having thus returned to the diplomatic arena as an advocate of Arab causes, Gorbachev at least tried to maintain the standing of the Soviet Union as superpower that was necessary for peace to be made. At the same time, Soviet-Israeli relations were developing along the careful, but positive, path set forward by Shevardnadze, but the Soviets stopped short of resuming diplomatic relations, which had been broken after the 1967 war. Instead, the new Soviet foreign minister Besmertnich visited Israel in Spring 1991, the first Soviet visit of that kind, in conjunction with Secretary Baker's efforts to activate the peace process, in which both Washington and Moscow were supposed to play a formal role as well as an asymmetrical informal role behind the scenes.

On June 7, 1991, the Israeli press reported Prime Minister Shamir's response to Secretary Baker's peace initiative: Israel would not allow the U.N. any role in the proposed peace conference. The opening session must immediately be transformed to bilateral talks between Israel and the Arab states and/or a Palestinian/Jordanian delegation, not including PLO representatives or Palestinians from East Jerusalem. At the time, Syria remained adamant in its insistence on both seemingly "procedural aspects" of the talks. Former Israeli prime minister Rabin, an opposition leader, predicted that such a general Arab-Israeli peace effort, in which the "procedural aspects" would loom greatly from the beginning—later broken down though it might be into talks between the Arab states and Jerusalem, and talks between a Palestinian-Jordanian delegation and Israel—would not succeed, as too many partners were tied up at the same time to the most radical one (Syria, in this case). Rabin suggested bilateral negotiations between Israel and a Palestinian delegation alone to begin with. He felt that Syria should be the last partner involved, because he believed that if Syria were involved in an international conference, negotiations would immediately collapse because of the unresolvable issue of the Golan Heights.[24] Rabin didn't care who represented West Bank and Gaza residents and was ready to forgo the West Bank elections called for by his own peace plan of 1989, because he believed that representation of those communities could be achieved even without elections and that Israel and the Palestinians might both gain from a changed status quo. Shamir would not necessarily share these views, constrained as ever by Sharon and his more militant coalition partners and by his own ideology.

As minister of housing, Sharon did his best to enhance settlements in the occupied territory, and Gush-Emunim, the militant religious group, even timed announcements of their establishment to coincide with Baker's visits in the area, to demonstrate will. This prompted angry comments from Secretary Baker and President Bush, and a diplomatic argument that "freezing" the settlements could help Israel to extract more concessions from the Arab states, such as lifting the Arab commercial boycott and ending the state of war. Shamir, on his side, tried to capitalize on Syria's less compromising stance, warned against the growing cooperation between Egypt and the more radical Arabs such as Assad, and demanded in public that the nomination of Palestinian delegates to the actual talks be entrusted to Jordan with Israeli consent, in order to avoid negotiations with a PLO-appointed delegation.

While for the immediate time being the peace process seemed to have reached an impasse, the Israeli press continued to quote actual and potential cases of missile and nuclear proliferation on the Arab and the Iranian side. An Italian news agency reported that Libya and North Korea, combining Qaddafi's money and Kim-Il-Sung's technological potential, had signed a "secret agreement" to develop SCUD missiles into something like IRBMs, capable of hitting targets "thousands of miles away." The North Korean bomb was reported to be just two to three years away. Early in June, it was reported that Piongiang flatly denied even the shipment of SCUD-Cs to Syria in March.

Iran had already been reported by Washington and Jerusalem to be pursuing an extremely ambitious foreign political and armaments program, including nuclear weapons and ballistic missiles to be purchased or produced with North Korean and Chinese help.[25] General David Ivry, director general of the Israeli Defense Ministry, describing Iran as seeking "regional hegemony" in place of Iraq, warned that the Gulf War proved that missiles launched from far away could hit Israel (and thus required Israeli retaliation by similar means, one may conclude), thus rendering Israel's previous land-force option irrelevant. He also warned against Syria's growing missile and conventional force.

Then came an official Chinese statement, early in June 1991, that Beijing would join the proposed five-power conference on arms limitation in the Middle East, i.e., accept Bush's initiative in principle. But soon afterward the *New York Times* reported that China would sell the M-9 to Syria and Pakistan, and that Damascus had partially financed its development.[26] Another short-range Chinese missile, the M-11, was reportedly sold to Pakistan as well. This report was made shortly before an important visit of a high American official to Beijing. One could see here Chinese maneuvers to encourage the U.S. to lift the embargo on China regarding specific items that remained in force in spite of the "most favored nation" commercial status granted by the United States as a precondition to limit weapons exports. The actual arms sales to the region, in which the Chinese army was reported to be very much interested, must remain monitored to reach any clear conclusion in this regard.

The Algerian reactor was not mentioned again in Israeli sources, but Iraq was reported to have warned Algiers, plagued by serious Moslem fundamentalist riots early in June, that "Israel was planning to attack its reactor." On June 10, 1991, an IAEA spokesman in Vienna publicly announced Algiers' acceptance of IAEA inspection of its reactor. No details have been disclosed as yet, in spite of the fact that neither China, the supplier, nor Algeria had joined NPT. At the same time, the, *New York Times* reported that North Korea had turned to the IAEA to sign a safeguards agreement. If these reports were true and Algeria and North Korea sincere, both may have been prompted by Chinese-American understandings—or by fear of a South Korean attack on the northern facility—and by Algiers' willingness to legitimize its reactor in the wake of Bush's initiative, leaving Israel isolated in this regard.

Interestingly enough, Labor's chairman Shimon Peres remained publicly silent during the period after President Bush proclaimed his unconventional arms control initiative, although, according to *Ha'aretz*, Peres had endorsed such an initiative in advance. Instead the Labor leader endorsed Baker's new peace efforts. Attention was shifting now to Assad's promised answer to Bush's and Baker's pleas for him to join the peace conference.

At the same time, conditions in the Soviet Union were rapidly deteriorating. Gorbachev tried to reassert himself in mid-July by finally signing START, hoping for Western compensation in the G-7 summit in London. And later he moved as far as trying to transform the Communist Party into a Western-like social-democratic party. Obviously, if Assad had not already been convinced that he could no longer count on Moscow, in the traditional sense, he must have been convinced now. Late in July, he agreed to attend the peace conference, thus accepting U.S. supremacy in the region and forcing Shamir to reconsider his own, rather negative, view of that idea. Due to the ongoing effort to put an end to Saddam's nuclear program, Bush's arms control initiative for the region was left aside in the meantime, but remained very much alive, seemingly with Peres' support.

Washington seems to have returned to Kennedy's nonproliferation campaign, this time much more determined. And this time Washington had the political and economic tools to enforce its campaign on Israel, with no Soviet threats to blur its intentions and with the acceptance of Peres (Kennedy's adversary in this respect).

Yet the future of the Bush initiative is uncertain. It is still not clear whether U.S. supremacy and leadership in the region will suffice to prevent other Arab nations, not just Iraq, from going nuclear. They could then—unless they had other incentives, such as complete economic dependence on the United States—use the peace process to attain the "ultimate power" in the nuclear age. Israel's consent to the new regime is thus doubtful, even in the case of Peres, who may have used rather opaque language, and press fillers, when he was reported to have endorsed it earlier. Even the Bush initiative was not explicit, and in fact demanded the "freezing" of Israel's existing nuclear option by allowing inspection of its facilities to prevent future production, but not the actual, duly controlled, removal of what had been accumulated before. Furthermore, throughout his public life, Peres' nuclear stances have varied greatly. He started with an open nuclear strategy, moved to an "ambiguous" posture, and then to an opaque one. Having endorsed what seemed to be a "balance of terror," he might have finally adopted the view that since an Arab bomb could not be prevented and since a "balance of terror" was probable, it should at least be accompanied by a peace process. Within such a context Peres might have adopted Weizmann's and General Tamir's view that Arabs should not be openly confronted with Israel's nuclear option, but should be approached in a reasonable way about peace before one of them went nuclear—by itself an unavoidable fact that must be tackled within, not outside of, a political process. Such an approach may even entail agreement to a NWFZ—and possibly to inspection at Dimona.

A more updated version of Peres' position would be the acceptance of Bush's initiative, even if by default—i.e., by not angrily rejecting it as Energy Minister Ne'eman did, by demanding inspection "in twenty-one Arab and twenty Moslems states" first, or by casting doubts on it as Rabin did. Whether Peres was sincere about supporting the initiative is unclear. Peres' cunning character and tricky appearance could lead a foreign observer to the conclusion that he may agree to the Dimona inspection—especially if its life expectancy indeed is about thirty years—and concentrate instead on laser-enriched uranium bombs. Spector cautiously mentions such an option, and that it might have been initiated in 1974 and could yield "two to three highly enriched uranium [bombs] per year."[27] Thus the retirement of Dimona, one may speculate, would deny Israel access to tritium and lithium 6 (whose half-life is rather short), which are necessary for fusion (big hydrogen and small neutron) bombs and could be produced in reactors only. Plutonium bombs could remain for longer and uranium ones added, if Israel had a definite lead over the Arabs in these highly sophisticated techniques, without Arabs being humiliated and challenged by Israel's possession of a publicly unsafeguarded reactor, which is forbidden to them. In this respect Peres could hope that the Bush initiative would deny Arabs the bomb better than Israel could, and believe that this positive development should be met with some Israeli concession to make it work—and to ease the peace process.

This approach could be congruent with the expectations of some members of the nonproliferation lobby, who have complained in conferences and publications abroad that Israel did not need "200 bombs" (if one believed Vanunu and Barnaby's estimates), and that the proposed "freeze" on production would greatly benefit Jerusalem in the first place, due to the proposed restrictions on the "have nots"—the Arabs.

In the meantime, on June 20, 1991, the *Washington Times* published a leaked report submitted to President Bush by the American intelligence community which stated that Israel's arsenal contains sixty to eighty bombs. This report asserted the fact that India and Pakistan had military nuclear capabilities defined as being "much smaller than Israel's" and that Iran and Algeria were working on a military nuclear program. Shortly before, on May 5, 1991, the same newspaper published a story about the deployment in Israel of Jericho II missiles.

Mr. Rabin expressed his skepticism about the Bush arms control initiative in public, and had publicly criticized Shamir's otherwise rather hawkish government for not "having publicly declared that large Arab cities ["capital cities," in another published version] would be destroyed if their leaders, specifically Iraq, resorted to use of weapons of mass destruction."[28] For Rabin, Shamir was too vague in this regard. Thus another circle seems to have fully, and adversely, closed. Peres, the executive officer in charge of Ben-Gurion's Dimona and an advocate of an open, or "opaque" but clear enough, nuclear option seemed ready to minimize its public role, while Rabin, the conventionalist disciple of Allon, missed an open threat in Likud's behavior in the most recent war. The one, who had tried to get around Kennedy's antiproliferation efforts, seemed ready to accept Bush's arms control initiative, while the other, who had seemed to be more interested in American jets and tanks, was now underlining a threat aimed at entire Arab cities.

Rabin's case, however, is rather consistent and explicit. In a public lecture on the lessons of the Gulf War, Rabin said that Israel's deterrent power was not affected during the war, because the circumstances of that war were irrelevant to Israel's power of deterrence:

> Israel will deter an Arab leader such as Assad from attacking her, when he knew that in response Israel was capable of harming his army and occupying territory in his country to the degree that may endanger his regime. Such a threat could be possessed only by an army capable of offense ... When the Arab states respond to the growing Israeli qualitative edge by invoking push-button weapons, Israel's answer should be the cultivation of conventional compellence in the air and on the ground, rather than building systems that will bury the whole Israeli home front underground.[29]

The message was clear: unconventional deterrence, rather than passive defense, by taking Arab capitals hostage, is necessary to protect the home front. Conventional war, in the spirit of Allon's doctrine, is necessary to compel, not just to deter, the enemy, and thus the option of waging it "would contribute to the peace process." This, of course, required American weapons and money and a degree of Israeli flexibility vis-à-vis Washington.

In the same conference, Minister of Energy Ne'eman complained that after the war the United States was doing "in the U.N. as it pleased, in contrast to the past ... The Israeli nuclear power was presented as a danger to the Middle East, while Washington was about to sell the Arabs conventional weapons worth $24 billion." Elsewhere Ne'eman said that he deeply suspected the United States, and thus Israel must turn to China and the Soviet Union for military and technological aid. When he toured a Soviet-made reactor, the Kremlin denied any intention to sell Israel such equipment. But some kind of scientific cooperation between the two nations was agreed upon, including in the nuclear field. These rude maneuvers, combined with Ne'eman's support for renewed West Bank settlement efforts, must have offended Washington a great deal.

In conclusion, I would like to reiterate that the purpose of this book was to discuss, historically, existing and projected deviations from the internationally accepted norm of nonproliferation and the quasi-norm involving the prevention of open nuclear threats, aside from the actual use of nuclear weapons. Such deviations have been called by other scholars "undeclared" and "ambiguous" postures, whereas I have advanced the term "opaque" posture, giving it my own interpretation.

I have dealt with these issues historically, in regard to a specific region, from an Israeli perspective, but have tried to be as objective as possible. At first, I discerned a variety of opaque nuclear postures, compared to the open ones and related to the praxis and theory of conflict, which was developed at first in the West.

It is possible that two kinds of nuclear opacity exist, at least in Israel's case: self-imposed opacity and foreign-imposed opacity. Self-imposed opacity may result from opposing reasons. On the one hand, it may represent a political decision by a nation such as Israel not to use open, crude, and humiliating threats against the enemy, while at the same time giving it enough information to influence its will to fight. This is the stand that would have been taken by Ben-Gurion, as I see it without having access to his closed files: Ben-Gurion's policy was to use the notion of "bomb in being," rather than adopting a nuclear warfighting doctrine. He simply avoided the issues of credibility and of implementing one's nuclear options in terms of targeting, escalation, etc. He was working within a historical framework that emphasized winning the race to get the option first and then seeking political arrangements that would solve or lower the level of the Arab-Israeli conflict, thanks among other things to the assumed role of the superpowers and to Israel's own relatively low territorial profile and domestic development. He thus pursued primarily political goals by sticking to the principle of the partition of western Palestine at the same time.

On the other hand, self-imposed opacity might result from grave doubts about the usefulness of nuclear threats in conflict with "irrational" Arabs and aim at avoiding the possibility of Soviet nuclear aid to them and incentives for them to go nuclear and maintaining a "last resort" option should they go nuclear, while seeking more conventional security guarantees in terms of territory and conventional weapons. I have argued that General Allon was the representative of that view.

Another form of self-imposed opacity could be discerned among politicians of the Israeli Right, whose nuclear expert, Professor Yuval Ne'eman, reiterated in public early in May 1991 his conviction that Israel's nuclear option should remain opaque "now more than ever." One could see here two motives: the fear that nuclear options could substitute for occupied territory—which Ne'eman would never give up—and the fear that the new nuclear "regime" for the Middle East, based on "freezing" the status quo, would impose restrictions on Israel, including its missile program, without affecting the Arabs too much. Ne'eman also initiated an international campaign to prevent "nuclear terrorism," should a Palestinian or Moslem guerrilla outfit succeed in obtaining a nuclear device and use, or threaten to use, it. From his point of view—and this is yet another reason for opacity—Arabs in the occupied territories might suffer as a result of any use of unconventional weapons by Arabs against Israel, a proposition that would become less viable if Israel withdrew from the occupied territory and removed its settlements therein. The very mixture of the populations in these areas was supposedly a kind of guarantee against unconventional attack, while the segregation of them by returning to partition would identify purely Jewish targets for these purposes.

In the case of the United States in the recent crisis, American nuclear power was not declared to be, nor actively used as, a factor in the conflict, unless the Iraqis used unconventional capabilities first—although the United States could have used nuclear threats and ultimately tactical nuclear weapons such as neutron bombs against a numerically superior conventional land force such as Saddam's army. The reasons for such self-imposed opacity in this case could be political-moral, bureaucratic, or both. The Soviets were not a real issue here for the United States. It could expect no Soviet support of any kind for the opposition—which was not the case in Vietnam with the North Vietnamese. On the contrary, the Soviets imposed an embargo on weapons deliveries to Iraq at the beginning of the crisis, although they did maintain their military advisers in the Iraqi Army for the time being. The use of nuclear threats by the United States against a Third World nation—abrasive and inhumane as Saddam's behavior was—would have been a deviation from established norms and habits, the breaking of self-imposed taboos, and a threat to the nonproliferation "regime" itself, although Saddam's own nuclear ambitions might have contributed heavily to his decision to invade Kuwait in the first place. And angry Soviet, Chinese, even radical Pakistani, and Indian reactions to such an American decision could not be ignored.

At first, it seemed that the Bush Administration found it acceptable not to use Saddam's nuclear ambition as a master variable to justify its efforts against him. Publicly other factors were stressed by the administration, such as oil, Saddam's breaking of the rules of international behavior, and the political calculations related to the creation and the maintenance of the coalition that finally fought him. Upon the opening of the air war on January 8, 1991, President Bush did explicitly mention the danger of a future Iraqi bomb if Saddam prevailed, but denying it from Iraq by using force was not his publicly articulated main goal, which was the liberation of Kuwait.

In fact, the United States seemed not to have a policy of using force against potential nuclear adversaries to eliminate their capabilities, unless they committed other crimes. This policy was based on political reasons, such as adverse effects on the existing nonproliferation regime, and on existing traditions regarding the use of force against foreign countries. The United States used public nuclear threats only against those who had already acquired the bomb, and mainly against great powers such as the Soviet Union and China.

Yet the Americans in fact made the unconventional weapons issue, including missiles, a major element—spelled out in the relevant Security Council decisions—in their anti-Saddam campaign. After the war, the Security Council tried—through IAEA inspectors—to disarm Iraq in this respect. But we cannot judge whether these efforts would be crowned with verifiable success. Thus the nuclear/missile complex became a major issue in the Gulf War, and the use of force to eliminate it, conditioned by political circumstances, became a precedent, to be followed by American efforts to establish a new "regime" in the area to control such weapons in the future.

Yet Saddam's survival, and apparent willingness to adhere to Allied conditions, is coupled with his hope to defy them to an extent that would allow him to return to the big game. This was given top priority over his other ambitions.

Should Saddam Hussein lose his nuclear potential, it would be as a result of the recent war in which he suddenly behaved as a "madman," and his goals—oil, the bomb, and regional hegemony—were examined in the cultural-historical framework of his "subjective rationality" and deemed unacceptable to the United States.

When the hostilities were suspended, Secretary of State Baker returned to his prewar activity, aimed at regional-political arrangements that would tackle the root of the conflict and the causes of proliferation, such as the Palestinian problem, which is linked to the instability in the region. These "arrangements" seem to be close to the Soviet idea of a "regional security system" for the Middle East, whose implementation first required Saddam's failure in his Kuwaiti adventure. The ensuing process is still in the making.

I have dealt with the Palestinian problem itself in the unconventional context, arguing that it could be analyzed as a real problem or used to justify ideological and political—"high" and "low"—arguments in Israel. I further explained the issue of sovereignty in the nuclear age in this context. That is, Palestinian—as well as Iraqi—sovereignty would have to be limited to achieve in the Middle East a peace that is not based on the balance of terror alone. Such limitations are usually incompatible with the concept of "self-determination," which has, however, already been partially limited by NPT. Yet the mechanism of enforcing NPT, and the opacity that was a part of it, almost allowed Saddam to get the bomb.

Thus it is possible that one of the reasons for self-imposed American opacity in its nuclear behavior in the Gulf crisis, and possibly for maintaining Israel's "reduced opacity" in this regard, was the established, bureaucratic rule which held that the issues involved, including Israel's nuclear option, should be discussed behind the scenes to prevent other Arabs and Third World nations from developing an obsession in regard to this highly sensitive matter. One could of course argue that the Arabs who were obsessed with it—such as Heikal, Qaddafi, and Saddam—were a hopeless case anyway. One could also argue that the public denial of Israel's right to possess nuclear weapons—in the sense of maintaining an official curtain of silence on the issue, which every now and again was lifted by Israel—just complicated the matter and did not contribute to any moderation on Qaddafi's or Saddam's side.

Therefore the time may have come, from Washington's viewpoint, to concentrate on a regional security system that would guarantee stability in the region by direct involvement of the superpowers, the Europeans, and the U.N. This may be reflected in Bush's arms control initiative more than in Secretary Baker's diplomatic efforts. Israel's nuclear option relieves others from using nuclear threats to defend Israel, and it relieves Israel from asking others to do so, in a unique circumstance in which the opposing side may use any means—especially conventional ones—to destroy Israel. Indeed, Israel's nuclear option has constrained the other side's freedom of action against Israel, and therefore the Israeli option remains a challenge to radical Arabs and an incentive for coexistence for moderate ones. The odds here are not necessarily even, but Israel has the nuclear option after all, and the others do not. When the "others," such as Saddam and Qaddafi, get the bomb, they might quote the Israeli challenge as their reason for needing it, but in fact their aim will be regional hegemony and international power. This could bring them—armed with nuclear weapons—into a conflict with the United States anyway. They may try to take regional American clients as hostages or be maneuvered into a nuclear conflict with them. Opacity would soon be the first casualty of such a development, because in anticipating such a development, the involved regional powers might feel that they must "draw the lines," just as Western deterrence theory caused the superpowers to do long ago. Yet such developments would have occurred among radical Arabs not because of Israel but because nuclear weapons are the ultimate symbol of power in the nuclear age. Without a nuclear option, Israel was doomed; with it, at least Arabs became divided—among other reasons—into "moderates" and "radicals," and the superpowers became involved in the conflict in a complex fashion and helped to defeat a nuclear-eager Arab regime.

Another complication, which will surely influence developments in the region in the post-Gulf War period, is the Iranian nuclear program; coupled with a fierce anti-Israeli accent, this revitalized program may be seen as primarily aimed against Saddam's Iraq, against the pro-Western Arab states, and toward regional hegemony in a degree of cooperation with Syria and radical Palestinians. Iran took the lead against the American-sponsored Middle East peace process late in 1991 and publicly justified its exposed nuclear efforts by invoking Israel's nuclear option. Israel's willingness to agree to any "new order" in the nuclear sense will be affected by American moves to counter the Iranian development, and by the growing fear that the disintegration of the Soviet Union has already contributed to the emergence of an international "black market" in which Soviet plutonium and uranium could be freely purchased and Soviet nuclear experts might offer their services to everyone.

From an Israeli point of view, self-imposed opacity may represent two additional kinds of negative approaches: a total rejection of nuclear options as valid tools for conducting one's foreign policy, and a conscious decision to deny or blur any positive significance attached to them. In my view, such an approach, as it was adopted by Israeli radicals and some scholars who used deterrence theory as a negative model, took on a life of its own and contributed to the confusion among Israelis—though not among Arab leaders and the superpowers—regarding Israel's nuclear options. A less radical approach adopted by Israeli politicians and proliferation scholars—the opaque "last resort" posture—was the result of foreign input, both theoretical and practical, combined with domestic ideological and political input.

At the time this approach was adopted, our foreign sources reported that missiles and a variety of nuclear options had been added to the arsenal, following the importation of foreign strategic-technical arguments and as a result of the Arab interest in the bomb and their response to the initial "bomb in being" option. Thus, one may maintain that Egypt risked a general war when it was not sure that viable Israeli nuclear options really existed, and when Egypt believed that it had enough Soviet support to at least provoke a limited war in 1967. In order to eliminate such options, Egypt at first took the chance of a limited war, which, however, seemed to Arab and Jew alike to be a general war to destroy Israel. In 1973 Egypt might have believed that it had enough means to render Israeli nuclear options impractical due to Egyptian air defenses and self-imposed limits on military behavior, plus some Soviet involvement, when it fought to liberate occupied Egyptian land and start a political-diplomatic process toward the liberation of other occupied territories. Yet very few Israelis understood the peculiar working of the nuclear issue in this regard, and their political behavior was influenced accordingly. Thus, scholars in Israel are still fighting against any expectations from this option by invoking "historical opacity," and by distorting historical facts thanks to the prevailing official opacity.

The most typical form of opacity is "political opacity," or "Jewish opacity," which combines arguments from the other postures, with the addition of political and group interests, personal ambition, and the like, which are only indirectly related to the real strategic-political matter. Similar traits are found among Arabs as well, although nuclear weapons lend themselves less successfully to such traditional games among ancient and clever nations, emotional and self-righteous as they may be, who are divided among themselves and lack Western rules of the game.

The final, and most recent, form of official opacity is the "reduced" or "minimal" opacity that was adopted by Prime Minister Shamir during the Gulf crisis. Here, Israelis started to look at the matter as it was, and some public credit was even given to David Ben-Gurion and to Ernst Bergmann in this regard. Yet even then, no public debate or fresh wave of academic discussion followed Shamir's counterthreats of a "terrible, horrible response" to Saddam's threats. The reason could have been, among those discussed elsewhere in this book, that the Gulf still seemed to be an American affair. And the prospect of an Israeli first strike, in the spirit of the Begin Doctrine, seemed unreal, due to the direct American presence and overwhelming might (even though this might could not prevent the launching of conventional SCUDs against Israel when the war began). While the Israeli government refrained from any response, some Israelis, including many usually liberal personalities, called for a response, as if Israel had lost its traditional, self-sustaining spirit. One of such liberal, a literary critic, even hinted vaguely toward the nuclear mirage, and was duly criticized by other liberals. Other Israelis, such as General Sharon, claimed that Israel had the means to eliminate the launchers, which a press fantasy described as "clean" nuclear weapons and others described as conventional tools. But the policy of nonintervention was maintained.

Then came the Bush initiative, which seems to have brought our discussion, beginning with John Kennedy, full circle. This book could give readers food for thought. Has the circle been fully closed? The similarities to the Kennedy era—during which Israel alone was the target and Soviet support to the Arabs was the main fear—seem to remain valid only on the face of it, as Israel alone still seems to be the target. But the dissimilarities are many, as the United States itself followed Israel's example and destroyed Iraq's nuclear capabilities as best it could, and is now trying to keep that potential capability under control. The Bush initiative could work not only as a CBM (confidence-building measure) but also to create a legal measure to use force against a proliferator of weapons of mass destruction, whereas Israel's own Begin Doctrine proved irrelevant. Thus the limits of NPT, with which we started this book, and of LSG, and of MTCR, in the Middle East, have been at least indirectly acknowledged. At the same time, all of us who study the Middle East must learn to address ourselves, each of us in his or her own way, to the subject matter of this book as an inseparable part of the reality, opaque as it may be, of that troubled area. And this seems to be the case, in that the problem seems solvable by means of American security guarantees to Israel, coupled with progress in the peace process, in which the Palestinian question is declared to be the key to the conflict.

In June 1991, an impressive group of American foreign policy, arms control, and strategic experts conducted a study of this problem, published by the School of Advanced International Studies of Johns Hopkins University in Washington, D.C. Similarly, a Council for Phased Peace, calling for the creation of a Palestinian state in phases, was established by Israeli doves in mid-June. A *Davar* story, published next to the report of the Johns Hopkins group, told Israeli readers that "most Palestinians" in the occupied territories, young and old, believe that the occupation is the result of an American (British, too, in the case of the elderly) and Jordanian conspiracy that resulted in the 1967 (or 1948) war. Most Palestinians seem to have no idea of what really happened, and most, according to Palestinian intellectuals quoted in that liberal daily, prefer to "blame others" rather than bear the responsibility for Palestinian mistakes. No attempt has been made to educate them, even if Palestinian intellectuals seem to be ready and able now to learn from the use of violence by uncontrolled youngsters during the Intifada, from the mob rule that accompanied the uprising, and from Arafat's mistakes in supporting Saddam Hussein.

This book has dealt a great deal with history, not just with strategy. Strategy and foreign policy are intimately connected to history, to culture, and to politics. Could the United States guarantee security to Israel in present circumstances, when it is perceived by Palestinians to be the source of all evil? Would a West Bank state resolve the issue of exiled Palestinians, without destroying Jordan sooner or later? Would Israel— not just Likud, but Ben-Gurion's Israel, the Holocaust-conscious Israel, and the Israel that watched Kuwait being overrun and salvaged as it was—allow the source of her very survival, as perceived by Ben-Gurion, to be "phased out"?

Notes

Introduction

1. See Leonard S. Spector, *The Undeclared Bomb: The Spread of Nuclear Weapons 1987-1988*. For the Carnegie Endowment for International Peace. (Cambridge, Mass.: Ballinger, 1988), pp. 161-95. And cf. Spector's *Nuclear Ambitions: The Spread of Nuclear Weapons 1989-1990* (Boulder, Colo.: Westview Press, 1990). Regarding the cases of Pakistan and India, see Spector's "New Players in the Nuclear Game," *Bulletin of the Atomic Scientists* (January/February 1989), pp. 29-32, and his annual reports on nuclear proliferation published by the Carnegie Endowment. Spector is less interested in the politics of proliferation—i.e. in the motives and goals of nations who seek nuclear weapons—than he is in registering facts about their activities (mostly quoted from public sources written in English or from translations).

For further information on "undeclared bombs," see, Congressional Research Service (CRS) "Issue Briefs"; the publications of Programme for Promoting Nuclear Non-Proliferation (PPNN), a London-based antiproliferation group; and see the regular attention paid to the subject in the *Bulletin of the Atomic Scientists*; for a recent report published by the Aspen Strategy Group of the Aspen Institute, see *New Threats: Responding to the Proliferation of Nuclear, Chemical, and Delivery Capabilities in the Third World* (Lanham, Md.: University Press of America, 1990), especially Geoffry Kemp's contribution, "Solving the Proliferation Problem in the Middle-East," pp. 197-222.

There are also a number of technical publications (such as *Nucleonics Week, The Energy Daily,* etc.) that publish data regarding the acquisition of nuclear-related technologies by nations involved. However, these publications are not principally concerned with the political or the strategic significance of nuclear weapons in areas such as the Middle East, nor are they antiproliferation as a matter of course. Whereas I am interested in the sources of antiproliferation philosophy itself and in its implementation in a specific area in the world as a practical-theoretical and as a political-strategic problem. A source of some importance in this connection are the reports of the Secretary General of the United Nations to the General Assembly; see, for example, *Establishment of a Nuclear-Weapon-Free Zone in the Region of the Middle East* (a study on effective and verifiable measures that would facilitate the establishment of a nuclear-weapon-free zone in the Middle East), Report of the Secretary General, U.N. General Assembly, doc. A/45/435, October 10, 1990.

2. Frank Barnaby, *The Invisible Bomb: The Nuclear Arms Race in the Middle East* (London: I. B. Tauris, 1989).

3. For the philosophy and the rules of the nonproliferation regime see, for example, Joseph S. Nye, "Maintaining a Nonproliferation Regime" in *Nuclear Proliferation—Breaking the Chain*, edited by George H. Quester (Madison, Wisc.: University of Wisconsin Press, 1981), pp. 15-38, and cf. his most recent publication in this regard, "Arms Control After the Cold War," in *Foreign Affairs* (Winter 1989/90), pp. 42-64. See also Jed C. Snyder and Samuel F. Wells, Jr., eds., *Limiting Nuclear Proliferation*. For the Wilson Center, Washington, D.C. (Cambridge, Mass.: Ballinger, 1985), pp. 43-58 (regarding Israel) and pp. 3-42 (regarding Iraq); and cf. Mitchel Reiss, *Without the Bomb: The Politics of Nuclear Nonproliferation* (New York: Columbia University Press, 1988), pp. 138-72 (concerning Israel). A major contribution to the nuclear history of the world, including the history of the nonproliferation "regime," is McGeorge Bundy's *Danger and Survival: Choices About the Bomb in First Fifty Years* (New York: Random House, 1988), pp. 513-16. An important contribution to the history of the British bomb, and to British influence on American strategic thinking, is Ian Clark and Nicholas J. Wheeler, *The British Origins of Nuclear Strategy 1945-1955* (Oxford: Clarendon Press, 1989); this book can be useful in understanding Israel's deliberations, due to some connections between the cases (including British leftwing criticism of the "national bomb," which was echoed in Israel). And see John Newhouse, *War and Peace in the Nuclear Age* (New York: Knopf, 1989), esp. pp. 136-37, 238-40, and 271-73 (regarding Israel); Newhouse's information about the French-Israeli nuclear cooperation and other issues related to the Middle East is however partial at best, due to his concentration on the superpowers and due to his sources, in the case of Israel.

Chapter One. Strategy, History, and Politics

1. See Robert Jervis's "Deterrence Theory Revisited" in *World Politics*, vol. XXXI, no. 3 (January 1979), pp. 289-324, and cf. his *The Illogic of American Nuclear Strategy* (Ithaca and London: Cornell University Press, 1984), and his "The Political Effects of Nuclear Weapons," in *International Security*, vol. 12, no.2 (Fall 1988), pp. 80-90. In a more recent book, Jervis seems to have accepted some premises of deterrence theory—especially the absolute importance of a second strike capability, as a *conditio sine qua non*—to make his point that nuclear

weapons "revolutionized" international politics, and hence should not be "conventionalized," in the spirit of Hans Morgenthau's warnings. See Robert Jervis, *The Meaning of the Nuclear Revolution: Statecraft and the Prospect of Armageddon* (Ithaca and London: Cornell University Press, 1989), esp. pp. 46-60.

2. I have used the English version of Pierre Gallois' *The Balance of Terror* (Boston: Houghton Mifflin, 1961). And see Kenneth Waltz, "The Spread of Nuclear Weapons: More May Be Better," *Adelphi Papers*, The International Institute of Strategic Studies, London, no. 171 (Autumn 1981).

3. In this connection (even though related to American nuclear strategy alone), see Colin Spencer Gray, *Nuclear Strategy and National Style* (Lanham, Md: Hamilton Press, 1986).

4. See in this context Yehezkel Dror, *A Grand Strategy for Israel* (Jerusalem: Academon, 1989), and its selected bibliography (including titles pertaining to deterrence), and see his discussion of "hidden nuclear stability," pp. 139-50.

5. For a recent psychological study in this respect based on Jervis's observations, see Steven Kool, *Minds at War: Nuclear Reality and the Inner Conflicts of Defense Policymakers* (New York: Basic Books, 1988).

6. See, for example, Frank Barnaby, *The Invisible Bomb: The Nuclear Arms Race in the Middle East* (London: I. B. Tauris, 1989), pp. 54-64.

7. See Peres' *Ha'aretz* article, June 2, 1989, "Economics without Boundaries," in which he criticized almost openly the official, conventional doctrine of the Israeli Army, which was formulated decades before by General Yigal Allon and seemed to be the official doctrine when his article was published (under Yitzhak Rabin as minister of defense). To a certain extent, Peres repeated here arguments put forward several years before by the late General Moshe Dayan, though some of the differences between Dayan and Peres remained unchanged. Still, as we shall see below, Rabin's security doctrine has been developed to combine nuclear options and conventional ones as well.

8. See Robert E. Harkavy, "Pariah States and Nuclear Proliferation," in *Nuclear Proliferation—Breaking the Chain*, edited by George H. Quester (Madison, Wisc.: University of Wisconsin Press, 1981), pp. 135-63.

9. Ibid., p. 151, and cf. Robert E. Harkavy, *Spectre of a Middle Eastern Holocaust* (Denver, Colo.: University of Denver Press, 1977).

10. See Kurt Gottfried and Bruce G. Blair, *Crisis Stability and Nuclear War* (New York: Oxford University Press, 1988), pp. 244-45.

11. Barnaby, *The Invisible Bomb*, pp. 65-66. Barnaby's main argument against neutron bombs is technical, based on the idea that boron-impregnated plastic covers will absorb most of the neutrons. When it was first published, I approached Sam Cohen, the "father of the neutron bomb," in Los Angeles to

verify Barnaby's "boron theory." Cohen brushed it aside as a "typical manipu-
lation [by Barnaby] of scientific data to advance political, or whatever, goals."
And cf. Cohen's June 1989 attack in the *Wall Street Journal* against conventional
battlefield PGMs (precision-guided munitions), as a return to "Goering's strategy" of wasting extremely expensive munitions (as compared to battlefield
nuclear weapons) on targets that could be easily substituted by the enemy with
decoys.

12. The Israeli case was referred to as "ambiguous" for the first time in the
scholarly literature by Yair Evron, "Israel and the Atom: The Uses and Misuses of Ambiguity 1957-1967," *Orbis*, vol. 17 (no. 4), p. 108ff. However, Evron
has since "extended" the period of Israel's ambiguity to the present. First, in his
"The Relevance and the Irrelevance of Nuclear Options in Conventional Wars,"
Jerusalem Journal of International Relations, vol. 7, nos. 1-2 (1984), pp. 143-76; and
second, in his Hebrew book *Israel's Nuclear Dilemma* (Tel Aviv: Hakibbutz
Hameuchad, 1987). The latter was sponsored (as Evron tells us in his introduction) by the late Israel Galili, a leading politician of the Israeli nationalist Left.
Galili harbored doubts about Israel's nuclear option, and was especially afraid
of its ramifications in terms of Soviet, American, and Arab responses. At the
same time, Galili adopted a view that was in opposition to Ben-Gurion's (which
lent more weight to his domestic battles with BG). Evron's strategic-technical
arguments and his membership in the nonproliferation lobby merged here with
Galili's political and strategic calculations, although both were ready to accept
a last resort option, which Evron, in a more recent publication, described as "a
very low probability situation—the complete collapse of Israel resulting from a
massive conventional onslaught by all the Arab world." See Yair Evron, "Israeli-
Palestinian-Jordanian Security Relations: The Idea of a Security Zone," *Emerging
Issues*, Occasional Paper Series, American Academy of Arts and Sciences, Cambridge, Mass., no. 3 (May 1990), p. 48. Evron's argument that "Israeli nuclear
developments were largely irrelevant to Sadat's decision to seek a political
accommodation with Israel" was repeated, without evidence, in his most recent
article, "Opaque Proliferation: The Israeli Case," in *The Journal of Strategic Studies*, vol. 13, September 1990, pp. 54-55.

It is also interesting here to note the input of Simcha Flapan, an active
politician and editor of the leftist Israeli journal *New Outlook*. Flapan, who had
endorsed the idea of binationalism—rather than Jewish independence in Palestine—was an early propagandist among those who blamed Israel for the creation of the 1948 Arab refugee problem. This school of thought made Israel
primarily responsible for Arab behavior (which as such justified Arab wrath).
Yet it treated Arabs as "irrational" enemies who might use the bomb first if
not appeased or if Israel introduced it first. Flapan thus endorsed an anti-bomb
posture as a matter of course, calling for regional nuclear disarmament as a
prelude to peace. In this connection, he adopted a public strategy of denying
Israel's nuclear option, from time to time, and stressing the role of foreign pressures and domestic anti-bomb activists in curbing Israel's nuclear options. As a
result, Flapan flatly published wrong information, as the reader may see when

comparing his information to my analysis below. See Flapan's "Nuclear Disarmament in the Middle East—The Only Solution," in *Humanity Under the Shadow of the Atom*, edited by Avner Cohen (Tel Aviv: Hakibbutz Hameuchad, 1987), pp. 194-204.

13. See Shai Feldman, *Israeli Nuclear Deterrence* (New York: Columbia University Press, 1982). And cf. Shlomo Aronson, "Israel's Nuclear Options," ACIS Working Paper, UCLA, no. 7 (1977), and Aronson, "Nuclearization of the Middle East—A Dovish View," *Jerusalem Quarterly*, no. 2 (Winter 1977).

14. For example, see Evron's "The Relevance and Irrelevance of Nuclear Options in Conventional Wars" (note 12, above), in which he offered a "speculative"—i.e., theoretical—interpretation of Arab behavior in 1973 (according to Professor Dan Horowitz of Hebrew University), denying (and ignoring) the enormous amount of published Arab sources proving the opposite (that nuclear weapons had a role in Arab planning for the war). And cf. my "Nuclear Dimension of the Yom Kippur War," *Jerusalem Journal of International Relations*, vol. 7, nos. 1-2 (1984), pp. 107-42. Among non-Israeli members of the antiproliferation scholarly lobby, the issue was a source of long-standing trouble. Some tried to use strategic-technical arguments to prevent Israel from "going nuclear," and some—such as George Quester in his *Politics of Nuclear Proliferation* (Baltimore: Johns Hopkins University Press, 1973)—seem to have registered the facts, but in order to maintain the momentum of the antiproliferation movement, refused to discuss their actual ramifications in the historical-political reality of the time. In *The Invisible Bomb* (1989), Barnaby contributed, in his way, to the maintenance of "ambiguous" postures by describing the actual capabilities in the bomb production sector—less so in the missile sector—and leaving out any historical-political understanding of the Middle East and of East-West deliberations.

15. The published Israeli sources on the nuclear cooperation between France and Israel are: (1) *The Diaries of Moshe Sharett*, vol. 2 (Tel Aviv: Ma'ariv Library, 1978), pp. 400, 483, 533-34, 565; (2) Ben-Gurion diaries, as quoted by Michael Bar-Zohar, in *Ben-Gurion* (Tel Aviv: Am-Oved Publishers, 1977); Mr. Peres, who according to his own public statement on April 10, 1990, was involved in the preparation of Bar-Zohar's Ben-Gurion biography, probably after the latter's death in 1973. (3) Shimon Peres' diaries and information related to the subject matter quoted by Matti Golan, in *Peres* (Tel Aviv: Schocken, 1982). Because of their affiliation with Mr. Peres, both Golan and Bar-Zohar must be used carefully; other primary sources, even those related to earlier periods, should be consulted first; see, e.g., Ben-Gurion's own *War Diaries 1948-1949* (Tel Aviv: Misrad Habitachon Press, 1982).

Ben-Gurion's 1954-1963 diaries, stored in the Ben-Gurion Memorial Archive, Kibbutz, Sde-Boker, are partially closed (completely beginning with 1961 and partially before that). I used the 1954-1958 diaries. Other unpublished sources used here are: public lectures given by important actors, interviews in the Israeli press, and specific talks with former officials conducted since the mid-1960s by the author in Israel, England, West Germany, France, and the United States. (These interviews were not necessarily always directly about the nuclear issue; sometimes the issue was raised by the people I interviewed.)

The main published sources related to the French side of the French-Israeli connection are: (1) Pierre Pean, *Les Deux Bombes* (Paris: Arthem Fayard, 1982); and cf. Lawrence Scheinman, *Atomic Energy Policy under the Fourth Republic* (Princeton, N.J.: Princeton University Press, 1965), and Bertrand Goldschmidt, *Les Rivalites Atomiques (1939-1966)* (Paris: Fayard, 1967), and his *Les Complex Atomique* (Paris: Fayard, 1980). Goldschmidt was personally involved in the Israeli venture, and therefore, his books must be used carefully and compared to Pean, whose information is usually compatible with other French and non-French primary and secondary sources, such as (2) Jean Francis Perrin (the former director of the French Atomic Energy Commission), as quoted in the London *Sunday Times*, October 5, 1986, in connection with Israeli nuclear technician Mordechai Vanunu's disclosures to that paper. Vanunu's own information will be discussed below, as published in more detail by Barnaby in 1989. Wilfrid L. Kohl's *French Nuclear Diplomacy* (Princeton, N.J.: Princeton University Press, 1971), is still very useful in understanding France's nuclear relations with the U.S. and Germany, but Kohl seemed not to have been aware of the Israeli-French nuclear sharing. This missing element was referred to in two major works dealing with the nuclear history of the world: McGeorge Bundy's *Danger and Survival* and John Newhouse's *War and Peace in the Nuclear Age*. Both of these authors quote foreign sources, but not fully; and Bundy also quotes relatively recent CIA estimates and other, sometimes undisclosed, sources, which give us a partial if not misleading picture.

Chapter Two. The American Paradigm and Early Efforts to Limit Proliferation

1. The publication of McGeorge Bundy's *Danger and Survival: Choices About the Bomb in the First Fifty Years* (New York: Random House, 1988) and John Newhouse's *War and Peace in the Nuclear Age* (New York: Knopf, 1989), as well as General Leslie Groves's biography by William Lawren—*The General and the Bomb* (New York: Dodd, Mead, 1988)—contributed a wealth of facts and sources about the nuclear history of the West. The first two authors dealt also with the Israeli nuclear program.

2. See Richard Rhodes, *The Making of the Atomic Bomb* (New York: Simon and Schuster, 1986), p. 579, regarding Bertrand Goldschmidt's early experiments in plutonium production in the United States.

3. Winston S. Churchill, *Triumph and Tragedy* (Boston: Houghton Mifflin, 1953), pp. 638-40. However, the original idea that the bomb "was perhaps the only grounds which the Japanese had for excusing themselves and thereby saving face" seems to have been argued by Lord Mountbatten in a conversation

with Churchill and others on July 30, 1945. During this conversation Churchill expressed grave moral doubts about the use of the bomb, according to Martin Gilbert's masterly biography, *Never Despair: Winston S. Churchill 1945-1965* (London: Heinemann, 1988), p. 249. Cf. Churchill's own "conventional" arguments about the defeat of Japan, and his adoption of Mountbatten's argument later in a letter to the assistant to Air Chief Marshal Sir Arthur Harris in connection with the controversy on British bombing policy in WWII (see Gilbert, p. 259).

4. Gilbert, *Never Despair*, pp. 156-57. For an American interpretation of British motives in pursuing the bomb under Atlee, see Bundy, *Danger and Survival*, pp. 463-65.

5. Gilbert, *Never Despair*, p. 157.

6. Ian Clark and Nicholas J. Wheeler, *The British Origins of Nuclear Strategy 1945-1955* (London: Oxford University Press, 1989), pp. 4-10. Also, in regard to British deliberations concerning development of their own bomb, see Agatha S. Y. Wong-Fraser, *The Political Utility of Nuclear Weapons: Expectations and Experience* (Washington, D.C.: University Press of America, 1980), pp. 138-48.

7. Clark and Wheeler, *British Origins of Nuclear Strategy*, p. 13.

8. Bundy, *Danger and Survival*, p. 508.

9. Ibid., "and among his [Ben-Gurion's] most important and steadfast supporters in this course were such notable Israelis as the soldier Moshe Dayan, the politician Shimon Peres and the scientific administrator Ernst Bergman." Dayan's early stance is not known, while Peres was at first an appointed official, not an elected politician. Recently, a Peres-inspired version of this list of credits omitted Dayan, at least in regard to the 1950s: See Dan Margalit, "The Name of the Game—No Choice," *Ha'aretz*, October 3, 1990; and cf. Matti Golan, *Peres*, p. 71. Accordingly, Dayan was rather opposed to Israeli-built missiles.

10. B. H. Liddell-Hart, *The Revolution in Warfare* (London: Faber and Faber, 1946).

11. B. H. Liddell-Hart, *Defense of the West* (London: Cassell, 1950).

12. Bernard Brodie, *The Absolute Weapon* (New York: Harcourt Brace, 1946).

13. Clark and Wheeler, *The British Origins of Nuclear Strategy*, pp. 70-71; and cf. official British history, M. Gowing, *Independence and Deterrence: Britain and Atomic Energy, 1945-1952* (London: Macmillan, 1964).

14. G. Herken, *The Winning Weapon: The Atomic Bomb in the Cold War. 1945-1950* (New York: Knopf, 1980), p. 221, quoted in Clark and Wheeler, ibid.

15. Herken, *The Winning Weapon*.

16. Clark and Wheeler, *British Origins of Nuclear Strategy*, p. 71.

17. Ibid., p. 70.

18. See Michael S. Sherry, *The Rise of American Air Power: The Creation of Armageddon* (New Haven and London: Yale University Press, 1987); cf. for a critical discussion of American nuclear strategy in the mid- to late 1980s, see Stephen J. Cimbala, *Nuclear Strategizing: Deterrence and Reality* (New York: Praeger, 1988).

19. Gilbert, *Never Despair*, p. 1010n; and cf. Bundy, *Danger and Survival*, pp. 470-71.

20. See Bundy, ibid., pp. 119-25.

21. Gilbert, *Never Despair*, p. 478; and cf. pp. 689-90, for Churchill's speech before the U. S. Congress on January 17, 1952, in which he stressed the role of the atomic bomb as the "supreme deterrent" against a third world war, and as the "most effective guarantee" of victory in such a war, while warning his audience "not to let go of the atomic weapon until you are sure that other means of preserving peace are in your hands. It is my belief that by accumulating deterrents of all kinds against aggression we shall, in fact, ward off the fearful catastrophes . . . which darken the life and mar the progress of all the peoples of the globe."

22. See Lord Zuckerman, "The Silver Fox, " which is a review of Strobe Talbot's *The Master of the Game: Paul Nitze and the Nuclear Peace*, in *New York Review of Books*, January 19, 1989; and cf. Zuckerman's previous publications in the *NYRB* on the impact of the United States Strategic Bombing Survey (USSBS) on early American nuclear strategic thinking.

23. For a much more detailed history of NSC 68 see Bundy, *Danger and Survival*, pp. 229-30, and his evaluation of President Truman's actual restraint in this regard, p. 231. Also cf. Zuckerman, "The Silver Fox."

24. Bundy, *Danger and Survival*, p. 587.

25. In Gilbert, *Never Despair*, see Churchill' s famous "Fulton" or "Iron Curtain Speech" of March 5, 1946 (pp. 197-203) and his private remarks later that year that the "'Russian Government is like the Roman Church: their people do not question authority . . . We ought not to wait until Russia is ready. I believe it will be eight years before she has these bombs.' His face brightened. 'America knows that fifty-two per cent of Russia's motor industry is in Moscow and could be wiped out by a single bomb. It might mean wiping out three million people, but they would think nothing of that.' He smiled. 'They think more of erasing an historical building like the Kremlin'" (from Lord Moran's diary of August 8, 1946, quoted by Gilbert, p. 258). And for an updated version of Soviet military thinking during the peak years of the cold war, see *Soviet Military Strategy*, edited by Marshal Vassily D. Sokolovsky (New York: Prentice-Hall, 1963). At the same time, as we learn from Gilbert's biography, Churchill perceived the

Russians to be "realists" to the highest degree, and therefore he was always seeking a political agreement, or at least an ongoing dialogue with them (pp. 1010ff), even if such an agreement had to be based on a position of strength, including Britain's own nuclear power.

26. The earliest and probably the best-known Arab nuclearist is the Egyptian Mohamed Hassnein Heikal, whose ideas will be referred to in specific notes below. The Soviet/Chinese-based concept of mass "wars of liberation" in the nuclear age was adopted by the Syrian Ba'ath regime around 1966. The Syrian adoption of this concept was very much inspired by the Algerian struggle for independence against a "nuclear" France, by the lessons drawn from earlier victories of non-nuclear nations such as China, and the growing, contemporary success of the Vietcong in Vietnam.

For the Algerians themselves, see *Al-Gish*, Algiers, March 27, 1968, as translated in *Hazav Daily Collection of Published Arab Information* (HDCI—the Israeli Army's Intelligence Branch translation service from the Arabic, available at the Truman Institute for Peace Research, Hebrew University, Jerusalem, and at the Dayan Center for Middle East Research at Tel-Aviv University). The author, "an Algerian officer," dismissed Japan's capitulation with "all her army intact" with contempt, but his main argument was that the Soviets and the Chinese found ways and means to fight and win against the nuclear West, as Algeria itself did against France. In order to cope with what he termed the Israeli nuclear threat and neutralize it, he argued, the Arabs must unite and produce a counterbomb that would guarantee their victory over Israel, following China's own nuclearization and open-atmosphere testing in 1964. In addition, he called for the mobilization of the Arab conventional might necessary to liquidate the Zionist threat, while underlining the "fanaticism" and the "criminal mind" of those Jews who fought to establish themselves as a separate state in the Arab Middle East. The writer thus gave the Israelis a very high credibility in terms of actually using their nuclear option, even if the Arabs developed their own nuclear weapons—a problem that Heikal, too, was struggling to resolve.

27. Bundy, *Danger and Survival*, p. 255ff.

28. In this regard, see Philip A. G. Sabin, "Shadow or Substance? Perception and Symbolism in Nuclear Force Planning," *Adelphi Papers*, International Institute of Strategic Studies, London, no. 222 (summer 1987).

29. See Thomas C. Schelling, *The Strategy of Conflict* (Cambridge, Mass.: Harvard University Press, 1960); here the 1963 Oxford paperback edition is quoted unless otherwise mentioned. And cf. Schelling's most recent publication in this regard: "The Thirtieth Year," in *Daedalus* (Winter 1991), pp. 21-31, in which he explains his original strategic thinking in relationship to arms control and nuclear proliferation, using a possible nuclear Arab challenge as an example, in the context of the 1973 war. Cf. my different description and analysis of Arab behavior at the time below.

For Kissinger's own contribution to the American nuclear debate at the time, see his *Nuclear Weapons and Foreign Policy* (New York: Anchor, 1957). For Komer's involvement in Schelling's simulation games, see Fred Kaplan, *The Wizards of Armageddon* (New York: Simon and Schuster, 1983), p. 302. For Bundy's reflections on the bomb from the vantage point of his experience and later studies, see his *Danger and Survival*.

30. See Schelling, *Strategy of Conflict*, p. 4, and an earlier criticism in Stephen Maxwell, "Rationality in Deterrence," *Adelphi Papers*, International Institute of Strategic Studies, London, no. 50 (August 1968). And cf. the discussion in Alexander L. George and Richard Smoke, *Deterrence in American Foreign Policy* (New York: Columbia University Press, 1974), pp. 58-83. For a more recent criticism of the deductive and status quo-oriented nature of the theory, see Robert Jervis's "Deterrence Theory Revisited" and his "The Meaning of the Nuclear Revolution."

31. Schelling, *Strategy of Conflict*, 1980 edition, p. 260.

32. See Churchill's March 1954 letter to President Eisenhower with regard to the hydrogen bomb, quoted from Eisenhower's papers in Gilbert, *Never Despair*, pp. 959-60.

33. See Jervis, "Deterrence Theory Revisited," pp. 296-301.

Chapter Three.
The Israeli Paradigm: American Controlled Opacity?

1. Mrs. Ghandi is quoted by Professor Alex Keynan of Hebrew University, Jerusalem, from a Pugwash meeting with her in the mid-1960s in which he participated. India's actual capabilities and nuclear history will be covered briefly in Chapter 13.

2. See "Eretz Israel, history" in *Encyclopaedia Hebraica*, supplementary volume to vols. 1-17, 1967, p. 522. This entry was written by Eliezer Livne, the secretary of a public group that fought the introduction of the bomb into the Middle East in the early 1960s. Livne created a link here between West German interest in the acquisition of nuclear weapons and Israel's relations with Bonn, thereby explaining Israel's troubles with the Soviets, as well as those with the Americans at the time. This link will be discussed in the next chapter.

3. In addition to the sources mentioned above regarding Israel's cooperation with France, see further: Fuad Jabber's *Israel and Nuclear Weapons* (London: Chatto and Windus, 1971), which was based in part on some public information made available by Ernst Bergmann, the "founding father" of the Israeli nuclear complex at Dimona, according to the *Encyclopaedia Hebraica*, supplementary volume to vols. 1-32, 1983, pp. 300-301, and by Yoram Nimrod, an Israeli activist in a far-left antinuclear group who adopted a strategy of exposing

Israel's nuclear capability and then denying its military significance. Cf. Sylvia K. Crosby, *A Tacit Alliance* (Princeton, N.J.: Princeton University Press, 1974).

4. See Pierre Pean, *Les Deux Bombes* (Paris: Arthem Fayard, 1982), p. 60ff, 82; and cf. Georges-Henri Soutou, "Die Nuklearpolitik der Vierten Republik," in *Vierteljahreshefte für Zeitgeschichte*, 4 (1989), pp. 606-10; and see sources cited in Chapter 1, note 15.

5. See Jean Francis Perrin, as quoted in the *Sunday Times*, London, October 5, 1986; and cf. Pean, *Les Deux Bombes*, pp. 76, 83.

6. Yitzhak Ben-Aharon. Interview with the author, Tel Aviv, Israel, June 1989.

7. Since the terms under which heavy water was supplied by the U.S. to France, and some to Israel, specified that it be for peaceful use only, and allowed for American verification of its use, the U.S. might have been seen to have a direct legal claim against Israel. (See Frank Barnaby, *The Invisible Bomb*, pp. 9-10.) This may explain the great effort invested by the Wisconsin Arms Control lawyer Gary Milhollin in studying this specific issue; see his "Heavy Water Cheaters" in *Foreign Policy*, no. 69 (Winter 1987).

8. Pean, *Les Deux Bombes*.

9. Ibid., pp. 38-39.

10. *Foreign Relations of the United States*, vols. XIV and XV (Washington, D.C.: U.S. Government Printing Office, 1989).

11. The Western powers, Great Britain included, imposed a rather effective embargo on arms deliveries to all the nations involved following Israel's declaration of independence in 1948 and the ensuing Arab invasion. However, at that juncture Israel had very little in the way of medium and heavy equipment; the Arab armies were regular forces of semi-independent states, most of which were equipped by the British. In response to British advice and in accordance with his own interests, King Abdulla of Jordan refrained from sending his Arab Legion to invade the territory allotted to Israel in the 1947 U.N. partition plan, but he did lay siege to Jewish Jerusalem, which—as a part of an international zone—was outside the jurisdiction of both Israel and Jordan.

Israel was able to purchase large quantities of modern arms (mostly made for the *Wehrmacht*) from Czechoslovakia and fly them to the front using American chartered planes and crews, with Truman's knowledge and Soviet permission. The sources for the information can be found in the U.S. National Archives, CIA files pertaining to the Middle East.

12. See as a background analysis in this regard, Bernard Lewis, *The Political Language of Islam* (Chicago: University of Chicago Press, 1988), and Lewis' *Semites and Anti-Semites* (New York: W. W. Norton, 1986).

13. McGeorge Bundy, *Danger and Survival*, p. 508.

14. This issue is too sensitive to be mentioned here without references: See Bernard Lewis, *Semites and Anti-Semites* (New York: W. W. Norton, 1986), p. 140ff, and cf. *Staatsmänner und Diplomaten bei Hitler*, Hrsg. u. erl. von Andreas Hillgruber (Frankfurt/Main: Bernard & Graefe Verlag für Wehrwesen, 1967), pp. 662-67, regarding Hitler's meetings with Haj Amin; and cf. Hitler's own remarks following his meeting with Haj Amin in *Adolf Hitler: Monologe im Führerhauptquartier 1941-1944*, hers. von Werner Jochman (Hamburg: Die Aufzeichnungen Heinrich Heims, 1980), p. 187.

15. For an in-depth discussion of the "triple trap" see Shlomo Aronson, "Die Dreiface Falle: Hitler's Judenpolitik, die Alliierten und die Juden" in *Vierteljahreshefte für Zeitgeschichte*, 1 (1984), pp. 29-65; and cf. my English summary of the same argument, "Nazi Terrorism: The Complete Trap and the 'Final Solution'" in *The Morality of Terrorism: Religious and Secular Justifications*, edited by David C. Rapoport and Yona Alexander (New York: Pergamon Policy Studies, pp. 169-85), or second edition (New York: Columbia University Press, 1989).

16. American (and British) raw intelligence reports and analyses from occupied Europe and the Middle East during WWII and "expert opinions" related to them recently released by the U.S. National Archives in Washington, D.C., and in Suitland, Maryland, are very enlightening here (OSS SI [Secret Intelligence] and R&A [Research and Analysis], U.S. Army G-2 and Counter-Intelligence Corps, and British ISLD, MI5 and SIS or MI6 reports, delivered to American agencies). And see Martin Gilbert's *Auschwitz and the Allies* (New York: Holt, Rinehart and Winston, 1981), Bernard Wasserstein's *Britain and the Jews of Europe 1939-1945* (London: Clarendon, 1979), and David Wyman's *The Abandonment of the Jews* (New York: Pantheon, 1984). The most recent research was published in London by Tony Kushner, *The Power of Prejudices: Antisemitism in the British Society During WWII* (London: Manchester University Press, 1988).

17. Ben-Gurion's *War Diaries 1948-1949*; see entry about meeting on November 27, 1948, with front and brigade commanders (p. 853).

18. Ibid., pp. 964-65.

19. Ibid., p. 964.

20. Ibid., p. 902.

21. See *The Diaries of Moshe Sharett* (Tel Aviv: Ma'ariv Publishers, 1977), p. 400; I have also used notes from Professor Israel Dostrovsky's presentation "David Ben-Gurion and the Development of Science in Israel" held at the National Academy of Sciences, Jerusalem, April 23, 1987. Also cf. *United Nations Study on Israeli Nuclear Armament* (New York: United Nations, 1987); and Roger F. Pajak, *Nuclear Proliferation in the Middle East* (Washington, D.C.: National Defense University, 1982).

22. Ben-Gurion, *War Diaries 1948-1949*, pp. 902-3, 964-65.

23. There are many published Arab sources in this respect; some based on Jabber's and Nimrod's publications (see note 3, above), others based on Simcha Flapan. In fact, however, all press organs in the Arab world published historical and actual evaluations of the Israeli nuclear efforts much before the publication of Jabber's work, in which they referred to Ben-Gurion's initiative as early as 1948. See, among many other examples, HDCI translations from *Al-Manar*, Jordan, January 3, 1966; PLO Radio Cairo, December 27, 1965; *Al-Gumhuria*, Cairo, May 5, 1965; *Al-Hayat*, Beirut, May 10, 1965; Baghdad Radio, March 13, 1966.

24. See, for example, Mohammed Hassnein Heikal, "The Bomb," in *Al-Ahram*, Cairo, November 23, 1973, which was inspired among other things by Mr. Jabber's earlier visit to Egypt and the latter's discussion with Heikal of Schelling's theories and terminology; and cf. Heikal's series of articles: "The Israeli Nuclear Threat" in *Al-Rai*, Amman, and *Al-Nahar*, Beirut, June 12, 15, and 19, 1977.

25. See Ephraim Inbar, "Israel and Nuclear Weapons Since October 1973," in *Security and Armaggedon: Israel's Nuclear Strategy*, edited by Louis René Beres (Lexington, Mass.: Lexington Books, D.C. Heath, 1986), pp. 61-78. Inbar is a product of the Wohlstetter school, which adopted nuclear nonproliferation for others (especially Israel) after contributing to the massive nuclear rearmament of the U.S. itself. An American-inspired "moral" view is expressed in Beres' collection, which was intended to fight Shai Feldman's advocacy of open nuclearization for Israel, by Avner Cohen; cf. Cohen's changed views in this regard in the Hebrew collection of which he is editor, *Humanity Under the Shadow of the Atom* (Tel Aviv: Hakibbutz Hameuchad, 1988). Barnaby, who in turn used Inbar and Cohen extensively and almost exclusively, for his own purposes in rendering Israel's nuclear options ineffective or at least highly questionable, was not aware of Cohen's Hebrew collection.

26. See Pierre Gallois, *The Balance of Terror*.

27. The most recent research on Israeli missiles is contained in Seth Caruss's *Ballistic Missiles in the Third World* (Washington, D.C.: Center for Strategic and International Studies, October 1990); and cf. *Ma'ariv* report in this regard, October 25, 1990.

28. See Matti Golan, *Peres*, p. 53.

Chapter Four. American Intervention

1. For sources related to the nuclear cooperation between France and Israel, see Chapter 1, note 15. Also, see William Bader, *The United States and the Spread of Nuclear Weapons* (New York: Pegasus Press, 1968), which is the first American study to discuss the Israeli nuclear option and explain the French connection in some detail, correctly in my view.

2. See Hans-Peter Schwarz, "Adnauer und die Kernwaffen, " in *Viertel-jahreshefte für Zeitgeschichte*, 4 (1989), pp. 567-93; and cf. Ben-Gurion's 1958 diaries, especially the entry made on March 11, 1958, regarding a possible secret meeting between him and the German defense minister Strauss, and a later meeting between BG's deputy Peres and the Italian minister of defense; and cf. Newhouse, *War and Peace in the Nuclear Age*.

3. Schwarz, ibid., p. 576.

4. See Pierre Pean, *Les Deux Bombes*, p. 64.

5. Ibid., p. 65.

6. See Michael Bar-Zohar, *Ben Gurion*, in which the uranium supply is mentioned as the main problem (vol. III, p. 1373). Cf. a similar formulation in Matti Golan, *Peres*, p. 100. For my interpretation, see Jean Francis Perrin, as quoted in the *Sunday Times*, London, October 5, 1986, and Pean, *Les Deux Bombes*, pp. 127-28, 133-38.

7. In his *Israel and Nuclear Weapons*, Fuad Jabber (following Flapan's earlier arguments in this regard) creates the impression that the IAEC had a united anti-bomb motive for resigning. The real diversity of opinion—including the issue of basic vs. applied research, the use of financial resources, the problems of control and influence, and as usual, personality differences—is mentioned, but not fully spelled out, in a letter from the IAEC members to Ben-Gurion dated February 17, 1958 (according to testimony of Professor Shmuel Sambursky, first director of the Israeli Council of Science and member of the IAEC, to the author, June 3, 1989). According to the original letter of resignation, dated February 17, 1958, made available to the author by Sambursky, the IAEC was established in 1952, and although it had not met since 1956, "things were allegedly done in the name of the IAEC, which in fact did not exist, without the Israeli scientists who were close to the profession participating in the planning, if such planning existed." The signatories were Franz Ohlendorf of the Haifa Technical University, The Technion; Israel Dostrovsky of the Weizmann Institute; his colleagues S. G. Cohen, Zvi Lipkin, and Yigal Talmi; and Julio Rackach and Shmuel Sambursky of Hebrew University. Amos de-Shalit of the Weizmann Institute had already resigned, according to the letter.

8. See Agatha S. Y. Wong-Fraser, *The Political Utility of Nuclear Weapons*, pp. 140-41.

9. Crossman to Professor Dan Horowitz of Hebrew University; and Efraim Evron (Israel's ambassador in London, later minister and ambassador in the U.S.), testimony to the author, June 1989; and cf. Peres' interview with *Ma'ariv Weekly Journal*, August 1, 1988: "the whole academic community was against the Dimona reactor."

10. John Newhouse, *War and Peace in the Nuclear Age*, pp. 131-32; and cf.

Catherine McArdle Kelleher's *Germany and the Politics of Nuclear Weapons* (New York: Columbia University Press, 1975), whose view of the Franco-Italian-German consortium at that time is that it had not reached maturation in regard to nuclear matters when General de Gaulle took over and promptly killed it.

11. Schwarz, "Adenauer und die Kernwaffen", pp. 578-83.

12. Bar-Zohar, *Ben-Gurion*, p. 1357.

13. Ben-Gurion's diary, entry made on August 24, 1954.

14. Yair Zaban. Interview with the author, Jerusalem, Israel, November 1991. Zaban, one of the leading pro-Moscow leftist politicians at the time, verbally confirmed this picture in my interview with him. In the early 1960s, Zaban was secretary to the late Dr. Moshe Sne, a leftist turned Communist, who volunteered his aid to Prime Minister Eshkol in 1963, according to Zaban, in order to "calm the Russians down in regard to the nuclear issue."

15. Yigal Allon, *A Curtain of Sand* (Tel Aviv: Hakibbutz Hameuchad, 1959); and cf. 1968 edition, quoted later in the text.

16. Former minister Yitzhak Ben-Aharon. Interview with the author, June 16, 1989. The published information is contained in the *Encyclopaedia Hebraica*, pp. 676-77, entry "Ben-Gurion, David," which was written by yet another opponent of the nuclear project, Isiah Leibowitz, a political ally of Eliezer Livne. It should be noted here that the Manhattan Project itself was first financed from a special presidential fund in order to deliberately bypass Congress. See William Lawren's biography of General Leslie R. Groves (director of the Manhattan Project), *The General and the Bomb*, p. 26.

17. The minority was comprised of Ben-Aharon, Bar-Yehuda, and Barzilai of both left-wing parties, according to the author's interview with Ben-Aharon (see preceding note).

18. And see Yigal Allon, *Contriving Warfare*, with an introduction by Yitzhak Rabin (Tel Aviv: Hakibbutz Hameuchad Press), 1990, pp. 190-209.

19. Mrs. Meir's rivalry with Peres is described in a pro-Peres fashion by Bar-Zohar, *Ben-Gurion*, pp. 1373, 1389, 1481, 1497; and cf. Golan, *Peres*, pp. 90-92. Both lead the reader to the conclusion that Mrs. Meir was against the nuclear option and Peres' efforts to develop military ties with Bonn. An anti-Peres version is offered by former minister and Mapai's secretary general Yosef Almogi in *The Struggle Over Ben-Gurion* (Tel Aviv: Edanim, 1988), and by Isser Harel, director of Israel's Intelligence Services at the time and a political ally of Mrs. Meir's, in his *Crisis of the German Scientists 1962-1963* (Tel Aviv: Ma'ariv, 1982), pp. 182-87, and in his *Security and Democracy*, Yediot Aharonot edition (Tel Aviv: Edanim, 1989). In these sources the reader is led to the conclusion that Mrs. Meir was against Peres' methods and his personal traits, rather than against the nuclear option, but that she indeed feared serious trouble with the

U.S. due to Peres' handling of the issues. The main point may have been Peres' rather open talk on these matters and his exclusive control over them, which included personal intrigues against those who "invaded" his territory. The German complex was related to domestic resentment of the Jerusalem-Bonn ties. Harel supported this impression in so many words in an interview I conducted with him in 1988, which was further substantiated by ambassador Efraim Evron, who is not Harel's political or personal friend, in my interview with him.

20. See Golan, *Peres*, pp. 75-79; accordingly, Peres was contemplating "border changes" in the period between 1958 and 1959, mainly in the north, to secure water resources. In view of the relative decline of the Arab challenge and the major French and German breakthroughs achieved by Israel at the time, Golan describes Peres' behavior at the time as being conducted in "certain loss of senses."

21. Originally sent by Chancery at Tel Aviv to Levant Department as doc. no. (1192/59), VR 1241/1. Archival source: Public Record Office, Fo371/142379 tc169410; and see attached department minutes in regard to Peres and his "influence on Ben-Gurion," to decisions pertaining to future follow-up, and to copies sent to other relevant agencies. The original message was related to another letter from London to Washington regarding "Israel's efforts to buy uranium."

22. Bergmann was reported to have suddenly displayed, at international conferences, knowledge in nuclear physics that was unrelated to his actual field of research; this was brought to the attention of the American authorities.

According to Professor Horowitz, quoting British Labour leader Richard Crossman, Peres apparently spoke to Crossman quite openly about Dimona. A rather frightened Crossman informed his Israeli friends, mostly leftists and/or Peres' personal enemies, about it.

Crossman also uncovered the Strauss-Chaban-Delmas agreement of 1958; see Newhouse, *War and Peace in the Nuclear Age*, p.132.

23. See Yoram Nimrod, "Nuclear Fog and Arab Response," *Davar*, December 2, 1980. Mr. Nimrod was mentioned above as an antinuclear activist, who followed Flapan in blaming Israel for the plight of the 1948 Palestinian refugees; he also followed Flapan's lead in the antinuclear campaign by exposing Israel's nuclear efforts and then obscuring or dismissing them as dangerous and useless, both on his own and by quoting Mr. Allon.

Simcha Flapan tells us that the "opponents of the nuclear deterrence approach" were numerous, and that the issue transcended traditional party lines; see Flapan, "Nuclear Disarmament in the Middle East," in *Humanity Under the Shadow of the Bomb*, ed. by Avner Cohen, pp. 194-204. He counts among them the leaders of the two leftist parties, Galili, Allon, Hazan, and Barzily, and several other politicians, among them Abba Eban of Mapai. Flapan also gives us some details on the antinuclear committee, whose secretary was

Eliezer Livne, a controversial ex-member of Mapai and later an exponent of the most aggressive Israeli expansion into the West Bank. Another activist in the committee was Isaiah Leibowitz of Hebrew University, a controversial figure and an obsessive opponent of Ben-Gurion's at the time, who later dropped the nuclear issue in favor of extreme criticism of Israel's occupation of the West Bank. Other members, according to Flapan, were people of such caliber as Gerhard Scholem and Martin Buber, as well as several Hebrew University professors who were also embroiled in the Lavon Affair, such as S. N. Eisenstadt and E. E. Urbach.

24. Bar-Zohar, *Ben-Gurion*, pp. 1522-23.

25. Professor Shmuel Sambursky. Interview with the author, 1989.

26. See volume 7 of the *Diaries of Moshe Sharett*. Years later, one of Lavon's staunchest supporters, Professor Dan Horowitz of Hebrew University (who was at the time political correspondent for *Davar*), confirmed knowledge of Lavon's unauthorized radical schemes in other various cases against Arab countries; but he still believes that Lavon was not involved in the Egyptian debacle. He added that the case seemed politically useful for fighting Ben-Gurion, Dayan, and Peres.

27. Regarding the nuclear—or the hidden—aspect of the Lavon Affair, see Haggai Eshed, *Who Gave the Order*, Yediot Aharonot edition (Jerusalem: Edanim, 1982) p. 284. According to Eshed, who helped Ben-Gurion in his inquiries into the Egyptian affair and was close to Peres: "The construction of the reactor in Dimona caused strong opposition in Mapai's leadership. The storm gathered in October, 1957 immediately following the signing of the agreement with France . . . and it gathered unparalleled sharp momentum afterwards . . . Some see in it the main . . . motive behind the "affair" and the war of succession in Mapai which took place in combination with and in parallel to each other. It [the nuclear issue] also united former political adversaries into a broad united front . . . against Ben-Gurion." Other sources, such as Efraim Evron, Lavon's closest aide during the 1960 "affair," deny this categorically, as an ex-post-facto rationalization of a pure power struggle.

28. Livne and Leibowitz were spreading rumors to journalists about "Dimona's ruins" when the official Israeli-French connection was going to be terminated. One of these journalists was Dan Margalit of *Ha'aretz*, according to his disclosures to the author. At the time, Margalit was a reporter for the sensationalist, anti-Ben-Gurion weekly *Haolam Haze*. Margalit, in his own words, did not publish anything, because he did not grasp the significance of the information.

29. In addition to Harel's version (see note 19, this chapter), there is an authoritative published version of the secret Israeli-American-Egyptian talks and the inner-American deliberations with regard to Dimona and the Egyptian missiles in Mordechai Gazit's *President Kennedy's Policy Toward the Arab*

States and Israel (Tel Aviv: The Shiloah Center for Middle East and African Studies, Tel-Aviv University, 1983). This source is partially based on resources in U.S. presidential libraries. Mr. Gazit was a close aide to Foreign Minister Meir in the 1960s and served in the Israeli Embassy in Washington during the period covered in his book. He was later director general of Prime Minister Meir's Office. However, Gazit's version must be compared to the original American primary sources, and to a more recent study based on various American primary sources and oral history collections; see Beat Bumbacher, *Die USA und Nasser: Amerikanische Aegypten-Politik der Kennedy und Johnson Administration 1961-1967* (Wiesbaden: Steiner, 1987).

30. Golan, *Peres*, p. 71.

31. Ibid., p. 74.

32. Ibid., p. 102.

33. Ibid.

34. Pean, *Les Duex Bombes*, pp. 113-21. Perrin's testimony to the London *Sunday Times*, op. cit., is less explicit.

35. Pean, *Les Duex Bombes*, pp. 140-41.

36. Herbert Krosney and Steve Weismann, *The Islamic Bomb* (New York: The New York Times Book Co.; Hebrew translation, Jerusalem: Adam and Castel Communications, 1982), p. 111.

37. Pean, *Les Deux Bombes*, p. 120. Cf. Barnaby, *The Invisible Bomb*, p. 31. In a March 11, 1989, State Department draft prepared in anticipation of press inquiries regarding Vanunu's revelations (partially censored), we find a very definite American view of de Gaulle's behavior based on Perrin "that Israel and France had actually cooperated on developing atomic weapons for two years [1957-1959]. In 1959 General de Gaulle stopped cooperation on nuclear weapons with Israel, *but allowed the completion of the reprocessing plant which gave Israel the ability to extract plutonium* . . . [italics added]." See State Department briefing paper dated Nov. 18, 1986, "Israeli Nuclear Issues," National Security Archive, Washington, D.C., catalogue #9049.

38. Pean, *Les Deux Bombes*, pp. 123-40.

39. For secondary American sources, see *The New York Times* as early as 1966, *Time* magazine in 1976 (quoted below), and Robert E. Harkavy's *Spectre for a Middle East Holocaust: The Strategic and Diplomatic Implications of the Israeli Nuclear Weapons Program*. Monograph Series in World Affairs, vol. 14 (4), Denver, Colorado, 1977.

40. Bar-Zohar, *Ben-Gurion*, p. 1357.

41. See William Bader, *The United States and the Spread of Nuclear Weapons*,

chapter 3; and cf. McGeorge Bundy, *Danger and Survival*, and Newhouse, *War and Peace in the Nuclear Age*.

42. For details of the McMahon Act and its amended version, allowing aid to those who "joined the club" on their own, see Kohl, *French Nuclear Diplomacy*, pp. 106-7.

43. Kohl, ibid., pp. 112-13; and cf. Bundy, *Danger and Survival*, p. 489ff, which tells us the story of the origin of MLF (multilateral force), when Kennedy "came to office opposed to the spread of national nuclear forces"; Bundy then later describes the development of the British-American relations, leading to the sale of Polaris missiles to the former, and General de Gaulle's sharp reaction to this later on. One could speculate, without any evidence to prove it—except for Pean's assertion that de Gaulle was involved in developing missiles for Israel—that the general was repeating here his own method of "sharing" with Israel, that is, he felt discriminated against by the Anglo-American sharing agreement in regard to the Polaris missiles.

44. Kohl, *French Nuclear Diplomacy*, p. 113.

45. Regarding this formulation, see also Bar-Zohar, *Ben-Gurion*, p. 1373.

46. *Divrey Haknesset* [proceedings of the Knesset], December 21, 1960.

47. Gazit, *President Kennedy's Policy Toward Arab States and Israel*, p. 40.

48. The main Israeli published source for this is Gazit, ibid., p. 39, in addition to Bar-Zohar, *Ben-Gurion*, p. 1393ff and Golan, *Peres*, p. 123ff.

49. Gazit, *President Kennedy's Policy*, pp. 49-56.

50. Department of State, "Memorandum of Conversation Between President Kennedy and Mrs. Meir, Foreign Minister of Israel," May 8, 1963, JFK Library, NSCF, box 119, quoted by Gazit, ibid., p. 52n.

51. Bundy, *Danger and Survival*, p. 510.

52. See details in Gazit, *President Kennedy's Policy*, based on records contained in JFK Library, POF, box 119A, folder 9; and cf. Bumbacher, *Die USA und Nasser*, pp. 58-59.

53. Pean, *Les Duex Bombes*, pp. 104-7.

54. Pean, ibid., pp. 117-18; and cf. the data in the British *Sunday Times*, October 5, 1986, based on Vanunu's photographs and his oral testimonies, and also those made with much more detail (which explains his heavy punishment in Israel) to Barnaby. The latter contained information about the chemical and technical processes of building nuclear and thermonuclear weapons (as Barnaby interpreted them) and the exact location of each piece of equipment, its way of operation, the treatment of nuclear waste, and more. The disclosure of this kind

of information might make Dimona more vulnerable to precision attacks, among other things; such information is regarded as secret by every nuclear nation. Barnaby, however, could not resist the temptation of using Vanunu as a possible "tool" of the Israeli government in making Dimona's potential known. See Barnaby, *The Invisible Bomb*, pp. ix-xi.

55. Isser Harel. Interview with the author, 1988; confirmed by Ambassador Efraim Evron, June 1989.

56. According to Hanan Bar-On, Israeli minister in Washington, when interviewed by the author on March 11, 1978: "The trouble was that the Syrians had never read Schelling and Kahn, and Rabin's signals aimed at deterring them were perceived in Damascus as arrogant provocations and direct threats." According to Fred Kaplan in *The Wizards of Armageddon*, pp. 334-35, Schelling himself was "stumped" when faced with "a real life" problem of signalling to the North Vietnamese in 1964 (but his, and Kahn's, theory of signalling was implemented anyway by the "whiz kids" in Kennedy's and Johnson's administrations, who usually opposed nuclear proliferation by using conventional means).

57. Bar-Zohar, *Ben-Gurion*, pp. 1522-23.

58. Yair Evron, *Israel's Nuclear Dilemma*, p. 17. Evron quoted "publications abroad" as his source in this regard, but according to his note 12a, his foreign sources were his own article in *Orbis*, "Israel: The Uses and Misuses of Ambiguity" (Winter 1974), p.22. I have added to this published source an oral testimony by former minister Yitzhak Ben-Aharon, whose opinion was very close to Allon's in rejecting the nuclear option as totally valueless, if not self-defeating, from Israel's viewpoint.

59. Yair Evron, *Israel's Nuclear Dilemma*, ibid.

60. Yitzhak Ben-Aharon. Interview with the author, June 15, 1989.

61. Yair Evron, *Israel's Nuclear Dilemma*, p. 18.

62. See Michael R. Beschloss, *The Crisis Years: Kennedy and Khrushchev 1960-1963* (New York: HarperCollins, 1991), p. 574.

63. Confidential, LBJ Library NSF (National Security File), Committee on Nuclear Proliferation, containers 1-2, problem 2.

64. See U.S. Department of State, *Foreign Relations of the United States 1955-1957*, The Arab-Israeli Dispute, vols. XIV-XV (Washington, D.C.: Government Printing Office, 1989).

65. Assistant Secretary of State Phillips Talbot to Secretary Rusk (top secret, sanitized), May 14, 1963, subject: "Arms Limitations in the Near East, including summary of recommendations by a working group which had studied the par-

ties, their interests and past experience under the direction of State's Middle East men including CIA and ACDA representatives," JFK Library, NSF, box 119.

66. See Amembassy [American Embassy] Tel Aviv #724 of April 4, 1963, to Secretary of State (two parts, two documents), confidential, JFK Library NSF, box 119, summary of meeting between Ambassador Barbour and Ben-Gurion, especially sections related to Arab refugee issue; BG said that "Israel no longer asks recognition of its existence by Arabs as precondition" for allowing Arab refugees to return to her territory, but "an agreement on refugee operation" with Arabs must conclude this issue for good, including in U.N and the media. "I interjected that direct 'agreement' between parties not possible. What may be possible is understanding between Israel and US and between Arabs and US." BG agreed, stressing that "the main question" was the number of the refugees returning, and added that in his recent talks with Kennedy "we understood each other that most refugees must go to Arab countries." BG then returned to the security situation in the area, and said that "Arabs virulently anti-Israel . . . if Nasser should break Israel's Air Force, war would be over in two days. Both Eisenhower and de Gaulle 'had agreed it may be too late' for them to come to her aid on time . . . In two years, when he [Nasser] has missiles, he will [be] strong enough to attack." Cf. further Embtel [Embassy telegram] Tel Aviv # A-675 of May 1, 1963, regarding Israeli views of Kennedy's Middle East policy, which included favorable assurances about maintaining military balance of power in the region; however, the Peres-Meir rivalry was clear to the embassy (in terms of who secured what from Kennedy and thus was better suited to succeed BG), and whether the president had warned BG not to intervene in Jordan (at the time King Hussein had serious domestic troubles with pro-Nasserite elements that would soon produce a demand that the West Bank be demilitarized if the Hashemite regime was to disappear). Yet the main point in this Embtel was a lengthy summary of General Dayan's (at the time minister of agriculture) article in the right-wing daily *Ma'ariv*, published on April 12, 1963. In that article Dayan argued publicly, in connection with Egypt's missile program, that "no army had yet supplied itself with ground-to-ground missiles in order to arm them solely with conventional warheads . . . the UAR is either developing or will develop nuclear warheads . . . [which] would suit Nasser's ambitions in two ways: eliminating Israel and establishing his hegemony over an Arab bloc from the Atlantic to the Indian oceans [sic]. Israel must diligently develop these [missiles plus conventional and nuclear warheads, spelled out in the article] . . . so that it will not lag behind." Then followed Kennedy's answer to a letter sent earlier by BG, dated April 26—Deptel (Department telegram) 59-52 of 4-26-63— suggesting US-USSR joint guarantee to Middle East security issue, which BG did not accept as "very favorable." Embtel 833, May 5, 1963, to Secretary of State (secret, eyes only, JFK Library as above), signed by ambassador Barbour.

67. For the internal deliberations regarding McCloy's visit, and how to package it publicly in order to maintain secrecy, see JFK Library, ibid.

68. See Gazit, *President Kennedy's Policy*, p. 52n.

69. Bumbacher, *Die USA und Nasser*, pp. 58-59. A comparison of the original documents at the JFK Library could lead us to both interpretations, as many parts of Ambassador Badeau's reports to the Secretary of State in McCloy's name were censored; see Embtels #2470 and #2491, Amembassy Cairo, June 28 and June 30, 1963 (secret, eyes only, JFK Library, NSF. UAR/Israel Arms Limitations, box 159), in which Nasser was first reported to have asked for more time to consult with his army chief of staff Marshal Amer, who was abroad at the time. Then Nasser was reported to have been disinterested in McCloy's offer to supply Egypt with nuclear reactors for peaceful use (if he made concessions in regard to his unconventional efforts). In response to McCloy's own—not very wise—suggestion that Nasser might have been "a little suspicious of the Americans," Nasser said that "he had 'a little more than a little suspicion'" that the U.S. was too favorably disposed to Israel, having accused Israel of aggression since 1952 and the West of refusing to sell him arms. McCloy concluded that "the main motivation of his attitude toward our proposal was based on political sensitivities as he sensed them both in Egypt and in the Arab countries. Sheer military considerations were not the main factors." And cf. Deptel #19 to Athens, Greece, of July 3, 1963, concurring with McCloy's own recommendation "not visit Israel now pending consultation Washington," signed Rusk (JFK Library, NSF, UAR/Israel Arms Limitations, box 159). BG had resigned on June 16, 1963.

70. Gazit, *President Kennedy's Policy*, pp. 116-20: CIA Memorandum dated March 6, 1963, "Consequences of Israeli Acquisition of Nuclear Capability," Office of National Estimates, Memorandum to the Director, signed by Sherman Kent, Chairman (secret), esp. pp. 119-20.

71. See, for example, incoming telegram, Amembassy London, #21619, March, 28, 1963, signed by Ambassador David Bruce, regarding Israeli ambassador meeting with British Lord Privy Seal (Edward Heath), concerning "UAR rocket capability," confidential, JFK Library, NSF, box 119.

72. See former ambassador John S. Badeau, Oral History Interview, February 25, 1969, for JFK Library; and cf. Isser Harel, *The Crisis of the German Scientists*, pp. 71-76, regarding "new evaluation" presented by the Israeli Military Intelligence to Prime Minister Ben-Gurion.

73. See Harel, ibid., p. 77.

74. Ibid.

75. Memorandum for Record, conversation between Robert W. Komer, NSC, and Israeli Minister Mordechai Gazit, May 15, 1963, JFK Library, NSF, box 119, secret. In response to Komer's suggestions, as quoted above, "Gazit grinned."

76. Bar-Zohar, *Ben-Gurion*, p. 1506.

77. Ibid., p. 1554.

78. In this connection one could examine—which is impossible to do on the Israeli side—the inquiry results of the U.S. Nuclear Regulatory Commission and the related documentation beginning with a memorandum from the director, Thomas McTiernan, to Chairmen Hendrie of February 17, 1978, and the related Congressional activities, and CIA, FBI, and other agencies' documentation (some of which remained classified or censored), regarding the possible diversion or theft of highly enriched uranium from NUMEC, a nuclear enrichment facility at Apollo, Pennsylvania. This "diversion" became known in 1965 and might have started earlier in the 1960s. Israel was mentioned in these partially public and partially "secret/sensitive" documents as the target country of the diverted uranium.

79. Ambassador Efraim Evron's interview with the author.

80. Embtel #55 of June 27, 1963, to Secretary of State, unclassified, JFK Library, NSF, box 119.

Chapter Five. The 1967 War

1. Mordechai Gazit, *President Kennedy's Policy Toward the Arab States and Israel*, p. 54. The document itself, writes Gazit, is still classified: "What Kennedy wrote was, in essence, what he had said to Minister Meir in December 1962 and what Under-Secretary Harriman told [a] delegation of American Jews in May 1963, namely that the United States would militarily assist Israel in case of attack."

2. In public, Kennedy repeated the text of "the old and discredited 1950 U.S.-U.K.-France declaration," as Gazit puts it (ibid., p. 47), that "in the event of aggression or preparation for aggression . . . we would support appropriate measures in the United Nations, adopt other courses of action on our own to put a stop to such aggression." Cf. *Documents on American Foreign Relations*, edited by Richard Stebbins (New York: Simon and Schuster, 1963), doc. 68 (b), p. 268. And cf. relevant JFK Library files, NSF, Israel, box 119, which discuss in detail the legal meaning and possible effects of executive agreements with foreign countries, especially in regard to Israel.

3. This point is important in order to understand Barnaby's historical confusion about Israel's motives in regard to a nuclear option, which he explains in terms of the American weapons embargo on Israel following the Suez War of 1956 (*The Invisible Bomb*, p. 6). In fact the U.S. never "cut-off its arms supplies to Israel" at that time because it had not yet supplied any arms to Israel, but only did so later, "thanks" to this option.

4. Letter from Eugene Rostow, at the time professor of law at Yale Uni-

versity, to the author regarding President Johnson, October 14, 1976; and according to testimony by Ambassador Evron to the author, June 1, 1989, which fully concurs with the primary sources cited below, Johnson refused even to see his own emissary McCloy before he departed for his second mission on disarmament talks in Egypt.

5. See Moshe Dayan, "Germany, Dimona and the Jordan," *Ha'aretz*, March 26, 1965. Cf. the *New York Times* report on Dayan's article, March 27, 1965.

6. Bar-Zohar, *Ben-Gurion*, p. 1550.

7. Ibid.; and cf. "Memorandum for Record by R. W. Komer, Luncheon with Israeli Minister Gazit, 23 September 1963," dated September 24, 1963 (secret), JFK Library, NSC files, Israel, box 119. In this meeting Gazit said "he hoped we would make appropriate reference to BG's deeply felt desire to provide for long-term 'survival' of the Jewish people in a home in Israel before he [BG] died . . . he [Gazit] thought it important we express agreement in principle to, or at least willingness to discuss, demilitarization of the West Bank should a change of regime occur in Jordan."

8. Yuval Ne'eman, "Why I Resigned from the Defense Ministry, " *Ha'aretz*, February 6, 1976. In the article, Ne'eman explained his 1976 resignation as special adviser to Mr. Peres, who was then minister of defense, as being because Peres failed to embark upon a missile program capable of launching Israel's own intelligence satellite. Later, Ne'eman helped to found the nationalist Tehiya party and served under Begin as minister of science from 1981.

9. Pierre Pean, *Les Deux Bombes*, pp. 140-41; Pean cites in this respect American press disclosures as well.

10. "Meeting, Ministry of Defense, Gen. E. Weizmann, and Gen. Toufanian of Iran, " record #37193, nonproliferation catalogue, National Security Archive (a private declassification institute), Washington, D.C. This source is from U.S. intelligence reports captured by the Iranians in the U.S. Embassy following Khomeini's ascendance; the very existence of such documents in American hands could mean that either side provided them, or that the Americans had other means to obtain them.

11. The impact of the Egyptian launching on Ben-Gurion, Peres, and other security people is vividly described by Isser Harel, in his *Crisis of the German Scientists 1962-1963*, pp. 14-19. Harel accused Peres of having responded to the Egyptian launching ahead of it by improvising a makeshift Israeli missile, "Shavit 2, " which was nothing serious, but whose firing created the impression that Israel was the first to introduce missiles to the area.

12. See Steven E. Gray in *Aviation Week*, May 10, 1989; and cf. Steven E. Gray, "Israeli Missile Capabilities: A Few Numbers to Think About, " October 7, 1988 (Lawrence Livermore Laboratory/Z Division); and cf. further *London*

Times, September 16, 1989; *IISS Annual Report,* October 6, 1989; and the CIA-originated NBC stories on Israeli-South African missile cooperation, broadcast late in October 1989. For more updated versions, see Leonard S. Spector, *Nuclear Ambitions: The Spread of Nuclear Weapons 1989-1990* (Boulder, Colo.: Westview Press, 1990), p. 20, and pp. 161-64, and Seth Carus, *Ballistic Missiles in the Third World* (Washington, D.C.: Georgetown University Center for Strategic Studies, 1990), pp. 20, 32, 46.

13. See Pean, *Les Deux Bombes,* p. 143.

14. The memoranda, dated March 13 and 14, 1964, was titled "Tanks for Israel." Archival source: LBJ Library, NSC File, McGeorge Bundy, container 1, item 33c.

15. Regarding earlier estimates of Israel's nuclear and missile capabilities, see Peter Pry's *Israel's Nuclear Arsenal* (Boulder, Colo., and London: Westview and Croom Helm, 1984); Pry not only minimized both Israel's nuclear and missile capabilities, compared to other foreign analysts, but he also accused the Israeli government of having misused a fully safeguarded, small American research reactor at Nahal Soreq for bomb production. Similar accusations were repeated in April 1987 in a document entitled "Critical Technology Assessment in Israel and NATO Nations," prepared by the Institute of Defense Analyses in Alexandria, Virginia, which was publicly quoted in late October 1989 in connection with the South African story, a controversy related to selling supercomputers to Israel.

16. Simcha Flapan, "Nuclear Disarmament in the Middle East—the Only Solution," in *Humanity under the Shadow of the Bomb,* edited by Avner Cohen, pp. 194-204.

17. See Senator Robert F. Kennedy's speech in the U.S Senate, "Hazards of Nuclear War," *Congressional Record,* June 23, 1965, Proceedings and Debates of the 89th Congress, First Session, in which Israel and India were mentioned by name as if they "already possess weapon-grade fissionable material, and could fabricate an atomic device within a few months"; and cf. ACDA Director William C. Foster's article, "New Directions in Arms Control and Disarmament," in *Foreign Affairs* (July 1965), pp. 587-601.

18. LBJ Library, DSDUF, container #1, item #3, memo, "Committee on Nuclear Proliferation, third meeting," with cover letter dated 1-28-1965 (sanitized, secret, limited distribution).

19. In regard to Wohlstetter's work pertaining to the alleged "bomber gap" and "missile gap," which "had greatly impressed [Paul] Nitze," see Lord Zuckerman, "The Silver Fox," *New York Review of Books,* January 19, 1989; and cf. Nitze's own memoir, *From Hiroshima to Glasnost: At the Center of the Decision* (New York: Grove Weidenfeld, 1989).

20. I was unable to locate an official, source for Eshkol's first declaration

that Israel "would not be the first to introduce nuclear weapons to the Middle East." However, it was reported in the *New York Times*, May 19, 1966, that the prime minister *repeated* this pledge. About Bergmann's resignation, see Fuad Jabber, *Israel and Nuclear Weapons*, pp. 48-49. Jabber adopted the speculation offered in Aubrey Hodes' "Implications of Israel's Nuclear Capability," *The Wiener Library Bulletin*, XXII (Autumn 1968), p. 3, that Eshkol offered President Johnson "to freeze operations at the Dimona plant at the point they had reached—reportedly in exchange for arms," Jabber, p. 49.

In his "Nuclear Disarmament in the Middle East," Flapan goes even further and tells us that "Israel was forced to freeze her plans to develop nuclear weapons due to heavy pressure exercised on her by Presidents Kennedy and Johnson, and due to criticism at home" (p. 197). Such assertions—one coming from an Arab author interested in minimizing the actual Israeli nuclear threat while awakening the Arabs to it, the other from an Israeli antinuclear politician—contributed to the confusion and ambiguity that clouded Eshkol's policy for several years afterward. One could of course speculate that Bergmann was removed and the whole nuclear option made to seem "frozen" in 1965 as a result of the American investigation of the NUMEC affair (see Chapter 4, note 78).

21. Outgoing Deptel (Department of State telegram), May 30, 1964, to Amembassy Cairo, top secret, signed Ball, copy to Mr. Komer in the White House; archival source: LBJ Library, NSF, UAR, container 158, item la.

22. Archival source: LBJ Library, NSF, UAR, container 159-161, Cables, vol. 2, item 99a.

23. Department of State, incoming airgram A-737, April 11, 1964, from Amembassy Cairo, signed by the American ambassador, John S. Badeau, subject U.S.-UAR relations (secret); archival source: LBJ Library, NSF, UAR, container 158, item 39.

24. Deptel circular 2447 to Vienna for IAEA, June 26, 1964, confidential, repeated to all Arab capitals; archival source: UPA Microfilms, "Israel: National Security Files 1963-1969," K4-128b [Kathy], Library of Congress Microfilm Reading Room, 86-892624 (85/4561 MICRR).

25. Copies of this cable were sent to the White House, the Joint Chiefs, and several other government agencies; archival source: LBJ Library, DTG 0312152 March 1965, NSF, Israel, vol. IV, cables 2/65 to 11/65 (secret).

26. SECRET/NOFORN, limited distribution; archival source: LBJ Library, NSF, Committee on Nuclear Proliferation, container #1-2, problem 2, item 1.

27. See Heikal's *Sphinx and Commissar* (New York: Harper and Row, 1978), p. 15. Incidentally, Heikal maintains that one of the German scientists who worked on the Egyptian missile, Dr. Wolfgang Pilz, left for China following the failure of the Egyptian project, and was believed by the Russians to be the

"coordinator" of the successful Chinese guided nuclear missile program.

Concerning Egypt's economic problems and tribulations with the American PL-480 grain export aid, combined with Nasser's other foreign policy priorities, see Beat Bumbacher, *Die USA und Nasser*, pp. 145-267.

28. Embtel to Secretary of State 2379, copy in sanitized form, signed by [Ambassador Lucius D.] Battle; archival source: LBJ Library, NSF, UAR File, containers #159-161, item 20.

29. Hazav, special appendix to summary 46, February 23, 1966; and cf. HDCI translation, March 18, 1966, of *Al-Gumhuria*, Cairo, March 12, 1966: "A Preventive War Is the Only Way to Preempt Israel's Acquisition of Nuclear Force," which is only one among many similar Arab press disclosures.

30. Haselkorn was the first to suggest the Soviet Union as a target of Israel's nuclear program in his "Israel: From an Option to a 'Bomb in the Basement'?" in *Nuclear Proliferation: Phase 2*, edited by R. M. Lawrence and J. Larus (Lawrence, Kansas: University of Kansas Press, 1975), pp. 149-82.

31. Yair Evron, *Israel's Nuclear Dilemma*, p. 18.

32. See Ely's nuclear "war-fighting" views in Wilfred L. Kohl, *French Nuclear Diplomacy*, pp. 44-45.

33. HDCI translation (May 15, 1966) of a report published in *Al-Yaum*, Beirut, May 1, 1966.

34. Department of State, NEA:NE:MSterner:rwc, February 24, 1966 (secret, sanitized); archival source: LBJ Library, NSF, UAR, container #159-161, item 156a.

35. Bar-Zohar, *Ben-Gurion*, p. 1560.

36. See Haselkorn, "Israel: From an Option to a 'Bomb in the Basement'?"

37. Yitzhak Rabin, *A Service Record*, vol. I (Tel Aviv: Ma'ariv, 1979), pp. 129-30.

38. The participants of the 1964 Arab summit had decided to divert the sources of the Jordan River to Syria, Lebanon, and Jordan, in response to Israel's Negev irrigation project (in which water was pumped from the Sea of Galilee, which is fed by the Jordan River); the irrigation project followed complex negotiations in which American mediators had been involved since Prime Minister Sharett's tenure.

39. UPA/Library of Congress, February 25, 1965 (secret, sanitized).

40. Deptel 5632, March 18, 1965 (secret, sanitized NSC copy); archival source: LBJ Library, NSF, Country File UAR, container #159-161, item 6.

41. Embtel 3653, Amembassy Cairo to Secretary of State (secret); archival

source: LBJ Library, NSF, UAR, container #159-161, item 2la.

42. United States Arms Control and Disarmament Agency, "Memorandum of Conversation on Prospects of Non-Proliferation Agreement and Related Matters," July 13, 1965 (limited official use), copies to the White House, to the American embassies in Moscow, Cairo, Paris, U.S. UN Mission, Mr. Harriman . . . ; archival source: Library of Congress/UPA.

43. See Isser Harel, *Security and Democracy*, pp. 450-51.

44. See Matti Golan, *Peres*, pp. 136-38. According to Golan, Peres was not enthusiastic about Ben-Gurion's campaign to reform the Israeli political system, perceiving in it, rather, a personal vendetta; nor did he believe in the new party's chances. But Ben-Gurion made his decision for him, leaving Peres without a choice; if he stayed in Mapai, he would be left to the mercy of all his enemies, without his old mentor to protect him and against the latter's explicit wishes. The nuclear issue was, however, introduced, among others, by Peres as a major dividing issue between his new party and Mapai, even if it was never spelled out in public.

45. PLO chairman Ahmed Shuqairi was the most active Arab leader in this regard, at least publicly, both before and after the 1966 summit. See for example *Filastin*, Beirut, November 17, 1966 (HDCI translation, November 27, 1966): "Preparations should be made to destroy the nuclear reactors in Israel"; and cf. *Al-Muharar*, Beirut, November 11, 1966: "An Arab Preventive War Against Israel Would Be Launched by Missiles and a Surprise Aerial Attack against the Reactor in Dimona."
Cf. Nasser's own repeated threat of a preventive war "if the Israelis continued to work toward production of an Atomic bomb" in an interview with the British *Observer* as quoted by Cairo Radio, February 6, 1967.

46. Regarding the better-known reasons and decision-making procedures on the Israeli side, see the disclosures in Eitan Haber, *"Today War Will Break Out": The Reminiscences of Brig. General Israel Lior, Aide-de-Camp to Prime Ministers Levi Eshkol and Golda Meir*. Yediot Aharonot edition (Tel Aviv: Edanim, 1987).

47. See *Al-Hayat*, Beirut, November 24, 1966. In his *Sphinx and Commissar*, p. 149, Heikal speaks of the Syrian Ba'ath regime at that time as a group of hot-headed fanatics and risk-takers, which concurs with Syrian Foreign Minister Ibrahim Mahus's dismissal of the Israeli bomb as "a paper tiger": "Look, the U.S. has tons of atomic bombs which do not prevent the Vietnamese people from fighting a war of liberation . . . and also France together with NATO, which have atomic weapons, withdrew with this weapon when faced with the heroic Algerian revolutionaries" (quoted in *Al-Mussawar*, Cairo, December 16, 1966, HDCI translation, December 25, 1966).

48. See Heikal, ibid., pp. 174-80.

49. See Haber, *"Today War Will Break Out,"* pp. 146-47.

50. Ambassador Evron's testimony to the author, June 1989, which fully concurs with Rabin's description of this incident in his memoirs, *A Soldier's Record*, pp. 169-70.

51. Haber, *"Today War Will Break Out,"* p. 161.

52. See Lior, in Haber, ibid., quoting Eshkol's fears that the Egyptians intended to stop Israeli shipping in the Straits of Tiran, bomb the nuclear reactor in Dimona, and then start an all-out offensive. It could be assumed that the fears regarding Dimona were intensified following the Egyptian flight over the reactor site on May 17, 1967, and the interpretation given to it by Chief of Army Intelligence, General Aharon Yariv, and possibly also by the chief scientist of the Ministry of Defense, prompted the decision to call up the reserves. Allon himself added "attacks against Israeli nuclear installations" to his list of casus belli, such as the resumption of the blockade on Eilat or Arab military presence in Jordan; the reason must have been the maintenance of the "last resort" option and the protection of the Israeli population from the ensuing fall-out. See Janis Gross Stein and Raymond Tanter, *Rational Decision-Making: Israel's Security Choices 1967* (Columbus: Ohio State University Press, 1980), p. 143; and cf. Michael Brecher, *Decisions in Crisis: Israel 1967 and 1973* (Berkeley: University of California Press, 1980), pp. 104n, 107-10. All three writers, however, gave Dimona only a limited meaning in influencing the call-up decision, and refused to deal with the nuclear factor as the main, or rather, the master variable explaining the Six-Day War (perhaps another example of "ambiguity" regarding this issue in academic research). Frank Barnaby, in his *The Invisible Bomb*, speculates that the decision "to go nuclear" was made after the 1967 war, and as a result of it (p. 24).

Chapter Six. The Road to the Yom Kippur War

1. May 25, 1967, letter from NSC Chief W. W. Rostow to President Johnson (and attached, "sanitized," documents); archival source: LBJ Library, NSF, Egypt, container #159-161, item 11b.

2. Bundy, *Danger and Survival*, p. 510.

3. Yosef Burg, in a meeting with the author, June 1991, in which he explained his refusal to attack the Iraqi reactor in this context in 1981.

4. See Yitzhak Rabin, *A Soldier Record* (Tel Aviv: Ma'ariv, 1979), p. 150, according to which Ben-Gurion was doubtful as to whether Nasser was aiming at war at all, and extremely critical of the mobilization decision, among the other decisions of the Eshkol-Allon-Galili cabinet; cf. Bar-Zohar, *Ben Gurion*, vol. III, pp. 1588-89, and Moshe Dayan, *Story of My Life*, Yediot Aharonot Edition (Jerusalem: Edanim, 1980), pp. 410-11. Dayan agreed with Ben-Gurion that Nasser was not aiming at an invasion at that time and that the West would not

support an Israeli preemptive war. He disagreed with Ben-Gurion's conclusion, however, and preferred preemption. Otherwise the strategic initiative would completely pass to Nasser's hand—implying a future Egyptian offensive—while Egypt maintained pressure on Israel with its regular army in Sinai; Israel's reserve army could not be mobilized indefinitely.

Bar-Zohar omits here the Dimona variable from Ben-Gurion's calculations, and fails to mention Peres' complete endorsement of Ben-Gurion's posture (see Rabin, p. 166); he describes the posture as "completely wrong" and as a sign of old age, which Peres merely conveyed to others and Dayan "sharply rejected" (pp. 1590-93). Bar-Zohar, whose third volume of Ben-Gurion's biography was published in 1977, was a political associate of Peres; he would not challenge the usual Israeli perception of the Six-Day War as a just, emergency measure to save the nation from complete annihilation by quoting his own hero.

5. Cf. Abba Eban and Moshe Carmel (at the time minister of transportation), interviews in *Davar*, June 3, 1976.

6. See Bar-Zohar, *Ben-Gurion*, pp. 1588-93, regarding Ben-Gurion's analysis of the crisis, for which he put the onus of the blame squarely on Eshkol's cabinet. Yet Bar-Zohar, in the spirit of the uncritical praise of the 1967 war victories typical of that time, dismissed Ben-Gurion's behavior as "out of touch" due to old age alone; other considerations, such as the defensive posture relating to Dimona, are not mentioned in his narrative. Ben-Gurion refused, however, to rejoin Mapai in 1968 as Dayan and Peres did, and Bar-Zohar, who also joined that party and became a practicing Labor politician, had to explain his hero's refusal to fight in 1967 and his rejection of the Labor Party later on. Bar-Zohar chose an easy explanation, as did Matti Golan (*Peres*).

8. Ibid., pp. 177-90.

9. Ibid.

10. For details, see *"Today War Will Break Out": The Reminiscences of Brigadier General Israel Lior*, edited by Eitan Haber, pp. 212-22.

11. The term "bomb-in the basement," which became rather popular among scholars, was coined by the Israeli analyst Avigdor Haselkorn; see his "Israel: From an Option to a Bomb in the Basement, " in *Nuclear Proliferation: Phase 2*, edited by R. M. Lawrence and J. Larus, pp. 149-82. Haselkorn was also the first analyst to draw our attention toward the Soviet Union as a target of Israel's nuclear deterrent. However, since he left Israel and settled in Los Angeles, his more recent interpretations of Israel's nuclear behavior seem to be beside the point; see the *Los Angeles Times*, November 11, 1986, regarding the Vanunu affair, which he described as an official change in Israel's opaque nuclear policy: a government-inspired leak to move the bomb from the basement to the living room.

12. See Yigal Allon, *Curtain of Sand* (Tel Aviv: Hakibbutz Hameuchad, 1968 edition), pp. 70-71, 401.

13 Arieh Naor, "The Jewish Wars," *Monitin* (May 31-June 15, 1991), pp. 12-18.

14. Ibid. Naor was cabinet secretary under Prime Minister Begin. His version is cited here—although there are many others in print—because of his use of official documents and his reliability.

15. Heikal, *The Sphinx and the Commissar*, p. 191.

16. See chapter 2, note 26.

17. Moshe Dayan, *A New Map, Different Relations: A Collection of Dayan's Speeches and Writings, 1967-1969* (Haifa: Shikmona Press, 1969).

18. The contents of this exchange was published by the author in the February 24, 1968, issue of *Ha'aretz.*

19. See Department of State, NEA: LDBattle: lab 10/25/67 (secret, sanitized) no. 18402; archival source: LBJ Library, "Memorandum of Conversation, dated October 24, 1967, between President Johnson and aides and Israel's Foreign Minister Abba Eban, and an aide." Following a long censored part, the document quotes President Johnson as assuring Eban that both nations "in general" share the same objectives: "We share the feeling of need to fashion a peace structure for the Middle East and will do all possible to help bring it about." However "a peace structure" was not necessarily an Arab-Israeli entente of the sort many Israelis hoped for; it could possibly have meant a detente, which could leave the 1948 Arab refugee problem open due to the irreconcilable positions of all sides (as indeed no agreement on final peace could be achieved in the framework of Security Council Resolution 5/242 of November 22, 1967). Despite his public stance, which seemed closer to Israel's demands to end the conflict in return for occupied territory, Johnson—in his meeting with Eban—seemed to be very skeptical about the war itself and angry at Israel's reluctance to counsel with the United States at the time, and warned his interlocutor that boundaries could not be changed, aggression not accepted by the U.S., nor had Washington great influence over the Russians. "The President wished to caution the Israelis that the further they get from June 5 [1967] the further they are from peace." This kind of terminology was used by Johnson's advisers at State and in the NSC. But he personally might have expected Israel to take care of itself without embroiling him too far in its dilemmas—as he indeed did on the eve of the 1967 war, according to Ambassador Evron.

20. See Hans-Peter Schwarz, "Adenauer und die Kernwaffen," and cf. Michael Eckert, "Die Anfänge der Atompolitik in der Bundesrepublik Deutschland," *Vierteljahreshefte für Zeitgeschichte* (1/89), pp. 115-43. For other aspects of West German nuclear activities, cf. Dan Charles, "Exporting Trouble—West Germany's Freewheeling Nuclear Business," *Bulletin of the Atomic Scientists* (April 1989), pp. 21-27.

21. For an Indian discussion of NPT as primarily an American-British-

Canadian, rather than Russian, concept, with obvious "discriminatory" provisions in favor of the nuclear weapon powers themselves, see K. Subrahmanyam, ed., *Nuclear Myths and Realities* (New Delhi: ABC Publishing House, 1981), pp. 5-8; cf. the discussion of the London Supplier Group (LSG) in the same book, pp. 32, 35.

22. See Bundy, *Danger and Survival*, p. 510.

23. Ibid. p. 512.

24. See, for example, Jed C. Snyder and Samuel F. Wells, Jr., eds., *Limiting Nuclear Proliferation* (Cambridge, Mass.: Ballinger, 1985), p. 56: "The United States will still have accomplished something quite significant for arms control if it achieves nothing more than holding Israel where it has been on the nuclear front—holding Israel indeed where it has been for the last twenty years."

25. Such arguments were made several years before by Arab circles who simply expressed the opinion that "the West" was interested in creating a "balance of terror" in the Middle East in order to prevent the Arabs from exploiting their decisive conventional power in their struggle to eliminate Israel. See among many other examples, *Al-Ahrar*, Beirut, "Preaching for a Preemptive War to Destroy the Reactor in Dimona. But if Israel Would Acquire an Atomic Bomb a Guerrilla War Should be Started," HDCI translation August 20, 1966, no. 384.

26. Kissinger is quoted by General Elad Peled as having expressed such views in the mid-1960s when a guest of the Israeli Defense College; see Shlomo Aronson, *Conflict and Bargaining in the Middle East* (Baltimore: Johns Hopkins University Press, 1978), p. 397n.

27. Helmut Sonnenfeldt. In an interview with Oded Brosh, March 1991, Brookings Institution, Washington, D.C.

28. "The Bush Program: Between Shamir and Mubarak," *Ma'ariv*, May 31, 1991.

29. Regarding the end of inspection in 1969 see Simcha Flapan, "Nuclear Disarmament in the Middle East—the Only Solution," *Humanity under the Shadow of the Atom*, edited by Avner Cohen, p. 198, who is following an open statement to *Ma'ariv* made by Prime Minister Rabin in 1976.

30. According to American sources, when the Johnson Administration was first approached by Israel in regard to the Phantom sale, it tried to link it to an Israeli obligation with regard to the acquisition of surface-to-surface missiles; see Deptel [State Department telegram] 00971 to Secretary of State from Amembassy Tel Aviv, September 28, 1967, "Memorandum of Conversation November 4, 1968 and November 5, 1968," especially p. 3., LBJ Library: NSF, Israel, vol. x, memos, container #142-143, item 145g. Archival source: Library of

Congress/UPA. On the ensuing diplomatic process I have used, among many other sources, oral testimony given to me by former Under-Secretary of State Joseph Sisco, March 31, 1977.

31. See Mohamed Heikal, *The Road to Ramadan* (London: Collins, 1975), pp. 76-77. In his 1977 *Sphinx and Commissar*, Heikal suggests a typical "nuclear" explanation for Soviet behavior in 1967 and several years afterward, in comparison, one may suggest, with their bolder behavior in 1973 in favor of the Arabs; see pp. 153-54. Accordingly, Khruschev calculated that since nuclear weapons could not be used militarily, they could be used politically, "and this required a special technique. At the time of Hungary and Suez he threatened the use of nuclear weapons, leaving it to others to escalate the conflict whichever way they wanted to, but knowing very well that they would not. On the other hand, in Cuba, Kennedy called his bluff in an area where the Americans enjoyed military superiority, and so his political use of nuclear weapons proved ineffective . . . After Cuba . . . Marshal Gretchko . . . accused Khruschev of failing to appreciate that nuclear weapons could not be used as a political weapon unless there were conventional forces to back them up." That is how Admiral Sergei Gorshkov transformed the Soviet navy into a worldwide force, and that is why the Soviets had "nothing to match the Phantoms" for years.

This way of thinking would have led Heikal to believe that the Arabs needed the bomb first, in order to be at all able to bring their potentially much larger conventional power back to the scene.

32. For a comprehensive, if rather pro-Kissinger, discussion of detente in retrospect, which fits the 1973 Middle East war into its framework, see Raymond L. Garthoff, *Detente and Confrontation* (Washington, D.C.: Brookings Institution, 1985), and cf. McGeorge Bundy's version in *Danger and Survival*, pp. 510, 518-25, 540, 542.

33. Yigal Allon, *A Curtain of Sand*, p. 401.

34. See Heikal's "The Bomb, " essay in *Al-Aharam*, November 1973. Heikal was unable to mobilize the masses to follow him as did Nasser. His adoption of an old Nasserite nuclear concept might have been sincere; or it might have been an alternative to Sadat's "minimalist" course in comparison with Nasser's grand designs; or it might have been the lesson he had learned from Soviet restraint under conditions rather favorable to them in terms of both the conventional and nuclear power at their disposal during the 1973 war, which left the Arabs with less than what they might have hoped for at the time; or it might have been the adoption of Qaddafi's line, which, however, endangered Egypt and was, in fact, adopted by Iraq, Egypt's older rival.

35. Dayan even maintained that "the Soviets" encouraged the Egyptians and the Syrians to fight Israel following the 1967 war; see Dayan, *A New Map, Different Relations*, p. 512; and cf. Heikal's distinction between the Soviet military and the party leadership in this regard in *The Sphinx and the Commissar*, pp. 190-220.

36. See *Sadat's Memoirs* as serialized in *October*, Cairo, and in *Al-Sayassa*, Kuwait, January 7, 1977: "All of a sudden a magician emerged on the international political stage . . . He hit the hat with a stick and a rabbit came out. This rabbit was called detente between Russia and the United States . . . This was a surprise." Heikal (*The Sphinx and the Commissar*, pp. 181-82), argues that "detente" was already the reason for the Arab defeat in 1967, an argument which does not concur with Sadat's timing, above, of the "surprise. " See further in the January 19, 1977, edition of Sadat's memoirs relating to the Moscow detente agreements of 1972: "I was not optimistic. What could the Soviets possibly say [to the Arabs] after the 'detente' agreement about a new thing called 'military relaxation' . . . ?"

In *The Road to Ramadan*, p. 169, Heikal quotes himself in a meeting with Sadat about detente: "One day I said [to the president] I'm afraid it looks as though detente is going to become a reality and impose itself on us before we can impose ourselves on it . . . [Sadat answered,] 'Maybe we will just be able to catch the last part of the tail of the detente.'"

37. See Garthoff, *Detente and Confrontation*, pp. 289-355; and cf. a more updated specific study: Albert Carnesale and Richard N. Haass, eds., *Superpower Arms Control: Setting the Record Straight* (Cambridge, Mass.: Ballinger, 1987).

38. In 1971, Fuad Jabber, later Professor Paul Jabber of UCLA, published his *Israel and Nuclear Weapons*, which was conceived in terms of a "suspended" Israeli nuclear option, but in fact Jabber went to Cairo later in the early 1970s, as he told me several years later, and acquainted Heikal with Schelling's theory of conflict and other deterrence-theoretical aspects of what he must have regarded in fact as a real Israeli nuclear option.

39. See Heikal's article "The Bomb" in *Al-Aharam*, November 1973.

40. This analysis completely contradicts Barnaby's arguments in 1989 that the Soviets and the Americans are so involved with their clients that they might be drawn to nuclear war among themselves; see *The Invisible Bomb*, p. xii. The Arabs, at least, were much less confident than Barnaby is during the much more aggressive Soviet foreign policy under Brezhnev, and thus Barnaby's argument seems to serve his general campaign against nuclear weapons, regardless of the historical truth.

41. See Sadat's speeches of July 18 and July 24, 1972 (in the files of the Dayan Center, Tel Aviv University), explaining the "pause" (*waqfa*) in his relations with the Russians.

42. In October 1972, seventy-two senators cosponsored the Jackson Amendment, and Senator Jackson, a contender in the 1976 elections, pursued the matter in 1973 and afterward "portending serious . . . difficulties in managing the diplomacy of detente." See Garthoff, *Detente and Confrontation*, pp. 309-10.

Chapter Seven. The Walls of Jericho

1. See Louis René Beres, *Security or Armageddon: Israel's Nuclear Strategy*, p. 202n. According to Vanunu and Barnaby (*The Invisible Bomb*, p. 31), the plutonium separation plant that had begun production in 1966 reached its full capacity in 1972, "producing about 1.2 kilograms of plutonium a week for 34 weeks a year, or about 40 kilograms a year." This estimate led Barnaby to calculate in 1986 that about two hundred Israeli bombs of all kinds had been built to date.

2. See Yair Evron, *Israel's Nuclear Dilemma*, pp. 100-101: "As mentioned above, Dayan was probably in favor of Israeli acquisition of nuclear weapons and of developing a strategic doctrine based on nuclear deterrence."

3. In a speech at the Israeli Defense College on July 24, 1973; see Aronson, *Conflict and Bargaining in the Middle East*, pp. 164-65 and p. 408, note 85.

4. Qaddafi was reported to have first opposed the Egyptian-Syrian offensive which, on the face of it, he should have endorsed. Such an attitude could not be explained except by his fears that they might be defeated again and by his rejection of the concept of a limited war. If a war was embarked on at all, it should be an all-out offensive, and this required nuclear weapons as a precondition. See for an example of his continued nuclear efforts, HDCI of January 14, 1981, p. 3, and cf. Leonard S. Spector, *The Undeclared Bomb: The Spread of Nuclear Weapons 1987-1988*, pp. 402-406, and Spector's *Nuclear Ambitions* (1990), p. 178.

5. See Moshe Dayan, *Story of My Life*, Yediot Aharonot Edition (Jerusalem: Edanim, 1980), p. 594.

6. Charles Wakebridge, "The Syrian Side of the Hill," *Military Review* (February 1976), pp. 20-30.

7. Dayan, *Story of My Life*, pp. 598, 600-601.

8. Ibid.

9. Ibid., pp. 595-96.

10. Regarding the impact of the Yom Kippur War on Israeli politics, see D. Caspi, A. Diskin, E. Guttman, eds., *The Roots of Begin's Success* (London: Croom-Helm and New York: St. Martin's Press, 1984), especially pp. 3-20.

11. See Stephen Green, *Living by the Sword: America and Israel in the Middle East, 1968-87* (London: Faber and Faber, 1988), as quoted by Amir Oren in *Davar*, May 27, 1988. In regard to the dispatch about Jericho testing on the Ile de Levant, see Chapter 5, note 25.

12. Stephen Green, *Taking Sides: America's Secret Relations with a Militant Israel* (New York: Morrow, 1984).

Green is very much interested in the alleged diversion of enriched uranium from NUMEC (Nuclear Materials and Equipment Corporation) in Apollo, Pennsylvania, to Israel in the mid-1960s. Again here, however, his selective use of primary sources is a case of "historical opacity," in which nuclear-related primary sources are used against Israel, while Israel is officially silent and must register the damage to its interests without being able to set the record straight in regard to the picture as a whole. For a follow-up on Green's book and a more up-to-date version of the NUMEC affair based on primary sources and private information, see Andrew and Leslie Cockburn, *Dangerous Liaison: The Inside Story of the Israeli-U.S. Covert Relationship* (New York: HarperCollins, 1991), pp. 71-97. (However, the subject is presented in an overall biased framework; the authors seem to lack the necessary linguistic tools to look at Hebrew or Arabic sources and to lack knowledge of the Middle East in general and Israel in particular.)

The NUMEC episode is also referred to in Spector's most recent proliferation biannual report, thus: "The episode has remained controversial, and conclusive evidence that Israel obtained the material is still lacking." (Yet he quotes a former CIA official to the contrary, as if the agency had concluded already in 1968 that "the most likely case" was that the NUMEC material had been diverted and had been used by the Israelis in fabricating weapons.) See Spector, *Nuclear Ambitions* (1990), p. 154, and his notes 38-39.

13. Green, *Living by the Sword*.

14. William B. Quandt. Interview with the author, Brookings Institution, Washington, D.C., October 26, 1979.

15. See Bundy, *Danger and Survival*, p. 510.

16. Dr. Joseph Sisco. Interview with the author, March 1977.

17. Dan Margalit, *Message from the White House* (Tel Aviv: Otpaz, 1971). At that stage Margalit was close to Begin, and in a way to Dayan, and his book might have served them both to argue that a withdrawal to the pre-1967 lines was out of the question, thanks to secret American commitments.

18. Moshe Dayan. Interview with the author in the Knesset, Jerusalem, November 11, 1980.

19. See Margalit, "The Name of the Game—No Choice," in *Ha'aretz*, October 3, 1990.

20. See Matti Golan, "Walking Confidently," in *Ha'aretz*, May 8, 1981.

21. Bundy, *Danger and Survival*, pp. 510, 511.

22. See Aronson, *Conflict and Bargaining in the Middle East*, pp. 183-96, in which the diplomatic side of the Yom Kippur War is discussed.

23. U.S. Congressional sources to the author; and cf. an Egyptian interpre-

tation of Israel's nuclear strategy both at the time and since by Dr. Butrus Butrus A'ali in *Al-Aharam Aliqtisadi*, May 1, 1976: "According to foreign sources [the *Time* magazine April disclosure earlier that year], Mrs. Meir had decided to use . . . [nuclear weapons] against the Egyptian onslaught . . . If all the experts agree that Israel could in principle use nuclear weapons, they further agree that this would not serve her interest because the dropping of a nuclear bomb over an Arab capital would bring about the killing of tens of thousands of civilians, which would trigger a sharp reaction in the Arab and the global spheres. It would justify a more concentrated attack against Israel in order to destroy her, and this would be accepted by world opinion as understandable. If that is so . . . it seems to us that Israel wanted to signal that she could produce . . . or that she had already produced . . . nuclear weapons, in order to threaten the U.S. more than the Arabs . . . The Israeli nuclear strategy is aimed against the . . . American[s] and not directly against the Arab nation. This means that in peace time Israel wants . . . to pressure the U.S. government to obtain from her large financial and military aid . . . [for otherwise she] will go nuclear . . . [or threaten] to involve the region in a nuclear race. In a war situation if Israel would face . . . defeat it would threaten to use nuclear weapons to make the American superpower intervene, and come militarily to her aid . . . The October victories render the Israeli conventional and the [meager quantity of] nuclear weapons not a real danger to the Arab nation . . . [who] has military and financial capabilities both in the conventional and in the nuclear field." It seems that A'ali, a Copt close to Sadat, was not so close to him at the time, or that Sadat had several, interchangeable moods with regard to the Israeli nuclear threat. However, his analysis of the nuclear factor as being helpful in securing conventional American aid was true at the time, as far as Meir's own action was concerned, and was not illegitimate in the eyes of Allon's school. Dayan, of course, tended to see in it an autonomous strategic asset.

24. Aronson, *Conflict and Bargaining*, esp. pp. 191-96 and the relevant notes; and cf. Raymond L. Garthoff, *Detente and Confrontation*, pp. 377-78, and Bundy, *Danger and Survival*, pp. 518-25. See further John Newhouse, *War and Peace in the Nuclear Age*, pp. 238-39.

25. The formulation is quoted from Newhouse, ibid., and cf. Aronson, ibid., pp. 192-93, and Garthoff, ibid., p. 378n, according to which "Some subsequent accounts have played up the possible Soviet supply of nuclear weapons, perhaps for Egyptian SCUD ballistic missiles, but this was never a serious possibility." Bundy, whose later version of the Washington scene at the time is very close to Garthoff's, does not mention the "radioactive cargo" at all. Cf. Frank Barnaby, *The Invisible Bomb*, in which Barnaby transforms-the "subsequent accounts" reported by Garthoff to facts, and simply maintains that Soviet nuclear weapons were transferred to both Egypt and Syria (pp. xii, 24), without quoting any sources in this regard. "It was not a principal consideration at the meeting at which an alert was decided upon," says Garthoff, in apparent disagreement with Barnaby.

26. As I explain it, rejecting Garthoff's interpretation to the effect that the 1973 war was fully conducted within the "rules" of detente, see Aronson, *Conflict and Bargaining*, pp. 368-69. The arrival of the Soviet "nuclear vessel" in Alexandria did touch upon the very heart of detente, following Brezhnev's threats of unilateral intervention; both must have been rejected in principle by Washington, even if the Soviets could blame Israel for their threats, so that the issue was blurred, and remained both within and without the rules of detente. Paul Nitze, of course, had his own view of Soviet behavior since the outbreak of the 1973 war: "The Soviets, who had advanced knowledge of the attack, did not advise us. It was evident that their commitment to detente and to the various statements of principle we had negotiated with them was nil. That there would be repercussions in the Arms Control field I had no doubt." See his *From Hiroshima to Glasnost: At the Center of Decision, A Memoir*, p. 337. Nitze's memoir is no doubt his response to Bundy's *Danger and Survival*, as one may deduce from the typical remark on nuclear proliferation: "Nuclear proliferation was another problem, but again I disagreed with my colleagues, who seemed to feel that nuclear proliferation was a greater danger than the growing imbalance and instability in the nuclear and conventional balance between the United States and its allies and the USSR. In my opinion, it was that growing imbalance which made the possession of nuclear weapons appear necessary to third countries" (p. 347). Helmut Sonnenfeldt, in his interview with Oded Brosh (see Chapter 6, note 27), fully concurs with the opinion that "DEFCON 3 alert . . . was the result of Soviet nuclear activities" at the time; he—like Nitze—saw the problem of proliferation grounded primarily in superpower behavior, as article 6 of NPT "increases rather than decreases incentives for proliferation among those who rely on the U.S. for protection."

27. See Aronson, *Conflict and Bargaining*, pp. 193-95 and the relevant notes.

28. For an English version of this theory, see Yona Bendman and Yishai Cordova, "The Soviet Nuclear Threat Towards the Close of the Yom Kippur War," in *The Jerusalem Journal of International Relations*, vol. 5 (1980), pp. 94-110. The authors—two former IDF intelligence officers—maintain that the first report of a neutron-radiating cargo carried by that vessel reached Washington only after the alert. Garthoff tells us (*Detente and Confrontation*, p. 378n) that they were wrong about this.

29. Bundy, *Danger and Survival*, p. 52?.

30. Bundy, *Danger and Survival*, p. 521.

Chapter 8. Sadat's Peace

1. Bundy, *Danger and Survival*, p. 506.

2. Ibid., pp. 506-7.

3. Ibid., p. 507.

4. Dayan's most visible approaches in this regard were made in a press conference in Paris, March 19, 1976, and in a lecture in Tel Aviv on March 29, 1976; each received due attention by the French and Israeli presses the day after being made.

5. Bundy, *Danger and Survival*, pp. 510-11.

6. See details in Aronson, *Conflict and Bargaining in the Middle East*, pp. 180-232. Kissinger's memoirs, which were published in the meantime, do not essentially change the picture drawn there.

7. In the 1960s, Iraq had been very close to Nasser's initial strategy of acquiring some kind of a nuclear option, either because Nasser wanted one, because of its own aspirations for Arab leadership, or as a response to the Israeli nuclear challenge. However, it succeeded only in obtaining a small Soviet research reactor of no military significance. Baghdad then endorsed Nasser's open threats of a preventive war against Israel should Israel go nuclear; cf. *Al-Thawra al-Arabia*, Baghdad, HDCI translation, February 1966. After the Six-Day War, Iraq was the only Arab nation (Qaddafi was second only to the Iraqis in this respect) who publicly concentrated on the nuclear issue as the key to the conflict. See Dr. Haddi Aude, Secretary General of the Iraqi Atomic Energy Commission, Middle East News Agency, April 4, 1968, HDCI translation, April 5, 1968, and cf. Iraqi press reports to the effect that the Arabs would "obtain" nuclear weapons from foreign sources if necessary, quoted by Radio Baghdad, HDCI translation, January 16, 1969. During the period in which NPT was implemented, Iraq and other Arab nations put pressure on the superpowers to force Israel to join the treaty, and thus cancel its nuclear program. In 1971, a large-scale geological survey of uranium was conducted in Iraq. In 1972, Iraq joined NPT and started initial negotiations toward the acquisition of nuclear power stations. In 1973, however, Saddam Hussein was speaking openly of a far-reaching modernization process necessary to fight Israel. See Iraqi News Agency, HDCI translation, March 19, 1972; *Al-Thahi*, Baghdad, HDCI translation, March 8, 1973; Middle East News Agency, HDCI translation, July 4, 1973; and Radio Baghdad, HDCI translation, June 13, 1973, respectively. The Iraqi agreement with France to purchase a large research reactor rather than a nuclear power plant was signed, however, on November 18, 1975, and might have been the result of several developments related to the 1973 war and the ensuing oil crisis. These gave Iraq the financial means to go ahead with the project, and gave the French the motives to supply the reactor, in part due to their resentment of the pressure Kissinger brought to bear on the Europeans in 1974 not to conclude their own deals with the Arabs.

8. See Heikal, "The Bomb," in *Al-Aharam*, November 1973.

9. Fuad Jabber, the author of *Israel and Nuclear Weapons*, traveled to Egypt at that time and acquainted Heikal with Schelling's writings, according to Profes-

sor Jabber (who later changed his first name to Paul) in a conversation with the author at UCLA in 1977.

10. HDCI translation, January 6, 1977.

11. HDCI translation, January 20, 1987.

12. See Efraim Inbar, "Israel and Nuclear Weapons Since October 1973," in *Security or Armageddon*, edited by Louis René Beres, pp. 202-3.

13. Frank Barnaby, *The Invisible Bomb*, p. 28, and cf. Spector's analysis of Barnaby's estimates in his *Nuclear Ambitions*, pp. 160-62.

14. Spector, *Nuclear Ambitions*, p. 162.

15. See Aronson, *Conflict and Bargaining*, p. 431n.

16. Dayan, at a press conference in Paris on March 19, 1976, and in a lecture in Tel Aviv on March 29, 1976. See Shlomo Aronson, "Nuclearization of the Middle East: A Dovish View," in *The Jerusalem Quarterly*, 2 (Winter 1977), pp. 25-44.

17. Inbar, "Israel and Nuclear Weapons," in *Security or Armageddon*, edited by Beres, p. 203.

18. See the above-mentioned *Time* magazine cover story, "How Israel Got the Bomb," April 12, 1976; and cf. Inbar, ibid. p. 202.

19. Moshe Zak, "Bush's Program: Between Shamir and Mubarak," *Ma'ariv*, May 31, 1991.

20. Spector, *Nuclear Ambitions*, pp. 161-62.

21. Barnaby, *The Invisible Bomb*, p. 39.

22. See *Toward Peace in the Middle East* (Washington, D.C.: The Brookings Institution, 1975).

23. In his *Decade of Decision* (Berkeley: University of California Press, 1977), p. 80n., William B. Quandt, the American Middle East expert, who was a member of the Brookings group, quoted Israel's nuclear option as one of the reasons for the urgency of seeking a comprehensive solution to the Arab-Israeli conflict.

24. "Top Secret, Ministry of Defense, Tel Aviv, July 18, 1977," The National Security Archive, Washington, D.C., nonproliferation catalogue, record #28683. The source of this document is U.S. intelligence reports found by the Iranians in the U.S. Embassy in Tehran. See Chapter 5, note 10.

25. Ibid.

26. The texts of the initial Camp David accords of September 17, 1978, and of the Israeli-Egyptian Peace Treaty of March 26, 1979, are contained as

appendixes in William B. Quandt, *Camp David—Peacemaking and Politics* (Washington, D.C.: The Brookings Institution, 1986).

27. An official demand to this effect was made by Egypt's Foreign Minister Ismail Fahmi, addressing the U.N. General Assembly; see *New York Times Index*, 1977, September 29, 3:1: "[Fahmi] insists that to attain peace Israel will have to forgo atomic arms, to accept a limit on traditional weapons and to end its 'open door' immigration policy." "Open door . . . policy" refers to Israel's "Law of Return," which gives Jews everywhere the legal right to immigrate to Israel. Since 1974, Fahmi has publicly repeated many times that Israel's signature on NPT was a precondition for peace; see, for example, his interview with *Al-Ahbar*, Cairo, HDCI translation, June 6, 1974. Fahmi resigned his office upon Sadat's visit to Jerusalem in November 1977, but, according to General Weizmann, the Egyptian delegation that accompanied Sadat to Israel raised the nuclear issue almost upon arrival; see Uri Dan in *Ma'ariv*, March 20, 1981; cf. Moshe Zak in *Ma'ariv*, March 20, 1981; according to his information, "Sadat's worry about the Israeli nuclear capability was one of the motives for his visit to Jerusalem, and in his first meeting there he raised this subject and did not let loose even in the [ensuing] Camp David talks."

28. Ismail Fahmi became one of Sadat's most outspoken critics, and was joined by General Sa'ad al-din Shazli, Egyptian Chief of Staff during the initial stages of the October 1973 war. Shazli was fired by Sadat—and later exiled—during the hostilities because Shazli wanted to extend the hostilities beyond the president's intentions. He accused Sadat of yielding to Israel's nuclear blackmail. Regarding the above-quoted defense of Sadat, see *Al-Ahbar*, Cairo, November 23, 1977, HDCI translation, December 1. 1977.

29. Zak, in *Ma'ariv*, May 31, 1991.

30. Heikal, himself, became the target of pro-Sadat factions in his own *Al-Aharam* paper and among members of the research center of the paper. They accused him of manipulating the nuclear issue against Sadat, after contributing more than anyone else to warning Egypt against the possible, catastrophic results of the Israeli nuclear threat. In one sense, Egypt had nothing to win from acquiring the bomb but a risk to its very existence, and in another, peace could allow Egypt to gain limited objectives by neutralizing the Israeli bomb and later by cultivating close ties with the Americans—and eventually driving a wedge between Washington and Jerusalem—while obtaining its own nuclear infrastructure. This is based on 1986 conversations between the author and Dr. Ali Dessuki, a former member of the Al-Aharam center in California and a then-active member in Brussels.

31. See Oded Brosh, "Nuclear Aspects of the Arab-Israeli Conflict," master's thesis, Hebrew University, Jerusalem, 1984, in which Brosh uses many HDCI quotations to analyze the various differences between Arab rejectionists and to differentiate between the more "opaque," almost totally silent, Syrian

treatment of the issue (to avoid giving Israel's option legitimacy and credibility) and the much louder Iraqi treatment of the issue.

32. George Quester suggested some years ago that the Saudis had taken on financing the Pakistani bomb project on condition that the latter sever their ties with Libya. This fits in well with the overall pattern of Zia-ul-Hak's relationship with the Arab world, and his stormy ties with Qaddafi. Oded Brosh throws more light on both these matters, and also suggests that the Saudis are paying for the Pakistani bomb by footing the bill for major economic projects in Pakistan, thus allowing the Pakistanis to divert major portions of their own budget to the nuclear program; see Brosh, "Perceptions and Public Attitudes Toward the Nuclear Dimension in the Multilateral Regional Conflicts," Ph.D. dissertation, Hebrew University, 1990.

Chapter Nine. The Doctrine of Opaque Nuclear Monopoly

1. The cabinet secretary at the time was Mr. Arieh Naor. The details of the proceedings that resulted in the adoption of what Mr. Naor calls the "Begin Doctrine" are quoted from Naor's article "A Risk Too High," *Yediot Aharonot*, April 2, 1989, in which he warned against Iraq's revitalized nuclear program.

2. Cf. *Newsweek* magazine story on Finance Minister Yoram Aridor's memo regarding Israel's military nuclear option, April 27, 1981, according to which Aridor was considering nuclear substitutes for Israel's expensive conventional arsenal.

3. Stated in a television interview, February 14, 1982.

4. Sharon was quoted by Israeli television in the summer of 1982 as saying that he had informed U.S. Defense Secretary Caspar Weinberger that "Israel has [unilaterally] terminated the arms race." That is, foreign procurement was terminated, not home industries; cf. "An Undelivered Speech," *Ma'ariv*, December 18, 1981.

5. See Telem Party platform, Tel Aviv, 1981; and cf. Shlomo Aronson, "The Nuclear Option and Election Slogans," *Ma'ariv*, March 30, 1981.

6. Jed Snyder and Samuel F. Wells, *Limiting Nuclear Proliferation*, p. 4.

7. See, for example, *Al-Watan al-Arabi*, Beirut, January 20, 1978, HDCI translation, January 29, 1978, #848/21.

8. For Saddam Hussein's career, see Fuad Matar, *Saddam Hussein: The Man, the Cause, and the Future* (London: Third World Center, 1981); and cf. Samir al-Khalil, *Republic of Fear: The Politics of Modern Iraq*, paperback edition (Berkeley: University of California Press, 1990), and Christine Moss Helms, *Iraq: The Eastern Flank of the Arab World* (Washington, D.C.: Brookings Institution, 1984).

9. HDCI translation, October 20, 1975.

10. Published October 17, 1977, in *Al-Usbua al-Arabi*, Beirut, HDCI translation October 26, 1977.

11. See *Al-Watan*, Kuwait, July 27, 1980, HDCI translation August 5, 1980. This statement was related, among other things, to the recent murder by unknown agents of an Egyptian nuclear scientist in the service of the Iraqis.

12. See A. James Gregor, *Contemporary Radical Ideologies*.

13. HDCI translation, August 11, 1981.

14. To gain a picture of Israeli activities, American diplomatic efforts with the French, the decision-making process leading to the bombing of Osiraq, and technical details regarding the Iraqi reactor, see Shlomo Nakdimon, *Tammuz in Flames*, Yediot Aharonot edition (Jerusalem Edanim, 1986); and cf. Leonard S. Spector, *Nuclear Ambitions*, p. 187, especially with regard to the Iraqi order placed in 1980 with NUKEM, a West German firm, to obtain more than eleven tons of depleted-uranium metal fuel pins, which were sized to fit into Osiraq, where they could be irradiated to yield plutonium, "and were unsuited to any other purpose—including its stated end-use."

15. Regarding the French deliveries, which did not include a separation plant, see Pierre Pean, *Les Deux Bombes*, 1982, pp. 170-73. Regarding the Italian role in supplying "hot cells" and training Iraqi nuclear engineers, see Nakdimon, *Tammuz in Flames*, pp. 101-2.

16. See Pierre Gallois' *The Balance of Terror*.

17. See "Saddam Has an Atomic Bomb Already," *Yediot Aharonot*, October 12, 1990. In this report, which remained unconfirmed, the paper quoted an official Portuguese statement to the effect that "10 years ago the Government of Portugal signed an agreement with Iraq to supply the latter with natural uranium. 252 tons were indeed sold . . . to Baghdad, as Iraq committed itself not to use the uranium to produce nuclear weapons."

18. See "Iraq Mines Uranium for Nuclear Weapons," *Ha'aretz*, October 14, 1990, which quotes from British ITV, channel 4 program broadcast on October 13, 1990. According to British scientists who reportedly had access to Soviet spy satellites, the mine—which is located in Kurdistan's Gara and was held by Kurdish rebels until 1988, when the local population was gas-bombed—could be the source for natural uranium enriched by gas centrifuges or by calutrons.

19. See Nakdimon, *Tammuz in Flames*, pp. 147-48.

20. The original, handwritten letter, marked "personal and top secret," was published on August 15, 1990, by the weekly *Haolam Haze*, following the

Iraqi occupation of Kuwait earlier that month; and cf. Nakdimon, *Tammuz in Flames*, p. 175.

21. In a public speech on February 14, 1991, broadcast by the Israeli Radio, Peres claimed that President Mitterand indeed refused to supply the second installment, due to Peres' own contacts with the newly elected Socialist French head of state. He further argued that the French enriched uranium was at the time the source of the immediate danger.

22. Leonard S. Spector. Interview with the author, Washington, D.C., September 24, 1990.

23. Ibid., p. 283.

24. See Nakdimon, *Tammuz in Flames*, pp. 149-87, about this and Begin's cabinet deliberations. Nakdimon was Begin's press secretary, and his book benefited from his relations with the former prime minister and his successor, Yitzhak Shamir.

25. Waltz's "The Spread of Nuclear Weapons: More May Be Better." Shortly after its publication in 1981, Shai Feldman, a disciple of Waltz's, who has privately claimed some proximity to Mr. Peres, published his *Israeli Nuclear Deterrence*, in which he advocated an open Israeli nuclear posture on the basis of his interpretation of NATO's strategy in Europe in the 1960s and early 1970s with its status quo situation. He also added his opinion that Israeli withdrawal to the pre-1967 lines would give Israel's nuclear threat the optimal credibility. Feldman was, however, ready to wait with the open posture until at least one Arab state acquired the bomb—an approach that takes such acquisition for granted. His study is yet another example of scholarly refusal to deal with what we believe to be the actual, historical-political reality of nuclear threats in the Middle East; other than using some HDCI Arab press reports and published advocacies, Feldman did no actual research into Israel's own behavior in the past and present, or into the role of the superpowers in this regard, or into inter-Arab relations and deliberations concerning Israel's actual behavior since the introduction of its nuclear option in the mid-1960s. He argues against an ambiguous Israeli nuclear posture while retaining the basic ambiguity to which it is opposed by using American deterrence-theoretical arguments derived from a bipolar reality, rather than the multipolar one in which Israel lives. Thus his study could be criticized as having taken deterrence theory out of its context, and as having totally ignored its warnings against actors such as the Middle East politicians.

26. Cf. Shlomo Aronson, *Conflict and Bargaining in the Middle East*.

27. See *Ma'ariv*, March 12, 1982: "Deputy Foreign Minister [Ben-Meir] in the Knesset: We shall not live with nuclear weapons of any kind and of any origin in an Arab state which perceives itself as a belligerent of Israel." Yehuda Ben-Meir of the National Religious Party was addressing the House in regard to

the renewed Iraqi effort to obtain a new reactor from the French government to replace Tammuz 1.

28. Eitan was quoted by *Hadashot*, an Israeli tabloid, to this effect on April 2, 1990, in connection with published information about Iraq's renewed nuclear effort.

29. See Nakdimon, "The Mishap—Wrong Quotation," in *Tammuz in Flames*, appendix 2, pp. 313-14.

30. The Americans protested openly against the use of U.S.-made F-16 fighter bombers and F-15 fighters in the raid, and argued that Iraq was far from a military nuclear capability. Washington suspended the shipment of four more F-16s. For details, and Begin's angry reaction, see Nakdimon, ibid., pp. 222-33.

31. In *Nuclear Ambitions: The Spread of Nuclear Weapons 1989-1990*, pp. 158-61.

32. See Butrus Butrus A'ali, in *Al-Aharam Aliqtisadi*, May 1, 1976, and cf. Peter Pry's book, *Israel's Nuclear Arsenal*.

33. See a more recent sample of this opinion in *Al-Qabas*, Kuwait, September 25, 1986, HDCI translation, October 10, 1986; and cf. Abdalla al-Achmar, Deputy Secretary General of the Syrian Ba'ath Party, further in the text.

34. Interview with a pro-Libyan paper in Beirut on January 3, 1983, HDCI translation, February 10, 1983, #843/41.

35. See HDCI translation, January 14, 1983, quoting *Al-Thawra* of November 24, 1982; and cf. HDCI, November 30, 1982, quoting Syrian commentator Naziah Alsuffi in *Tishrin*, November 3, 1982. Both Al-Achmar and Alsuffi underlined Soviet support and growing involvement as a precondition for Syria's "North-Vietnamese" strategy.

36. Leonard 5. Spector, *The Undeclared Bomb: The Spread of Nuclear Weapons 1987-1988*, pp. 18, 166; and cf. his updated analysis in *Nuclear Ambitions*, pp. 158-60.

37. Spector, *Nuclear Ambitions*, p. 161.

38. In regard to the Jerusalem-Pretoria nuclear cooperation, cf. Spector, *Nuclear Ambitions*, p. 164, and his *Undeclared Bomb*, pp. 383-84; and cf. Frank Barnaby, *The Invisible Bomb*, pp. 13-19.

39. For the most recent evaluation, see Spector, *Nuclear Ambitions*, p. 162.

40. Theodore Taylor, quoted in Spector, ibid.

41. "Israel Said to Deploy Jericho Missile," *Aerospace Daily*, May 1, 1985.

42. Spector, *The Undeclared Bomb*, pp. 26-27.

43. For the most recent summary of American opinion and evaluation, see Spector, *Nuclear Ambitions*, pp. 158-60.

44. Sam Cohen. In a telephone interview with the author, Los Angeles, May 1986, following the publication of a technical argument by Barnaby that neutron bombs could be neutralized by using boron-covered coats.

45. Sharon, "An Undelivered Speech."

46. See his "Satellite Photographs in Real Time," *Ma'ariv*, November 16, 1990. Zak is sometimes a spokesman for Likud's highest officials, and his article was published in response to the news about difficulties in Israeli-American relations late in November 1990, about which he tried to set the record straight.

Chapter Ten. Lebanon and the Demise of the Begin-Sharon Cabinet

1. See Uzi Benziman, *Sharon: Israeli Caesar* (Tel Aviv: Adam Publishers, 1985), for further biographical details.

2. Sharon and his chief of planning, General Avraham Tamir, were behind the leak, according to former high officials in the Israeli Foreign Ministry. The document itself remained officially classified.

3. For details, see Zev Schiff and Ehud Ya'ari, *Israel's Lebanon War* (New York: Simon and Schuster, 1984).

4. See Yosef Harif, "An Important Message to President Reagan," *Ma'ariv*, February 19, 1982.

5. HDCI translation, July 8, 1981.

6. See *Al-Watan el Arabi*, Beirut, July 24, 1981, HDCI translation, August 9, 1981.

7. See *Al-Aharam*, Cairo, July 24, 1981, HDCI translation, August 6, 1981.

8. See *October*, Cairo, July 11, 1982, HDCI translation, July 19, 1982.

9. Spector, *Nuclear Ambitions*, p. 20.

10. Obtained by the National Resources Defense Council, a private environmental group that monitors nuclear issues under the Freedom of Information Act, according to Spector, *Nuclear Ambitions*, p. 160 and p. 161n.

11. Spector, ibid., p. 20.

12. For details, see Schiff and Ya'ari, *Israel's Lebanon War*.

13. It should be noted that Shamir had suggested, as Begin's Foreign Min-

ister, a nuclear disarmament regime for the Middle East, which was officially submitted, on October 31, 1980, by Ambassador Arieh Ilan to the U.N. General Assembly; it was a diplomatic maneuver that accompanied the "Begin Doctrine." When he succeeded Begin, Shamir seemed to Mr. Yoram Nimrod to have seriously endorsed a rather radical, new approach; see, for example, Nimrod's article, "Shamir Gives Up the Nuclear Option," in *Al-Hamishmar*, November 15, 1987.

14. See, for example, General Mustafa Tlass, "We Shall Use Missiles to Destroy the Reactor in Dimona," quoted in *Yediot Aharonot*, February 13, 1984.

15. See, for example, *Ma'ariv*, June 2, 1985: "The Syrian Defense Minister to ABC Network: 'We have the Right to Develop Nuclear Weapons. Israel has Boosted the [capacity of] the Reactor in Dimona; Syria has a Soviet Nuclear Guarantee.'"

16. For a more recent statement to that effect, see *Ma'ariv*, November 1, 1987, "Shamir: Israel Has No Nuclear Weapons," regarding his use of the old Eshkol formula that "Israel will not be the first to introduce nuclear weapons to the Middle East."

17. Peres, as quoted in a meeting with the editorial board of *Ma'ariv*, in the June 29, 1984, issue.

18. See *Monitin* monthly, July 1984.

19. See President Reagan's statement and Shamir's response during the latter's visit to Washington, in the *New York Times*, November 19, 1983. According to Israeli Foreign Ministry sources, this agreement was followed by a specific National Security Memorandum issued by the president establishing an American-Israeli Joint Planning Military Group to coordinate cooperation in conventional areas of mutual interest such as Israel's contribution to Reagan's SDI, or "Star Wars," program.

Chapter Eleven. From Lebanon to the Intifada

1. *Aerospace Daily*, May 7, 1985.

2. Spector, *Nuclear Ambitions*, p. 20.

3. Ibid., and cf. pp. 162-63.

4. For details, see Wolfram F. Hanrieder, *Germany, America, Europe: Forty Years of German Foreign Policy* (New Haven: Yale University Press, 1989), pp. 467-70.

5. A comprehensive summary of these attitudes is contained in Nimrod Granit, *The Perceptions of Israeli Unconventional Efforts in Arab Eyes and in the*

Scholarly Literature and Arab Activities in this Respect 1960-1988, a master's thesis written under my supervision at the Department of Political Science, Hebrew University, Jerusalem, 1989. The Syrian press, in Syria itself and abroad—such as *Al-Farsan*, which is published simultaneously in London and in Paris—reacted in the most vehement fashion to Vanunu's disclosures, and to the missile deployment and testing in the second half of the 1980s.

6. See Spector, *Nuclear Ambitions*, p. 165, and cf. *Ha'aretz*, March 3, 1990: "Israeli ambassador in Washington Mr. Moshe Arad has advised American Congressman about the cessation of military relations with South Africa." In the story itself NBC network was quoted as saying that the issue was that of the timetable for the implementation of the decision to end military relations, and that of the "cooperation between South Africa and Israel regarding development of a nuclear ballistic missile [which] continues."

7. See, for example, *Ha'aretz*, September 23, 1987, Peres's statement in Boston: "Israeli Missiles Are Not Targeted at the Soviet Union."

8. See, for example, among other commentaries, Foreign Broadcast Information Service Daily Report (FBIS) SOV-87-188, September 29, 1987, "Commentary Views Israel's 'Nuclear Option,'" in which General Allon's rejection of the nuclear option is mentioned when that option was "still in its infancy"; which means that the situation has changed after all.

9. FBIS Daily Report: Soviet Union, August 11, 1987, page E5.

10. See note 7, this chapter. The very fact that such a major statement was made abroad signifies either domestic disagreement or a not very original method of undercutting Israel's own military censorship.

11. Regarding the actual implementation of INF and the verification of the Spider-related part of it, see *Bulletin of the Atomic Scientist*, October, 1989, p. 47.

12. The improvements were the result of German labor, as reported by *Ha'aretz* on October 22, 1990, from Bonn.

13. Spector, *Nuclear Ambitions*, p. 164.

14. Ibid.

15. See the summary of foreign press reports (mainly from *Aviation Week*, the first week of October 1988, and *International Defense Review*, July 1987), and the description of the launching's possible ramifications on Soviet-Israeli relations by Reuven Pdezur, *Ha'aretz*, October 13, 1988.

16. Spector, *Nuclear Ambitions*, pp. 163-64.

17. Ibid.

18. See Reuters' story from Abu-Dhabi, quoted in *Ha'aretz*, July 28, 1988, cit-

ing *Al-Itihad,* United Arab Emirates, in an interview with the former director of the Egyptian chemical-weapon warfare program, Mr. Mamduh Attieh, who said that the Arabs should obtain chemical and bacteriological weapons as the only means they have against Israel's nuclear threat. The best way to neutralize Israel's nuclear capability, he said, is the launching of an Arab nuclear force. "But as long as we cannot overtake Israel, we must possess an unconventional deterrent."

19. The writer A. B. Yehoshua, a leading Israeli dove, argued that Israel's nuclear weapons would guarantee its survival if Israel withdrew from the West Bank, in the spirit of Shai Feldman's book, *Israeli Nuclear Deterrence.* In response to Yehoshua, Binyamin Natanyahu, a leading Likud spokesman, argued in *Yediot Aharonot,* July 15, 1988: "Yehoshua's treatment of 'our nuclear weapons' as a guarantee to the success [of the] withdrawal scheme is no less surprising. Should we learn from that that 'peace lovers' such as he is would seriously consider the use of nuclear weapons in the case of a conventional attack? I hope that they will enlighten us as to whether they want to drop nuclear bombs on [West Bank cities in close proximity to Tel Aviv and Jerusalem], or on . . . Jericho or Nablus [just a little farther away]."

20. See, for example, Inbar and Yaniv's contributions to Louis René Beres, *Security or Armageddon,* in which Inbar remained skeptical about the very existence of an Israeli nuclear option; Yaniv later published a whole book advocating conventional deterrence; Evron's most recent antinuclear treatise was published in 1990, having reluctanty accepted a "last resort" nuclear option.

21.See Peres' *Ha'aretz* article of June 2, 1989: "Economics Without Boundaries," quoted in Chapter 1, note 7.

22. Regarding the Arrow, see *Ha'aretz,* June 30, 1988: "Director-General of Defense Ministry Signed Memorandum of Understanding to Develop 'Arrow' Missile." See further *Ha'aretz* of July 3, 1988, quoting a senior member in Rabin's mission to Washington: "The 'Arrow' could not give an immediate answer to Saudi, Syrian and Iraqi missiles, and we shall have to continue relying upon a preemptive strike against their bases or upon a general nuclear deterrence."

23. For a version of the Soviet "Regional Middle East Arrangement," see text of Soviet Foreign Minister Shevardnadze press conference in Vladivostok, September, 9, 1990; and cf. interview by Sergei Rogow, Director, Military and Political Department, Institute of American and Canadian Affairs, Soviet Academy of Sciences, in *Ha'aretz,* September 9, 1990. Mr. Rogow was in fact a high-ranking KGB official, according to Dr. William Quandt of the Brookings Institution, in an interview with the author, Washington, D.C., September 18, 1990.

24. Dennis Ross, the Chief of the Planning Staff at the State Department, as reported by Israeli Radio from Washington, October 20, 1990; Dr. William Quandt, Brookings Institution, to the author, September 19, 1990.

25. See *Ha'aretz*, June 22, 1988, "Rabin . . . : We have the Means to Punish the Arabs Ten Times Harder." The direct quote is related to press reports regarding the alleged purchase of M9 Chinese-made IRBMs by Syria (which Rabin dismissed following the purchase of more obsolete Chinese missiles by Saudi Arabia) and regarding the radius of Syrian SCUD-B missiles that could hit targets in Israel "north of Beersheba," a definition that is not clear enough to include or exclude Dimona. Rabin then said: "The Arab states must calculate that Israel is ready to protect her back, both defensively and offensively, and I suggest to [their] leaders [that] if any one of them considers the use of chemical weapons, [they must] realize that Israel has the means to inflict a ten-times larger punishment on the populations of the belligerent Arab states."

This could be described as the adoption of a countervalue, or countercity strategy by Israel, in response to Iraqi missile attacks against Teheran, in case Syria—or Iraq itself—might believe that such precedents could be repeated in Israel's case.

26. In an Israeli TV Interview on February 19, 1991, reprinted in *Yediot Aharonot* on Feb. 20, 1991.

27. *Ma'ariv*, "Our Deterrent Power Has Proved Itself."

28. Weizmann criticized Shamir's cabinet, however, for its decision not to respond to the Iraqi SCUD missile attacks at the outbreak of the Gulf War, lamenting the decline of Israel's deterrent power thereby; in this he found himself in the same boat as General Sharon.

29. See *Davar*, January 17, 1991.

30. Tamir, "My Talks with Members of the Iraqi Leadership," *Yediot Aharonot*, February 15, 1991.

31. Ibid.

32. General Amnon Shahak, Director of Military Intelligence, quoted in *Yediot Aharonot*, March 8, 1990.

33. See Chapter 1, note 7.

34. See soviet Defense Ministry announcement, September 14, 1989, as quoted the next morning by *Ma'ariv*.

35. October 26, 1989, and *New York Times* of October 27, 1989. See *Ma'ariv* for Israeli comments and follow-ups regarding the Congressional hearings.

36. See Spector, *Nuclear Ambitions*, p. 165, especially in regard to "Israel's possible involvement in a scheme to smuggle advanced U.S. missile gyroscopes to that country"—i.e., South Africa.

37. See Moshe Zak, "The Senator from Kansas," in *Ma'ariv*, April 20, 1990.

38. NBC and CBS reports quoted in the Israeli press, March 29-30, 1990;

reports on testimony by the director of U.S. Naval Intelligence regarding Iraq's "advanced nuclear program," and about an Egyptian, "even more advanced" nuclear effort by the DNI; and cf. the British *Independent on Sunday*, April 1, 1990, and the American *Time* and *Newsweek* magazines of that weekend.

39. See Shomron's interview with *Yediot Aharonot* on Friday, April 6, 1990; in an Israeli television interview of General Ehud Barak, his deputy, on the same date, General Barak analyzed Saddam's public warnings against Israeli attacks and threats to "destroy half of Israel," by using chemical means, as rather defensive postures.

40. For Saddam's speech, see Israeli translation and Rabin's response—in opaque nuclear terms—in *Yediot Aharonot*, April 4, 1990.

41. Spector, *Nuclear Ambitions*, p. 163.

42. See reports in the British press, quoted in *Yediot Aharonot*, December 15, 1989, about Iraq's missile testing—which was later described as a failure—and Iraq's own claims to have developed an antimissile missile (also regarded as premature by Israeli experts); and cf. Saddam's warning that superpower detente required Arab cooperation and constrained Arab freedom of action, a summary of which is in the same issue of *Yediot Aharonot*.

43. The interview with Rageb Gibril appeared in Mapam's newspaper *Al-Hamishmar*, February 26, 1988.

44. See texts of Foreign Minister Shevardnadze's speeches in Damascus and in Cairo on March 1988, and cf. Robert Turdiev, a high official in the Soviet Foreign Ministry, as quoted by the Kuwaiti paper *El-Anba*, reported by Reuter's on April 2, 1988: "Israel endangers the Arab states more than they endanger her . . . The Soviet Union tries to verify the stories that Israel has nuclear weapons, and suggests a combined system of regional security."

45. See text of a televised press conference held by Dennis Ross, chief of the planning staff, Department of State, and broadcast to three Arab capitals, as reported in *Ha'aretz* on June 15, 1989.

46. Advanced parts of an interview with *Vanity Fair*, as quoted in *Ha'aretz*, June 11, 1989.

47. *Ha'aretz*, June 11, 1989, Shaul Zadka reporting from London on Iraqi overtures to Israel regarding help to the Maronites in Lebanon against Syria.

48. *The National Interest*, Washington, D.C., Summer 1989.

Chapter Twelve. The Rebirth of Pan-Arabism?

1. See Yehoshua Porat, "A Lesson in History and Its Falsification," *Ha'aretz*, February 21, 1991.

2. Ibid.

3. This general history of Iraq and Kuwait is based on British and American intelligence field reports during WWII in OSS archives, and on Dr. Amazia Bar-Am of Haifa University, "Uniqueness and National Integration (*Watania*) in the Thought and Political Praxis in Iraq under the Ba'ath 1968-1982," Ph.D. diss., Hebrew University, Jerusalem, 1986; and cf, Bar-Am's article in *Ha'aretz*, "The Realization of a Dream, " August 26, 1990.

4. See A. James Gregor, *Contemporary Radical Ideologies*, among Gregor's other works on Fascism. In a public lecture at the Van-Leer Institute, Jerusalem, June 4, 1981, Professor Gregor referred specifically to the Ba'ath Party in this connection. He also mentioned Sukarno's regime in Indonesia, Nasserism, and to an extent Soviet Communism as "tools of modernization" using Fascist methods, but he was careful to distinguish between what he called "Fascism" and German Nazism.

5. Stanley Hoffmann, "A New World," in *Foreign Affairs* (Fall 1990), p. 115.

6. See Yosef Harif, "We Knew That We Did Not Know," *Ma'ariv*, February 8, 1991; and cf. Eyal Erlich, "Did Israel Miss a Chance of Peace with Iraq?," ibid.

7. According to Spector's 1990 report, *Nuclear Ambitions*, "By early 1989, it appeared that as part of this overall trend, Iraq had revitalized its efforts to acquire nuclear arms" (p. 191); and see the open declaration by the director of U.S. Naval Intelligence, Admiral Brooks, before a congressional committee to this effect in February 1989. In 1989, says Spector, both American and Israeli authorities believed that Iraq was five to ten years away from producing nuclear devices, whereas other sources quoted by him were less sure about it and reduced the necessary period of time to develop the Iraqi bomb to "two to five years."

8. *PPNN Newsbrief*, no. 10, p. 6. This report has been officially confirmed by the Argentinian Minister of Foreign affairs, Domingo Cabillio, upon arriving for an official visit in Israel on September 3, 1990. Mr. Cabillio said that the termination of the Condor project was agreed upon by the presidents of the U.S. and Argentina "about a year before." He further said that his country would avoid supplying "dictatorial regimes with military technologies."

9. *PPNN Newsbrief*, ibid, p. 7.

10. *New York Times*, June 26, 1991.

11. See *Davar*, January 24, 1991, quoting a document submitted to the U.S. Senate Committee on Foreign Relations, according to which West German firms played a leading role in supplying Saddam with electromagnets and centrifuges for uranium enrichment.

12. See Yevgeni Primakov, *The War That Could Be Avoided*, partially pub-lished by *Time* magazine and *Yediot Aharonot*, March 1, 1991; Primakov was President Gorbachev's special envoy to Iraq before and during the Gulf War; according to his report, Saddam told him that since he "won the war against Iran in 1988," Iraq had become the target of a "multinational conspiracy"; "nei-ther the U.S. nor Israel could accept an Iraq with strong military muscles." Saudi Arabia and the Gulf states were involved in the "conspiracy," since they have ignored the oil export quotas fixed by OPEC, and thus the low oil price meant the "destruction of Iraq." Primakov responded by saying that Saddam probably had a "Massada Complex" (fear of imminent destruction) similar to Israel's, and the Iraqi ruler agreed, sensing some understanding of the claims and demands that accompanied his self-proclaimed state of desperation.

13. According to well-informed *Ma'ariv* staff writer Moshe Zak, Yassir Arafat was supposed to be instrumental in Saddam's plan to take control of Kuwait's assets abroad, but was preempted by the Western governments who immediately froze them. As far as Egypt was concerned, President Mubarak was quoted by Senator Frank Lautenberg, Democrat of New Jersey, in mid-August, as if the Iraqi ruler had promised him personally some of the money, and more for Egypt's own purposes.

14. The emergence of American consciousness of Saddam's nuclear ambi-tion at this stage and the role played in this regard by several key figures, both public and official—such as Henry Kissinger, Richard Perle, Ann Lewis (former head of the Democratic National Committee), Richard Haass (a senior NSC aide), and Congressman Stephen Solarz—is described by Michael Massing, "The Road to War," *New York Review of Books*, vol. 38 (no. 6), March 28, 1991. One could, of course, argue—as was the case in some American post-war press analysis—that Saddam's nuclear capabilities were purposely inflated by the Bush Administration to justify an oil war. However, Saddam's own disclosures of nuclear potential after the war quickly put this argument to rest. For a detailed list of these disclosures, which the IAEA and the Bush Administra-tion still regarded as misleading and incomplete, see the *Washington Post*, July 26, 1991, "Iraq Accused of Not Meeting U. N. Deadline," and cf. in the same paper "Eliminating Iraq's Weapons of Mass Destruction," a detailed list of Sad-dam Hussein's disclosed weapons of that kind, based on a U.N. Special Com-mission finding and IAEA information, which those bodies described as "far away from a conclusion in any of these fields."

15. *PPNN Newsbrief*, ibid.

16. Ibid.

17. President Hosni Mubarak was quoted by Israeli Radio on September 9, 1990, to the effect that "Egypt's goal in the current crisis [is] to prevent Iraq from acquiring the atomic bomb."

18. Press conference on September 4, 1990, quoted by Israeli Radio "Kol-Israel."

19. The letter was signed by a presidential aide, and reprinted in the *Yediot Aharonot* local weekend supplement, October 19, 1990.

20. For details see *Ma'ariv* columnist Moshe Zak, "Yossi and Yanush," August 31, 1990. Mr. Zak, who is close to Prime Minister Shamir's views and reflects his opinions, also criticized an Israeli reserve general—"Yanush" Ben-Gal—who had suggested in public that the Americans should use "clean," i.e., neutron bombs against Iraq. He further hailed Mr. Yossi Sarid, a leftist member of the Knesset, who had given up on Arafat's PLO following the latter's support of Saddam' s invasion of Kuwait.

21. Ibid.

22. "The Egyptian President in the National Assembly," Israeli Television tape, August 6, 1990.

23. Mr. Arens on Israeli Television on August 20, 1990. It was later reported in *Yediot Aharonot*, September 6, 1991, that during this visit, on which the IDF's Director of Military Intelligence and the head of the Mossad accompanied him, Arens warned the U S. about the huge extent of Saddam's nuclear project. Thus according to this report, Israel was actively involved prior to the Gulf War.

24. Israeli Television interview, August, 22, 1990.

25. Zack in *Ma'ariv*, November 16, 1990.

26. *Ma'ariv*, November 15, 1990.

27. See *Yediot Aharonot*, September 4, 1990: "Saddam . . . declares his intention to use unconventional weapons, but the world was never more ready to face such threats as it is now, and Israel is even more . . ."

28. See *Pisqei Din*, "Verdicts of the Israeli Supreme Court," in criminal appeal 172/88, Mordechai Vanunu against the State of Israel, September 1990, reprinted in *Ha'aretz*, September 2, 1990.

29. See Shaul Zadka, reporting from London; "[The Supreme Court's] Revelations Deter Saddam," *Ha'aretz*, September 2, 1990.

30. See Avigdor Feldman, "Something Erotic in the Air," *Ha'aretz*, August 31, 1990.

31. *Journal de Brazil*, quoted in an Israeli Television news broadcast, September 5, 1990.

32. Baker's testimonies before the House and the Senate's Foreign Relations committees, September 4 and 5, 1990.

33. Leonard Spector. In a conversation with the author, September 24, 1990.

34. Spector, *Nuclear Ambitions*, p. 197.

35. William B. Quandt. Interview with the author, September 19, 1990.

Chapter Thirteen. India, Pakistan, North Korea, Algeria, Iran, and the Rest

1. See Yan Kong and Tim McCarthy, "The Proliferation of the PRC-Supplied Algerian Reactor, " *Eye on Supply*, no. 4 (Spring 1991), pp. 71-73.

2. Indian scholars have been ambivalent about the value of a nuclear guarantee implied in the August 1971 Indo-Soviet Treaty. See especially Raju G. C. Thomas, "India's Nuclear and Space Programs: Defense or Development?" in *World Politics* 28 (2), January 1986, p. 326. This author discounts the value of such a guarantee.

3. See Leonard S. Spector, *The Undeclared Bomb*, 1988, p. 102; cf. *Time* magazine, April 6, 1987, the *New York Times*, March 26, 1987; and final launching reports in the world press in Spring 1989.

4. The report was published by Dan Raviv and Yossi Melman on April 8, 1990; both are journalists, one American and one Israeli, specializing in Israel's secret activities abroad.

5. See Ashok Kapur, *Pakistan's Nuclear Development* (London: Croom-Helm, 1988), and cf. Spector, *The Undeclared Bomb*, pp. 120-53. See also P. K. S. Namboodiri, "Pakistan's Nuclear Posture," in *Nuclear Myths and Realities*, edited by K. Subrahmanyam (New Delhi: ABC Publishing House, 1981), pp. 139-94.

6. See, for example, George Quester in "Some Pakistani Problems and a Nuclear Non-Solution," *Journal of Strategic Studies*, 8 (4), December 1985, p. 102ff.

7. For U. S.-Pakistani relations in this regard and congressional involvement in trying to curb Pakistan's nuclear program, see Warren H. Donnelly, "Pakistan and Nuclear Weapons," *Issue Brief* IB86110, updated November 6, 1987, Congressional Research Service, Washington, D.C., and Mr. Donnelly's subsequent reports.

8. See, for example, Mushahid Hussein, former editor of *The Muslim*, Islamabad, "Why Pakistan Needs a Nuclear Option," *Washington Post*, July 29, 1987; and cf. Stephen P. Cohen, "South Asia," in *Superpower Competition and Security in the Third World*, edited by Robert S. Litwak and Samuel F. Wells, Jr. (Cambridge: Ballinger, 1988), p. 163. Cf. further an interesting, if perhaps melodramatic, scenario sketched by Rodney W. Jones in "Strategic Consequences of Nuclear Proliferation in South Asia: Outlook from the United States," *Journal of Strategic Studies*, 8 (4), December 1985, pp. 30-36.

9. See Nayar-Hussein controversy in Spector, *The Undeclared Bomb*, pp. 133-35ff, and congressional deliberations in this regard, including the Reagan Administration's final decision not to expose Pakistan as a nuclear nation; and cf. Donnelly, "Pakistan and Nuclear Weapons."

10. See Yitzhak Shichor, "Unfolded Arms: Beijing's Recent Military Sales Offensive," in *Pacific Review*, vol. 1 (no. 3), 1988, pp. 320-30, and Yitzhak Shichor, *East Wind Over Arabia: Origins and Implications of the Sino Saudi Missile Deal*. China Research Monograph 35, Institute of East Asian Studies (Berkeley: University of California, 1989).

11. See Far Eastern Economic Review (FEER) report on April 27, 1989, p. 8, to the effect that U.S. officials were investigating a report that Pakistani technicians have been working alongside Chinese counterparts in setting up CSS-2 East Wind missiles in Saudi Arabia. On China's involvement in Pakistan's conventional and nuclear systems, see Yaakov Vertzberger, *The Enduring Entente: Sino-Pakistani Relations 1960-1980*, The Washington Papers, no. 95 (Boulder, Colo.: Westview Press, 1983); and especially B. K. Kumar, "Nuclear Nexus between Peking and Islamabad: An Overview of Some Significant Developments, in *Issues and Studies*, Taipei, vol. 21 (8), August 1985, pp. 140-50; and cf. Yan Kong and William C. Potter, "Comments on Beijing's Defense Establishment," *Eyes on Supply*, no. 4 (Spring 1991), pp. 74-76.

12. Shichor, "Unfolded Arms," p. 59.

13. Reuter's dispatch from Islamabad, December 27, 1988.

14. In this regard, see Spector, *Nuclear Ambitions*, p. 118.

15. For the dates see Spector, *Nuclear Ambitions*, p. 273.

16. Spector, *Nuclear Ambitions*, p. 284.

17. Ibid.

18. Quoted in *Ma'ariv*, October 27, 1989.

19. "Today" show details appeared in *Ma'ariv*, October 27, 1989.

20. Peter Pry, *Israel's Nuclear Arsenal*, pp. 7-13, 21, 26, 38, 66-67.

21. See Bundy, *Danger and Survival*, p. 505ff. Here Bundy reconciled himself with the Israeli bomb, as he put it: "The Israeli case may be one more demonstration of the preposition [sic] that what you oppose before it happens is something which it is wise to accept when it becomes real" (p. 512). Bundy does not implicate himself fully (as a high U.S. government official) in the efforts to stop or delegitimize the Israeli nuclear program; he explains the U.S. failure in this regard as being the result of U.S. domestic politics and Israel's determination to pursue the bomb at all costs—and even use it. "A still deeper question [writes Bundy] is whether the United States would wish to accept the moral and polit-

ical responsibility of forcing the abandonment of the Israeli nuclear weapons program, even assuming that it could. If the abandonment should take place, and if at some time in the future only a nuclear threat or even a nuclear response could prevent Israel from being overrun, would the United States do for the Israelis what it had made them unable to do for themselves?"

22. See Spector, *Nuclear Ambitions*, p. 127.

23. Spector, *Nuclear Ambitions*, p. 124.

24. Ibid.

Epilogue. The End of Opacity?

1. Baghdad Radio, February 2, 1991.

2. In an interview with *Ha'aretz*, May 17, 1991.

3. Baghdad Radio, February 2, 1991.

4. Concerning Cheney's harmless remark, a former Israeli chief of staff, General Mordechai Gur, now a Labor politician, commented on Israeli Radio, February 4, 1991, that the secretary's interview meant "abrasion of Israel's conventional power of deterrence and hence we remained catastrophically dependent on nuclear deterrence alone."

5. Yosef Cohen, "A Time Bomb," *Kol-Hair*, Jerusalem, February 8, 1991.

6. According to Israeli Radio, Foreign Minister David Levy demanded, in a letter to Secretary Baker, that far-reaching limits be imposed on Iraq's military capabilities, conventional and unconventional alike, following Saddam's threats to "destroy Israel" during the war; on Israeli Television, on February 28, 1991, Deputy Foreign Minister Natanyahu demanded control mechanisms to ensure the same purpose; shortly beforehand he mentioned "four Arab states" who were engaged in developing unconventional weapons—he probably meant, other than Iraq, Libya (nuclear, chemical), Syria (chemical, nuclear?), and Egypt (chemical, nuclear?)—and argued that such weapons should be denied "from dictatorships."

7. Quoted in *Ha'aretz*, June 10, 1991.

8. See *Ha'aertz* of May 12, 1991, Reuven Pdehzur from Washington: "Iraq Had Before the War Enough Enriched Uranium to Build a Nuclear Bomb," about 45 kilograms of 80 percent and 93 percent enriched; and cf. *PPNN Newsbrief*, no. 13 (Spring 1991), p. 6, according to which Iraq had just 20 kilograms of highly enriched uranium, fully accounted for by the IAEA before the war: "Most experts, accordingly, meanwhile remain unconvinced that even with the extensive assistance Iraq is said to have been given . . . it could have acquired

the capacity to produce a significant quantity of weapons-usable material in less than five years. " Yet the above-quoted Washington story, based on an Iraqi letter to the IAEA dated April 27, 1991—following the agency's refusal to accept an initial Iraqi letter to the U.N. Secretary General, requested on the basis of Security Council Resolution 687—doubles the amount of the Iraqi enriched uranium in comparison to the PPNN report, and at least half of it was not accounted for; what was missing, probably, were the weaponization mechanisms for something like two Iraqi bombs, even though Saddam pretended to show some kritrons (triggering devices) in public which were partially confiscated by the British authorities on their way to Baghdad (he boasted that he "has already had them anyway").

9. See "U.S. Shows Photos to Argue Iraq Hides Nuclear Material," *New York Times*, June 27, 1991; and cf. "U.S. Says Iraq Still Runs Nuclear Arms Program," *Boston Globe*, June 27, 1991.

10. In this regard, see Leonard Weiss, "Tighten Up on Nuclear Cheaters," *Bulletin of the Atomic Scientists* (May 1991); and cf. "Baghdad Gave Up: U.N. Arms Control Inspectors Would Be Allowed Free Access," *Ma'ariv*, May 20, 1991.

11. See "Cheney—The U. S. Would Finance 72% of the 'Arrow' Project and Supply 10 More F-15s," *Yediot Aharonot*, May 31, 1991.

12. *Defense News Weekly*, quoted in *Ha'aertz*, June 10, 1991.

13. The Bush initiative was preceded by a variety of leaks, some close to the spirit of the initiative itself, some of which could be seen as "trial balloons," and some as specific responses to Israeli signals, such as Energy Minister Ne'eman's publicly proclaimed interest in a "Soviet-made reactor for peaceful use," or rather in an Israeli-made reactor; cf. *Wall Street Journal*, May 8, 1991, quoting Paul Leventhal, chairman of an American-based arms control institute, to the effect that Ne'eman's interest in the Soviet is because of growing "maintenance and safety problems" at Dimona (he was quoted as having said that it was "started" in 1957). The timely publication of this item could represent the opinion of the nonproliferation lobby, which was active on its own (1957 is of course the wrong date). A good example of the nonproliferation lobby's activity in connection with the Bush initiative is "Defusing the Nuclear Mideast," by Avner Cohen and Marvin Miller, *New York Times*, May 30, 1991.

14. See in this connection Cathleen S. Fisher, "Build Confidence, Not Weapons," *Bulletin of the Atomic Scientists*, vol. 47 (no. 5), June 1991.

15. Former minister of energy, Labor MK Moshe Shahal, was severely censured by the committee chairman Eliahu Ben-Elissar (Likud) for that indiscretion. See *Ma'ariv*, May 30, 1991—"Ben-Elissar: Shahal the Liar Discloses Secrets; Shahal: Ben-Elissar Uncredible and Pompous as a Balloon." In fact, Shahal was probably active here to cover up his previous support of a "Saddam-oriented" policy, which he reportedly endorsed before the war.

16. Yeshiahu Ben-Porat, "Bush Worries Rabin," *Yediot Aharonot*, May 31, 1991.

17. According to the Spring 1991 *PPNN Newsbrief*, Saddam had obtained about 30 centrifuges before the war; many more are necessary to produce weapons-grade uranium. According to the American National Public Radio, June 3, 1991, an Iraqi expert who deserted to the U.S. disclosed that parts of Iraq's nuclear infrastructure remained intact, since the Allies were unaware of them or some were protected in underground shelters.

18. For an in-depth survey of Egypt's domestic and foreign policy choice before the Gulf War, see William B. Quandt, *The United States and Egypt* (Washington: The Brookings Institution, 1990).

19. This analysis is taken from Ora Koren, "Money and Power, Too," *Ha'aretz*, June 4, 1991. Ms. Koren is an expert on Arab affairs.

20. Zev Schiff from Washington in *Ha'aretz*, June 3, 1991: "Assad advised the U.S. and the Soviet Union that he was against the formula offered by President Bush regarding arms control in the Middle East."

21. See *U.S. News and World Report*, June 3, 1991, according to which President Bush supposedly protested in Cairo, but not publicly, in this regard.

22. *Ha'aretz*, reporting from Washington, June 3, 1991.

23. London *Sunday Times*, June 2, 1991.

24. In *Yediot Aharonot* interview, ibid.; Rabin's view was similar to Henry Kissinger's opinion in this regard, as before.

25. Cf. *Ma'ariv* and *Ha'aretz*, May 31, 1991, both reporting on Bush's announcement of his initiative for the Middle East.

26. On June 10, 1991.

27. Spector, *The Undeclared Bomb*, p. 192.

28. Israeli Radio broadcast, May 8, 1991.

29. Reported in *Davar*, June 11, 1991.

Bibliography

Many of the works listed here were published in Hebrew-language editions only. For the convenience of the reader, titles are given in English.

Archival Sources

Ben-Gurion Memorial Archive, especially Ben-Gurion's personal diaries 1953-1958. Kibbutz Sde Boker.

Lyndon B. Johnson Memorial Library, Austin, Texas.

John F. Kennedy Memorial Library, Boston, Massachusetts.

Library of Congress, Washington, D.C.

National Security Archive, Washington, D.C.

Public Record Office (PRO), Surrey, England.

U.S. National Archives, Washington, D.C.

Published Primary Sources

(including primary sources contained in or referred to in biographies, memorabilia, scholarly literature, and the media)

Allon, Yigal. *A Curtain of Sand.* Tel Aviv: Hakibbutz Hameuchad, 1959, rev. ed. 1968.

——— . *Contriving Warfare: Defense Related Statements.* Tel Aviv: Hakibbutz Hameuchad, 1990.

Barnaby, Frank. *The Invisible Bomb: The Nuclear Arms Race in the Middle East.* London: I. B. Tauris, 1989.

Bar-Zohar, Michael. *Ben-Gurion.* Vol. III. Tel Aviv: Am-Oved Publishers, 1977.

Ben-Gurion, David. *War Diaries 1948-1949.* Tel Aviv: Misrad Habitachon Press, 1982.

Brecher, Michael. *Decisions in Crisis: Israel 1967 and 1973.* Berkeley: University of California Press, 1980.

Bumbacher, Beat. *Die USA und Nasser: Amerikanische Ägypten-Politik der Kennedy und Johnson Administration 1961-1967.* Wiesbaden: Steiner, 1987.

Bundy, McGeorge. *Danger and Survival: Choices About the Bomb in the First Fifty Years.* New York: Random House, 1988.

Churchill, Winston S., *The Second World War.* Vol. VI, *Triumph and Tragedy.* Boston: Houghton Mifflin, 1953.

Clark, Ian, and Nicholas J. Wheeler. *The British Origins of Nuclear Strategy 1945-1955.* Oxford: Clarendon Press, 1989.

Congressional Record, Washington, D.C.

Dayan, Moshe. "Germany, Dimona and the Jordan," *Ha'aretz*, March 26, 1965.

————. *A New Map, Different Relations: A Collection of Dayan's Speeches and Writings 1967-1969.* Haifa: Shikmona Press, 1969.

————. *Story of My Life.* Yediot Aharonot edition. Jerusalem: Edanim, 1980.

Divrei Haknesset [Official Record of the Knesset]. Jerusalem: Government Printing Office, 1960.

Evron, Yair. *Israel's Nuclear Dilemma.* Tel Aviv: Hakibbutz Hameuchad, 1987.

Foreign Relations of the United States 1955-1957. Vols. XIV-XV. Washington, D.C.: Government Printing Office, 1989.

Garthoff, Raymond L. *Detente and Confrontation.* Washington, D.C.: The Brookings Institution, 1985.

Gazit, Mordechai. *President Kennedy's Policy Toward the Arab States and Israel.* The Shiloah Center for Middle East and African Studies. Tel Aviv: Tel Aviv University, 1983.

Gilbert, Martin. *Never Despair: Winston S. Churchill 1945-1965.* London: Heinemann, 1988.

Golan, Matti. *Peres.* Tel Aviv: Schocken, 1982.

Haber, Eitan, ed. *"Today War Will Break Out"*: *The Reminiscences of Brigadier General Israel Lior, Aide-de-Camp to Prime Ministers Levi Eshkol and Golda Meir.* Yediot Aharonot edition. Tel Aviv: Edanim, 1987.

Harel, Isser. *The Crisis of the German Scientists 1962-1963.* Tel Aviv: Ma'ariv, 1982.

———. *Security and Democracy.* Yediot Aharonot edition. Tel Aviv: Edanim, 1988.

Heikal, Mohamed (Hassnein). "The Bomb," *Al-Aharam,* Cairo, November 23, 1973.

———. *The Road to Ramadan.* London: Collins, 1975.

———. "The Israeli Nuclear Threat" in *Al-Rai,* Amman, and *Al-Nahar,* Beirut, June 12, 15, and 19, 1977.

———. *The Sphinx and the Commissar.* New York: Harper and Row, 1978.

Hillgruber, Andreas, ed. *Staatsmänner und Diplomaten bei Hitler.* Frankfurt/Main: Bernard und Graefe Verlag für Wehrwesen, 1967.

Jewish Observer and Middle East Review, "An Independent Deterrent for Israel." Unsigned editorial. December 28, 1962.

Jochmann, Werner, ed. *Adolf Hitler: Monologe im Führerhauptquartier 1941-1944.* Hamburg: Die Aufzeichnungen Heinrich Heims, 1980.

Kohl, Wilfrid L. *French Nuclear Diplomacy.* Princeton, N.J.: Princeton University Press, 1971.

Nakdimon, Shlomo. *Tammuz in Flames.* Yediot Aharonot edition. Jerusalem: Edanim, 1986.

Naor, Arieh. "A Risk Too High," *Yediot Aharonot,* April 1, 1989.

———. "The Jewish Wars," *Monitin,* May 31, 1991, through June 15, 1991.

Newhouse, John. *War and Peace in the Nuclear Age.* New York: Knopf, 1989.

Nitze, Paul H., with Ann M. Smith and Steven L. Rearden. *From Hiroshima to Glasnost: At the Center of Decision.* New York: Grove Weidenfeld, 1989.

Pean, Pierre. *Les Deux Bombes.* Paris: Arthem Fayard, 1982.

Peres, Shimon. "Economics Without Boundaries," *Ha'aretz,* June 2, 1989.

Perrin, Jean Francis. Quoted in the London *Sunday Times,* October 5, 1986.

Primakov, Yevgeni. *The War That Could Be Avoided,* partially published by *Time* magazine and *Yediot Aharonot,* March 1, 1991.

Quandt, William B. *Decade of Decision.* Berkeley: University of California Press, 1977.

———— . *Camp David—Peacemaking and Politics.* Washington, D.C.: The Brookings Institution, 1986.

———— . *The United States and Egypt.* Washington, D.C.: The Brookings Institution, 1990.

Rabin, Yitzhak. *A Soldier Record.* Tel Aviv: Ma'ariv, 1979.

al-Sadat, Anwar. *Memoirs.* Serialized in *October,* Cairo, and in *Al-Sayassa,* Kuwait, December 1976 through January 1977.

Sharett, Moshe. *Diaries.* Vol. 7. Tel Aviv: Ma'ariv, 1978.

Sharon, Ariel. "An Undelivered Speech," *Ma'ariv,* December 18, 1981.

Stebbins, Richard P., ed. *Documents on American Foreign Relations.* New York: Simon and Schuster, 1963.

Stein, Janis Gross, and Raymund Tanter. *Rational Decision Making: Israel's Security Choices 1967.* Columbus: Ohio State University Press, 1980.

Tamir, Avraham. "My Talks with Iraqi Leaders," *Yediot Aharonot,* February 15, 1991.

U.S. Department of State, *Foreign Relations of the United States 1955-1957,* The Arab-Israeli Dispute, Vols. XIV-XV. Washington, D.C.: Government Printing Office, 1989.

Wakebridge, Charles. "The Syrian Side of the Hill," *Military Review,* February 1976.

Zak, Moshe. "The Bush Program: Between Shamir and Mubarak," *Ma'ariv,* May 31, 1991.

Deterrence, Arms Control, and Proliferation Research and Nuclear "Sharing"

Aspen Strategy Group. *New Threats: Responding to the Proliferation of Nuclear, Chemical, and Delivery Capabilities in the Third World.* Appendix 7, "'Solving' the Proliferation Problem in the Middle East," by Geoffrey Kemp, pp. 197-222. Lanham, Md., and London: Aspen Strategy Group, 1990.

Bader, William. *The United States and the Spread of Nuclear Weapons.* New York: Pegasus, 1968.

Carnesale, Albert, and Richard N. Haass, eds. *Superpower Arms Control: Setting the Record Straight.* Cambridge, Mass.: Ballinger, 1987.

Carus, W. Seth. *Ballistic Missiles in the Third World: Threat and Response.* The

Washington Papers. New York: Praeger, with the Center for Strategic and International Studies, Washington, D.C., 1990.

Cimbala, Stephen J. *Nuclear Strategizing: Deterrence and Reality.* New York: Praeger, 1988.

Donnelly, Warren H. "Pakistan and Nuclear Weapons," *Issue Brief* IB86110, Congressional Research Service, Washington, D.C., November 6, 1987.

Eckert, Michael. "Die Anfänge der Atompolitik in der Bundestrepublik Deutschland," *VJH*, January 1989, pp. 115-43.

Evron, Yair. "Israel and the Atom: The Uses and Misuses of Ambiguity 1957-1967," *Orbis*, vol. 17 (no. 4), p. 108ff.

Gallois, Pierre. *The Balance of Terror.* Boston: Houghton Mifflin, 1961.

George, Alexander L., and Richard Smoke. *Deterrence in American Foreign Policy.* New York: Columbia University Press, 1974.

Goldschmidt, Bertrand. *Les Rivalites Atomiques (1939-1966).* Paris: Fayard, 1967.

———. *Les Complex Atomique.* Paris: Fayard, 1980.

Gray, Colin Spencer. *Nuclear Strategy and National Style.* Lanham, Md.: Hamilton Press, 1986.

Gupta, Bahbani Sen. *Nuclear Weapons: Policy Options for India.* New Delhi: Sage, 1984.

Harkavy, Robert E. *Spectre of a Middle Eastern Holocaust.* Denver: University of Denver Press, 1977.

———. "Pariah States and Nuclear Proliferation," in *Nuclear Proliferation—Breaking the Chain*, edited by George H. Quester. Madison: University of Wisconsin Press, 1981, pp. 135-63.

Jervis, Robert. "Deterrence Theory Revisited," *World Politics*, vol. XXXI (no. 3), January 1979, pp. 289-324.

———. *The Illogic of American Nuclear Strategy.* Ithaca: Cornell University Press, 1984.

———. "The Political Effects of Nuclear Weapons," *International Security*, vol. 12 (no. 2), Fall 1988, pp. 80-90.

———. *The Meaning of the Nuclear Revolution.* Ithaca: Cornell University Press, 1989.

Kapur, Ashok. *India's Nuclear Option.* New York: Praeger, 1976.

———. *Pakistan's Nuclear Development.* London: Croom-Helm, 1988.

Kissinger, Henry A. *Nuclear Weapons and Foreign Policy.* New York: Anchor, 1957.

Kong, Yan, and Tim McCarthy. "The Proliferation Risks of the PRC-Supplied Algerian Nuclear Reactor," *Eye on Supply,* no. 4 (Spring 1991), pp. 71-73.

Kong, Yan, and William C. Potter. "Comments on Beijing's Defense Establishment," *Eye on Supply,* no. 4 (Spring 1991), pp. 74-76.

Liddell-Hart, Basil Henry. *The Revolution in Warfare.* London: Faber and Faber, 1946.

———. *Defense of the West.* London: Cassell, 1950.

Maxwell, Stephen. "Rationality in Deterrence," *Adelphi Papers,* no. 50. London: International Institute for Strategic Studies, August 1968.

Nye, Joseph S. "Maintaining a Non-Proliferation Regime," in *Nuclear Proliferation—Breaking the Chain,* edited by George H. Quester. Madison, Wisc.: University of Wisconsin Press, 1981.

———. "Arms Conrol After the Cold War," *Foreign Affairs* (Winter 1989-1990), pp. 42-64.

Quester, George H. *The Politics of Nuclear Proliferation.* Baltimore: Johns Hopkins University Press, 1973.

———. "Some Pakistani Problems and a Nuclear Non-Solution," *Journal of Strategic Studies,* vol. 8 (no. 4), December 1985, p. 102ff.

Reiss, Mitchell. *Without the Bomb: The Politics of Nuclear Nonproliferation.* New York: Columbia University Press, 1988.

Sabin, Philip A. G. "Shadow or Substance? Perception and Symbolism in Nuclear Force Planning," *Adelphi Papers,* no. 222. London: International Institute for Strategic Studies, Summer 1987.

Scheinman, Lawrence. *Atomic Energy Policy Under the Fourth Republic.* Princeton, N.J.: Princeton University Press, 1965.

Schelling, Thomas C. *The Strategy of Conflict.* Cambridge, Mass.: Harvard University Press, 1960; New York: Oxford, 1963.

———. "The Thirtieth Year." Arms Control: Thirty Years On. *Daedalus* (Winter 1991), pp. 21-31.

Schwarz, Hans-Peter. "Adenauer und die Kernwaffen," *VJH* (April 1989), pp. 567-93.

Shichor, Yitzhak. "Unfolded Arms: Beijing's Recent Military Sale Offensive," *Pacific Review,* vol. 1 (no. 3), 1988.

————. *East Wind Over Arabia: Origins and Implications of the Sino-Saudi Missile Deal*. China Research Monograph 35, Institute of East Asian Studies. Berkeley: University of California, 1989.

Snyder, Jed C., and Samuel F. Wells, Jr., eds. *Limiting Nuclear Proliferation*. Cambridge, Mass.: Ballinger, 1985.

Sokolovsky, Vassily D., ed. *Soviet Military Strategy*. New York: Prentice-Hall, 1963.

Soutou, Georges-Henri. "Die Nuklearpolitik der Vierten Republik," *VJH* (April 1989), pp. 606-10.

Spector, Leonard S. *The Undeclared Bomb: The Spread of Nuclear Weapons 1987-1988*. For the Carnegie Endowment for International Peace. Cambridge, Mass.: Ballinger, 1988.

————. "New Players in the Nuclear Game," *Bulletin of the Atomic Scientists* (January/February 1989), pp. 29-32.

Spector, Leonard S., with Jacqueline R. Smith. *Nuclear Ambitions: The Spread of Nuclear Weapons 1989-1990*. For the Carnegie Endowment for International Peace. Boulder, Colo.: Westview Press, 1990.

Subrahmanyam, K., ed. *Nuclear Myths and Realities*. New Delhi: ABC Publishing House, 1981.

Thomas, Raju D. C. "India's Nuclear and Space Programs: Defense or Development," *World Politics*, vol. 28 (no. 2), January 1986, p. 326ff.

United Nations General Assembly, *Establishment of a Nuclear-Weapon-Free Zone in the Region of the Middle East*. Study on effective and verifiable measures which would facilitate the establishment of a nuclear-weapon-free zone in the Middle East. Report of the Secretary General. Document A/45/435, 10 October 1990.

Waltz, Kenneth N. "The Spread of Nuclear Weapons: More May Be Better," *Adelphi Papers*, no. 171. London: International Institute for Strategic Studies, Autumn 1981.

Wong-Fraser, Agatha S. Y. *The Political Utility of Nuclear Weapons: Expectations and Experience*. Washington, D.C.: University Press of America, 1980.

Zuckerman, Lord. "The Silver Fox" (review article based on Strobe Talbot's *The Master of the Game: Paul Nitze and the Nuclear Peace*). *New York Review of Books*, January 19, 1989.

Secondary Literature on Israel's Nuclear Program and Behavior

Albright, David. "Israel's Nuclear Arsenal," *FAS* (May 1988).

Aronson, Shlomo. "Israel's Nuclear Options," *ACIS Working Paper No. 7*, Los

Angeles: University of California, 1977.

——— . "Nuclearization of the Middle East—A Dovish View," *Jerusalem Quarterly*, no. 2 (Winter 1977).

——— . *Conflict and Bargaining in the Middle East*. Baltimore, Md.: Johns Hopkins University Press, 1978.

——— . "The Nuclear Dimension of the Yom Kippur War," *The Jerusalem Journal of International Relations*, vol. 7 (no. 12), 1984, pp. 107-42.

Bendman, Yona, and Yishai Cordova. "The Soviet Nuclear Threat Toward the Close of the Yom Kippur War," *The Jerusalem Journal of International Relations*, vol. 5 (1980), pp. 94-110.

Cohen, Avner, ed. *Humanity Under the Shadow of the Atom*. Tel Aviv: Hakibbutz Hameuchad, 1987.

Crosby, Sylvia K. *A Tacit Alliance*. Princeton, N.J.: Princeton University Press, 1974.

Encyclopedia Hebraeica. Appendix volume to vols. 1-17. Entries "Eretz Israel—History," p. 522ff, and "Ben-Gurion, David," pp. 676-77.

Eshed, Haggai. *Who Gave the Order*. Yediot Aharonot edition. Jerusalem: Edanim, 1982.

Evron, Yair. "The Relevance and the Irrelevance of Nuclear Options in Conventional Wars," *The Jerusalem Journal of International Relations*, vol. 7 (nos. 1-2), 1984, pp. 143-76.

——— . "Israeli-Palestinian-Jordanian Security Relations: The Idea of a 'Security Zone,'" in *Emerging Issues, Middle East Security: Two Views*. Occasional Paper No. 3. Cambridge, Mass.: American Academy of Arts and Sciences, 1990, pp. 23-49.

——— . "Opaque Nuclear Proliferation; The Israeli Case," in *The Journal of Strategic Studies*, vol. 13 (no. 3), September 1990, pp. 45-63.

Feldman, Shai. *Israeli Nuclear Deterrence*. New York: Columbia University Press, 1982.

Flapan, Simcha. "Nuclear Disarmament in the Middle East—the Only Solution," in *Humanity Under the Shadow of the Atom*, edited by Avner Cohen. Tel Aviv: Hakibbutz Hameuchad, 1987, pp. 194-204.

Golan, Matti. "Walking Confidently," *Ha'aretz*, May 8, 1981.

Green, Stephen. *Taking Sides: America's Secret Relations with a Militant Israel*. New York: Morrow, 1984.

———. *Living by the Sword: America and Israel in the Middle East, 1968-1987*. London: Faber, 1988.

Haselkorn, Avigdor. "Israel: From an Option to a 'Bomb in the Basement,'" in *Nuclear Proliferation: Phase 2*, edited by R. M. Lawrence and J. Larus. Lawrence, Kan.: University of Kansas Press, 1975, pp. 149-82.

Hodes, Aubrey. "The Implications of Israel's Nuclear Capability," *The Wiener Library Bulletin*, vol. XXII (Autumn 1968).

Inbar, Ephraim. "Israel and Nuclear Weapons Since October 1973," in *Security and Armaggedon: Israel's Nuclear Strategy*, edited by Louis René Beres. Lexington, Mass: D. C. Heath, Lexington, 1986.

———. *War and Peace in Israeli Politics: Labor Party Positions on National Security*. Boulder, Colo.: Lynne Rienner Publishers, 1991.

Jabber, Fuad. *Israel and Nuclear Weapons*. London: Chatto and Windus, 1971.

Krosney, Herbert, and Steve Weissman. *The Islamic Bomb*. Jerusalem: Adam and Castell Communications, 1982.

Millholin, Gary. "Heavy Water Cheaters," *Foreign Policy*, no. 69 (Winter 1987).

Nimrod, Yoram. "Nuclear Fog and Arab Response," *Davar*, December 2, 1980.

Pajak, Roger F. *Nuclear Proliferation in the Middle East*. Washington, D.C.: National Defense University, 1982.

Pry, Peter. *Israel's Nuclear Arsenal*. Boulder, Colo., and London: Westview and Croom-Helm, 1984.

United Nations. *A Study on Israel's Nuclear Armament*. New York: The United Nations, 1987.

Israeli and Western Periodicals and Media Used

Aerospace Daily, Washington, D.C.

Al-Hamishmar, daily newspaper, Tel Aviv

Aviation Week, New York

Baltimore Sun, daily, Baltimore, Md.

Bulletin of the Atomic Scientists, Chicago, Ill.

Daedalus, Cambridge, Mass.

Davar, daily newspaper, Tel Aviv

Eye on Supply, quarterly review, Emerging Nuclear Supplier Project, Monterey Institute of International Studies, Monterey, California

Foreign Broadcast Information Service (FBIS), Soviet Broadcasts, Washington, D.C.

Foreign Policy, Washington, D.C.

Ha'aretz, daily newspaper, Tel Aviv

Hadashot, daily newspaper, Tel Aviv

The Independent, London

International Defense Review, London

International Institute of Strategic Studies (IISS) Annual Reports, *Adelphi Papers,* London

Issue Brief, Congressional Research Service, WAshington, D.C.

The Jerusalem Journal of International Relations

The Jerusalem Quarterly

Jewish Observer and Middle East Review, London

The Journal of Strategic Studies, London

Ma'ariv, daily newspaper, Tel Aviv

Monitin, bimonthly, Tel Aviv

Newsweek magazine, American edition

The New York Times, New York Times Index

The Observer, London

The Sunday Times, London

Time magazine, American and European editions

Vierteljahreshefte für Zeitgeschichte (VJH), Stuttgart and Munich

World Politics, Princeton, N.J.

Yediot Aharonot, daily newspaper, Tel Aviv

Arab Newspapers and Other Printed Sources and Arab Broadcasts

All Arab sources listed below were translated by the Israeli Intelligence Branch Translation Service, code-named "Hazav." I have referred to it as HDCI

(Hazav Daily Collection of Published Arab Information). HDCI translations are available at the Truman Institute for Peace Research, Hebrew University, Jerusalem, and at the Dayan Center for Middle East Research, Tel Aviv University.

I have also used Hazav material gathered by Oded Brosh in his master's thesis "Nuclear Aspects of the Arab Israeli Conflict," Hebrew University, Jerusalem, 1984, and by Mr. Nimrod Granit in his master's thesis "The Perceptions of Israeli Unconventional Efforts in Arab Eyes and in the Scholarly Literature and Arab Activities in This Respect 1960-1988," Hebrew University, Jerusalem, 1989.

Al-Aharam, Cairo

Al-Aharam Aliqtisadi, Cairo

Al-Ahbar, Cairo

Al-Ahrar, Beirut

Al-Anba, Kuwait

Baghdad Radio

Filastin, Beirut

Al-Gish, Algiers

Al-Gumhuria, Cairo

Al-Hayat, Beirut

Al-Ittihad, United Arab Emirates

Al-Manar, Amman

Middle East News Agency, Cairo

Al-Nahar, Beirut

October, Cairo

PLO Radio Cairo

Al-Qabas, Kuwait

Radio Cairo

Al-Ray, Amman

Rooze al-Yusuf, Cairo

Al-Thahi, Baghdad

Al-Thawra, Damascus

Al-Thawra al-Arabia, Baghdad

Tishrin, Damascus

Al-Usbua al-Arabi, Beirut; Paris

Al-Watan, Kuwait

Al-Watan al-Arabi, Beirut

Al-Ziad Beirut

Miscellaneous Printed Works

Almogi, Yosef. *The Struggle over Ben-Gurion*. Tel Aviv: Edanim, Tel Aviv, 1988.

Aronson, Shlomo. "Die Dreifache Falle: Hitler's Judenpolitik, die Alliierten und die Juden," *VJH* (January 1984), pp. 29-85.

———. "Nazi Terrorism: The Complete Trap and the 'Final Solution,'" in *The Morality of Terrorism: Religious and Secular Justifications*, edited by David Rapoport and Yona Alexander. Pergamon Policy Studies. New York: Pergamon, 1982, pp. 169-85; second edition, New York: Columbia University Press, 1989.

Benziman, Uzi. *Israeli Caesar*. Tel Aviv: Adam Publishers, 1985.

Beschloss, Michael R. *The Crisis Years: Kennedy and Khrushchev 1960-1963*. New York: HarperCollins, 1991.

Caspi, Dan, Avraham Diskin, and Emanual Guttman, eds. *The Roots of Begin's Success*. London: Croom-Helm; New York: St. Martin's Press, 1984.

Dror, Yehezkel. *A Grand Strategy for Israel*. Jerusalem: Academon, 1989.

Gilbert, Martin. *Auschwitz and the Allies*. New York: Holt, Rinehart, and Winston, 1981.

Gregor, A. James. *Contemporary Radical Ideologies*. New York: Random House, 1968.

Hanrieder, Wolfram F. *Germany, America, Europe: Forty Years of German Foreign Policy*. New Haven, Conn.: Yale University Press, 1989.

Kaplan, Fred. *The Wizards of Armaggedon*. New York: Simon and Schuster, 1983.

Kelleher, Catherine McArdle. *Germany and the Politics of Nuclear Weapons*. New York and London: Columbia University Press, 1975.

Kool, Steven. *Nuclear Reality and the Inner Conflicts of Defense Policy Makers*. New York: Basic Books, 1988.

Kushner, Tony. *The Power of Prejudices: Antisemitism in the British Society During WWII*. London: Manchester University Press, 1988.

Lawren, William. *The General and the Bomb*. New York: Dodd and Mead, 1988.

Lewis, Bernard. *Semites and Anti-Semites*. New York: W. W. Norton, 1986.

———. *The Political Language of Islam*. Chicago and London: Chicago University Press, 1988.

Margalit, Dan. *Message from the White House*. Tel Aviv: Otpaz, 1971.

Massing, Michael. "The Road to War," *New York Review of Books*, vol. 38 (no. 6), March 28, 1991, pp. 16-21.

Porat, Yehoshua. "A Lesson in History and Its Falsification," *Ha'aretz*, February 21, 1991.

Rhodes, Richard. *The Making of the Atomic Bomb*. New York: Simon and Schuster, 1986.

Schiff, Zev, and Ehud Ya'ari. *Israel's Lebanon War*. New York: Simon and Schuster, 1984.

Sherry, Michael S. *The Rise of American Air Power: The Creation of Armageddon*. New Haven, Conn.: Yale University Press, 1987.

Wasserstein, Bernard. *Britain and the Jews of Europe 1939-1945*. London: Clarendon, 1979.

Wyman, David. *The Abandonment of the Jews*. New York: Pantheon, 1984.

Name Index

A'ali, Butrus Butrus, 180, 246, 333n, 341n
Abdulla, King, 307n
Abdulla, Sabbah abu, 233
Abu-Nidal, 253
Abul-Abbas, 216, 217, 253
Achmar, Abdulla, 181, 341n
Adanauer, Konrad, 63, 64
Aldin, Haled Muhi, 187
Allon, Yigal, anti-nuclear stance & conventional strategy of, 22-25, 33, 64-67, 73-76, 81, 85, 97, 98, 101, 113, 117, 131, 140, 146, 155, 158, 159, 213, 288-290, 299n, 311n, 312n, 326n, 329n, 333n
   and domestic politics, 118
   as foreign minister, 157
   and "last resort" nuclear strategy, 97, 102
   and partition of Palestine, 119, 120, 193
   and peace plan, 134
   and war of 1967, 108, 118
   and war of 1973, 146, 147, 325n
Almogi, Yosef, 311n
Alsuffi, Naziah, 341n
Amer, Abd al-Hakim, 99, 318n
Aoun, Michel, 256
Arad, Moshe, 344n

Arafat, Yassir, 107, 121, 122, 160, 203, 204, 209, 213, 216, 218, 220, 221, 226, 246, 247, 283, 296, 349n, 350n
Arens, Moshe, 191, 212, 247, 250, 350n
Aridor, Yoram, 338n
Arnet, Peter, 271
Aronson, Shlomo, 301n, 308n, 333n-336n, 358n, 340n
Attiah, Mamduh, 345n
Aude, Haddi, 335n
Assad, Hafez, 12, 122, 143, 179, 181, 198, 202, 206, 226, 231, 256, 268, 271, 281-283, 286
Atlee, Clement, 21, 22, 25, 303n
A'zala, Ibrahim Abu, 223
Azariahu, Arnan, 74
Aziz, Tarak, 171, 214, 215, 240

Badeau, John S., 93, 101, 318n, 322n
Bader, William, 70, 309n, 314n
Baker, James III, 219, 220, 221, 224, 240, 253, 254, 282, 284, 285, 286, 292, 350, 353n
Barbour, Walworth, 317n
Ball, George, 91-92
Bar-On, Hanan, 316n
Barnaby, Frank, xi, 13, 69, 157, 159, 179-182, 213, 288, 298n-300n, 302n,

171, 232, 235, 329n
and Arab world, states, 74, 79, 81,
 85, 232, 235, 254
and France, 43, 92, 107
and Israel, 108, 122, 129, 134, 171,
 317n, 324n
and Israeli nuclear option, 74, 96,
 100, 105, 131-132
and missiles, 66, 91
and Egyptian unconventional
 options, 37, 66, 79, 82, 92, 155,
 269, 335n
and Palestinians, 122
and Soviet Union, 76, 79, 84, 85,
 114, 115, 120, 134, 136
and United States, 92, 104, 105,
 134, 151, 318n, 323n
and war of 1967, 108-111, 113-115
Nakdimon, Shlomo, 174, 339n-341n
Naor, Arieh, 167, 327n, 338n
Ne'eman, Yuval, 86, 179, 195, 250,
 267, 273, 287, 289, 290, 320n
Nehru, Jawaharlal, 41
Netanyahu, Benyamin, 245, 345n,
 353n
Newhouse, John, 18, 28, 63, 70, 298n,
 302n, 310n, 333n
Nimrod, Yoram, 306n, 309n, 312n,
 343n
Nitze, Paul, 26, 28, 80, 245, 321n,
 323n
Nixon, Richard M., 85, 127, 128, 129,
 136, 146, 157, 159, 187
Nye, Joseph P., 298n

Ohlendorf, Franz, 310n
Oppenheimer, Robert J., 46, 228
Oren, Amir, 144, 331n
Oswald, Lee Harvey, 81

Pean, Pierre, 69, 71, 81, 86, 87, 94,
 114, 117, 121, 189, 302n, 307n,
 310n, 314n, 315n, 320n, 321n, 329n
Peled, Elad, 328n
Peres, Shimon,

and Arab world; Palestinians;
 strategy towards, 158, 193-195,
 198, 203, 214-216, 287, 299n
as director general, Ministry of
 Defense, 51, 63, 64, 66-70, 73,
 80, 313n
and domestic politics, 311n, 317n,
 324n
as deputy minister of defense, 80,
 81, 85, 105, 310n
as finance minister, 197
as foreign minister, 212
and Hussein I of Jordan, 204, 207
and Israeli nuclear option 74, 77,
 78, 97, 98, 101, 104, 147, 158,
 159, 176-179, 195, 213, 245, 247,
 286-288, 303n, 311n, 312n,
 324n, 326n, 340n, 343n, 344n
as Labor Party chairman, 8, 202
as minister of defense, 157, 320n
as opposition leader, 8, 195, 224
and peace process, 219, 286
and Osiraq (Tammuz 1) bombing,
 167, 173, 174
as prime minister, 196, 198, 200-
 203, 236, 263
and Rafi party; war of 1967, 106,
 117
rivalry with Rabin, 193, 207, 213-
 215, 225
and war of 1973, 147, 159
and West Bank, 86, 193-195, 201,
 204, 207, 212, 215, 345n
Perle, Richard, 349n
Perrin, Jean-Francis, 43, 44, 69, 302n,
 307n, 314n
Pilz, Wolfgang, 322n
Plato, 52
Porat, Yehoshua, 347n
Potter, William C., 352n
Primakov, Yevgeni, 349n
Pry, Peter, 321n, 352n

Qaddafi, Muammar, 130-134, 140,
 145, 161, 180, 181, 198, 201, 222,

Subject Index

Israel (continued)
258, 296, 300n, 337n
and nuclear weapons, ambiguous
& opaque stances, deterrence,
strategy of, x, xii, xiii, 4, 5, 7, 9-
12, 14, 20-23, 25, 36-38, 41-43,
50-58, 60-62, 64-70, 73-83, 89-
97, 99, 102, 105, 106, 114, 117,
119, 120, 125-127, 132, 133, 135,
136, 139, 145, 146, 148, 152-154,
158-160, 162, 163, 167, 172, 175-
185, 188, 189, 191, 192, 194, 195,
197, 199-200, 205-209, 213, 216,
220, 225-228, 230, 245-247, 250,
251, 257, 258, 263, 266, 267, 272-
276, 278, 279, 283, 287-291, 293-
296, 300n, 319n, 333n, 340n,
352n
and "balance of terror," 58, 74,
131, 172, 173, 175, 178, 179,
252, 287
and fusion (hydrogen,
thermonuclear) bomb, 160,
181, 225, 274, 287
and "last resort" strategy, 33,
97, 102, 157-160, 163, 183,
185, 188, 213, 274, 275, 294,
300n, 325n
and monopoly of in Middle
East, 177-179, 188, 193, 194,
212, 215, 230, 279, 283
and neutron, tactical nuclear
bomb, 13, 78, 182, 188, 189,
198, 272, 274, 288
and occupied territories, 177,
183
and open posture, 177, 208, 288
and strike capability, second,
12, 28, 74, 175, 178, 189
and strike capability, first, 11,
189, 192
and occupied territories, 86, 98,
135, 185, 192, 195, 200, 255, 274,
284, 290, 292, see West Bank;
Gaza Strip; Golan Heights;

Sinai; territories in exchange
for peace
and annexation policy, 120,
167, 194
and autonomy in, see West
Bank
and nuclear aspects of, 175-
177, 197, 206
and settlement effort in, 120,
164, 165, 221, 289
and strategic depth, value of,
119, 208, 218, 221
and Palestinians, 37, 164, 185, 194,
210, 214, 215, 284, 285, see also
Palestine Liberation
Organization (PLO)
and PLO, 204, 212, 215, 218,
219, 221, 246, 285
and statehood for, 123
and peace process, 97, 129, 131,
163, 187, 188, 190, 193, 194, 219
and reactor for peaceful use, see
Soreq reactor, 91, 94, 157, 266
reprisal & retaliatory policy, 76,
85, 108, 115
and satellite program, see "Ofek"
and Saudi Arabia, 151, 184
"small," 206
and "smart" weapons, 275
and South Africa, 201, 266, 267,
277
and Soviet Union, 11, 12, 64-67,
123, 127, 195, 201, 216, 289, 295,
354n
and missile & nuclear threats
by Israel against Soviet
Union, 78, 102, 129, 134, 181,
198, 201-203, 205
and missile & nuclear threats
by Soviet Union against
Israel, 76, 78, 86, 87, 97, 98,
104, 123, 124, 135, 136, 181
statehood, problem of; Israel as
"pariah" state, 3, 10, 11, 13, 45,
46, 62